A FLAG UNFURLED

THE WAR LETTERS OF JOHN L. HOBSON II

Authored by

STEPHEN GALE HOBSON

Edited by

ANITA L. GAUNT

Maps by

THADDEUS LYFORD

Dedication

This work is dedicated to my children:

Benjamin Gale Hobson
Nathaniel Cary Hobson
Adam Noyes Hobson

And the family of John L. Hobson II

Remember Where You Came From

And, Dad, wherever you are, "where the war drums beat no longer and the battle flags are furled", this is for you.

Table of Contents

Foreword   vii

1. Memories   1
2. Introductions   11
3. Prologue to War   21
4. National Guard Training Camp   45
5. Camp Curtis Guild, Jr. - Boxford, Massachusetts   75
6. Over There   103
7. Somewhere in France   119
8. Chemin des Dames Sector   183
9. Toul Sector   243
10. The Million Dollar Raid   297
11. The Second Battle of the Marne   327
12. Saumur Artillery School   373
13. Fini la Guerre!   407
14. Rest & Relaxation   435
15. Spur Camp   461
16. Embarkation Camp   533
17. Little Boar's Head - And Beyond   551

Epilogue   563
Appreciation   573
Sources   577
About The Author   579

2nd Lieutenant John Lambert Hobson II, Le Mans, France, 1919.
Stephen G. Hobson Collection - Hobson family photograph

The Lone Trail
Robert Service

Ye who know the Lone Trail would follow it,
Though it lead to glory or the darkness of the pit.
Ye who take the lone trail, bid your love good-bye;
The Lone Trail, the Lone Trail follow till you die.

The trails of the world be countless, and most of the trails be tried;
You tread on the heels of the many, till you come where the ways divide;
And one lies safe in the sunlight, and the other is dreary and wan,
Yet you look aslant at the Lone Trail, and the Lone Trail lures you on.

And somehow you're sick of the highway, with its noise and its easy needs,
And you seek the risk of the by-way, and you reck not where it leads.

And sometimes it leads to the desert, and the tongue swells out of the mouth,
And you stagger blind to the mirage, to die in the mocking drouth.

And sometimes it leads to the mountain, to the light of the lone campfire,
And you gnaw your belt in the aguish of hunger-goaded desire.

And sometimes it leads to the Southland, to the swamp
where the orchid glows,
And you rave to your grave with the fever, and they
rob the corpse for its clothes.

And sometimes it leads to the Northland, and the scurvy softens your bones,
And your flesh dints in like putty, and you spit out your teeth like stones.

And sometimes it leads to a coral reef in the wash of a weedy sea,
And you sit and stare at the empty glare where the gulls wait greedily.

And sometimes it leads to an Artic trail, and the snows
where your torn feet freeze,
And you whittle away useless clay, and crawl on your hands and knees.

Often it leads to the dead-pit; always it leads to pain;
By the bones of your brothers ye know it, but oh, to follow you're fain.

By your bones they will follow behind you,
till the ways of the world are plain.

Bid good-bye to sweetheart, Bid good-bye to friend;
The Lone Trail, the Lone Trail follow to the end.
Tarry not, and fear not, chosen of the true; Lover of the Lone Trail,
The Lone Trail waits for you.

Foreword

Honor Thy Father - 5th Commandment

"Soldiers are the epitome of believers. They believe so much in the cause for which they fight that they are willing to die for it."

                                        - ANONYMOUS

IF

Rudyard Kipling

If you can keep your head when all about you
Are losing theirs and blaming it on you;
If you can trust yourself when all men doubt you,
But make allowances for their doubting too;
If you can wait and not be tired by waiting,
Or being lied about, don't deal in lies,
Or being hated, don't give way to hating,
And yet don't look too good, nor talk too wise:

If you can dream- and not make dreams your master;
If you can think- and not make thoughts your aim;
If you can meet with Triumph and Disaster
And treat those two imposters just the same;
If you can bear to hear the truth you've spoken
Twisted by knaves to make a trap for fools,

Or watch the things you gave your life to, broken,
And stoop and build 'em up with worn out tools;
If you can make one heap of all your winnings
And risk it on one turn of pitch-and-toss,
And lose, and start again at your beginnings
And never breathe a word about your loss;
If you can force your heart and nerve and sinew
To serve your turn long after they are gone,
And so hold on when there is nothing in you
Except the Will which says to them: "Hold on!"

If you can walk with crowds and keep your virtue,
Or walk with kings- nor lose the common touch,
If neither foes nor loving friends can hurt you,
If all men count with you, but none too much;
If you can fill the unforgiving minute
With sixty seconds' worth of distance run-
Yours is the Earth and everything that's in it,
And- which is more- you'll be a Man, my son!

During the process of putting this book together, one of my three sons asked me, "Why are you doing this?" I answered that I was doing this for him, his brothers and all the members of the Hobson family so that everyone will know something about my father - my son's grandfather, who he never had the pleasure of meeting. My father died before my sons were born.

I went on to explain to my son that my father accomplished many notable things during his life. The letters he wrote while serving in the Army during the First World War capture the essence of him, and publishing these letters not only preserves the letters themselves, but also preserves his character so that he will be appreciated by future generations of our family. I explained to my son that I think we can all benefit from his letters.

I pointed out to my son that what makes my father's letters so interesting and poignant is that war creates extraordinary events that bring out extraordinary things in ordinary people. War and combat is a virulent breeding ground for human-interest stories. You couldn't make this stuff up! These letters demonstrate that conflict, especially war, creates defining situations. During a time of war the landscape changes, heroes made and villains destroyed. True personalities and character are revealed, the best and worst are brought out. A split second decision can define a person for the rest of his life as courageous or a coward. Sometimes a person's moment of truth happens so quickly that there is no chance to think about it. What makes one person grasp the opportunity and another impotent? I think it's something visceral, something deep inside, it's bred into our character. This was a defining period for my father and these letters are a journal of that time.

These letters were written at a time when much of the communication was done by the hand written word. Discipline and mental organization were required. Those elements were cultured and part of a basic education. There was no cut/paste, delete, or spell check that came with this period's communication tools; a brain, a pen or pencil, and a sheet of paper. Because of the circumstances under which they were written, I doubt any of these letters had the luxury of a draft. Some of the letters are 10-15 pages or more in length, mostly written in ink, and there is not a grammatical, spelling, or punctuation error in them, and there are no cross outs. We should appreciate the writing style, discipline, and the ability to eloquently express his thoughts.

The letters my father wrote could have been written by any soldier in any war at any point in history. In reading these letters, it is interesting to note just how consistent the emotions and human experiences of war actually are. The emotions, the hopes and the fears expressed by this young man are timeless and universal. It would have been nice to have the use of a non-violent paradigm for the flowering of my father's character. I wish upon wish that this horrific war had never become part of his life. However, it did. This historic world event became a crucible for defining him and creating his character and his letters give us a front row seat to that passage.

I hope that in these letters you will see an example of love and respect shared among a family. No family is perfect, and ours is no different, but love, respect and support among family members is always a good place to begin. My father was a leader by example, and throughout his life's roles as a son, brother, husband, father and man, he was an example of family values.

I said to my son that indeed it is difficult to reason and justify going to war, especially when we are sending a loved one into harm's way, or when the enemy's threat is perceived as being remote since the enemy has not attacked our shores. Why would a peace-loving people want to go to war anyway? Why did men like my father chuck the prospect of a good and safe life and volunteer to go to war - possibly to die for a cause? Was patriotism so simple to understand in 1917 during the First World War and again in 1941 during the Second World War, yet so difficult and complicated to understand today? According to the patriotism expressed in my father's letters, it's not difficult to understand at all if you believe in freedom, human rights and protecting a democratic way of life.

When the United States declared war in 1917 and entered The Great War, The World War, World War I, there was no personal benefit or selfish agenda for the soldiers, sailors and airmen who were putting their lives on the line other than the belief that, if they were successful, this war would be "The war to end all wars." and democracy and their families would be safe and the hope that you and I would never have to endure the same again. It was a pure sacrifice for a noble cause. There were no government backed entitlement programs for soldiers or veterans. There was no GI Bill. There wasn't even a government sponsored life insurance policy for military personnel. It was only after the American troops embarked for France that a modest life insurance program was instituted. My father writes home from France how wonderful this new benefit was.

I shared with my son that, while doing research for this book and poring through newspapers of the day, it was interesting to learn about the deep division among the American people that surrounded the nation's entry into the First World War. This dissent is nothing new; it goes all the way back to the Colonists' dissension over the American Revolution! Debate, dissension and controversy have apparently been a part of every war with which the United States has ever been involved! I came away with the feeling that the difference between the World Wars and the "conflicts" I have lived through - Korea, Vietnam and Iraq - is that, when war was declared in 1917 and 1941, the American people came together as a fighting unit. They volunteered en masse to fight on the front line. Those who weren't serving on the front line made the necessary sacrifice on the home front. And everyone, including the media, publicly supported a deserving government. A public anti-war demonstration would have been treason.

To underscore to my son why the United States, his grandfather and so many like his grandfather made it their responsibility to defend the cause of freedom throughout the world, I referred him to 1943 - the Second World War - to the wisdom and eloquence of Sir Winston Churchill. Churchill had come to the United States at the height of England's battle against the Nazis to address the graduating class of 1943 at Harvard University. Many young men in his audience that day would subsequently be fighting and dying on battlefields, on the seas and in the air of the European or Pacific theaters. He used the opportunity to explain how he felt about the role of the United States among the nations of the world and why the fate falls to us, the United States, to defend freedom in the world. Of the United States' involvement, Churchill said to the graduates,

> "There was no use in [the people of the United States] saying, 'We don't want it; we won't have it; our forebears left Europe to avoid these quarrels; we have founded a new world which has no contact with the old.' There is no use in that.

> "…I will offer you one explanation…The price of greatness is responsibility. If the people of the United States had continued in a mediocre station, struggling with the wilderness, absorbed in their own affairs, and a factor of no consequence in the movement of the world, they might have remained forgotten and undisturbed beyond their protecting oceans: but one cannot rise to be in many ways the leading community in the civilized world without being involved in its problems, without being convulsed by its agonies and inspired by its causes. If this has been proved in the past, as it has been, it will become indisputable in the future. The people of the United States cannot escape world responsibility."

Churchill also said, "The day may dawn when fair play, love for one's fellow man, respect for justice and freedom, will enable tormented generations to march forth serene and triumphant from the hideous epoch in which we have to dwell. Meanwhile never flinch, never weary, never despair." Churchill said that "Courage was the essential virtue…" because "…it guaranteed all the others." Sir Winston's words ring true today just as they did in 1943 and in 1917.

And that, I told my son, is why his grandfather felt compelled to join the fight. We should aspire to the patriotic ideals expressed in these letters. Soldiers are the epitome of believers. They believe so much in the cause for which they fight that they are willing to die for it. Today we have the advantage of looking back on this world event through the retrospective of history. We know how it all turned out. We know that democracy and freedom prevailed and that "…His truth goes marching on." But, when these men went off to war in 1917, they didn't know they were destined to come out on the winning side. There is no simpler time in history, just different circumstances. This was a courageous time in America's history.

These letters send the message that we should never lose the hunger for adventure. We should have courage and constantly seek new experiences and knowledge. We should follow our dreams, take The Lone Trail referred to in one of my father's favorite poems and, most important, have the courage to live by our principles and make every moment worthwhile. There is nothing like a war to remind us that life is very short.

Finally, I said to my son, the most important reason why we should read your grandfather's letters is simply because we will never see his kind again. We should not forget him. Not ever.

Being of proud Yankee stock, the Hobson family had a strong tradition of keeping to themselves. They were simply private people. It was uncharacteristic for the Hobson family to talk about family outside of the family. Evidence of this is written in a letter Father received from one of his boyhood friends, Dick Thompson. After Father had departed for the battlefields of France, Dick Thompson inquired of the Hobson family about my father's well-being and asked if perhaps they would share a letter or two. Dick Thompson later wrote to my father about the exchange, "Experience has given me sad evidence of the fact that it is easier to get a tooth out of any of your tribe than a letter!"

However private the family may have been, information did leak out through the tales of returning local servicemen and by comments in letters sent home by other soldiers. For the community's benefit and supporting the war effort, the Hobson family shared some selected letters with the local newspaper and, given the way my grandmother kept my father's original letters and had them transcribed and bound in a notebook, in addition to the pride she had in her oldest son, I suspect she planned to share or perhaps someday even publish the letters. If sharing the letters with family or publishing them was her intent, this effort of mine is doubly rewarding. I have fulfilled her wish. The passage of time and changing world events has made the letters more poignant.

In their entirety, the letters are a mosaic, many pieces coming together to form a picture. Some of the letters are more poignant than others. Some make us smile, some make our hearts ache, some are examples of how our lives have changed, but they all are interesting to some degree. And they all fit together. Such is life.

Only a few of the letters Father received while serving in the military survived. It was impossible to save them in combat living conditions. It would have been ideal to have been able to chronologically match up both sides of the correspondence in this work, the letters both sent and received. But, even in reading only the letters Father wrote home to his family, one side of the conversation, we can well imagine what sentiments were contained in the letters he received.

CEMBER 8, 1917.

CORPORAL HOBSON SEES A NEW RACE OF PATRIOTS IN THE MAKING

Haverhill Boy Who Enlisted in the Second Day of Recruiting for Battery A, 102nd Field Artillery, Is Enjoying Life on the Western Front and Has a Vision of Something More Than a Glorious Fight and High Adventure

CORP. JOHN LAMBERT HOBSON, 2d.
Who Writes of Experience With Battery A in France.

Although literary interests have dominated most of his twenty years, Corporal John Lambert ("Jack") Hobson 2d. of Battery A, 102nd Field Artillery, true to the ideals of American manhood that he has developed, enlisted in the battery on April 9, the second day of its recruiting.

This son of Mr. and Mrs. Arthur L. Hobson of 129 Arlington street, is a quiet unassuming youth, whose high patriotism is founded on strength of character and deep thoughtfulness. He is deeply interested in all literary movements, and until he had enlisted, only his most intimate friends were aware of the spirit of patriotism that must have been crying out against the wrongs perpetrated by the Prussians long before this nation made its declaration of war.

Corporal Hobson approached the national crisis with seriousness and with calm, dispassionate thought, despite his splendid loyalty as is evidenced by his letters. He sees a vision of something more than a glorious fight and high adventure, for in one letter he writes: "I am coming back to you all safe and well and a better and broader thinking man."

Information to the effect that the Corporal has been transferred to the Headquarters Company, 102nd Field Artillery, was received by friends yesterday.

Corporal Hobson was born in Berlin, N. H., 20 years ago, and he received his education in the Noble and Greenough school, Boston, the Fessenden school, Newton and Phillips-Exeter academy and attended the Plattsburg military camp during the summer of 1916. At the time of his enlistment he was a student in the Bryant and Stratton business school, Boston. His life has been rather uneventful, but his mind has been gathering the treasures of literature. Poems that he has written bespeak years of quiet thoughtfulness.

His lively literary instinct prompts him to dwell in his letters on those personal touches and those intimate scenes of the life he sees about him that give his letters a peculiar charm. At the same time he is thoroughly alive to the great issues that are involved in the present struggle. In a letter written to his father on the fourth of November he says:

"News of the second war loan reached camp a few days ago, and when we heard it had gone over five billion it made us all feel pretty good. It just goes to prove that the people of America are behind us, and that's all we ask. We'll deliver the goods over here when called upon to do so if we get a backing like that right through to the end. It is wonderful and certainly has put the heart into us."

In the midst of the havoc that has been wrought in France Corporal Hobson perceives the beautiful spirit that actuates the French people, he has a keen appreciation of those little characteristics that have always endeared the French people to the whole world, and the prospect of grim warfare has not dulled his sensibilities.

Corporal Hobson's letters are unusual, but the excerpts below do not do them full justice. The letters are to the members of his family, and they are in great part personal. The dates given with the extracts are of the days on which the letters were written.

September 21, 1917.

I am really on my way to somewhere. It seems very funny indeed to be riding along on a train without a ticket and not knowing where you are going. It is

turned on eight men had to be ready to jump in so that no water would be wasted.

Another thing which was scarce was wood. No food could be cooked which required over two hours cooking. We did not suffer from lack of food, nevertheless, but got all we could eat without being pigs. War bread is being used all over the country, and I personally like it very much; in fact, I like it fully as much as American bread, the taste of which I long since have forgotten—so really I should not try to judge.

The trains over here are the queerest things I ever saw and maybe they are not rough riding How these little cars ever stay on the track is beyond me, but somehow they do. I saw a first class sleeping car in the freight yard yesterday, and it doesn't look any more like ours than black looks like white. The day coaches have four wheels and the pullmans six.

The French people are very nice indeed to the American soldiers and we are greeted with a smile everywhere we go. Cheering is not the style over here, but hand waving and a look of welcome greet us and keep spirits well up as we march through the town. Black is to be seen on a great many ladies while a look of heart-felt suffering marks their faces. There are almost no men to be seen who are not in uniform, and those who are not are either unfit or too young.

I saw a very impressive sight yesterday. A little boy was out plowing a field with two oxen while a woman, whom I took to be his mother, was hoeing. The women seem to be filling the men's places around here and seem glad to do it to serve France.

The French children are very much like the American children. The French soldier boys are very friendly indeed with us, and we have a fine time exchanging smokes and trying to make each other understand what we mean.

October 23, 1917.

You ought to see the boys of Battery A now. They are all in wonderful condition, happy, and really doing some work

got up at Boxford, 5:30. But my! what a change in the light and air!

More mail came yesterday which makes the third bunch we have received. Three cheer! I have got my letter from Art, papers. Be sure and let me know about the Exeter and Andover game. I may be miles away, but my heart and hopes are all with the boys in Red just the same, and Johnny intends to have a celebration all his own over here if the good old school comes through with another victory.

November 4, 1917.

George Croston arrived in camp a few nights ago. He left Boxford after us, you know, and hence had some very interesting town news to tell us.

November 8, 1917.

We now have stoves so when we are not out on duty we are able to keep warm. The wood over here is green and wet so at times we have quite a job to keep our fires going, but somehow or other we have done it. It is getting colder over here every day, and our overcoats feel mighty good. It has rained almost every day this week, and the mud is awful.

THE CHANCE

Life was just a game to me—
Just a game I somehow started,
Open-handed, reckless-hearted * * *
Just a game I played and played,
Never heeding where I strayed—
Life was just a game to me!

Just a game—and I was losing—
That which seemed at first all choosing,
Grew on me until no daring

Article from Haverhill Gazette, 8 December 1917.
Stephen G. Hobson Collection - Stephen G. Hobson photograph

Article from Haverhill Evening Gazette, 1 February 1919.
Stephen G. Hobson Collection - Stephen G. Hobson photograph

From the beginning of history, word and song have stirred men to battle and to weep in reflection afterward. I have included in this work Father's favorite poems - some are lighthearted, and some are not so lighthearted - as well as several of his favorite period songs and barracks ballads. These have been placed in the text where I felt they would set the tone for some of the situations described in the letters.

The poem "IF", by Rudyard Kipling, that is placed at the beginning of this work is actually one of my favorites. The reason it is in here at all is because it reflects much of the wisdom my father passed on to us kids over the years and, whenever I read it, I can hear my father talking to me. The poem correctly mirrors his image and wisdom, so I pass it along to you in the spirit of this work.

Most of the poems I have included are from Robert W. Service's "Rhymes of a Red Cross Man", which Father carried with him in France. Robert W. Service was a prolific writer born in 1874 to Scottish parents living in England. During the early part of the Great War, he served as an ambulance driver and correspondent. He wrote and published work before the United States declared war in 1917, thus the British perspective for most of Service's poems.

In his letters, Father specifically mentions Service's poems I have included herewith as being his favorites. In fact, he had marked his favorites with a check mark in his compact, leather bound copy of Service's book he carried with him in France. Apparently, even before going overseas in 1917, my father was inspired by Service's poems. He would read them at home in his father's study in the Haverhill house sitting in front of the fireplace.

In regard to the songs and ballads included in this book, "Taps" holds an especially poignant place. "Taps", originally composed as a military return to quarters piece during the American Civil War, became the official military funeral piece in 1891. At the playing of this bugle call, which was Union Army General Daniel Adams Butterfield's signature, I could look into Father's eyes and see in them the flashback in his mind of his entire experience in the First World War. When my father heard "Taps" it would bring a tight jaw upon his kind face; a reminder of the human cost of this war and the horrific things he witnessed. "Taps" makes an appropriate last entry in this work. I feel that it is Father's message that, as much of an adventure as he may have found it at the time, war is a sometimes necessary but always horrible business. When "Taps" was played, the look in Father's eyes was a clear message that there is nothing glorious about war.

The title of this book, A Flag Unfurled, came to mind because Father was a modest, unpretentious man. He did not talk very much about his experiences during the war. He writes in one of his letters that anyone who had not actually experienced war on the front lines, seen the death and destruction and experienced what he called the "adventure," could never understand it, nor believe it. What he saw and experienced on the front line in France was beyond his Christian, civilized, rational boundary of acceptance. Those who were there formed a bond, a bond based on shared experiences. They understood what we on the outside could not. They placed their lives in each other's hands. They understood each other, what happened and why. In order to understand, or even have an inkling of perception, you had to be there and be part of that bond. As a result, outside of that bond - the band of brothers - he just didn't talk about his experiences. He was never one to wear his emotions on his sleeve. Father kept his flag furled, so to speak. In this work I am unfurling and flying his flag.

This work is not a re-telling of Father's stories. The centerpiece of the work is the compilation of the actual letters Father wrote home to his family and the letters are surrounded by an historical overview. This is his adventure, in his words and without interpretation. The letters are complete and unedited. All the words, phrases, grammar and expressions are exactly as my father originally wrote them.

My small contribution to this work - my remembrances of my father, the overview of the Hobson family cast of characters, the historical activities of his battery, regiment and division, the description of the three campaigns in which he fought and my notes and the clarifications in brackets - were added only where I felt it was beneficial to round out the character of the man or to bring understanding or clarity to the letters. With the censorship of mail during a time of war, soldiers could not reveal in their letters information about their location or tell about the battles they were in, hence the location reference in the letters as just "Somewhere in France". I felt that by explaining the references made in the letters and what events were surrounding my father when he wrote each letter, this work would have more juice and be more meaningful.

With every keystroke I have tried to keep in mind for whom I have written this book and why. The introduction portion of this work may initially to the reader seem a bit lengthy, but all the information in this portion is relevant to what follows and understanding the letters.

So not to overwhelm the reader with too much history and lose focus, I have concentrated only on the historical events that directly affected my father and his adventure. I salted in interesting and amusing facts and, for illustrative purposes, inserted relevant pictures when I found them. My intent was to make the background interesting, simple and understandable. I wanted my part of this work to be more like a story than a history lesson and to keep this work focused on my father's letters. The First World War and all its political theories and geo-political nuances are way too vast a subject and the analysis is far beyond my purpose.

I hope in reading my father's letters you will come to know this wonderful man and the times in which he lived and gain appreciation for what and why his generation sacrificed for their country and the world so that subsequent generations could live in freedom.

My father is literally "remarkable," and so are the events that formed his character. Enjoy!

CHAPTER ONE

Memories

"To live in hearts we leave behind is not to die"

Thomas Campbell, Hallowed Ground

My father was 49 years of age in 1946, the year I was born. Growing up, my friends' fathers were generally much younger than my father, and many of their fathers had served in the Second World War which had ended in 1945. When I answered the question so often asked in those days "…and what did your father do in 'the war?'" I got a look like I didn't understand the question and I was constantly explaining that my *father* - no, no, not my *grandfather*, my *father* - had indeed fought in the *First* World War, and that in our house, the *First* World War was *the war*.

While other kids were singing the songs in honor of their fathers' respective Second World War military service - the Marine Corps Hymn, the Navy's "Anchors Away" or the Army Air Corps' "Off We Go Into The Wild Blue Yonder" - I would pipe up and sing the Army's "Field Artillery March" or the "Caisson Song" which went, "Over hill, Over dale, We will hit the dusty trail, As those caissons go rolling along…" and then inevitably someone would stop me there and ask what a caisson was. So, for all my friends who thought to ask but didn't: a caisson is a two-wheeled carriage or cart that was trailed behind the limber as part of the support trail for an artillery piece. The caisson generally held ammunition.

My father's war was very different from the Second World War in which my friends' fathers served. Several branches of military service, such as the air forces, were in fledging stages during the First World War or of minor size compared to the Second World War military brances. Unlike the major role of the naval engagements and air bombing during the Second World War, the First World War, while it was fought on many fronts by many different military service branches, was mostly a brutal, head-to-head confrontation of land-based, boots-on-the-ground, entrenched Army infantry and artillery hammering away at each other in a mass slaughter across No Man's Land in France. When compared to my friends' fathers' war stories, my father's stories must have seemed archaic. Relatively, they were.

As a young boy I would sit for hours at Father's feet and beg him to tell me war stories. If his mood was right or he just got tired of me pestering him, he would indulge me.

When I was very young, the stories Father told us about his experiences during the war were light and self-effacing. At that time he didn't engage in the serious side of his experiences. The stories were just right for a sleepy little boy at bedtime, or for all three of his children sitting on his lap listening to him wide-eyed and spellbound on a stormy weekend afternoon.

There were stories of him being thrown from a horse during a steeplechase at Saumur Artillery School. For this horsemanship training exercise (All Army officers were expected to be proficient horseback riders.) Father had drawn, by chance, the biggest horse on the line and, during the steeplechase, the horse balked, stopping abruptly short of a jump, and Father came out of the saddle, sailed right over the big animal's head and landed in a pond.

There were stories about his favorite Army horse, Kid, a mare that he rode when he arrived in France. He had affectionately named the horse after his sister, Alice, whom he had nicknamed Kid. The remarkable horse became a pet. On many rainy nights when the regiment was on the move, changing positions or going to another sector or front, Kid, faithfully and with sure-footed ability, transported Father many miles on muddy, slippery French roads while Father, shrouded in a poncho and a helmeted head bent against the night's weather, slept in the saddle. But, alas, Kid the horse who was high-spirited, like Father's perception of his sister, was apt to be gun shy.

At several inopportune times when the battery guns fired, the horse threw him or ran off. Once, he told us, he was climbing into the saddle just as the battery fired and Kid spooked and took off at a gallop with Father hanging on her side with one booted foot in the stirrup, galloping away with him hanging on like a rodeo stunt rider.

There were funny stories about the other "pets" they encountered. There were refugee dogs, the pants rabbits or coo-coos (body lice), and a cat, Miss Pussy, which he writes home about which epitomized the definition of being a survivor. And there were the huge rats that roamed the dugouts at night. His nemesis rodent who for some reason he named Betty would jump on him in the middle of the night.

There were stories that made him very human. He confessed to the terror he felt as a very young and newly commissioned officer the first time he got a command with older men reporting to him. He would laugh at himself along with our delighted squeals of, "Oh, Daddy!" when he told us about the blunders and gaffs he committed leading his men in review parades, often getting confused and giving incorrect commands sending the entire marching company into disarray. He confessed to marching his detail into a blind alley. When his commanding officer dressed him down for that, my Father took the criticism like the man he was, but thought it curious that the Captain didn't ask how he marched the detail in formation out of that alley.

Early newsreels that were made during the First World War we saw as kids on 1950s vintage television were comical; the speed of the film, probably taken with a hand-cranked camera, made the soldiers appear to move in fast, jerky motions. My brother and I wondered if they actually walked like that way back then. As a young boy seeing all this, it was often hard for me to imagine that Father was actually there.

Rainy, stay indoors Sunday afternoons were occasionally made exciting for my older sister, brother and me by an escorted trip to the dark, spooky attic in the big, old house where we grew up and the ceremonial unlocking, opening and viewing of the hidden treasures in Father's Army trunk, the contents of which I figured were unsorted since the day he returned from France forty years before.

In the trunk were his officer's Colt 45 pistol and holster; a wristwatch with a sweat rotted canvas strap and a protective wire grid over the glass crystal; his dog tags which were round metal disks with stamped lettering; collarless, white, fine cotton shirts that were yellowed with age but still starched, folded and bound in a neat bundle and tied with string by the French laundry that last laundered them; an assortment of rifle and pistol cartridges with the brass having turned green from mold (the significance of keeping these particular cartridges was never made clear); his carefully folded Army officer's uniform, including handmade leather riding boots, and his Sam Browne belt that was so emblematic to him and he was so proud to have worn.

The Sam Browne belt was only issued to warrant and commissioned officers. It is a broad leather waist belt with a leather strap that went over the right shoulder diagonally across the chest to the left hip. It was originally designed to help carry the weight of a pistol or sword. General Sir Sam Browne of the British Army in India first introduced the Sam Browne belt to the military in 1861. It had two straps, each coming straight over each shoulder from the back to the front. General Browne had lost his left arm in battle and needed assistance in carrying his sword and side arm or pistol and he designed and wore this belt for that purpose. The belt design was later modified into the familiar single strap across the chest model and, as the swords and such of Browne's era gave way to modern weapons of war, the belt became more ornamental than functional.

Also in the trunk were Father's overseas cap and "puttees" (long strips of wool cloth that were wrapped around the lower leg and worn to form a gaiter); a few medals and ribbons; assorted flags, the most impressive being a large, white linen flag with a deep blue YD on it for the Yankee Division, and several banners with a red border surrounding a white field bearing a single blue star in the center of the field (These banners were hung in a window by the families of soldiers servicing overseas, the number of stars indicating the number serving.); a pair of wire rimmed "spectacles" that appeared to be painful to wear (I tried them on. They were!); documents yellowed with age; old coins; pictures of rows and rows of soldiers in undisclosed locations; and souvenirs, including a German soldier's belt buckle and cigarette lighter. Whenever I saw these particular "souvenir" items, I had an amusing imagined vision of a hapless German prisoner of war my father encountered being relieved of these possessions and, as my father walked away with his prize belt buckle and lighter, the prisoner being left to hold his trousers up with one hand and asking for a light for the cigarette he held in the other hand! There were also glass picture slides and a wooden viewing box that, when you looked into the box with a light behind, produced the most amazing three-dimensional images of French battlefields and architecture.

And, most startling to me, carefully placed in an envelope tucked away in the bottom of the trunk were his molar teeth. The teeth had become decayed and were extracted while he was in France. With the expediency of combat situations and absence of proper oral hygiene and dentistry on the front lines coupled with father's love of sweets, the teeth had simply been pulled out rather than properly repaired, probably by some itinerant Army dentist with crude tools and no pain killer. In his letters, my father makes one reference to an anticipated visit to the dentist that didn't sound like he was looking forward to it. The first time I saw the teeth I remember that I privately wondered why someone would hang onto his old teeth this long, and one day I remember that I asked my father if he was waiting for the Tooth Fairy to come. A chuckle and a gentle hand on my shoulder acknowledged my youthful, but nevertheless sincere, question.

I imagine that, for Father, every time he opened that trunk it was a virtual tornado of nostalgia. But for us kids, it was like opening the most incredible time capsule. It was fascinating stuff, no matter how many times I saw it. And then, triggered by the nostalgia of the moment, and only for the moment, there would be the stories.

As I got older, the awareness of war grew real. Pictures of actual combat in the Korean War, albeit sanitized by the media for public consumption, came right into our living room on the televised evening news programs.

The Korean War directly and tragically touched our family when, in 1952, our older cousin, Philip Hobson, Jr., was killed fighting with the Marines in Korea. The story of Philip Hobson Jr. going into the military paralleled my father's. Young Phil had completed his secondary education at Groton and was on his way to college at Yale but, with patriotism in his heart and the Korean War underway, he felt he should do his duty for his country instead, and he enlisted in the Marines. Philip Hobson, Jr., a corporal, was killed by artillery shrapnel while retaking one of those numbered hills in Korea that kept changing hands.

As the 1960s unfolded, I went off to boarding school and then to college. The "conflict" in Vietnam began and escalated from the United States just having "observers" in country into war, regardless of what our government wanted to call it. The threat of the draft loomed large in every young man's life. It was about this time the subject matter of my father's stories about his experiences in the First World War became more serious and grim. I noticed that those stories came out of him more slowly and deliberately and that he had a harder time telling them. These stories were obviously closer to the bone. In thinking about this, I've often wondered if he felt that we were finally old enough to understand the gravity of war. Perhaps, at that time in his life, he had come to the realization that the horrible war he fought was not the war to end all wars after all and his own sons, now grown and eligible for the draft, may have to go to war too. I'm sure the tragedy of his youngest brother's son getting killed in Korea weighed heavily on him as well. Perhaps he came in touch with the same feelings his father had for him when he marched off to war.

When he told these later stories, they were not stories of blood and guts. He would favor telling stories about human nature. The stories were of how men *really* behaved in combat conditions. It was certainly not the Hollywood-generated image of war or the Hollywoodglory stuff we were exposed to at the local movie theater's Saturday matinee or on early television. He would tell us how men reacted when they were on the receiving end of a deafening, earth shaking, horrifically terrifying, chaotic and inescapable artillery barrage. It was a nightmare of the senses. I asked him if he was afraid and he said it wasn't the fear of getting killed so much as the realization that you were probably already dead that kept you going! He told us what it was really like to have machine gun bullets fired at you — sounded like bees flying around your head he said, artillery shells exploding all around, shrapnel whizzing through the air, fragmentation shells bursting overhead and deadly gas shells bursting about spreading their drifting horror. At any time, a random shell burst could result in instant death and, should that happen, there would be few, if any, body parts remaining to identify or bury with honor. And, in the midst of all the horror, there was the urgency in the voices of men in command, the screams of men overcoming fear, and also the primal, haunting screams of the wounded - both human and animal. He would describe watching from the artillery positions the courageous but murderous infantry charges across No Man's Land - of men charging headlong into a hail of enemy machine gunfire and being cut down like wheat in the wind.

There were stories of other men's heroism and cowardliness that he had witnessed, and not always on the battlefield. Courage and bravery were also there when the bullets weren't flying. Men had their personal demons to deal with, too.

He said that in combat they didn't have time or the facility to deal with deserters. They didn't put together firing squads or deal with processes. When a man turned and ran under fire they simply caught him and then put him in the front line trenches, at bayonet point if necessary. You see, he would explain, in the trenches life expectancy was short because there that man would be the first to go "over the top," over the trench's parapet on the next charge across No Man's Land. One way or another, Father would say with a wry smile, the matter simply took care of itself. The man either found courage and faced the enemy and fought, or the enemy killed him in the charge.

He would tell us about the good and bad officers he served with and what leadership characteristics he felt they possessed or lacked that made them that way.

He would describe the adrenalin rush he would get from night artillery duels, when the big guns on both sides fired alternately at each other. He described the muzzle blast, the explosions, the chest thumping concussion and the light show put on by the muzzle flashes. In a letter to his brother Arthur he described it as looking "...as if the doors of Hell had opened." When I was a boy, while sitting on Fisherman's Beach in Swampscott, Massachusetts, watching the grand finale of a July Fourth fireworks, Father looked at me and winked, knowing I would get it without specific reference, and said to me, "*That* is what it looked like." I haven't been able to watch the finale of a fireworks display since without thinking about that.

He told about spies from French villages who were German sympathizers caught infiltrating the battery's artillery observation posts and how they were discovered and dealt with, usually with immediate execution. In an unusual, reflective mood one day late in his life, he revealed that he had carried out swift justice to a spy with that Colt 45 pistol that resided in that old trunk in our spooky attic.

Father's stories were spellbinding. They were full of adventure. They were real. They were an education.

When I reached my late teen years, my interests were elsewhere and I stopped asking him to tell me war stories. Because he was never one to come forth with the stories without being encouraged, it all just stopped. Certainly today, as I am writing this, I wish upon wish that I had been more persistent in asking him about his experiences. I have so many questions now.

The last time I remember something coming up in Father's life about his military experience was an incident that took place in the mid-1960s during the last few months of his life when he was in a hospital for surgery. He discovered that the young man cleaning his hospital room was a conscientious objector to the Vietnam War. This person was opposed to serving in the armed forces or bearing arms on the grounds of moral or religious principles. So, instead of submitting to the draft and serving his country in the military, this young man was assigned by the Selective Service to perform alternative service in this New Hampshire hospital. It must have been hard for Father to understand. Not to fight for the country was offensive to his very foundation and, you see, there was no conscientious objector status during the First World War.

Upon discovery of the man's draft status, Father, from his hospital bed the day before going into surgery, quietly and calmly confessed to the young man that he didn't agree with the Vietnam War either. My Father said he would not, however, tolerate a person who would not do his duty and fight for the country in which he lived and enjoyed the privileges of freedom and democracy. He told the young man to leave his room and to never come back. The man packed up his cleaning cart, picked up his pail and mop and quietly shuffled out of the room. My dear mother, forever the peace maker, feigned interest in a book and witnessed this conversation from her corner chair. She was horrified.

A few days later, I traveled from Boston, where I was attending college, to Hanover, New Hampshire, to visit my father in the hospital, who was by then recovering from the surgery. In the presence of my father, who was unable to talk at the time because of the surgery performed on his throat, my mother told me about the incident.

After hearing the story from my mother, I made no verbal comment. It was the Sixties and there were many mixed emotions about the Vietnam

War and life in the United States. In hindsight, perhaps none were more or less patriotic than another, just a different opinion of what was best for the country. But, I was a Baby Boomer. I was part of a new generation. And, because of the age difference, I was perhaps *two* generations of thinking away from my father. It was a time of rapidly changing morals and mores. We witnessed a President assassinated. Many of our childhood heroes and ideals were unmasked. Previously taboo topics and subjects were now discussed openly. The military and government was vilified. My generation did the unthinkable: we brashly challenged authority, men wore long hair, women shed their bras and demanded equality in the workplace, birth control in the form of a pill changed sex relations, Civil Rights movements were underway and the leader of the movement assassinated. But, my generation, being "Masters of the Universe," we were changing the world! Given the situation in that hospital room, it made perfect sense for me to remain silent. In that circumstance, there was nothing that *anyone* of my age could have said to someone of my parent's generation that would have been acceptable.

However, while my mother went on telling the story in scolding tones, I stood at the foot of Father's hospital bed looking at him. Lying there with all those tubes coming out of him, he looked like a fallen giant, a medical Gulliver. He was intense with frustration at not being able to talk. He was looking up at me with urgency, searching my face with his blue eyes for some signal. Not a signal of forgiveness, but some communication that I understood what he had done and why. With a prideful smile I touched his bed, gave him a knowing look, and simply nodded at him. It was my communication of understanding. It was my communication that what he had tried to instill in me for the past 19 years had taken hold; that I got it. His example had not been lost on me. Knowing his message was received, he relaxed his gaze, nodded, and sank his head restfully into the pillow, and he smiled back.

When this incident happened, the family had been told, but he had not (I always felt he probably knew), that he was fighting a rapidly losing battle with the most insidious enemy; an enemy he couldn't see and which defeated even the seemingly invincible. He was facing terminal cancer. This enemy didn't charge across a battlefield. It couldn't be vanquished by even the best artillery barrage, battle plan or all the courage a wise, strong character could muster. Life without my father seemed unimaginable. And I thought to myself: with all there was to think about with *that* on his mind, to the end, here was a man with principles.

Standing there at the foot of his bed looking at him in that light, several things occurred to me. The differences between our generations became clear. I realized there is something more important in life than self. I felt my generation had somehow bungled the passing of the torch of ideals from his generation, and I felt the defiance, bravado and that youthful feeling of invincibility slipping away. I realized that they just weren't building them like him anymore. I wondered: do I, do *we*, have this man's measure of resolve, ethical conduct, strength and conviction that it took to survive through unprecedented crisis and hardship, economic depression and world wars? I thought to myself: when he falls, who will pick up the flag? Who will walk the parapet at night guarding us while we sleep? I realized that my comfort in life existed because of the vigilance and sacrifice of my father and other men like him. I felt weight upon me, and I found all that very frightening. I didn't realize it at the time, unknowingly; my Father had just escorted me through a passage of maturity.

To have known my father, to have been his son, to have felt and seen his influence not only on my life but also on the lives of others, is the greatest gift I could ever have asked for.

CHAPTER TWO

Introductions

"It seemed a very great world in which these men lived..."

SIR WINSTON CHURCHILL

"His loveable and affable nature..."

RALPH EVERETT BRADLEY

In 1916, the year before the United States declared war, at age 19, my father, John Lambert Hobson II, a.k.a. John, "Johnny" or "Jack", was attending Bryant & Stratton Business School in Boston, Massachusetts. That same year he enlisted in the National Guard.

When he joined the National Guard, America's involvement in a war with Germany was imminent. The thought of becoming part of this event was very exciting to my father and it played a merry, enticing tune to his wanderlust and to his youthful, adventurous spirit. Although his decision to join the National Guard and the possible interruption of his education was not popular at home, he attended a National Guard training camp in Plattsburgh, New York, during the summer of that year.

To understand who my father was, what motivated him to march off to war and what the mood of the nation and the times were like, I need to take you through his personal background information and a literary painting of the historical scenery of the times.

John Lambert Hobson II was born in his family's home at Edge Hill in Berlin, New Hampshire, at six o'clock in the evening of 17 August 1897. He was the first child born into the Arthur Lambert Hobson, Sr. family and the namesake of his paternal grandfather, John Lambert Hobson, Sr.

As a boy, my father attended private schools in the Boston area: Noble and Greenough's in Boston, Fessenden School in West Newton and Phillips Exeter Academy in Exeter, New Hampshire. He then went on to Bryant & Stratton Business School in Boston.

Although Father was a bright and well-read lad with a strong sense of purpose in life, by his own admission he was never an academic and his interest by 1916 was not in book learning. He had a wandering spirit and a hunger to touch life, not just read about it.

At age 19, John Hobson II was tall - six foot one, with most of his height in his long legs - and he was very thin, almost frail in stature. But, generally being the tallest man in the room, he got noticed. He had kind, blue eyes and wore pince nez spectacles for reading. He had large ears and thick, dark, straight hair that he usually parted in the middle of his head or nearly so, like his father. He was considered a handsome man.

John played tennis on school teams and won several championship competitions. He also played tennis at the family's club at their summer residence at Little Boar's Head. With his long legs and slim torso, he was a very competitive distance runner while on the track team at Phillips Exeter Academy. At one point while serving in France, his ability to run would play a significant part in performing a very courageous act.

With the discipline and privilege of his background he was well bred, educated and a gentleman. However, beyond the privileges allowed by his inherited background, he had a definite, strong character of his own. He had a kind and gentle nature and a wonderful sense of humor. He also possessed a terrific sense of balance in his personality. I never saw him take himself too seriously, and he never took his situation in life for granted. His older, future brother-in-law, Everett Bradley, observed of him at the time that he was "…a lovable, affable fellow" and he was popular with all people. He was a "…keen and well balanced young man," a "…regular 'feller' " and "…a man in every sense." He could walk and talk with any man of any station in life. I'm sure his character got him through many of his military experiences.

John had good prospects for the future. Being the oldest son, there was some traditional certainty that he would follow in his father's footsteps and, following completion of his education, transition into the family paper manufacturing business. The interruption of this linear life plan process by joining the military - possibly on a permanent basis - probably played heavily on his father's emotions.

Father came from a loving, close knit, locally prominent and influential family and they all - his grandparents, parents, sisters and brothers - were a big part of his life in 1916-1919. They are mentioned frequently in his letters so it is appropriate that we have a profile of these people, the circumstances of the family and the social, political and economic atmosphere that shaped the times so we can understand the context of the letters.

Father's maternal grandfather, Stephen Henry Gale (1846-1920), was born in East Kingston, New Hampshire, into a Scots-Irish family that had its roots in American soil going back four generations to the 1600s. His father, Elbridge Gerry Gale, was a farmer of modest circumstances, mainly dependent upon his own exertions for the support of his family. Stephen's great grandfather, Jacob Gale, was a delegate to the First Provincial Congress of New Hampshire in 1774, and later served as Lieutenant Colonel of a regiment under the command of Colonel Josiah Bartlett; he later succeeded Colonel Bartlett as colonel.

Stephen Henry Gale in partnership with his older brother, John Elbridge Gale, was the co-founder of Gale Brothers, Incorporated, a large, successful shoe manufacturing company with plants located in Haverhill and Exeter.

In the late 1800s, with his shoe manufacturing business secure and enjoying a high profile in the community and being a popular local employer, Stephen Henry Gale became active in local and New Hampshire state politics. In 1893, he was elected Commissary-General (the head of the state's substance department who has charge of the purchases and issue of provisions for the army), hence the title General was awarded to him, and as such, he served on the staff of Governor John B. Smith. General Stephen Henry Gale was elected and served as a state senator from 1895 - 1897, and was elected and served as a representative to the state legislature from 1905 - 1907. In 1902, he made a short but spirited campaign for the Republican gubernatorial nomination.

Stephen Henry Gale would marry Anna Marie Brown. My father's mother, Alice Cary Gale, was their only surviving child of three children, her two brothers dying in infancy.

The Hobson family's roots can be traced back to 14th Century England and the immigration of William Hobson of Yorkshire to Rowley, Massachusetts, in the mid-1600s. My father's paternal grandfather and namesake, John Lambert Hobson, Sr. (1841-1921), was born in Rowley and moved with his family to Haverhill at the age of ten. In 1871, he married Ida Noyes. They had two children, one of them a son, Arthur Lambert Hobson, Sr., my grandfather.

John L. Hobson, Sr. was Vice President and a Director of the Merrimack National Bank and founded several paper manufacturing companies in New England: Haverhill Paper Company in Bradford, Massachusetts, Glen Manufacturing Company in Berlin, New Hampshire, and the St. Croix Paper Company in Woodland, Maine. He served as a Director of Bradford Academy, which became Bradford Junior College. He was a member of the Haverhill School Board and a Trustee of the Haverhill Library.

My grandfather, John's father, Arthur Lambert Hobson, Sr. (1872 - 1946), was born in Haverhill and was graduated from Haverhill High School and Harvard College. Following graduation from Harvard, he went into the paper business at his father's paper mill in Berlin, New Hampshire, the Glen Manufacturing Company, and served as General Manager. In 1898, the mill was sold to International Paper Company.

In 1896, he married Alice Cary Gale and they would have five children. One of the children, Clifford, died in infancy. The oldest child was my father, John Lambert Hobson II.

Following the sale of the Berlin mill, John L. Hobson, Sr. quickly became interested in building another paper mill and his son, Arthur, joined in this new venture. Taking advantage of an abundant supply of pulpwood and power available, a new mill, the St. Croix Paper Company, and a town named Woodland were built at Sprague's Falls on the St. Croix River located on the Canadian border in the northeastern-most corner of the United States - Washington County, Maine.

Arthur L. Hobson, Sr. was now serving as an officer of the new venture and, following the sale of the Berlin mill, the family moved from the relative wilderness of Berlin to the Boston area. Arthur ran the Maine mill's business from his office located in downtown Boston.

Arthur Hobson, Sr. traveled constantly between Boston and the mill in Maine. His family, however, would now live in Haverhill, Massachusetts, a suburb 33 miles north of Boston and the same town as where his father and father-in-law lived. Their ten-bedroom house on Arlington Street was sold to Arthur by the North Congregational Church after the church built a new parsonage. The family would also have a summer home at Little Boar's Head at Rye Beach, New Hampshire.

In 1906, the new St. Croix mill in Woodland started up and, at the age of 34, Arthur L. Hobson, Sr. was appointed Vice President and Treasurer and a director. Twelve years later, during the First World War, Arthur, now 46, was running the fledging paper manufacturing operation which took a great deal of his time - he was very devoted to his business.

In 1926, Arthur would become President of the St. Croix Paper Company, a position he would hold until his death in 1946. He also succeeded many of the directorships of his father at the bank and at Bradford Academy.

My grandmother, John's mother, Alice Cary (Gale) Hobson (1872 - 1959), grew up in Haverhill, was graduated from Bradford Academy in 1891 and spent a year at the Robinson Seminary in Exeter, New Hampshire. She was an accomplished, energetic woman, a supportive wife to her busy husband and a loving mother. The traditional role of women at the time was not in the business world, so she vented her capabilities through supporting her family, strong service commitments in public and civic affairs and as a generous patron of the arts.

Alice Cary (Gale) Hobson's lifetime achievements are prodigious. Had she been born one or two generations later and not constrained by the limits of gender and social order of the time, she would have been a formidable force in either business or government.

Among the many of her achievements, she made possible the Gale Memorial Park in Exeter and the Gale City Hospital in Haverhill. She wrote a history of Bradford Academy. She founded the Little Boar's Head Music Festival for the education and advancement of music and young musicians. A young Boston violinist, Arthur Fiedler, who would subsequently become the conductor of Boston Pops for 50 years, was a frequent participant and visitor to the house in Rye Beach. She was a board member of the New Hampshire Federation of Women's Clubs, the Haverhill Women's Club, the Children's Aid Society, and the National Women's Country Club of Washington, DC. She was a member of the Music Lovers Club of Boston and the North Congregational Church of

Haverhill. During the First World War she worked with the Red Cross and the local hospitals. At this time, however, she was busy managing the household and raising her family.

The status of my father's younger sisters and brothers at the time of the First World War follows.

His oldest sister, Alice Gale Hobson, was born in 1898 also in Berlin, one year after my father. Alice was nineteen years old in 1918 when my father left and is referred to in my father's letters as "Sis" or "Sister", or as "Kid", my father's nickname for her. Alice, like her mother, was graduated from Bradford Academy. At the beginning of the First World War, she was still attending Bradford Academy and, during the war, she worked with the Red Cross and local hospitals. In 1918, Alice was engaged to marry First Lieutenant Ralph Everett Bradley. From her brother John's perspective, their long distance romance unfolds in these letters while Everett was serving with him in France.

Arthur Lambert Hobson, Jr. was the second son and the namesake of his father. He was born in 1902. He is referred to in the letters as "Art." Arthur, Jr. was fifteen and sixteen years old in 1917-1918 and was in his "middle" and "upper" (junior and senior) years at Phillips Exeter Academy during the First World War. He was a good student and athlete. He played football and rowed crew at Exeter. Following his graduation in 1919, he would go on to Harvard, row at Henley and graduate from Harvard Law School.

Katherine Brown Hobson was born in 1905 in Brighton, Massachusetts, and was twelve and thirteen years old during the First World War. After the war, following the tradition of her older sister and mother, Katherine also attended Bradford Academy, graduating in 1922, and then went to Garland School in Boston, graduating in 1925. Katherine loved horses and horseback riding. She is referred to as "Kay" or "K" in my father's letters.

Philip Noyes Hobson was the third son and the youngest child of Father's family. Philip was born in Boston in 1909 and was nine years old in 1918. His nickname was "Buster" and is referred to as such in my father's letters. During this time, Philip was at home and being tutored in his education.

Father's future brother-in-law Ralph Everett Bradley's place in my father's life at this point is significant. He is mentioned frequently in my father's letters. Ralph Everett Bradley was born in 1891, was 25 years old in 1916, seven years older than my father and was a Harvard College graduate.

He was called Everett and in my father's letters is sometimes referred to as "Ev". Aside from being future in-laws, the Bradley and Hobson families were Haverhill neighbors. Marjorie Bradley, referred to as "Marj" in my father's letters, was Everett's sister.

My father and Everett Bradley served together with the 26th Division in France and, for a time, they were both part of Battery A of the 102nd Field Artillery Regiment. Everett was with my father from the beginning, starting in the summer of 1917 at the training camp, Camp Curtis Guild, Jr., in Boxford, Massachusetts. In recognition of his age, education and carriage, Everett was initially enlisted as a sergeant at the training camp. While at the training camp Everett was given a commission and promoted to second lieutenant and a command position with Battery A. When the Division landed in France, Everett was promoted again to first lieutenant but was shortly transferred to the U.S. Engineer Corps where he supervised the building of airfields in France and volunteered to be an aerial observer, scouting enemy positions and directing artillery fire from airplanes.

While they were serving together in France, my father and Everett Bradley lead very different lives. For the most part, Father served on the front lines as a non-commissioned artillery officer. Everett was a commissioned officer doing important work behind the front lines. Everett's own modest, self-effacing description of his duties while he was in France was that he was the "…pampered pet of Fortune." The two men performed very different work under very different circumstances and they were not always in the same location. However, rank, duty and distance never kept them apart for very long, spiritually or physically. The letters reveal that while serving together in France they saw each other as frequently as possible and whenever apart wrote to each other. They had a solid friendship and held a tremendous mutual respect for each other.

Everett was a big brother figure and confidant for my father. And for Father, who was constantly exposed to instant death on the front lines, Everett was more than a mentor. Most important, he was a touchstone. In a world of army life and in the thick of a horrific war, living in a world seemingly gone mad with death, violence and destruction, Everett Bradley was a reminder to my father of things that were sane: the love of his family and home. It created a lasting bond between the two men, as sharing a war experience can do, and the relationship never wavered.

Alice Cary Gale Hobson and John Lambert Hobson II, Berlin, NH, 1898.
Stephen G. Hobson Collection - Hobson family photograph

Arthur Lambert Hobson, Sr. family - Undated. Left to right: Katherine Brown Hobson, Arthur Lambert Hobson, Alice Gale Hobson (back row), Alice Cary (Gale) Hobson, Arthur Lambert Hobson, Jr. (back row), John Lambert Hobson II, Phillip Noyes Hobson. Stephen G. Hobson Collection - Hobson family photograph

John Lambert Hobson II, 1913 - Age 16. Stephen G. Hobson Collection - Hobson family photograph

129 Arlington Street, Haverhill, MA. Home of the Arthur Lambert Hobson, Sr. family, 1916.
Haverhill Public Library Collection

Arthur Lambert Hobson, Sr. summer house at Little Boar's Head, Rye Beach,
NH. Undated. Stephen G. Hobson Collection - Hobson family photograph

CHAPTER THREE

Prologue to War

America's Gilded Age

1916

"The lamps are going out all over Europe"

EDWARD GREY - BRITISH FOREIGN SECRETARY

"They shall not pass!"

FRENCH GENERAL ROBERT GEORGES NIVELLE FOLLOWING
THE BATTLE OF VERDUN

In 1916, the year before going to war, the United States was transitioning out of its Gilded Age. The Gilded Age was a term given by Mark Twain and Charles Dedley Warner to America's expansive and self-indulgent period that began in the late 1860s after America's Civil War, Reconstruction of the South and the Industrial Revolution. Great strides were made during this time. Manufacturing and service industries thrived. Private and public wealth expanded. Laws were passed that enforced free enterprise in business and improved the human condition.

It was a time of amazing accomplishments for the nation. A national rail system was completed, the Panama Canal was built, National Parks were established and expanded, agriculture was mechanized and the factory system of production spread across the country. Alexander Graham Bell invented the telephone and Thomas Edison developed the electric light. The Brooklyn Bridge was completed.

It was during its Gilded Age that the United States gained the economic strength and world political stature that ultimately played the decisive roles in the outcome of the First World War.

With the nation's seemingly unbridled prosperity and growth, many farming communities in the northeast became industrial centers. Cities and towns grew rapidly in size, number and ethnic diversity. There was, consequently, an environmental cost. Dams were constructed on rivers to harness the resource for power generation. Air-fouling coal was the economical fuel for firing factories' boilers and heating homes. Forests were decimated to build roads and houses and to make way for more farmland to feed the expanding population.

The Gilded Age was an economic opportunity for private fortunes to be made. American millionaires, fewer than 20 in 1850, numbered 40 thousand by 1900. Private wealth increased by a factor of 13. In some small measure, the Hobson and Gale families participated in this growth through the Northeast's thriving shoe, banking and paper industries. On a much, much larger scale, this period in American history saw the formation of mega-wealth through business organizations like Carnegie Steel Company, Standard Oil Company, General Electric Company and U.S. Steel Corporation. Personal fortunes, like those of the Rockefeller, Carnegie and Mellon families that were made during that time from railroads, steel (steel production rose from 13,000 tons per year to 11.3 million) and banking, continue to this day in the form of foundations.

The United States had emerged from the Gilded Age as one of the world's wealthiest nations. It was first in the output of timber, steel, coal and iron. Since 1860, before the American Civil War, the population of the United States had tripled and its exports tripled as well.

The condition of the nation's people and the conditions of the workplace, previously not a consideration in the economic advancement of the country, now came into the forefront. The Progressive Era would emerge and was the social conscience and legislative aftermath to America's rapid growth and industrialization during the height of the Gilded Age.

The progressive movement peaked during Theodore Roosevelt's presidency in 1901 - 1909. It became a time of change and reform when it was recognized that the common laws that existed in the United States no longer had the power to deal with the uncommon wealth that was building in this country. An eighth of the population held seven-eighths of the nation's wealth.

Roosevelt coined the term "muckrakers" to describe commentators who kept their heads down concentrating on raking the muck of America. Instead of holding their heads up and looking forward, they persisted in pointing out the inequities and poor conditions of the time. According to the period's leading muckraking journalist, Ray Stannard Baker of "McClure's Magazine", the guiding principle of the nation was: "Society cannot exist unless a controlling power upon will and appetite be placed somewhere."

And so it was that during the latter part of the Progressive Era, laws were passed to curb the excess and President Roosevelt, an enthusiastic Republican with a healthy social conscience, became famous as the "Trust Buster". Legislation included the Interstate Commerce Act and the Clayton Antitrust Act that curbed the activities of monopolies and trusts. The 17th Amendment was passed governing the election and term of Senators. The Federal Trade Commission was established to oversee the business of business. The organization of American labor started with the formation of the American Federation of Labor and the Industrial Workers of the World, giving the factory workers a voice and leverage in negotiating better working conditions and pay scales with management and business owners.

In this time of reform, the Child Labor Law, known as the Keating-Owen Act of 1916, would be passed protecting children in the workplace and improving the working conditions in American factories.

Enabling the collection of great wealth during the Gilded Age was the lack of sustaining income taxes. Federal income taxes on individuals and corporations were not permanently established until 1913 by the 16th Amendment to the Constitution. Prior to that time, the federal government was supported by sales taxes on distilled spirits, carriages, refined sugar, tobacco and snuff, property sold at auction, corporate bonds, tariffs on imported goods and, prior to the Civil War, slaves.

In the fiscal year 1866, the United States Government collected $310 million from tax revenues and had a budget surplus. In the fiscal year 1918, five years after the implementation of the Federal Income tax in 1913, annual internal revenue collections for the first time passed $1 billion. Two years later, in 1920, the revenue from tax collections was $5.4 billion! America's growth was expansive and expensive, and big government was now a rapidly growing business, and the politicians began their ride on the coattails of the working population and America's businesses. The struggle to maintain a balance between the wealth of the citizens and abuses of government and politicians had begun.

Big government, now supported by federal and state taxes leveled against the populous and businesses, and the emergence of career politicians was not what the Founding Fathers of the country had envisioned for their democracy. The country's Fathers originally set out a government, later reiterated by Abraham Lincoln, which was to be of the people, by the people and for the people, not of the government, by the government and for the politicians.

John Adams of Massachusetts, signer of the Declaration of Independence, the first Vice President of the United States under President George Washington and the second President of the United States, had some thoughts on this subject. Adams, addressing his son, Thomas, who was expressing an interest in public service, wrote to him,

> Public business, my son, must always be done by somebody. It will be done by somebody or other. If wise men decline it, others will not; if honest men refuse it, others will not. A young man should weigh well his plans. Integrity should be preserved in all events, as essential to his happiness, through every stage of his existence. His first maxim then should be to place his honor out of reach of all men. In order to do this he must make it a rule never to become dependent on public employments for subsistence. Let him have a trade, a profession, a farm, a shop, something where he can honestly live, and then he may engage in public affairs, if invited, upon independent principles. My advice to my children is to maintain an independent character.

Adams did not feel the country was well served by professional, career politicians who had never put their foot on a shovel. A profile of today's politician shows that since John Adams wrote this to his son the United States has gradually slipped down a long, slippery slope, far away from Adams' and the Founding Father's wisdom and vision.

Much of the industrial advantage enjoyed by the United States during the Gilded Age came from the great influx of immigrant labor that was further defining America and her character. Escaping the problems of their overseas homelands, humanity poured into America where they were told the streets were paved with gold and that opportunity existed for every man. For many, it would work out that way. For most, however, it would not, and they lived in slums, toiled in sweatshops and endured deplorable working and living conditions. Generally, it was a better condition than the one they left behind.

Many immigrants brought with them welcomed skills and trades from their homelands that were not found in America. The immigrants were willing to work in American factories and harvest the country's rich, natural resources in the fields, mines and forests for low wages and under poor conditions, in the process making huge profits for their employers. During the first decade of the 1900s, 8.8 million souls immigrated to the United States. Thus, in 1916 the population of the United States was more ethnically diverse than at any other previous point in its history.

This was an interesting and transitional time in American history. The First World War would be the trip wire that would push America into the 20th Century and a whole new way of thinking.

On the eve of America entering the First World War in 1916, newspaper headlines noted interesting events.

England's Sir Ernest Shackleton was exploring the Antarctic.

In Russia, the bizarre-appearing mystic, Rasputin, was gaining notoriety and a credible foothold with the ruling Czar's family.

In Dublin, Ireland, on Easter Sunday 2,000 Irishmen would start a rebellion against the rule of Great Britain to attain political freedom and eventually establish the Irish Free State.

On America's business front, in 1916 the Dow Jones Industrial Average broke 100 for the second time since its creation in 1896. The compilation of companies that made up the Average was expanded in 1916. The companies in the original compilation were selected to represent a profile of America's industry and their performance was a barometer and reflection of the condition of the American economy. As an indicator of America's growing and diversified business base, the compilation of the Average went that year from the original 12 industrial companies to 20 companies. Today, General Electric (GE) is the only surviving company of the original 12 used to compile Messrs. Dow and Jones' historic and most widely noted stock market barometer.

America's GDP (Gross Domestic Product - the value of all the goods and services produced in the country) grew 3.7% in 1915 and catapulted 16.2% in 1916. With America supplying the war in Europe, America's exports to Europe expanded from $1.479 billion in 1913 to $4.062 billion by 1917.

In 1916, with the expansive Atlantic and Pacific oceans protecting its borders from attacks from overseas, the United States was at peace, except for problems along its southern border with Mexico. Mexico had a history of unstable governments. The United States' relationship with Mexico was thorny at best, and would ultimately play a role in the decision to go to war in Europe the following year.

In 1916, the United States government recognized Venustiano Carranza as the head of Mexico's government and refused to recognize a dictator, Victorino Huerta, who in 1913 had seized control of the Mexican government. Germany had financed Huerta's movement to set up a pro-German Mexican government.

Early in 1916, Huerta's supporter, the infamous Mexican revolutionary, Francisco Pancho Villa, with his cavalry, Los Dorados (The Golden Ones), began raids along the Mexican border into New Mexico killing several Americans. President Woodrow Wilson subsequently sent a division of American troops commanded by General John J. "Black Jack" Pershing, a veteran frontier Indian fighter and a veteran of the Cuban War of 1898 and the Russo-Japanese War of 1904 - 1905, on a punitive expedition to chase Pancho Villa back into Mexico. The campaign started in June and ended in

October. Pershing's nickname, Black Jack, was a subtle accolade bestowed on him by his troops because of his pre-military experience teaching black students in the Missouri schools.

Pershing did indeed chase Pancho Villa out of the United States. But Pershing continued the pursuit and chased Villa across the border through Chihuahua, Mexico. Pancho Villa, whose real name was Doroteo Arango, was never captured. However, the Mexican government resented the United States' federal troops' uninvited intrusion into Mexico and the incident stressed relations between the two countries. A subsequently proposed alliance between Mexico and Germany against the United States made by the Germans would ultimately sway many isolationists and play a very decisive part in the United States' decision to go to war.

In 1916, the world population was approximately 1.8 billion (it was 6.8 billion in 2010). The population of the contiguous 48 United States was approximately 100 million, a third of what it is today including all 50 states. At that time, the population of the Commonwealth of Massachusetts was about 3 million. The population of New York State was about 10 million, more than three times that of Massachusetts. Three million of New York State's population - equivalent to the population of the entire Commonwealth of Massachusetts - lived in New York City.

In 1916, the median age in America was twenty-five, more than ten years younger than today. The life expectancy of a man was 50 years and 54 years for a woman.

In 1916, a rapidly shrinking third of America's population still earned a living from farming, although about half the population lived outside of cities in rural locations.

Life in one of America's small towns, Haverhill, Massachusetts, and home of the Hobson and Gale families, mirrored much of what was happening in the Northeast United States. Prior to 1640, Haverhill was an Indian village known as Pentucket. It was incorporated as a town in 1641 and as a city in 1869.

Haverhill, with a population in 1916 of 50,000 (almost 61,000 in 2010), was a northern suburb of the rapidly growing city of Boston. Haverhill began as a farming community settled by Europeans. Among its distinctions: it was the site of the original Macy's department store established as a dry goods store in 1851 and where Macy's held its first Thanksgiving Day Parade. Haverhill, ever socially conscious, was anti-slavery, as was most of the north pre-Civil War, but Haverhill was a stopover on the Underground Railroad during the Civil War, and in the 1850s was an early pre-prohibition center for the temperance movement and the Temperance Society.

During the industrial revolution, the town had evolved into an industrial center. Local area mills thrived for 180 years, including gristmills, sawmills, tanneries, shipbuilding, textile, shoe factories and paper mills that were attracted by the power that could be generated from the Merrimack (old spelling Merrimac) River that flowed through the town. The flush mill era for Haverhill would last until the Great Depression of the 1930s when much of the Northeast's manufacturing industries collapsed or went elsewhere.

Newspapers were the medium of record in 1916. To keep the reading public current with the day's events, most city newspapers were published and distributed twice each day with a morning and an evening edition.

The local Haverhill Gazette newspaper in 1916 gives a good picture of life in Haverhill. It advertised eggs costing 51 cents a dozen, beef steak at 40 cents per pound, butter for 53 cents per pound and a loaf of bread for 8 cents (although a store-bought loaf of bread was not pre-sliced until 1933 when the Taggart Baking Company began pre-slicing its brand, "Wonder Bread").

An entire Sunday chicken dinner with all the fixings served at a good Haverhill restaurant cost 75 cents. Men's suits cost 15 - 25 dollars; a dress shirt six dollars; a neck tie under two dollars; and dress gloves cost fewer than four dollars. You could top it all off with a fine felt Derby hat, very much the gentleman's fashion of the day, that cost five dollars.

For 11 cents, you could take in the matinee at the Majestic Theater in downtown Haverhill which was featuring Hollywood's latest silent movie production starring Helen Ware, "The Garden Of Allah". The theater had a piano by the stage where a live pianist played the background music for the movie.

In 1916, a good job in Haverhill paid about 35 - 50 dollars...per month.

In 1916, a five-bedroom house in a nice Haverhill neighborhood cost about 5,000 dollars.

The pictures of the Hobson and Gale families show that most of the gentlemen of the day had beards. Barbershop shaves were a regular item for men. A shave and hair cut was, in fact, "two bits" or 25 cents. Barbershop shaves were popular because the average man simply didn't have the know-how or the tools to properly sharpen a straight razor at home. Shaving at home with a dull straight razor was a painful and often blood-letting experience. Men went to the barbershop for a shave by a professional with a properly sharpened instrument, or men didn't shave at all and they simply grew a beard and trimmed their whiskers with scissors. Sporting a full beard or several days' growth of beard stubble between barbershop visits was considered acceptable at any social occasion and was actually born out of practicality and pain avoidance. Beards, therefore, were popular even though twelve years prior the "safety razor" with its disposable and consistently sharp blade was invented by King Gillette and manufactured in Boston. The safety razor would eventually make the "bald face" and a clean cut appearance popular and easier to achieve without requiring a blood transfusion. However, prior to American men going off to war in 1917, the use of the safety razor and the discipline of shaving every morning at home was a slow acceptance process. As any male will testify, not shaving is easier than shaving. And, besides, there was a social aspect to the regular barbershop visits.

Relevant to our subject, what finally gave acceptance to the safety razor and the fashion of being clean shaven every morning was the First World War. For hygiene reasons and to allow a rubber gas mask to seal tightly around the face, the U.S. government put a safety razor into the hands of every American soldier. And the soldiers readily and more than willingly used it.

Wherever it exists on the human body, hair is a breeding ground for lice, a nasty and abundant companion of life in the trenches. Being clean shaven prevented attracting lice, and the prospect of falling victim to a leaky gas mask and breathing lachrymator or asphyxiate (chlorine or phosgene) gas was too horrible to imagine.

As a young boy, John Hobson would ride horses for transportation like we would cars or bicycles today, and the family would regularly transport about town in horse drawn carriages in warm months and sleighs during the winter. Rather than the roads being plowed during the winter they were instead rolled to pack the snow so sleighs could slide on the surface. In 1916, horses were still evident for personal transportation and field work, and horse teams pulled streetcars for local public transportation. The resulting manure in the city's streets left a smell and an abundance of flies that one can only imagine today, but post First World War America would swap all that for automobile exhaust. What few automobiles there were on the streets in Haverhill in 1916 cost about 450 dollars each. Eight years prior, in 1908, Henry Ford had introduced the Model T Ford automobile. It mobilized America with affordable automobile transportation. The Model T car initially cost 260 dollars and 15 million would eventually be sold.

In 1916, cigarettes, unfiltered and fatter around than today's version, were 20 cents a pack. Pipes and cigars were the gentleman's preferred method of nicotine delivery. Oblivious to the health hazard, smoking tobacco was advertised to the public as healthy and an aid to digestion and relaxation. Women generally didn't smoke at this time.

Leisure time during this period for the average American was scarce. In 1916, there was a six-day work week. Saturday was just another work day. Sunday was a day dedicated to resting and at worship and with family. Families were more centralized and less mobile than today. Generations of Americans never left the town or county in which their ancestors first landed and settled. There would be large family Sunday dinners. Roast chicken was popular.

In 1916, there was also a large national interest in sports, especially America's national sport, baseball!

In the 1916 World Series, the American League's storied Boston Red Sox faced off against the National League Pennant-winning team from Brooklyn, NY, the Robins, which later became the Dodgers. In the second game of the series, the Red Sox's George Herman "Babe" Ruth made his pitching debut in front of 42,000 fans gathered at Braves Field in Boston, used that year for the World Series because of its larger seating capacity over Fenway Park. The Red Sox won the World Series 4-1.

The Red Sox would win the World Series again in 1918, and the team would subsequently sell Babe Ruth to the New York Yankees. The Red Sox would be denied another world championship for 86 years, until 2004, haunted, many said, by the curse of the "Bambino" (Babe Ruth).

The sporting events, equipment and records of the day certainly were different from today's. In 1916, amateur golfer Charles "Chick" Evans won the U.S. Open at the Minikahda Club in Minneapolis, Minnesota, with 286 strokes. He played with hickory-shafted golf clubs.

In 1916, a fourteen-year old boy from Atlanta, Robert (Bobby) Tyre Jones, Jr. played his first U.S. Amateur golf tournament. Bobby Jones didn't win that tournament, but he did finish in the top ten and then he went on to become perhaps the world's greatest and most beloved golfer, founding the Augusta National Golf Club and the U.S. Masters Championship golf tournament.

In 1916, Dario Resta won the Indianapolis 500 automobile race in a Peugeot automobile with a "breakneck" average track speed at Indy's "Brickyard" of 84 mph. The fastest winning speed in recent Indy 500 history was set in 1990 at 185 mph. The world land speed record in 1916 was 141 mph set in a Benz automobile. Today it is 458 mph.

In 1916, Richard Williams defeated William Johnston in tennis men's singles at the U.S. Open. Williams wore the gentleman's tennis "togs" of the day: long, white flannel pants; long-sleeved, white shirt; and a necktie. Because of the war in Europe, many international events were cancelled including tennis' international Davis Cup, which was not played from 1915 to 1918.

In 1916, Jess Willard was the World's Heavyweight Boxing Champion. Willard, called the Great White Hope by a bigoted America, had knocked out the Heavy Weight Champion, Negro pugilist Jack Johnson, during a 1915 boxing match in Havana, Cuba. The controversial Johnson was possibly the greatest heavyweight fighter in history and he was the first black Heavyweight Boxing Champion in boxing history. The famous and flamboyant Jack Johnson's effect and influence was felt worldwide. In the opening phase of the Great War, the French military nicknamed a powerful artillery shell that emitted prodigious black smoke The Jack Johnson.

During the summer of 1916, there was a heat wave along the east coast that extended from the Carolinas to Maine. As many that could sought relief at the ocean's shore. During the month of July, along the New Jersey coast the war news in Europe would be briefly eclipsed and the public's interest drawn by the news of a series of shark attacks at Beach Haven, Spring Lake and in Matawan Channel by Sandy Hook. The unprecedented and rapid succession of the shark attacks by the "Jersey Man-Eater" that was later caught and found with the human remains in its stomach, would 44 years later become the inspiration and genesis for Peter Benchley to write his best-selling book, "Jaws". The publication of Benchley's book in the 1970s had much the same effect on the nation as the original attacks did in 1916; it made people wary about swimming in the ocean and triggered a surge of revenge shark killing.

In 1916, Jeannette Rankin of Montana became the first woman elected to the United States Congress. This is remarkable because in 1916 women didn't even have the right to vote in national elections. That right wouldn't be given to women until 1920 under the passage of the 19th Amendment to the U.S. Constitution. A pacifist, when Congress was asked by President Wilson for a declaration of war in 1917, Senator Rankin would vote not to go to war, and, when Congress was asked by President Roosevelt for a declaration of war in December of 1941 after the attack on Pearl Harbor, Rankin cast the only dissenting vote, stating, "As a woman, I can't go to war and I refuse to send anyone else."

However situated people were in the beau ideal of American life in 1916, all the citizens of Haverhill and the United States had a wary eye looking eastward across the Atlantic Ocean. The storm still raging in Europe since 1914 threatened to draw the United States into a brutal war.

There had been no war in Europe for almost a century. German Chancellor Otto von Bismarck had historically presided and maintained a delicate balance of power among the great European powers. But, since the beginning of the 20th century, Germany, under the Second Reich ruled by Kaiser Wilhelm II, had been engaged in the imperialist pursuit of colonial possessions. The balance of European power had been upset. Formally, Frederick Wilhelm Viktor Albert of Hohenzollern, or William II (and known as Kaiser Wilhelm II, the Emperor of Germany and King of Prussia since 1888), was the successor of Frederick III. Not atypical of the time, there was close breeding among the crowned heads of Europe. Wilhelm II was the grandson of William I of Germany and Queen Victoria of Britain, a cousin to Czar Nicholas II of Russia and King George V of Britain and the uncle of King Edward VII of Britain. Wilhelm II was born with a withered left arm.

Kaiser Wilhelm II had a strong belief in the divine nature of kingship and a love of military display, possibly a personality trait developed as compensation for his physical shortcoming. Seeking a place in the sun for Germany with the other major nations of the world, Wilhelm led the German Empire to become imperialistic and a major naval, colonial and commercial power. In the process, Germany threatened neighboring Western European countries. The perceived threat sparked imperialist rivalry among nations, generated an armaments race and, with Germany's rapid naval expansion, threatened Great Britain's dominance on the high seas.

Feeling the need for protection against Germany's aggression, the international combination of Western European nations bound together in a series of alliances for defense: the Triple Alliance, the Triple Entente and the Entente Cordiale. Noted British author of the time, H. G. Wells, said of the state of affairs that everybody knew it was a situation that was going to lead to a war, but nobody knew how to stop it.

In June of 1914, the Austro-Hungarian heir to the throne, Archduke Francis Ferdinand, was assassinated by a Serbian teenager. Immediately following the assassination of the Archduke, Austria-Hungary swore retaliation against Serbia. Russia vowed it would protect Serbia. Allied with Austria-Hungary, Germany declared war on Russia. German military forces subsequently marched through Belgium, a Russian ally, to invade France. Great Britain, not attacked but threatened by the possible German dominance of France just across the Channel, was allied with France and on 4 August 1914 declared war on Germany. Signs went up over England seeking enlistment in their military saying, "England expects that this day every man will do his duty."

Thus began what was known at the time as the Great War. When the hostilities began, Edward Grey, the British Foreign Secretary, said in despair, "The lamps are going out all over Europe. We shall not see them lit again in our lifetimes."

The first fight of the Great War, known as the Battle of Mons, happened on 22 August 1914 at Casteau in Belgium. It was a fight involving a squadron of 120 cavalrymen of the 4th Dragoon Guards of the BEF, the British Expeditionary Force, who had landed in France the week before and were pursuing a large number of German troops reported to be advancing through Brussels toward the town of Mons. It would be the first engagement by British soldiers on Continental Europe since the Battle of Waterloo 99 years earlier that pitted the French army under Emperor Napoleon against the combined Anglo and Prussian armies of the Seventh Coalition.

When war first broke out in Europe, Alfred von Schlieffen developed the German's ambitious war strategy: The Schlieffen Plan. The plan called for an immediate and quick sweep from the Western Front (west of Germany) over the top of the continent and to the west through neutral and lightly defended Belgium to attack France's weaker, upper northeast corner, while Austria-Hungary maintained a defensive stance toward Russia on the Eastern Front (east of Germany). Schlieffen figured it would require the

Prewar Europe

Russian Army at least six weeks to mobilize and, by the time Russia had mobilized, Germany would have defeated the French army as the French defended Paris. The desired result would be Germany capturing France, and then the Central Powers would be ready to meet Russia's forces on the Eastern Front where they would prevail by superior force. It sounded simple enough, albeit characteristically arrogant. But nothing in this war would prove to be simple.

The plan faltered from the start. Believing that Germany's northwest advance into Belgium was a diversion, most of the French army moved directly east, straight across the continent, to the south and below the main force of the German attack. And Germany hadn't taken into account and greatly underestimated that Belgium, France, Russia and Britain - "that contemptible little army" as the Germans referred to the British - would fight back as strongly as they did. To the east, the Russians hurled men at the attack in huge numbers, and they were killed proportionately. But, the courageous Russian offensive on the Eastern Front drew German resources and upset the plan and was a diversion to the advance on the Western Front.

German plans for the offensive on the Western Front soon unraveled. Recognizing their vulnerability from the eastward-attacking

34

French army below their main force, Germany spread the main force of its offensive in northern France to defend against the French army's drive below them. The result was that the entire German offensive was split, strung out, and was fighting on two fronts and became weakened.

However, Germany quickly occupied Belgium. The Germans successfully advanced on France's English Channel ports through northern Belgium, but were stopped at the First Battle of Ypres in October 1914 and later at the Somme in July 1916.

German forces did penetrate far enough into France to threaten Paris. In September 1914, with the resounding battle cry of "They shall not pass!" the Allies stopped the German's dash only about thirty miles east of Paris in the bloody and hard fought First Battle of the Marne, which became known as the "Miracle on the Marne." The Germans had come dangerously close to taking Paris. Many civilians fled the city. At the outset of the battles around the First Marne, French Commander Marshal Joffre addressed his troops and said, "Soldiers of France, we are attacking. Advance as long as you can. When you can no longer advance, hold your position. When you can no longer hold your position, die!" Joffre wanted to make it clear to his soldiers that if the Germans did take Paris, there would be no tomorrow. As a result of the halt in the German offensive, thirty-three German generals were sacked.

The result of all this was that, after Schlieffen's initial sweep was stopped in 1914, both sides dug in and the war stalemated in a catastrophic, bloody, trench war along the Western Front along what was called the Hindenburg Line. Entrenched positions barely changed a full kilometer for almost three years. The Hindenburg Line - 400 miles of mud and appalling horror - snaked its way from north to south through continental Europe. Its northern point was on the North Sea's coast in Ostend, Belgium. From there, it ran south into France at Armentieres, then southeast across France to Soissions, Douai, Saint-Quentin, Reims, Verdun and Saint-Mihiel. The line then ran south across the southwest corner of the German border to Luneville on the northern border of Switzerland.

HINDENBURG LINE, 1914

German soldiers on their way to the Western Front.

By 1916, the Great War had been going on for two years between the Central Powers - Germany, Austria-Hungary, Japan, Bulgaria and the Ottoman Empire - and the Allied Powers - the United Kingdom, France, the Russian Empire, Belgium, Italy, Romania, Serbia, Italy and Montenegro.

Because so many nations were ultimately involved, the Great War would evolve and become known as the World War but, of course, it would not, or could not, be designated as the First World War until there was the unfortunate order of succession subsequently established twenty years later by the next world war, the Second World War.

From February to December of 1916, the horrific First Battle of Verdun yielded 700,000 total dead, wounded or missing soldiers within a ten kilometer square (approximately 16 square mile) battlefield. Several Allied defeats followed, the most awful around the Chemin des Dames in the Aisne Campaign. Battle-weary French soldiers being slaughtered in the trenches were saying, "We're lions being led by donkeys!"

On 1 May 1916, French General Petain, head of France's 2nd Army, took over command of the demoralized French troops from the head of the 3rd Army, General Nivelle, who had taken over as commander and Chief of the French Army from Joffre. Upon passing command, Nivelle said the immortal words to Petain, "My order after the Battle of Verdun was 'They shall not pass!' I transmit it to you…" Thus, "They shall not pass" became the rallying cry of the Allied troops.

In the ensuing German occupation of 11 million civilians in northern France and Belgium, the Germans murdered civilians, set up concentration camps and forced women and children into slave labor. It was not good public relations. The world was repulsed.

Beyond Europe, Germany attacked Britain's far-flung empire hoping that attacking the British Colonies would distract England from fighting on the Western front and on the North Sea. Germany had also devised a plan called Operation #3 that fortunately was never attempted; it called for the invasion of New York City and Boston.

On the Western Front in Europe, the French and British were losing 7,000 men per day in the trenches. This had become the mother of all wars of attrition, an exploration of how far men can be degraded. A British soldier marching up to the front lines at the Somme, where some of the costliest battles early in the war were fought, reportedly said, "We're not making a sacrifice. Jesus, you've seen this war. We are the sacrifice!"

By 1916, mired in trench warfare along fronts on the east and west sides of Germany, almost two million Europeans had already been butchered in the Great War. In the beginning, it appeared that on a global basis the war was going the Central Powers' way.

To break the stalemate on the Western Front, both sides kept intensifying their efforts. Each year casualties mounted in huge proportions as each side invented more terrible weapons and launched more reckless infantry charges across open country battlefields in a frustrated effort to break through the oppositions' trenched lines of defenses.

In the year 1916, 19,000 British soldiers were killed in a single day of combat on the Western Front along the Somme River in France. The Battle of the Somme raged for 140 days, eventually killing over 1.4 million soldiers on both sides, the largest death toll of any single battle in history. One day on the Somme, there were 50,000 soldiers killed in four and one-half hours! Of the vast loss of human lives, Winston S. Churchill, Britain's First Lord of the Admiralty during the First World War, said:

> War, which used to be cruel and magnificent, has now become cruel and squalid. Instead of a small number of well-trained professionals championing their country's cause with ancient weapons and a beautiful intricacy of archaic maneuver, sustained at every moment by the applause of their nation, we now have entire populations, including even women and children, pitted against one another in brutish mutual extermination, and only a set of bleary-eyed clerks left to add up the butcher's bill.

In the fall of that year, along with other military advances in an attempt to overcome the stalemate in the trenches, there emerged on the scene Germany's iconic fighter pilot and Air Ace (German qualification to become an Ace was 10 enemy planes shot down) who captured the imagination of many with the use of the airplane as a weapon, Baron Manfred von Richthofen, a.k.a. Red Knight of Germany, a.k.a. the Red Baron. He was, in fact, of minor nobility. His father was a cavalry officer in the Prussian Army, and Manfred did fly a red airplane.

In 1916, Richthofen shot down the first 15 enemy aircraft of the 80 he would ultimately shoot down in his career. It was remarkable progress for the development of aircraft being used for the first time in combat. The Wright brothers had experienced the first unassisted airplane flight only 13 years prior in 1903 at Kitty Hawk, North Carolina. But, upon success of the first flight, Orville and Wilber Wright did immediately begin marketing their invention to the United States military.

Fighting at the Somme. "We're lions being led by donkeys!" American Heritage History of World War I

Germany's iconic Air Ace Baron Manfred Von Richthofen, a.k.a. The Red Baron, a.k.a. The Red Knight of Germany, and the plane he made famous, the Fokker DR 1. Richthofen was credited with 80 victories (kills). At age 26, he was killed in pursuit of his 81ˢᵗ victory. www.worldwar1.nl

In 1916, Germany was using dirigibles - Zeppelins - in the first air raids on London.

In horror, America looked on from across the Atlantic at the Great War. The people of the United States were shocked at the news of the carnage, but they didn't have the appetite to fight. There was great anti-interventionist sentiment in the country. This sentiment was nothing new; it had been part of American foreign policy established by the greatest of our Founding Fathers. The issue touched on the very reasons the United States declared independence from England in the first place. In George Washington's Farewell Address in 1796 the core of his message was independence abroad and unity at home. Washington said, "Europe has a set of primary interests which to us have none, or a very remote relation. Hence she must be engaged in frequent controversies, the cause of which is foreign to our concerns… 'Tis our true policy to steer clear of permanent alliances with any portion of the foreign world." And Thomas Jefferson's first inaugural address made reference to America having "entangling alliance with none." Almost one hundred and twenty years later, American isolationists hurled this foundation of American history at President Wilson.

With America's diverse, ethnic and growing immigrant population, there were strong emotions among American citizens about participation in this European war. Many citizens who had recently immigrated to the United States still identified themselves as hyphenated Americans and they had not forgotten what difficult conditions brought them to America in the first place, many having been driven from their homeland by abuses of the Allied nations. Having found opportunity in America, they were not enthusiastic about making any sacrifice for the Allied nations or their German homeland that had tormented them.

Brutalized and abused for generations, the Irish-American immigrants loathed the British.

There were anti-Semitism repercussions with Russian-American Jews who had in persecution fled their homeland.

Having escaped Prussian militarists and settled in large numbers in America's Midwest, many German-Americans wanted to see their Fatherland delivered a lesson. And then there were those German-Americans with very strong family ties that transcended the Atlantic who did not want to go to war against their relatives. Many German-Americans returned to Germany to fight for the Fatherland.

The general population of America's western states, who were still forging the last American frontier, felt no affiliation whatsoever to what was going on in Europe. Ostrich-like, sticking their heads in the sand, to many American westerners this war was, in their minds anyway, something that possibly threatened things way over on the other side of the country, the east coast, and did not involve them at all.

Gender also played a role in the anti-intervention sentiment. A Civil War ditty sung by peace-loving American mothers, who had no vote at this time but whose souls always bore the brunt of war, went like this:

I didn't raise my boy to be a soldier
I raised him to be my pride and joy
Who dares to put a musket on a shoulder
To shoot some other mother's pride and joy

Was America neutral? Not completely. America was the banker and supplier of the war. About half of the British war budget was spent in the United States, and investors on Wall Street were betting on the outcome of the war. American exports and the economy grew.

All totaled, the attitude among the American people to spend America's treasure and blood in a war being fought on European soil to defend the Allied countries against the countries of the Central Powers certainly was not unanimous.

Many Americans were seeking a romantic adventure, as the war may have been perceived, and a cause. When American movie theaters showed newsreels containing film clips of the war in Europe, the theater management posted a notice on the movie screen stating, "The President has called for strict neutrality. Please do not hiss". Even so, the red-blooded American audience, spirited with indignation, would still give the German soldiers the raspberries. Many Americans were more than just sympathetic or just making noise about the horror that was taking place in France; they were doing something about it.

Before the United States entered the war, several thousand Americans, many of them college boys representing 50 schools, went to France during 1914 - 1916 to fight with the Allies in one capacity or another through two operations that mostly furnished ambulance drivers for the French Army: the American Field Service (AFS) and the Norton-Harjes. Through these services, these men were able to serve with the Allied Forces and still keep their American citizenship. Many became ambulance drivers, like the American author and adventurer Ernest Hemingway who subsequently used his experiences as a basis for his book, "A Farewell To Arms". "A Friend of France" was carved on the tombstone of one of many American ambulance drivers who gave his life for the cause during this time.

Many "Yanks" flew with the French and British forces in American-manned squadrons or escadrilles. The most well-known of these squadrons was the legendary French Service Aeronautique squadron. Originally named the Escadrille Americaine, in order to downplay America's involvement in the war it was later called the Escadrille Lafayette or the Lafayette Escadrille. There were 224 American pilots that served in the Lafayette Escadrille. By the end of the war, 11 died from illness or in accidents, 15 became prisoners of war, 51 died in combat and 11 became Aces.

While the majority of the American population stood passively by and did not support America's involvement with a war in Europe, the Germans remained truculent, generally ignoring the existing rules of naval warfare involving attacks on merchant vessels without warning. The United States was actively trading across the Atlantic with Great Britain and France, filling contracts to supply the Allies with food and weapons during wartime, which exposed the American merchant fleet to attacks on the sea.

In January 1915, the German auxiliary cruiser Prinz Eitel Friedrich sunk the William P. Frye, a hapless wooden, Bath, Maine-built sailing freighter and the first of a number of American merchant vessels that were sunk by the Germans in the Atlantic. At the time of her sinking, the William P. Frye was carrying a cargo of case oil (kerosene), coal, grain and sugar.

The loss of 128 American souls in the torpedoing and sinking of the British ship Lusitania off the coast of Ireland just south of Queenstown in May 1915 by a German submarine, or unterseeboote or U-boat, further weakened President Wilson's popular position of neutrality. It has never been resolved as to whether Lusitania was carrying contraband munitions.

Wilson's successful reelection campaign slogan in 1916 was "He kept us out of war." However, with the horrible slaughter taking place in Europe and now with innocent American lives being lost in attacks on the high seas, it was becoming apparent by 1916 that the United States would be involved in the Great War before long.

Just having subdued the Mexican border troubles and in anticipation of possibly going to war in Europe, the United States passed the National Defense Act of May 1916. The National Defense Act authorized doubling the size of the Army and quadrupling the organized militia or National

Guard over a five-year period. It also immediately established National Guard training camps and endorsed the Plattsburgh, New York, summer camp program, a program my father would attend, training for new National Guard troops.

In the end, the measures taken under the National Defense Act would prove to be nowhere near enough, but at least it gave the United States somewhat of a running start when war was declared the following year.

With these world events as a background, sensing that the United States' involvement in the Great War was eminent, seeking adventure, and certainly not enamored with school, in the summer of 1916 John L. Hobson II joined the National Guard.

For a month during the late summer and early fall of that year, from 8 September through 5 October, my father attended the National Guard training camp in Plattsburgh, New York, as part of Company B of the 10th Regiment.

And so it is here that we begin the first of the many letters my father wrote home to his family.

CHAPTER FOUR

National Guard Training Camp
Plattsburgh, New York

"...I can't say that I feel much like dancing."

JOHN L. HOBSON II - AFTER EXPERIENCING THE FIRST DAYS OF MILITARY LIFE

Corporal (U.S.N.G.) John Lambert Hobson II at Plattsburgh National Guard Training Camp, back row, fourth from the left - 1916. Stephen G. Hobson Collection — Hobson family photograph

OH! HOW I HATE TO GET UP IN THE MORNING
Lyrics and music by Irving Berlin

The other day I chanced to meet a soldier
Friend of mine
He'd been in camp for sev'ral weeks and
He was looking fine
His muscles had developed and his cheeks
Were rosy red
I asked him how he liked the life, and this
Is what he said:

Oh! How I Hate To Get Up In The
Morning,
Oh! How I'd love to remain in bed
For the hardest blow of all is to hear the
Bugler call:
'You've got to get up, you've got to get
up,
You've got to get up this morning!'"

Someday I'm going to murder the bugler
Someday they're going to find him dead
I'll amputate his reveille and stomp upon it
Heavily
And spend the rest of my life in bed!

A bugler in the Army is the luckiest of men
He wakes the boys at five and then goes
Back to bed again
He doesn't have to blow again until the
Afternoon
If ev'rything goes well with me I'll be a
Bugler soon!

Oh! How I hate To Get Up In The
Morning
Oh! How I'd love to remain in bed
For the hardest blow of all is to hear the
Bugler call:
'You've got to get up, you've got to get
Up
You've got to get up this morning!'"

Oh, boy! The minute the battle is over
Oh, boy! The minute the fore is dead
I'll put my uniform away and move to
Philadelphia
And spend the rest of my life in bed!

THE FOOL
Robert Service

"But it isn't playing the game," he said,
And he slammed his books away;
"The Latin and Greek I've got in my head
Will do for a duller day."
"Rubbish!" I cried; "The bugle's call
Isn't for lads from school."
D'ye think he'd listen? Oh not at all:
So I called him a fool, a fool.

Now there's his dog by his empty bed,
And the flute he used to play,
And his favorite bat... but Dick he's dead,
Somewhere in France, they say:
Dick with his rapture of song and sun,
Dick of the golden hair,
Dicky whose life had just begun,
Carrion - cold out there.

Look at his prizes all in a row:
Surley a hint of fame.
Now he's finished with, nothing to show:
Doesn't it seem a shame?
Look from the window! All you see
Was to be his one day:
Forest and furrow, lawn and lea,
And he goes and chucks it away.

Chucks it away to die in the dark:
Somebody saw him fall,
Part of him mud, part of him blood,
The rest of him - not at all.

And yet I'll bet he was never afraid,
  And he went as the best of 'em go;
For his hand was clenched on his broken blade,
  And his face was turned to the foe.

And I called him a fool... Oh, blind was I!
  And the cup of my grief's abrim.
  Will Glory o' England ever die
  So long as we've lads like him?
So long as we've fond and fearless fool,
  Who, spurning fortune and fame,
Turn out with the rallying cry of their schools,
  Just bent on playing the game.

A fool! Ah no! He was more than wise.
  His was the proudest part.
He died with the glory of faith in his eyes,
  And the glory of love in his heart.
And though there's never a grave to tell,
  Nor a cross to mark his fall,
Thank God! We know that he "batted well"
  In the last great Game of all.

Y.M.C.A. HEADQUARTERS
MILITARY TRAINING CAMPS
U.S. ARMY
PLATTSBURGH, NY
Undated

Dearest Mother

Well I am really here at last even if you all did have a good laugh at me before I left. The train ride was rather rough as we had to stop about every other mile or so but I had the good luck to fall in with a man before the train pulled out of Boston so I didn't mind it in the least. We were just one hour late arriving at camp and believe me breakfast went to the right place. Dinner tasted just as good as we were kept busy all the morning unrolling etc. This afternoon we drilled for almost three hours then just given an hour's rest and out working again only this time with those guns. Supper was fine and I ate like a pig. There was going to be a lecture tonight but a rain blew up in the later part of the afternoon and whereas it is not raining now it is no night for a lecture. We have not been stationed in our regular tents yet but will be tomorrow when the squads are made up. Eight men to a squad and eight men to a tent. There I guess I have told you just about all I know about this life so far except that I have to be back in camp at ten tonight and lights out at 10:30.

I suppose that you are all going up to the dance tonight but I can't say that I feel much like dancing. All the men are more or less tired and I bet eleven or before will find us all asleep.

Well Mother dear I want to buy a few things and look around so will close.

Please give my love to everyone and tell Arthur that some of these men look worse in their suits than I do.

Your soldier boy,
Jack

P.S. There is my address on the top of this page only add "Co H."

Tuesday

Dearest Mother

Just a few lines a day to let you know that your soldier boy is well and really having a good time. This life certainly is great and I am really very sorry now that I did not come up before. Well there is another summer coming and if all is OK at home believe me I am coming up here. Oh it is great Mother and all the men are enjoying themselves to the limit. Well now for the news.

Last night at sun down we had a parade with a band. That band put all kinds of pep into the men and everything went great. The lecture after supper was the thing that I have not the words to explain. That old moon was shining and all the camp around a fire with the speaker in the middle. It was great - just fine. Thank goodness it was warm last night and how I did sleep. Every man in the tent was in by nine and I was in bed by 9:15. The last thing I knew I heard a faint laugh in the bed next to me and then it was morning. Yes I had really gone to sleep at 9:30. The man who sleeps at my feet did the same thing.

The drill this morning was not as hard as yesterday's - guess that we are getting used to it a little.

After lunch

I just went for the mail and found your letter waiting for me. News from home seems good and I am mighty glad to get it.

I sent both grandparents a post card the other night and will try to write them a real letter before long. Yes, the candy arrived and every man in the tent agreed that it was the best fudge they had ever ate. This means that more would be welcome. I will write sister the very first chance I get but will you please thank her for it for me. Mother, Sister certainly is a thoughtful girl and I am proud of her. She does her best around the house but sometimes it is pretty hard. There is so much going on down there all the time that I don't see how she ever does the many things that she does every day.

I had my coat taken in at the neck this morning and now I look fine, and feel even better. I hope to get into town tonight if I am not too tired to get a shave. When I get that I will be tiptop all around.

Well Mother it is time for afternoon drill so good-bye for now.

Love to all.
Jack

Y.M.C.A. HEADQUARTERS
MILITARY TRAINING
U.S. ARMY
PLATTSBURGH, NY
Undated

Dearest Mother

At last I have got a few minutes to myself in which to write you a real letter and not merely a post card.

Mother, I am very tired indeed tonight in fact I am so much all in that I am going to make friends with my cot about nine o'clock or even before if I get through answering some of the many letters that I owe people. Some will have to wait a long time for an answer to their letters I am afraid if I don't have more extra time than I have had of late. Let them wait - I can't help it and some nights I feel like never writing again to anyone except you and the family. Night is always welcome believe me and there are very few times after lunch when rest does not feel mighty good. Well now let me tell you what we have been doing today that has been so hard.

We got up at the same old hour, 5:30 a.m. not p.m., and seven o'clock saw all of company B marching out of camp in "heavy marching order." Packs and guns. We walked for a good five miles and some of the ground we went over wasn't fit to build pigpens on. We had good roads at first, then turned down what was once a railroad bed and hence was very sandy and rough. How we ever got over this is beyond me but we did and then headed for the woods and wild land. At every other step you would hit a hole or old log and the bushes were fierce. We were all lead to the top of a small hill and at last called to a "halt". Then we were told that companies "A" and "B" were going to attack us and it was our job to hold the hill. My squad was first put in a trench, which was heaven because we could lean against the sides and smoke in peace but not be seen by the enemy. I guess the captain saw that life was too easy for us there so he pulls us out and puts us back of some bushes. This was not as comfortable as the trench but was not bad because we were forced to lie down. The captain again decides to change our squad and this time we got it for fair. We were placed on the side of the hill right in a pile of dirt. Yes we had to lie down but could not get comfortable on account of some sticks and stones, which kept getting in the way. Here we were forced to stay for almost an hour and then the fun began. The enemy began to come out of the wood from all sides and we were told to "open fire". We all had blanks and with a man on each side of you shooting away for all he is worth and the enemy shooting one's hearing soon fades half away. Everyone along our "firing line" was yelling, "Give them merry hell boys!" while the enemy was yelling something along the same line which I was unable to hear on account of the noise. After the sham battle was over we were marched back over the five miles we had come to camp. Almost everyone had cut his poor hands in one way or another and we were just plain brown or black from dirt. After mess the captain thought we all needed a little rest and so he gave it to us by having us take our tents down and then putting them up again. What the big idea was I could not say but orders are orders around here so we had to do and say nothing. Just as soon as the tents were up and everyone was expecting a few minutes rest we were ordered to fall in and drill and drill we did for 2 ½ hours with ten minutes for a smoke. After drill we had ¾ of an hour before "retreat" in which some took a swim but most of us lay down. Then retreat, which means more walking and then at six o'clock "mess" with a lecture after it and we were free. Outside of this I have done nothing today but yet every one of us are all in and ready to go to bed. Having told you the few things we have done today I will go on with something else.

I received your letter this a.m. and Mother dear you certainly have been fine about writing me. I have heard from you almost every day and now I look forward to your letters as I do mess. I know one is always waiting for me at noon and that letter is the first thing I head for when we return to camp after the morning's work. You always tell me something of interest and every letter is like the chapter of a book for it bears on the one before.

I wrote Dad a rather long letter some days ago and wonder if he ever received it. I wish you would ask him to just drop me a post card if he does not feel like writing a real letter because I should like very much to hear from him.

Please tell Arthur I received his letter but rather doubt if I get a chance to answer it. It was a fine letter Mother for a fellow of his age.

Well dearest Mother bed is calling your rookie son so he must obey and go. Just think of that wonderful sleep which is coming to me after a hard day's work. Won't it feel great in the good fresh air with never a care or worry and better yet being well and blame happy.

Remember me to McHenry and give my love to the family.

Love and kisses.
Jack

Y.M.C.A. Headquarters
Military Training Camps
U.S. Army
Plattsburgh, NY
Undated

Dearest Mother

Work has really begun up here and take it from one who knows we have very little time to oneself. What time we do have free we usually rest as being on your feet for four or more hours kind of takes the pep out of you. This morning's drill was very stiff and kind of took hold of us all. We have now just finished lunch and everyone is spread out on his cot smoking and reading or writing. Drill starts up again very soon and between you and me I guess that we will all be glad to see night come. It always goes kind of hard for the first two or three days but after that we all get used to it they tell me.

Yesterday I took a short car ride and walk with two other men. In the evening some of the men had fires at the head of their company's street. The moon was wonderful and the lake was very calm. Everything was great but the air was too cold. I got to bed about 9:30 and was asleep almost before my head touched the pillow. My how I did sleep after I got under those four blankets and the next thing I knew it was time to get up. There is where we all feel the cold and how a man ever shaves is beyond me. After eight o'clock it is warm and nice until about eight o'clock at night when it gets cold again.

My hay fever has been very bad today but I guess that it will go off in a few days. Here's hoping. Will write more tonight after this afternoon drill.

Well the day's work is over and now we are waiting for the lecture which starts in a little while.

The drill this afternoon was not quite as hard as this morning's but at the same time it was not too easy. Those guns are light enough when we first start out but before many minutes you are aware of the fact that you have something on your shoulder. Well it is all in a day's work so what if your shoulder is sore. My back is very tired from standing up straight and here's betting money I look better when I get home.

What is the news at Rye now days? I suppose that everything is going along about the same as when I left but there must have been a little excitement since Thursday so please keep me posted.

Well Mother dear I am well and happy and after all is said and done that is the chief thing.

Please give my love to all.

Love and kisses for yourself.
Jack

Y.M.C.A. Headquarters
Military Training Camps
U.S. Army
Plattsburgh, NY
Undated

Dearest Mother

Well night is here again and I shall take a few minutes of my evening to write you or one of the family my daily letter. I know you are all interested in what I am doing up here the same as you are when I am off on a visit so I have done my best to let some one of you hear from me every day. You must all overlook mistakes that may be made in these letters because as a rule I write them at night when my brain as well as my body is tired out from the day's work. Yes, work not child's play or boy's play but men's work.

Believe me Mother this life is wonderful but awfully hard - almost too hard in fact. We are going full force now and this pace is to be kept up until October 5th. Some of the men who were here in July and August told us tonight that we were being worked harder than the other camps. This is so because we are going on an eleven day "hike" instead of a six or seven day one as the other camps have done. There is a certain amount of work which has to be done before we leave hence we have to hurry right along or we will not be ready.

The hard work is beginning to show on some of the men and one man in our tent has foot trouble all ready. My feet are ok but my poor right arm is nearly all in tonight. This morning we carried our packs for the first time and mine got my right shoulder in such a way that it stopped the blood from flowing in the arm. Before half an hour was up my whole right hand was purple and that gun would have gone clean to the ground if I hadn't relieved my hand with my left. The gun is carried on the shoulder supported by the right hand and it must be carried that way. Oh no there was no resting, no let up, no kicking, nothing to do but grit those teeth of mine and stick. Most of the men had trouble with their packs and many were in the same box that I was in. After drill this afternoon the man next to me in line was gritting his teeth for fair and the expression in his face was one of trouble. He like all the rest of us was having his troubles but he stuck and that is what counts. "Stay with it" as Dad said, and stay I will as will the rest. The days are hard, blame hard but I would go through more than this for the sake of that wonderful sleep which follows the hard day's work. Oh that sleep it is just wonderful and the air can't be beat. I just love it up here and I really feel as if it was doing me good. It isn't the soft, easy going life of Rye but it is the life that will make men out of us all who are here and when we leave we will all have something to show for it. The few fellows my age who are here more than the older men because as you have often said now is the time of life that counts. It's all wonderful. Yes, wonderful and old Arthur wants to get here as soon as possible.

Well all is ok with me and here's hoping that all is ok at home. Let me hear from you every now and then just as you have and it will add to the pleasures and hard spots of Plattsburgh.

Love to all and lots for yourself.

Your happy boy,
Jack

Dearest Sister

Gee but life is a joke if only one looks at it in the right way. Here we all are up here working our heads off and every one of us is having our own little troubles. Yet every man here grits his teeth and laughs when the day is over. The whole blame affair strikes me funny and almost every night I lay awake for five or ten minutes, I can't stay awake any longer, and laugh to myself about some of the funny little things which have taken place during the day. The whole thing is too wonderful to even be a dream. I just love it all and every day holds out a new pleasure for me. Oh sister, I tell you I love it. Why aren't you a boy so that you might come up here to this place of joys and hardships and enjoy the wonderful life I am lucky enough to have. Now let me tell you what we have done today.

This morning when we got up it was almost raining but the sun was trying its best to come out and the lake was as calm as it could be. As I jumped from my cot I felt a bad pain in my left ankle and on looking at it I found that the fool thing was puffed up and very hot. After breakfast I answered sick call along with many other men some of whom had my trouble. The doctors up here have no time to throw away hence your long legged brother was put up on a long table, in turn of course, and before he could wink or flinch that doctor was pulling away at his ankle for all he was worth. You bet it hurt, but why yell? Grit your teeth again and bear it. Well that doctor had my ankle strapped up in no time at all and told me to get a move on and report again tomorrow morning. The company had left when we, five of us, got back to the company street and orders had been left for us to join the marching line as soon as possible on the Peru road. The bunch got quite a start on us so we fooled the whole outfit and hired a Ford for $.50 and rode out to where they were. You should have seen the look on our captain's face when we rode up in that funny little Ford. He laughed all the way over and said, "Good work men. I didn't expect to see you at all." We walked just nine solid miles over hard roads and my ankle never hurt me at all. The sun came out and it was mighty hot. Every puddle that happened to come in our way we would step in to cool our feet off. There were many of them because it had rained during the night. After lunch I did enjoy a good laugh. Everyone was kicking because they had bad feet and many of the men could barely walk their feet hurt them so. Mine were fine so I could laugh. We drilled all the afternoon and when some of those fellows came into supper tonight I don't believe they much cared whether their feet were on or off. Well today is over and tomorrow we fight another sham battle. This is very hard work but loads of fun.

Yes the big "hike" starts early Monday morning and we are gone right up to October 5th. The day we leave. We get back to camp about eleven o'clock on October 5th and the Boston train pulls out at six that night. You just bet that you can write me while we are gone - all you want. I doubt if I'll have any time for letter writing but I may. There is an auto that comes out to us from here which brings our mail out to us so please write even if I can't answer.

I wish that I had been at the house for that dance you folks had but to be frank with you I had rather lead this life than the life of Rye. I have forgotten all about dancing and would you believe it girls are out of my mind. Never once after the first four days here have I thought of a girl except my two loving sisters and my dear mother. There is not time for thoughts of girls up here and the men say very little about them. Last night however we got one fellow in our tent going on girls and after he raved on for half an hour giving us his opinion of the fairer sex I fell asleep.

Say sister what has Jeanne said because I have not answered her letter. I am so blame tired when night comes around that I only feel like writing one letter and I feel that one ought to go to some one of the family. Will you please explain to Jeanne and the rest how it is and tell them I will try to write Sunday when we get the day to ourselves.

Well, dearest, good night and write me again real soon.

Give my love to all the family and read them such parts of this letter, which you think will interest them.

Lots of love and kisses,
Jack

Y.M.C.A. Headquarters
Military Training Camps
U.S. Army
Plattsburgh, NY
Undated

Dearest Dad

Gee what a day this is in camp. Rain! Rain! Rain! It started in this morning so instead of having drill we all marched up to the gym and had a lecture on the "pack". This lasted for about two hours then we returned to camp. In the meantime the sun had come out and all was fine. We had only two hours left before lunch so the captain had us put our packs on and we went off for a two hour march with a ten minute rest in which to enjoy a smoke and rest our backs and legs. All I needed was the smoke but I guess the rest didn't hurt me any. At the end of the ten minutes we all formed a half circle while the captain gives us a talk on "marching order". We are allowed to smoke during this talk and as a rule the captain is puffing himself. Oh those old boys are human but when they get us out at drill and have us fall flat and fire then get up on the run and fall again in a few yards I began to think that for the time being their hearts are made of stone or something harder. I would give money to see you up here going through what we are. Dad, I am afraid that your poor legs would fall off before noon. We are falling down and getting up all the time and that pack gets very heavy indeed before the day is over. How some of these older men ever stand it is beyond me but they do and what is more they all wear the smile of the younger men when the day is over. Every one of them act like boys about my age. Two of the men in our tent are thirty years old and there is one fellow just my age. They are all fine fellows every one of them and we certainly get along fine. Laughing all the time when we are off duty and working our heads off when on. This afternoon we went out for some aiming practice but before we had been out an hour it began to pour and so we were forced to withdraw to our tents. Here we are with the afternoon free and only one thing to do before supper - clean our guns. They were mighty wet when we got in and hence they had to be all taken apart and cleaned. I have got mine all oiled up now and she looks great. Some of the other fellows have just got started on theirs and are this very minute working their heads off. Those guns have to be cleaned once every day and sometimes when we have been falling in sand and the like we have to clean them twice. There is always something to do and if time gets hanging heavy on our hands as it seldom does we just fall to cleaning our guns.

Dad this is really a wonderful life and I will be sorry when the month is over and I have to return to Bryant Stratton. I just love this outdoor life - working all day in the fresh air and sleeping in the clear cool air of night. Schoolwork will certainly go hard with me for a few days but I suppose I will get used to it.

Tonight I expect to go into Plattsburgh to get a haircut and look the girls over. I have to go into town every night so just to keep in practice of dodging the people on the sidewalks. It never would do for me to light into Boston next month and run into everyone I meet on the street.

Another thing I will have to brush up on is my table manners. Up here things are put on the table and it is almost a case of every man for himself. You and Mother would be landing hot and heavy on the neck of your older son if you saw his table manners up here. It is all right in camp but will I be able to get over it when I get home - that is the question. Well be easy on me for a few days after my return and I guess all will be OK. I will get over them - don't worry.

That man I came up here with, Mr. Ladd, has turned out to be a great friend. He makes all kind of plans with me for the evenings and we get along fine. He is going with me tonight. I never see the old fellow during the day as he is in another company but night usually finds us together.

Well Dad dear I must close as I owe some of those fair girls down there a letter so must tend to them.

Give my love to Mother and the rest.

Lots of love for yourself.
Jack

Y.M.C.A. Headquarters
Military Training Camps
U.S. Army
Plattsburgh, NY
Undated

Dearest Mother

I am sorry to say that I failed to write you or one of the family a letter last Saturday but conditions were such that I could not. Well I guess a slip up of one day won't hurt.

Last Saturday we were kept busy almost all day and the little time which we did have off was spent in washing. In the morning we went off on a ten-mile hike working out war problems all the way. It surely was great fun and at last I am beginning to get a little light on this war game. Every move we made was explained as well as the reasons. I got so interested in it that those ten miles went under my shoes like an auto tire would go over the same road. We shot all the afternoon and this whereas I was not as interested in it as the war problems made the afternoon pass very quickly. Dick Thompson showed up about five but I was very busy so only saw him for a few minutes until after supper when I went down to the hotel Champlain where he was staying. As good luck would have it he had not finished supper so I sat down and ate again. My but it did feel good to eat off real plates and drink out of a real glass. All our stuff is tin. We talked awhile after supper and I returned to camp about 9:30. Sunday was the day for both of us. I got up to the hotel about 10:30 after two hours of work on the range and found Dick ready and waiting for excitement. It was too late to take any of the regular trips so I'll be hanged if we didn't have a Ford and went to Ausable Chasm and had lunch. Oh that lunch it was great and what was better yet it was cheap. After lunch we went through the chasm and Mother I wouldn't have missed that sight for anything. I sent you some post cards of it but you can only get an idea of the chasm from them. You have got to really see it before you can fully realize the size and height of those rocks. You walk for about a mile and a half along this river. Sometimes you are right beside it and at others you are about

125 feet above it with rocks all around you. At the end of this winding walk you get into a boat and shoot some rapids and then get out. The way that water rushes along is just wonderful and the boat ride has got anything at Revere Beach beat coming and going. When we came out of the chasm we found our Ford waiting for us so we jump in and head for a silver fox farm. We took in a couple of towns on the way and landed back at the hotel about five or a bit before. Then heaven come to earth if it ever did - I for the first time since leaving home took a bath in hot water. Dick thought it was a great joke for him to introduce me to a bath and the poor fellow laughed until the tears were rolling down his face. There is not hot water in camp in fact the water we wash in is ice cold most of the time so that hot bath felt good - very good in fact. After my swim we had supper and then we said those parting words and I returned to camp after a perfect day. We went out on the range this morning but it began to pour so we had to return to camp where we have been since nine o'clock.

Say there goes the call for lunch so I must beat it.

Love to all and lots for yourself.
Jack

Dearest Mother

We have just pulled into camp for the second night of the "hike" and I must confess that I am tired. We had a very hard march this morning and what was worse yet we were forced to fight the last three miles of it. I am not over tired but just feel comfortable when laying down. Last night we camped out in an old field about eleven miles from Plattsburgh. There were enough stones in that hay field to build a house with but after much work my tent mate and I got our little lot almost stoneless. I slept like a log and I guess that everyone else did. We got up at 5:15 this morning and that sun rising over the mountains was just great. We left camp about 6:45 and arrived here (hanged if I know the name of the place) about one. After pitching our tents we had mess and my what a mess. I had to buy some food elsewhere. After mess I took a half-mile walk back to a steam where I bathed my hot dirty feet in some ice-cold water.

We are camped in another field for tonight and thank goodness it is free from stones and has long grass. I bet I sleep tonight even better than I did last night.

I received your long and interesting letter about an hour ago and at once sat down in front of our "pup tent" to read it. You can picture me sitting there with my gun across my knees reading it can't you?

Great guns a storm is coming up. I see where we have a wet and cold night of it.

Well there is yet work to be done so I must get busy.

Give my love to all and keep a lot for yourself.
Jack

Post Cards

Undated

To: Mr. Arthur L. Hobson, Esq., Little Boars Head, NH

Am very tired tonight as I have been shooting all day and it is not easy work. This is the hotel where Dick [Thompson] stayed and where I enjoyed three good meals. What do you think of it? I like this life even better than I did when I last wrote and I hate to think of October 5th except I shall be glad to see you all once again. Drop me a line if you have time.

Lots of love.
Jack

Undated

To: Mrs. Arthur L. Hobson, Little Boars Head, NH

This post card will show you very well the packs we carry on our backs when on the march. I have been on the "firing line" the greater part of today and my poor head feels it tonight. Those guns certainly go off with a loud bang. Expect to have a good sleep tonight. Shall be in bed at nine.

Undated

To: Master Philip Hobson, Little Boars Head, NH

How do you like this picture? I think it is fine. Will you please tell Mother that I have had a large picture of my company sent to Rye and tell her to open it. It is coming under my name. Do you get wet all over now when you go in bathing or have you stopped going in?

Lots of love.
Jack

To: Mr. Arthur L. Hobson, Little Boars Head, NH

Well Dad I am all here after a fairly hard day's work. They surely are trying to teach us a lot in one day and by the time I get out of here I ought to know something. I have been changed to "Co B" so tell Mother and the rest to send letters to "Co B" instead of "Co H". Received Mother's letter this a.m. and will try to answer it tomorrow.

Love to all.
Jack

Common Postal

Undated

Am very busy these days, Mother, so have not the time to write you a real letter. The big hike starts next Monday and we have started to get ready for it soon. I received your two letters this morning and they were more than welcome. Don't worry Mother dear your news is of great interest to me and without your letters I should be at a loss. Things here are going fine and I like it up here better every day I am here. This is the life for me all right even if I do miss a few of the comforts of home. Did Dad get my letter or did it go astray? Am in town tonight with Mr. Ladd. Went to bed at eight last night and was dead to the world at 8:15. Gee how I do sleep. I hate to get up at 5:30 though. Will try to write you a real letter very soon.

Lots of love.
Jack

Dearest Mother

This very likely will be the last real letter, which you will receive from your rookie son while he is at camp. We start off on the "hike" bright and early tomorrow morning and I rather doubt if I shall be able to find the time or place to write letters however, if I do, you will get one. Our mail is all brought out to us by auto so if you or any of the rest have time to write please do so. The address is just the same.

Yesterday was a day of rest in camp. We took a ten-mile "hike" in the morning and then were given the rest of the day to ourselves. I spent some of the afternoon in writing letters and the rest in having a shave and a rest. Last night I went down and fixed up my ticket for coming home. I have been lucky enough to get a drawing room with two other men. One I know and the other I do not. I guess that bed and sleep will be a mighty welcome thing when we get on that train. We leave here at 6:00 p.m. on October 5th and I cannot say what time we get into Boston but it will be somewheres around six the next morning.

Gee Mother but this "hike" is going to be a great thing if my feet will only hold out. They are all right now but how they will stand up under 10 or 15 miles a day remains to be seen. A lot of men are not being allowed to go at all on account of bad feet and my friend Mr. Ladd is leaving tomorrow. The poor man is very disappointed that he has to miss the eleven days "hike" but the doctor told him yesterday morning that there was no use even starting it. My real test starts in tomorrow and if I return from that "hike" with both feet in fair shape and all in I will consider myself in fine shape. We sleep on the ground in blankets and the fellow I am bunking with and myself are praying that we get soft ground. There are two men to a shelter tent each carries half of the tent in his pack.

You remember that just before I left home I made a wish that we would get a little rain while I was up here. Well, Mother we got it the other night before last for fair. A thunderstorm blew up about seven o'clock Friday night and my how it did pour. Our tent is on high ground and hence no water flowed in but some of the tents were flooded yesterday morning. All day yesterday black clouds over hung Lake Champlain but the sun stayed with us until about five o'clock last night and then another thunderstorm hit us which was a peach. It only lasted about an hour but during that one short little hour it certainly did rain cats and dogs. I thought that some of those thunderstorms we have at the beach were bad enough but these two had them all beat. We all sat around inside the tent and smoked until it was over. Let's hope that we don't have one of these storms while we are off on this "hike."

Before I forget it Mother there is one thing of mine that you may forget to pack so I am going to speak of it. In the drawer of the table in my room you will find a bunch of papers. I believe they are in the left hand corner if they have not been moved since my departure. On those papers are written different poems, which I have made up from time to time during the summer and also a few stray thoughts. These are all in a nice neat pile. Will you please see that they are brought to Haverhill when you come as I wish to copy them in with the rest. Thanks a lot.

I am going into Plattsburgh for lunch today with Mr. Ladd. This camp food is fine but I like a change every so often and believe me I get it. I like to eat off of real plates and have hot food every now and then so I make it a point to do it.

Well Mother dear I guess I have told you all the news so I will close.

Don't worry if you do not hear from me again for some little time. No news is good news you know.

Give my love to all the family and keep a lot for yourself.

Your rookie son,
Jack

To: Mrs. Arthur Hobson, Little Boars Head, NH

Was so busy yesterday that I did not have time to write. Dick arrived about four and so I spent the evening with him. Today (Sunday) we hired an auto and have now just finished lunch at a hotel about 15 miles from camp. Dick is staying at the Hotel Champlain and I am to have supper with him tonight. The hotel is three miles from the camp. Went for a long hike yesterday morning and shot in the afternoon. We shoot all day tomorrow I believe. The "hike" starts a week from tomorrow I believe and do not return to camp until the day we leave for home. Time certainly flies up here. It was very cold last night but we are all getting hardened to it now.

Will try to write a real letter tomorrow.

Jack

To: Mr. Phillip Hobson, Little Boars Head, NH

My dear Phillip:
    John and I are having a great time up here. We have been riding around all day in a Ford. Here is one place we saw.

Sincerely,
Dick

Undated

To: Mrs. Arthur L. Hobson, Little Boars Head, NH

I wrote Dad a long letter this p.m. so you can get the news from him. Just thought I would drop you this card for good luck. Dick Thompson and I may have lunch at this hotel Sunday. I have seen it several times but have not been inside yet.

Lots of love,
Jack

Undated

To: Mr. Arthur L. Hobson, Little Boars Head, NH

This is a very small part of the Chasm that Dick and I went through this afternoon. Dad it was just wonderful and a sight that was well worth seeing. I won't forget it in a hurry I know that. Never before have I seen such high rocks and never before have I seen water rush as it did in the chasm. I am to have supper with Dick now.

Love,
Jack

Undated

To: Mr. Arthur L. Hobson, Little Boars Head, NH

Well Dad everything is still fine and the work hard. The nights are warmer than they were and three blankets fill the bill. Is your friend Nolan a captain up here? There is one by that name in another company.

Jack

Undated

To: Mrs. Arthur L. Hobson, Little Boars Head, NH

This is the view of part of the camp and you can get a very good idea what it looks like from this. I just love this sleeping in a tent and believe me we get enough fresh air but are warm. Drill work all day tomorrow and a lecture at night. We rise at 5:30. Oh what an hour.

Jack

CHAPTER FIVE

Camp Curtis Guild, Jr. - Boxford, Massachusetts
And so it began...

"The world must be made safe for democracy"

PRESIDENT WOODROW WILSON

By 1917, Father had joined the National Guard and attended and completed training at the Plattsburgh training camp and had subsequently returned to school for the winter. In Europe, the Great War was grinding on and three years of a stagnated war had eroded Kaiser Wilhelm's political power. The British fleet had closed the North Sea. The German Navy and its merchant vessels had been bottled up, effectively creating a blockade and shortages of food and supplies for the now starving civilian population of Germany. In one day, Germany lost 41 ships.

The Kaiser had clarified his position on Germany's imperialist pursuits saying that his naval expansion had been directed at Japan and not Britain, and that he really did not share the sentiment of the German people against the British. After all, he was a blood relative of the British monarchy. In the Kaiser's faltering and weakness, military leaders Erich Ludendorff and Paul Von Hindenburg gained control of the government and became military dictators of Germany. In one of the more famous, or infamous, quotes in history, in 1914 when Kaiser Wilhelm was originally confronted by his general staff to initially mobilize the army, he was reported to have said to them, "Gentlemen, you will regret this."

Meanwhile, more nations had been drawn into the maelstrom.

In January of 1917, the German high command broke the Sussex Pledge which promised to limit submarine warfare. Germany declared unrestricted submarine warfare against all shipping vessels, neutral or hostile, destined for Great Britain. Prior to this, German captains gave warning and allowed the crew of merchant vessels to abandon the ship before she was sunk. In February and March of 1917, German submarines attacked without warning and sank several American vessels.

At the same time, German Foreign Minister Arthur Zimmermann proposed through a telegram sent through the German ambassador to the Mexican government a German-Mexican alliance, an overt act of aggression toward the United States, in which Mexico's reward in the alliance upon the defeat of the United States would be the recovery of the Texas, New Mexico and Arizona territories. Mexico, unable to organize its own government, later declined the offer. However, it was to be the last straw in the decision for the United States to go to war.

In view of these combined events, the United States could no longer remain neutral.

In all the saber rattling, Foreign Minister Zimmermann reminded the American Ambassador in Berlin that in the event of the United States going to war against Germany there were 500,000 German-born Americans in the United States who would rise up against the United States government. It is reported that the American Ambassador replied to Zimmermann that the United States had 500,001 lampposts from which to hang them!

When the call finally did come for Americans to go to war, there were two Midwestern National Guard divisions formed, the 32nd and the 89th, that were made up almost entirely of German-Americans who felt they wanted to defend freedom and democracy and the new life they were enjoying in their new homeland.

On 6 April 1917, the United States declared war on Germany. In his address to Congress requesting a declaration of war, President Wilson said, "The world must be made safe for democracy. The day has come when America is privileged to spend her blood and her might for the principles that gave her birth and happiness and the peace which she has treasured. God helping her, she can do no other."

Because many American citizens still maintained strong anti-interventionist feelings and were opposed to involvement in a European war, and President Wilson was cautious - even suspicious - of the underlying territory acquisition motives of even Britain and France, the United States joined the Allied Forces in the Great War as an Associated Power. In this role, the United States agreed to bring manpower, foodstuffs and, most important, money: $10 billion in U.S. Treasury loans toward the effort to defeat "The Beast of Berlin." However, unlike the events leading the United States into World War II, in World War I America was not the arsenal of democracy.

The other Allied nations did not depend on the United States for armament, leadership or victories in the field. It was the British and French that supplied the munitions, ships, aircraft and command for the overall Allied war effort.

U.S. Army recruiting poster.

In its role as an Associated Power and trying to keep its distance and not wanting to become amalgamated with the other Allied nations, the United States agreed initially to send only an expeditionary force to France. However limited it initially appeared, it would be the event that changed the outcome of the Great War.

At the time of the United States' declaration of war, under the strategy devised by Alfred von Schlieffen, Germany was defending the war on two fronts: on the Western Front against France and Britain, and on the Eastern Front against Russia. France was weakening under the prolonged strain of the war.

In the stalemated war on the Western Front in France, the German troops were being held behind the Aisne River, and the war had become a bloody, catastrophic trench war running along the 400-mile battle line, the Hindenburg Line.

With its huge reserves of manpower, food and money, it was hoped that the United States joining the Allied Powers would shore up the Allied effort, break the stalemate, quickly tip the balance in favor of the Allied Powers and bring a swift end to the war in Europe. As the United States' situation and morality was described in "The History of the 26th Division": "Then, suddenly we were at war. Not at war with a decadent kingdom or with heathen natives inhabiting an island, but at war with a race that was determined to subjugate all free people."

Wanting to keep America's involvement in this war in check and under control, the United States Congress took great pains to outline in detail the objectives of the United States and succinctly stated the objective as being: To bring the conflict to a successful termination by helping to compel, through force of arms and in cooperation with its associates, Germany and then other Central Powers to accept the following political terms:

- Evacuation of occupied territories by the Central Powers.
- Adjustment of Italy's border and an independent Poland.

- Open international covenants, openly arrived at.
- Absolute freedom of the seas in war or peace.
- Efforts to remove economic barriers, reduce armaments and form a League of Nations.
- Impartial adjustments of colonial aims.
- Nationalities be given a chance for autonomous development.

These objectives would later evolve into President Wilson's 14 Points of the peace negotiations at the end of the war.

The Allied forces were headed by Marshal Ferdinand Foch of France. Under him was Sir Douglas Haig for Britain, King Albert I for Belgium and General John J. Pershing for the United States. American commanders were not used to taking a back seat. Initially it was said of their French commanders that "They suffered from an inheritance from Napoleon; they arrogantly and bumptiously acted according to the assumption that what they didn't know about warfare couldn't be taught." That opinion would change before it was over.

General Pershing's initial military plan, hatched in April 1917 and proposed to the Allies for the United States to achieve its objectives, was for the United States to fight only on the Western Front, figuring that the war would be won or lost there. The plan would initially commit to General Foch and his French Army's command one million men of an American Expeditionary Force (A.E.F.) landing in France at the rate of four divisions per month, along with the 25,000 tons of supplies per day necessary for supporting the troops.

Pershing's modest initial idea of what was to be committed would be quickly raised to a four-million man National Army along with corresponding supply and service support systems. But, as it would turn out by the end of the war, of the four-million man army that was committed to, only 2,057,675 American troops would actually land in France - with a million plus of them combat effective - and 644,000 would be the logistical arm of services and supply. That meant that of the total four-million man force, there were approximately two million men that were recruited into the United States military that never made it to France and they were still in training or stationed stateside when the war ended.

When war was declared, men were quickly needed to swell the ranks of the existing 200,000 members of the United States Regular (Federal) military. Traditionally, the military looked to the State Militia, the Reserve and the National Guard for the additional manpower to staff an American Expeditionary Force to be sent to France.

The United States was certainly not the world's largest military power when it entered the Great War. The United States was not well prepared to go into a war of this magnitude.

Not maintaining a large, regular army is traditional in American history. In the late 1700s the Founding Fathers of this country, under their vision of a well-functioning democratic government to govern and for a free people to live in happiness, believed that in times of peace the maintenance of a large military force was not necessary and possibly even dangerous. World history had proven that a nation's citizenry maintaining a large, ponderous, peacetime military force often became tempted to misuse the military to overthrow an existing government. The government of the United States was designed so government officials were elected by the people to carry out the will of the people and power was transferred through a peaceful and democratic election process and not through a military takeover.

Thus the Founding Fathers believed in maintaining a small, regular, Federal Army and also in having a reserve in the form of a State Militia and/or National Guard that could become activated or recruited into the regular federal Army in times of war. So, it was in that spirit - a spirit that had been founded in the American Revolution and the tradition of the Minute Men rallying to arms at a moment's notice against the British at Lexington and Concord during the Revolutionary War in 1775, that the regular army maintained by the United States in 1916 - 1917 was small, but it held a reserve that could be called upon in times of war with the idea that the regular Army could be reduced again when peace was achieved. And, thus it was in the fall of 1917, the first United States troops that became the American Expeditionary Force and sent to fight in France were mostly volunteers.

During WWI, the U.S. Army was made up of many components. There are many references in this work to those various components. Combat formations for the U.S. Army were broken down by ascending size and decreasing specialization into:

- Battery - The smallest artillery combat formation (e.g. Battery A).
- Battalion - A unit of 300 to 1,300 soldiers (e.g. the 1st Battalion).
- Regiment - Comprised of a number of battalions (e.g. the 102nd Field Artillery Regiment).
- Brigade - Two or more regiments or battalions (e.g. the 51st Field Artillery Brigade).
- Division - A formation of combined military arms capable of independent operations and consisting of between 10,000 and 30,000 soldiers and made up of several brigades or regiments.
- Corps - Two or more divisions made up a corps.
- Army - Two or more corps made up an Army. There were three American Armies in World War I. The 26th Division was part of the First Army.
- Theater - the country in which the armed conflict was taking place (e.g. Europe).

A First World War United States Army Division was comprised of about 28,000 soldiers: 1,000 officers and 27,000 enlisted personnel. An American Division was larger than a French or a British division, each of which had about 16,000 soldiers.

Broken down by specialty of function, an American division was usually comprised of four infantry regiments of about 4,000 men each, three artillery regiments (two regiments of 75 mm guns and one regiment of 155 mm guns), three machine gun battalions and a host of other supporting units - supply, medical, etc.

In this war, the War Department decided that United States division numerical designations of 1-25 would be reserved for Regular Army Divisions. Division numbers 26-42 were reserved for the National Guard and 76 - 91 for the National Army (drafted troops). Of the 42 divisions that would eventually be "in country" (France) by the end of the war, only 30 would see combat.

The division with which my father served in the First World War, the 26th Division, also known as the Yankee Division, was originally formed in 1917 as part of the American Expeditionary Forces (A.E.F.), and was made up almost entirely of National Guard troops from the New England States.

The first five divisions to arrive in France were the 1st, 2nd, 26th, 41st and the 42nd Divisions. Each division gave itself a name.

The 1st Division was known as the Big Red One because it was, of course, the first Division. The 2nd Division was called the Indianhead Division. The 41st Infantry Division was the Sunset Division because they were from the west. The 42nd, named by its commander, Douglas MacArthur, was called the Rainbow Division because of the varied location and background of its soldiers (a rainbow across America) and was intended to be the first to be sent overseas, thus for public relations reasons denying any one state the honor of being the first to set foot on French soil. This division contained the famous Irish Brigade of New York State volunteers, the Fighting 69th Regiment. The famed battle cry of the 69th, "Faugh A Ballagh!" (Clear the Way!), their mascot, the Irish wolfhound, and their famed priest, Father Duffy, are the stuff of legend. And the 26th Division's name, the Yankee Division, was given to it because its original soldiers all came from New England and they considered themselves true Yankees. The Division almost named itself the Minutemen in honor of the Revolutionary War's New England heritage.

The commander of the 26th Division was Major General Clarence R. Edwards. Edwards had trained at West Point and had to stretch a bit to qualify as a Yankee. He was actually born in Cleveland, Ohio, but his father came from Springfield, Massachusetts. With a wink and a smile, a true Yankee would comment that just because the cat had the kittens in the oven, it don't make 'em biscuits! From all reports, Edwards was popular with his men, and today there is a statue of him in Hartford, Connecticut.

Organizing a division was a larger job than just laying it out on paper. Before the 42nd Division of volunteers or the 1st Division of regulars got straightened out and ready to embark for France, the 26th Division was ready to go. When the authorities called on 13 August, General Edwards was the only division commander who could promise to have a division organized and ready to ship out to France by 1 September. As a result, the Yankee Division has the distinction of being the first complete division to arrive in France, ahead of both the 1st Division and the 42nd Division. The 26th Division not only has that remarkable distinction, it was also the first to take the battle line as a division.

The 26th Division's battle record in the First World War was described in "A Brief History of the Fighting Yankee Division" as follows:

> The record of the New England Division, the 26th Division of the United States Army, will live forever as one of the most glorious in American annals. No Division in any army has ever fought with greater endurance and grit and bulldog tenacity: with greater cheerfulness and height of morale, than the Yankee Division, the Sacrifice Division, the "Saviors of Paris," to use the full-hearted sobriquet bestowed by the grateful French people: "the pick of the shock troops" to use the expression of French generals.

> The 26th was the first National Guard division and, in fact, the first full division to arrive in France…No other American division has seen so long and continuous service on the front. When the Armistice was signed and the guns ceased to roar, the Y.D. had had nine months of incessant fighting, interrupted only by passage from front to front, always in its travels, as it happened, under the most adverse of weather conditions.

> Always the 26th was given the most difficult task to do, for they were certain to do it right, as shock troops should. The post of honor was always theirs, and in war the post of honor is where the hardest, most resolute, most desperate fighting is to be done. The Y.D. earned the name given it by the Allied armies, the Sacrifice Division…When the full history is written of the Minutemen, as they came very near being called, there will be no more inspiring tale for red-blooded men of future generations to read.

When war was finally declared, my father wasted no time. He enlisted in the United States Army on 9 April, the second day of recruiting in Haverhill, Massachusetts.

Under Bulletin #27 NED 1917, on 4 August, Father, who in the National Guard had been a Corporal in Battery A of the 2nd Regiment of Massachusetts Field Artillery, was officially and honorably discharged from the National Guard of The United States and the "State" of Massachusetts (the printed government transfer form of the time allowed for only a State not a Commonwealth), and was transferred to the Regular United States Army.

Age and education determined the initial assignment of rank. Father maintained his rank as a corporal in the newly formed United States Army's 102nd Field Artillery Regiment of the 26th Division. My father had the education to qualify to be a commissioned officer but, being 19 years of age at the time of his enlistment, he was too young to meet the age requirement to qualify for a commission.

With the rest of the regiment, on 25 July, United States Army Corporal John Lambert Hobson II reported for training at Camp Curtis Guild, Jr. in Boxford, Massachusetts.

26th (Yankee) Division shoulder patch - 1917. Stephen G.
Hobson Collection - Stephen G. Hobson photograph

The 102nd Field Artillery Regiment was the offspring of the 1st Massachusetts Regiment of Field Artillery, MVM, which, upon the declaration of war, became the 2nd Massachusetts Field Artillery.

The new 102nd Regiment was made up of several batteries: Battery A that was recruited from Haverhill, Battery B that was recruited from Worcester, Battery C from Lawrence, Battery D from New Bedford, Battery E also from Worcester and Battery F from Lowell.

The regiment was comprised of 1,724 soldiers - 104 officers and 1,620 enlisted men - and, when they got to France, 1,235 animals - horses and mules - were added to the ranks.

The regiment was accepted by the War Department on 20 July and mobilized in Boxford, Massachusetts, on 25 July at Camp Curtis Guild, Jr.

Formally becoming the 102nd Field Artillery on 5 August, the regiment became part of the United States Army along with several other regiments: the 101st Field Artillery Regiment (formally the 1st Massachusetts Regiment of Field Artillery) and the 103rd Field Artillery Regiment from Rhode Island, New Hampshire and Connecticut. This combination of regiments made up the 51st Field Artillery Brigade of the 26th Division. Within the 51st Brigade, the 101st and 102nd Regiments would be destined to fire 75 mm artillery; the 103rd would fire 155 mm artillery. The 101st Regiment would also contain a trench mortar battery.

Immediately following the United States' declaration of war against the Central Powers, there was a massive increase in the United States' manufacture of ships and weapons and the recruitment of men into the military.

The arms manufacturers, Colt in Hartford, Connecticut, and the Springfield Armory in Springfield, Massachusetts, responded with an increase in the production of light weapons, the Colt 45 semiautomatic pistol and the famous and coveted Springfield rifle.

Government money was committed for the development of war tools: $200 million for the development of tanks (although only 15 American-built tanks ever made it to France and those weren't delivered until after the Armistice was signed), and $640 million for an aviation program that was set forth by the War Department to build 40,000 aircraft in the United States within one year.

Airplanes built in the United States with no way to transport them to France where the fighting was taking place were of little use to the pilots fighting on the Western Front. But the war did establish a new industry of products in the United States that could be easily exported: the manufacture and supply of aviation instruments and the supply of spruce wood for the frames of planes. Also, helium, a nonflammable gas used to inflate observation balloons, could be produced cheaply in the United States.

To accommodate the massive amount of war material and food supplies suddenly being moved across the country, and in order to insure smooth, priority delivery of war material to the ports, the Army Appropriations Act was passed and the nation's railroads were taken over by the government. Preference and right-of-way over passenger service was given to military use and the transportation of military supplies. Rail lines immediately became hopelessly congested. American harbors became choked with transatlantic supply ships that were exporting material to support the American troops that were soon to begin arriving in France. The transportation congestion jeopardized the delivery of the United States' winter coal supply that year. President Wilson said of the confused situation, "It is not an army we must shape and train for war. It is a nation."

Under the Selective Service Act, there was a draft established on 18 May 1917. Overall, the draft would supplement enlistments of regular and National Guard soldiers and bolster the ranks of the United States National military force from 200,000 in April 1917 to 4.7 million in November 1918. Approximately two million would volunteer and another 2.7 million would be drafted. Initially, the age to be eligible for the draft was 18 to 21. A year later, in May of 1918, a work-or-fight order was issued stating that anyone not employed in an essential industry would be drafted and the upper limit on the draft eligible age was raised to 45. The broadening of the eligibility made some of the fathers of the soldier sons already fighting with the A.E.F. in France eligible for the draft, including my grandfather, Arthur L. Hobson, Sr.

In the end, the United States military force was broken down by branches: approximately four million in the Army, 600 thousand in the Navy and 79 thousand in the Marines. Civilian men and women employees and volunteers used for support outside of the Federal military were another 42,644.

According to "The American Heritage History of World War I", "The treatment [initially] given Mr. Wilson's Army was hardly enlightened, even for that era. The Government gave the [new] troops nothing save their clothing, bedding, a toothbrush and a safety razor. Recruits from the backwoods were prone to employ the toothbrush for rifle cleaning..."

Also according to the "American Heritage History of World War I": The average soldier in the first million recruits was 67.49 inches tall and weighed 141.54 pounds. Compared to the Civil War figures of 67.502 inches and 136.05 pounds, it proved that Young America hadn't gotten very far in physical stature in one half-century. Few married men were taken by the draft boards. Of the 4,883,213 married men who registered, 74.12% were deferred. Of the 6,509 American Indians inducted from reservations, only 228 claimed deferment. Out of a total of 26,520 convicts and ex-cons in the nation, about 7,900 were taken into the service. Some proved quite expert at killing; the majority became problems for everyone else in the outfit. There were no "conscientious objectors" in the United States. The draft law did not recognize any such classification. But 1,697 individuals were judged reasonable facsimiles thereof, and 103 were judged to be "insincere" and seven "insane."

Boston Globe reporter Frank P. Sibley reported in his book "With the Yankee Division in France",

The time for training was terribly short, because by its prompt organization the [26th] Division was able to step to the head of the list of divisions going to France and waited only for transportation arrangements to be made. What could be done was done. Training and equipment were two great requisites. Equipment of the Division proceeded upon the principal that the requisite field and trench artillery, machine guns, automatic rifles, animal and motor transportation, special ordnance, engineer and signal property, with munitions of all descriptions, would be issued after arrival in Europe. Only small arms could be provided, and there were not enough of these to equip every organization throughout. Woolen uniforms and overcoats were taken; heavy tentage, cots, mosquito bars and cotton uniforms were left behind. Of individual equipment there was more than could be carried. At first, it seemed probable that there would not be enough, but state and city officials, municipal organizations, churches, societies, and individuals went heartily to work. From state arsenals and armories, from factories and warehouse stores, and from many unsuspected sources, uniforms and outfits were secured. Every soldier had an assortment of comfort kits, knitted gear, extra gloves and toilet articles - everything that lively imaginations could guess would be of service. Most of it had to be left behind; practically all the rest was lost at some time during the campaign, but all of it gave comfort to somebody while it lasted. During this time, the headquarters troop and the signal battalion remained at the armory on Commonwealth Avenue, Allston (Massachusetts), the engineers in the Cadet Armory on Columbus Avenue. The three artillery regiments went into camp at Boxford, Massachusetts. The 101st Infantry took camp on the old muster field at Framingham [Massachusetts]; the 102nd gathered at New Haven [Connecticut], and the two other infantry regiments at Westfield [Massachusetts] camp. Of the machine gun battalions, one was with the 101st Infantry at Framingham, one at Niantic, Connecticut, and one at Quonset Point, Rhode Island. The horses and mules had long before been sent to Newport News [Virginia], whence all our animals were to be shipped.

Camp Curtis Guild, Jr., where the three artillery regiments of the 26th Division trained, was located in Boxford, Massachusetts. It was a 300-acre, open field training facility named after a former Governor of Massachusetts. The camp was used during the summer of 1917 to process, vaccinate and inoculate against typhoid and paratyphoid, educate soldiers in the elements of sanitation, and, most important, train the 4,000 to 5,000 soldiers of the 26th Division's heavy artillery group. For the Division's artillery regiments, there would be further training upon arrival in France under French commanders.

The site would be named Camp Curtis Guild, Jr. only during that period of time, July - September of 1917, when the camp was used to train the 26th Division artillery. It was the largest artillery camp ever in New England.

The camp was built on a site originally established in 1775 as the Boxford Repository of Ammunition belonging to the cities of Salem and Beverly, Massachusetts. Initially, the site was used for the manufacture of bullets. During the 19th century, militia companies drilled there twice a year, in April and October. During the War of 1812 there was not much activity there to aid the government because the town didn't consider it in their best interest. The site was named Camp Stanton during the Spanish

American War and it maintained that name during the Civil War. The Corps Cadets of Salem, Massachusetts, also used the facility for summer maneuvers. In 1919, after the First World War, the facility was renamed Camp Robert Bacon. Today it is a wooded housing development. Looking at the site, unless you knew, you'd never guess what took place there almost a hundred years ago.

The camp was located only a few miles from the Hobsons' family home in Haverhill and about 30 miles from the family's summer home in Little Boar's Head. Family visits on weekends were frequent and convenient. It was estimated that 20,000 family members and friends visited the soldiers on one day about a week before the camp shipped out to France.

Corporal John Lambert Hobson II (left) and Sergeant Ralph Everett Bradley - August 1917.
Stephen G. Hobson Collection. A Short History & Photographic Record of
the 102nd U.S. Field Artillery 1917

Corporal John Lambert Hobson II (left), Sergeant Ralph Everett Bradley (center),
unidentified (right) at Camp Curtis Guild, Jr., Boxford, MA - August 1917.
Stephen G. Hobson Collection - Hobson family photograph

On 17 August, about a month before shipping out to France, my father celebrated his 20th birthday at home with his family. On this occasion, his paternal grandfather, John L. Hobson, Sr., sent him a check for his birthday accompanied by a note in which he wondered where his first grandson would be on his next birthday. My father's next birthday would, indeed, be celebrated under much difference circumstances. The note from his Grandfather Hobson counseled him, "…always be a man and a clean one at that."

His maternal grandfather, General Stephen H. Gale, would also write to my father on the occasion of his birthday. General Gale enclosed in his letter a copy of a letter written in December of 1862 sent by a father to his son who was about to enter the American Civil War as part of the 48th Regiment Massachusetts Volunteers. In his letter to my father, General Gale would write that the copy of the letter he enclosed expressed his feelings at this time more eloquently than he could.

The letter General Gale enclosed urged maintenance of good hygiene and mental habits, along with the caution not to use profanity. The concern with cleanliness and physical hygiene was because so many soldiers of that time died of disease. Medically speaking, it was a dangerous time to be going off to war. It was not surprising that his grandfathers would make such comments.

During the American Civil War (1861 - 1865), two men died of disease for every battle-related death. In the Boer War (1899 - 1902), ten British soldiers died of disease for every single combat death. And in the Spanish American War (1898), for every soldier killed in battle or who died of his wounds, six American soldiers died of disease, almost all from typhoid.

At the turn of the twentieth century, when compared to Europe, medical research, education and practice in the United States was slow to advance. As late as 1900, in the United States it was more difficult to get into a good college than medical school. Many medical schools would accept any man who could pay the tuition. Only one medical school in the United States required the prerequisite of a college degree, and many didn't require a high school diploma or any background in science to become bestowed with a medical degree.

At the beginning of the Great War, American medical standards were just beginning to transform to a higher level that would eventually become the highest in the world, and Germany's advanced medical research and drugs imported into the United States were now cut off.

First World War American military cantonments of 50,000 or more soldiers all living in extremely close quarters exposed men from diverse locations, hygiene and medical backgrounds to the vulnerabilities of different diseases. Compounding the dire situation at this time, the winter of 1917 - 1918 was the coldest on record east of the Rocky Mountains. The combined situations exhausted immunities, creating a potentially explosive disease mixture of humanity that set the stage for epidemic sweeps.

Without wonder drugs, common diseases killed many people. Drugs like penicillin, used to prevent death from what we consider today as being trivial injuries, diseases, minor infections, wounds and, most important, for the prevention of septicemia or blood poisoning and streptococcus germs that a person would come in contact with so easily in combat situations, would not become available until much later.

Wonder drugs would be discovered by Dr. Alexander Fleming in London, but not until the late 1920s and would not be available until the 1940s. The sulfa drugs, synthetic chemical substances used to fight bacterial infections like pneumonia, were discovered in Germany, but not until the 1930s.

Given these circumstances, it was no surprise that both grandfathers' birthday letters would comment on the importance of maintaining proper hygiene.

But most importantly, the letter enclosed with General Gale's birthday wishes also read, "I hope you are going with a love for your country, and your cause, and with a determination to be faithful to every duty you have undertaken. My boy, you bear the name of one who to the end of his honored life never shrunk from a duty, however painful, nor from a danger to which duty called him. Be sure that you do no discredit to it!"

While neither grandfather had served in the military, both had lived through the last great American war, the American Civil War. They had knowledge of war and no romantic vision of what their first grandson was about to experience.

And, so it began for a young Corporal John Lambert Hobson II. He would leave behind the comforts of home, school and the love of his family and friends and go off to fight the Great War and make the world safe for democracy.

It was to be the first step down "The Lone Trail" he longed to follow and provided the mold for the man he would soon become.

Caisson Song*
First Lieutenant (Later Brigadier General) Edmund L. Gruber - 1908

Over hill, over dale
As we hit the dusty trail,
And the Caissons go rolling along.
In and out, hear them shout,
Counter march and right about,
And the Caissons go rolling along.

Then it's hi! hi! hee!
In the field artillery,
Shout out your numbers loud and strong,
For where e'er you go,
You will always know
That the Caissons go rolling along.

In the storm, in the night,
Action left or action right
See those Caissons go rolling along
Limber front, limber rear,
Prepare to mount your cannoneer
And those Caissons go rolling along.

Then it's hi! hi! hee!
In the field artillery,
Shout out your numbers loud and strong,
For where e'er you go,
You will always know
That the Caissons go rolling along.

Was it high, was it low,
Where the hell did that one go?
As those Caissons go rolling along

Was it left, was it right,
Now we won't get home tonight
And those Caissons go rolling along.

Then it's hi! hi! hee!
In the field artillery,
Shout out your numbers loud and strong,
For where e'er you go,
You will always know

That the Caissons go rolling along.
That the Caissons go rolling along.
That the Caissons go rolling along.

*Originally written as the "Caisson Song" with the above words and transformed into a march by John Phillip Sousa in 1917 and renamed "The Field Artillery Song" in 1952, it was re-worded and adopted as the official song of the Army and re-titled "The Army Goes Rolling Along."

THE CALL
Robert Service

Far and near, high and clear,
Hark to the call of War!
Over the gorse and golden dells,
Ringing and swinging of clamorous bells,
Praying and saying of wild farewells:
War! War! War!

High and low, all must go:
Hark to the shout of War!
Leave to the women the harvest yield;
Gird ye, men, for the sinister field;
A saber instead of a scythe to wield:
War! Red War!

Rich and poor, lord a boor,
Hark to the blast of War!
Tinker and tailor and millionaire,
Actor in triumph and priest in prayer,
Comrades now in hell out there,
Sweep to the fire of War!

Prince and page, sot and sage,
Hark to the roar of War!
Poet, professor and circus clown,
Chimney-sweeper and fop o' the town,
Into the pot and be melted down:
Into the pot of War!

Women all, hear the call,
The pitiless call of War!
Look your last on your dearest ones,

Brothers and husbands, fathers, sons:
Swift they go to the ravenous guns,
The gluttonous guns of War.

Everywhere thrill the air
The maniac bells of War.
There will be little of sleeping to night;
There will be wailing and weeping to night;
Death's red sickle is reaping tonight:
War! War! War!

Camp Curtis Guild, Jr.
Boxford, Mass
Undated (July 1917)

Dearest Mother

Ye gods and little fishes but it was hot down here today. I don't think I ever felt the sun pour down so in my life as it did this noon but I imagine it will cool off tonight the way it did last night. Let's hope so anyhow because if it doesn't I see where very few of us slept a great deal tonight.

Mother dear, it certainly did seem good to sit down to supper with all of you folks again. I realize I have not been gone a week yet but home sweet home is always a welcome place to see and even more so now that I am living under conditions so much different than those which exist at home where everyone is free to come and go as they like.

We had a fine ride back to camp under that moon and both Everett and I were more pleased that you let the girls come with us. We two alone would certainly have been lonesome with a moon like that and no girls to enjoy it with.

This morning we were taken out for a short drill, it being altogether too hot to drill green men for any length of time. Percy Wendell was in charge and he did mighty well for a new man at the job. I don't know just what the plans are for us this p.m. but I guess it will mean hanging around until later when we may get a lecture on some subject or other.

Speaking about lectures, yesterday the camp doctor gave us one and, Mother dear, it was a wonder. Good plain English was used and things were brought out to me as never before. After hearing that Major talk I swear I don't see how a man can help but live a clean life but, alas, I realize only too well that many of them will not. This war game certainly does push one up against the very worst as well as the best. Clean living is a mighty important factor and God help the man who does not live as he should. The dirt on us won't hurt, that will wash off, but once our morals are lowered we can't wash it off like dirt. I have known this for some time but it certainly was driven home yesterday in a very strong way and my only prayer is that I can live the clean, high, moral life I have been taught to live at home, no matter what the conditions may be. You and Dad have done your share, now it is up to me.

Several men in our battery failed to pass their federal examinations and one poor soul in our tent is among them. He is, of course, very disappointed but I guess he realizes that he would be unable to stand up under the training. He is an awfully nice fellow and we all are sorry that he did not get by. I consider myself very lucky indeed that I got by as well as I did but let's not say a word until we are sure of it.

Everett has been working all day on the examination papers, getting them in shape. The doctors must have everything just so and it takes six or more sheets of paper to make a soldier out of a man. He (Everett) just came into the tent now and says he feels a bit tired as well as hot, also said that Hobby Lawton was over in the hospital tent. I guess this heat got him. He has been working his head off ever since we got here, so this may have something to do with it.

If you folks come down Sunday I wish you would bring me a fountain pen (which I, of course, forgot to buy or lift until the last minutes and then didn't have time) and some fountain pen ink, also those two bags.

There are an awful bunch of autos down here now but no one is allowed in the company streets until after six, so those who are not on duty have to visit in the autos. There are very few who are not hard on the job, however, so a great many just sit and watch whatever may be going on.

Well, Mother dear, give my love to all the family and come out here whenever you can.

Lots of love and kisses,
Jack

Some little storm* yesterday but I came through all right after twenty minutes of excitement. Things are getting under way slowly. No one slept a great deal last night. I slept fine once I got to sleep but that was not until late. The food so far has been very good and plenty of it. We expect to be here for about three weeks. No drilling as yet but everyone busy putting camp in shape. A great many people came down last night to see how their boys had come out of the storm. I believe you folks can come down any Sunday and I should not be surprised if you could see me oftener. We have a fine bunch in our tent. Everett and I are together.

Love to all and lots for yourself.
Jack

* The "some little storm" and "excitement" referred to in this letter was a severe electrical storm that swept through the area on 27 July which was described by newspaper reports as "hurricane gaited". As the storm front came through Boxford, the temperature dropped 28 degrees from the day's recorded high temperature of 92 degrees.

When the storm broke, a bolt of lightning with its 270,000 miles per hour of speed, 120 million volts of electricity and 50,000 degrees of temperature struck the ridgepole of a tent at Camp Curtis Guild, Jr. killing 22-year old private James F. Broderick, tearing the shirt off of another man and shocking several other men including then Sergeant Everett Bradley and Corporal John L. Hobson. Several other men wound up in the hospital.

The newspaper's account of the lightning's effect on neighboring tents reported that when the lightning bolt struck, it took the temper out of razors and the surgeon's instruments were found welded together.

I read somewhere that at any one time throughout the world there are approximately 1,800 electrical storms going on and there are a total of

40,000 electrical storms that occur each day. The odds of a person being struck by lightning are 0.0002%, or 1 person out of 500,000. To be struck by lightning in the first few weeks of training camp was not an auspicious beginning for Father's military career!

CHAPTER SIX

Over There

"Nous voila, Lafayette!" (Lafayette, we are here!)

LT. COL. CHARLES STANTON: UPON THE ARRIVAL OF
THE FIRST AMERICAN TROOPS IN FRANCE

"...try not to think of the sadness of the vacant chair"

CORPORAL JOHN L. HOBSON II: WRITING HOME BOUND FOR
THE BATTLEFIELDS OF FRANCE

"To all the world he was a soldier.
To me he was all the world."

UNKNOWN

OVER THERE
Music and lyrics by George M. Cohan
(1917)

Johnnie, get your gun, get your gun, get your gun,
Take it on the run, on the run, on the run,
Hear them calling you and me, ev'ry son of liberty
Hurry right away, no delay, go today
Make your Daddy glad to have had such a lad,
Tell your sweetheart not to pine, to be proud her boy's in line

Over there, over there!
Send the word, send the word, over there!
That the Yanks are coming, the Yanks are coming,
The drums rum-tumming ev'ry where!
So prepare, say a prayer, send the word, send the word to beware!
We'll be over, we're coming over,
And we won't be back 'till it's over Over There!

Johnnie, get your gun, get your gun, get your gun,
Johnnie show the Hun you're a son of a gun!
Hoist the flag and let her fly,
Yankee Doodle do or die
Pack your little kit, show your grit, do your bit
Yankees to the ranks from the towns and the tanks
Make your mother proud of you and the old Red White and Blue

Over there, over there,
Send the word, send the word, over there!
That the Yanks are coming, the Yanks are coming,
The Drums rum-tumming ev'ry where
So prepare, say a prayer, send the word, send the word to beware
We'll be over, we're coming over,
And we won't be back 'til it's over Over There!

General John J. "Black Jack" Pershing landing in France, June 1917.
The American Heritage History of World War I

After war was declared, the ingress of American troops to France was slow and in installments.

On 13 June, to cheers of "Vive L'Amerique!" from the French citizens, Pershing and his entourage of 190 soldiers, consisting of 67 enlisted men and 40 Regular Army officers, arrived at Bologne-sur-Mer. They were the first American troops in history to set foot on the continent.

Late in June, the first large deployment of the American Expeditionary Force arrived in France. It was a 14-vessel convoy containing 14,500 soldiers, the first wave of the 1st Division Regular Army troops and a battalion of Marines. They landed at the ancient shipbuilding town of Saint-Nazaire in the southwest of France.

In the days between his arrival and the arrival of the first wave of the 1st Division Regulars and Marines, Pershing became appalled at the deplorable state of morale of the French people and the French Army. For the downtrodden French people suffering from three years of a brutal war fought on their country's soil, the fresh, spirited American troops couldn't arrive fast enough. Pershing hoped the sight of fresh American troops landing on their soil would bolster the weakened French morale.

On 4 July, Pershing and his entourage were given a huge reception in Paris. At the event, a member of Pershing's staff, Lt. Col. Charles Stanton, raised his glass and exclaimed, "Nous voila, Lafayette!" ("Lafayette, we are here!"). It was received with thunderous applause and cheering. Lt. Col. Stanton's exclamation referred to the United States now reciprocating for France's Marie Joseph Paul Yves Roche Gilbert du Motier, better known to us as the Marquis de Lafayette, who came to America in 1777 at the age of twenty to assist the fledgling America's Continental Army and became one of the saviors of the American Revolution.

In August, another 25,000 men, the first wave of the 2nd Division Regulars, began arriving. Then the National Guard Divisions began landing in France. The 26th Division arrived in September, the 42nd (Rainbow) Division in October, followed by the 32nd Division from Michigan and Wisconsin and the 41st Division from the western states.

The complete embarkation of the 26th Division took a month. It started on 7 September and lasted until 9 October. The 101st Field Hospital went over first along with some infantry. The last to go were the Headquarters Troop, the 101st Machine Gun Battalion and the 101st Military Police. Troop movements and embarkation were done with the utmost secrecy - secrecy by the Army's standards anyway - and movement was generally at night and at a moment's notice.

Corporal John Lambert Hobson II at home on the Sunday before departing for France - September 1917. Stephen G. Hobson Collection - Hobson family photograph

Last walk with Dad the Sunday before departing for France - September 1917.
Katherine Hobson (right) watches as father and son begin an after dinner walk to grandparents'
houses to say good-bye. Note smoke trailing from the pipe his father had given him as a gift that day.
The pipe is mentioned in the letters. Stephen G. Hobson Collection - Hobson family photograph

The 102nd Field Artillery Regiment's departure overseas from the training camp in Boxford was recorded in the Regiment's History as follows:

> An early departure either for a camp in the South or for overseas was expected and Camp Curtis Guild, Jr. was the scene of many farewells. In the afternoon of September 21, 1917, the regiment struck tents and entrained for New York City. It was an impressive movement as the tents fell and each battery and company took up its packs and swung into line past crowds of relatives and friends.

On 21 September 1917, a year after first joining the National Guard, Corporal John Lambert Hobson II was now a member of the United States Army, serial number 134413. He was assigned to Battery A of the 1st Battalion of the 102nd Field Artillery Regiment; 51st Field Artillery Brigade of the 26th (Yankee) Division, a part of the First Army, under the command of Major General Clarence R. Edwards of the American Expeditionary Forces (A.E.F.) which was under the command of General John J. "Black Jack" Pershing. On that day, Corporal Hobson shouldered his pack, fell in and marched the short distance from Camp Curtis Guild, Jr. down a dirt road to the train station in East Boxford, Massachusetts, and boarded a troop train bound for the battlefields of France. But he did more than just march down a road and climb aboard a train. When he shouldered that pack and took the first step of that short march down what was to become a very long road, he was marching out of his existing life. He was leaving behind his loving family, his friends, his formal education, a comfortable life in Haverhill, enchanted summers at the family's summer home, an assured future - and his youth.

Through newspaper reports and the family's letters we get a more in-depth view of the day's events and the emotions that were expended that day.

At 4 o'clock that afternoon, the soldiers, looking very businesslike on the outside, swung their packs onto their backs and fell into formation marching past cheering and weeping relatives and friends,

down their battery street and out of the camp. They marched in formation a short distance down the dirt road from the training camp to the East Boxford train station.

A band playing patriotic songs accompanied the marching soldiers. Military bands seemed to have a way of accompanying men going to war. George M. Cohan's "Over There" was a popular patriotic song of the day. The song's stirring refrain, "Send the word, send the word over there, That the Yanks are coming, the Yanks are coming, … And we won't be back 'till it's over Over There!" must have set the jaw and quickened the step of every man marching to the train that day.

At the little East Boxford train station, the 26th Division's artillery boarded a troop transport train, bound for where they were not being told. The war was on and security was tight. Rumor among the soldiers had it that they were headed for New York where they would board a troop ship sailing to France. But there was also a rumor going around that they were on their way to another military camp in the southern United States for further training. Nobody official was talking.

At 5:25 that afternoon with the call "all 'board!", the conductors swung their lanterns and blew their whistles signaling forward to the engineer that the train was loaded and ready to depart. The civilian well-wishers that had crowded around the long string of passenger rail cars extending well beyond the station's platform backed away from the train.

Waiting impatiently at the front of the passenger cars was a huge, ominous looking steam locomotive: black and powerful with its gigantic, cylindrical boiler mounted on top of its massive iron drive wheels that were connected by powerful pistons and rods. Under building pressure the locomotive's boiler impatiently pinged from heat and it hissed and leaked steam that escaped from the valve gear through the undercarriage. Water dripped as the steam condensed when it hit the cool, fall air.

Located behind the boiler in the locomotive's square cab, the engineer and the fireman were busy making preparations for departure. The locomotive's tender had been topped off with water and loaded with coal; the oilers had checked and lubricated the wheels.

Many of the soldiers hung out of the train's windows and shouted one last good-bye. Several managed a last kiss from a girlfriend or mother standing beside the train. The girls stood on tiptoes and stretched to hug their soldier, one arm clinging around his neck, the other hanging onto a wide brimmed hat so it wouldn't fall off her tilted head.

Fathers, brothers and comrades stood in the background with a stiff upper lip and a choked throat, fighting to keep tears from flowing.

When the bystanders were clear of the train, the engineer pulled the whistle's cord and the locomotive's whistle gave a long, shrill warning blast of departure.

The engineer released the brake. He put his hand, sheathed in a greasy, leather glove, on the overhead throttle lever and squeezed the lever's brake, releasing it, and advanced the throttle lever forward, cracking it open just a few clicks. In response, the locomotive belched a huge cloud of black smoke from the smokestack. A jet of steam shot out from the valve gear as the hammer blow of initial steam pressure was delivered to the piston rods on the drive wheels. Slipping on the smooth iron rails, the drive wheels spun in place and then paused. The locomotive lurched forward.

With the initial forward lurch there was a series of banging noises repeated down the line of passenger cars as the couplings that linked the passenger cars together took up the slack that had set in between them while the train stood loading in the station. The couplings now were taking an even strain.

In earnest now, the locomotive's stack belched thick smoke, puffing faster and faster. The spinning drive wheels gradually gained a full purchase on the rails. Between the locomotive's huffing and puffing and the creaking noise of the weight-stressed passenger cars' iron axels and wheels, the train was a calliope accompanying the cheers and shouts of last farewells.

The train gained speed and departed this station bound for New York where a troop ship, the SS Finland, was waiting, docked and loading at a pier across New York's harbor in Hoboken, New Jersey, preparing to take these soldiers to France.

The journey began slowly. Giving to the ceremony of the occasion and caught up in the spirit of the masses that had gathered along the route, the engineer kept the locomotive at an idle speed for several miles down the line for the benefit of the cheering crowds gathered along the way and at the local Haverhill Bridge and Bradford stations. The engineer kept the whistle blowing and rang the brass bell as the train passed through the hometowns of many of the soldiers, who hung out of the passenger car windows, waving and cheering along with the crowd.

As the train passed through Bradford station, my father's sister, Alice, attending Bradford Academy that fall, was one of the many that had gathered beside the tracks. That night, Alice would write to her older brother that she had actually seen him in a passenger car window as the train slowly went by the cheering crowd at Bradford station.

Once the train had passed Bradford station, the engineer made preparations for joining the main rail line. Removing his glove for a moment, he reached into the top pocket of his overalls and pulled out his pocket watch. Pushing the top of the stem, he popped open the watch's cover. He quickly glanced at the time and, in one motion, snapped the cover closed and slid the watch back into his pocket. Because of all the rail traffic transporting military supplies and troops these days, they anticipated there would be congestion and delays on the route to New York. The engineer had a schedule to keep. A ship was waiting.

The engineer seated himself by the cab's window and leaned out. His elbow hung out of the cab. He looked down the tracks to assure it was clear ahead. The cool breeze on his hot, smutty face was a momentary relief from the intense heat inside the cab that was pouring out from the open door of the boiler's fire hole. Before pulling himself back into the cab and covering up for the long, dirty journey that lay ahead, he let the clean breeze cool his face. He pulled the red and white bandanna that hung loosely in a triangle around his neck up over his nose and mouth protecting him from breathing in the coal dust and soot that was swirling around in the cab. Using both hands, he reached up and pulled out and down the goggles that were previously resting on the top of the visor of his blue and white striped engineer's cap, placing them over his eyes. Having done this ritual, he resumed his official position seated by the cab's right side window. He leaned out and looked again down the track. Seeing the tracks were still clear, he eased the throttle further ahead. The smoke from the stack ran white now, streaming back over the passenger cars. They were on their way.

To the crowd gathered on the platform, the train appeared to get smaller and smaller as it gained speed. Eventually, the train's last car, the little red caboose with its little crooked, pot-bellied stove's chimney sticking through the roof, disappeared entirely from the sight of those still waving, but now silently. Finally, all that remained of the train and its soldier passengers were a few wisps of trailing smoke circling in the vacuum left behind. Then the locomotive's smoke disappeared entirely, evaporating into the evening's air. It was as if that ominous locomotive was pulling that trainload of soldiers into another dimension, a twilight zone of uncertain fate and destiny. According to the reports of that day, when the train left Bradford station, quiet reflection replaced the cheering and excitement of only a few moments earlier. An awkward silence overcame the crowd standing on the platform. In that moment, the familiar senses - the sight, touch, scent and the sound of the voice of their son, brother, father, fiancé, husband or comrade - morphed into something unfathomable to them: a person they loved going overseas to fight a war. These gentle men, these loved ones who were the husbands, fathers of their children, lovers, comrades of their youth, beloved brothers and sacred sons, would be called upon to kill other human beings and possibly be killed themselves. When they returned, if they returned, they would never be the same again. It was the end of innocence for a generation.

Alice Hobson, who was standing on the platform at Bradford Station as the train went by, wrote to her brother that night that she did not see the train's caboose disappear into the twilight. Although she was waving and shouting good-byes and farewell and looking down the tracks in the direction of the disappearing train with her brother and soon-to-be fiancé on board, she could not see through the tears that flooded her eyes.

Once past the local stations and the cheering crowds, in the fast fading light of the late summer evening the train steadily gained speed and joined up with the main rail line. Officers went up and down the aisles of the passenger car settling the soldiers down, instructing overzealous soldiers not to hang out of the windows and not to make cat calls or whistle at pretty women when they slowly went through stations. They handed out a meal.

The rhythmic clickety-clack sound of the train's wheels on the rails was hypnotic and conducive to the soldiers settling in, lulling them into private thoughts and dealing in their own way with their emotions and already missing what they had left behind.

One thought prevailed in the mind of every soldier aboard that train that night: they would all return. And, furthermore, they would bring honor to themselves and this place. It simply could not be any other way.

My father took this time to write a letter to his family.

Dearest Mother

I am sending this letter to you and of course you will read it to the rest of the family.

Well, dears, I am really on my way to somewhere. (Yes, it looks like New York now, but only land knows what kind of a game the government may be playing with us.) It seems very funny indeed to be riding along on a train without a ticket and not knowing where you are going. It is rather interesting to try to figure out where I am going to wake up tomorrow a.m. We left camp about 4:45 and I would not believe that we were really going until I heard the wheels rolling under me. The band led us down to the track while quite a few ladies and girls ran along beside the marching boys in khaki. Some were crying their poor eyes out and there were very few who did not show very marked signs of sorrow. Just as we turned out of our own battery street who should I catch sight of but Mrs. Newman. She looked very pretty all dressed in black and gave me a very cheery smile. Our progress on the train as far as Lowell was very slow indeed and at every station a little crowd had gathered to give us a cheer as we went by. At Lawrence we made quite a stop and one or two men were lucky enough to get some bystanders to buy them some pie and the like. We are not allowed to talk to anyone outside and are forbidden to put our heads out the windows. I however managed to catch the eye of an artilleryman while we were stopping at Ayer and slipped him a post card to mail to you. I shall do the same with this letter if possible. We had a fine little game of cards tonight, which managed to pass the evening. Supper consisted of two huge meat sandwiches, each one a meal in itself, one hard-boiled egg and coffee. I was very hungry as usual and it tasted mighty good. We are now on some siding where we have been for twenty minutes.

Poor Everett was very low indeed when we left Boxford, but now is doing fine. Up to date I have only swallowed hard once and that was last night when I kissed all you folks good-bye. Then the tears did their darnedest to flow, but I wouldn't let them come and that was all there was to it.

You folks have been so nice to me and have done so much to make things easy and comfortable for me that I don't know how I can ever thank you for all you have done. Mother dear has worked for all she was worth trying to think of little things that would help out that I never would have thought of and believe me Mother, they are going to come in handy. Nothing has been too good for Dad's soldier boy and he has put himself out a great many times that he might buy him a box of cigarettes or see that he is well supplied with money. Oh Daddy Dear you will never know how much your gifts and fore thought have been appreciated by your oldest son who is now on his way into the big world to make his own mark. If I can only live up to the high standards that you and Mother have set for me and if I can make half the success of life that you two have made of yours, I will be happy. I realize that your prayers and hopes are with me and that in itself will help guide me on the right road.

And now a word for the rest of the family - you have all done so much to make for my comfort and joy that I have a very great debt to pay to you on my return. I cannot forget it and once I get back it shall be paid in full. I have laughed and fooled with all of you but deep down beneath it was pretty hard to leave. I kissed you all good-bye last night without showing any very deep sorrow, but I was fighting within myself to hold back the emotion. So if I appeared cold on the outside please remember there was a very deep sorrow within.

Well dear ones left at home I will do my best to do you all credit while I am away and you at home try not to think of the sadness of the vacant chair which is there at the table and think of me as well and happy. God is with me and will bring me back a better and wiser man.

Love and lots of kisses,
Jack

KEEP THE HOME FIRES BURNING
(1914)

Music by Ivor Novello
Lyrics by Lena Ford

They were summoned from the hillside,
They were called in from the glen,
And the country found them ready
At the stirring call for men.
Let no tears add to their hardships
As the soldiers pass along,
And although your heart is breaking
Make it sing this cheery song:

Keep the Home Fires Burning,
While your hearts are yearning,
Though your lads are far away
They dream of home.
There's a silver lining
Through the dark clouds shining,
Turn the dark cloud inside out
'Til the boys come home.

Overseas there came a pleading,
"Help a nation in distress."
And we gave our glorious laddies,
Honour bade us do no less.
For no gallant son of freedom
To a tyrant's yoke should bend,
And a noble heart must answer
To the sacred call of "Friend."

Keep the Home Fires Burning,
While your hearts are yearning,
Though your lads are far away

They dream of home.
There's a silver lining
Through the dark clouds shining,
Turn the dark cloud inside out
'Til the boys come home.

As anticipated, there would be delays en route.

This is the post card to which Father referred in the letter he wrote on the train while en route to New York. The post card was handed out the window of the train to be mailed by another artilleryman at the Ayer, Massachusetts train station.

Postal
Undated (Sept. 21, 1917)
8:40 p.m.

We are at Ayer waiting for something. Feeling all right. Having a little card game. Everett and I are together. Will write more later.

CHAPTER SEVEN

Somewhere in France
Training at Coetquidan

*"Mother dear, life never meant so much to me
as it does now -I am really living and not just existing...
think of me as well and happy"*

Corporal John L. Hobson II

The ships used to transport the A.E.F. were of all sorts: from fruit boats to great, fashionable passenger racers. Some ships would be half filled with civilians, and in others the soldiers aboard would be of two or three military organizations. Some ships sailed in great convoys, some made it alone. Some ships went directly to France, others stopped en route at Liverpool or Southampton, England. Some went to Halifax, Nova Scotia, and waited there until it was reported that the chances of getting across the Atlantic through the submarines were good.

The A.E.F. troops would ultimately land at several French ports: Saint-Nazaire, Bordeaux, Marseilles and Harve; La Pallice was used as the horse port.

On 23 September 1917, the SS Finland sailed directly from Hoboken, New Jersey to Saint-Nazaire, France.

The voyage from the United States to France was perilous and made through submarine infested waters. During the previous three years, German U-boats had attacked twenty-eight U.S. ships. The large, lumbering U.S. troop transports made excellent targets for submarines lurking off the east coast. My father would tell stories about the voyage and the constant lookout for submarines. While at sea the soldiers conducted gun drills and abandon ship exercises and were assigned sentry duty to scan a sector of the horizon for signs of submarines. Untrained, anxious Army eyes saw submarines in every piece of flotsam and there were groundless alarms including one set off by a soldier who accidently leaned against the alarm handle in the middle of the night and set off a blast from the Finland's siren. The guilty man was nowhere to be found and, according to the History of the Regiment, the matter was dismissed by the ship's Finnish master with, "De gottamn Army blew dot vistle."

The Finland was part of a convoy along with other transports Henderson, Antilles and Lenape, all under the guardianship of the cruiser San Diego.

The SS Finland made port on 5 October. The troops disembarked the next day, 6 October.

The SS Finland was a 12,760-ton vessel (a vessel's "tonnage" is not its weight, it is a measurement of volume: one ton equals 100 cu. ft. of capacity) built in 1902 by W. Cramp & Sons of Philadelphia for the Red Star Line. She was 560 ft. in length and 60.2 ft. in beam. She had a straight stem, two funnels and four masts. She was a twin screw (propeller) with a speed of 15 knots. When used as a passenger ship from 1902 - 1917, she had accommodations for 342 first-, 194 second- and 626 third-class passengers. She sailed under the American flag until 1909 and then transferred to the Belgian flag. In 1912, she reverted to sailing under the American flag again. When America entered the war in 1917, she was taken over as a troopship.

The Regiment's History described their arrival in France:

Four days off the coast of France a fleet of destroyers met the convoy and took station and the cruiser San Diego turned back. It was reassuring to watch the destroyers to starboard and port, ahead and astern, cutting the water, rolling terribly in the heavy seas, and occasionally making a dash in some direction.

At last the welcome shore came in sight and we were met by an airplane which flew ahead and around, the observer searching for submarines. We crowded the rails for closer glimpses of the shore and as we passed through the locks into the Harbor of Saint-Nazaire peasants and French and American soldiers greeted us. We found a berth on October 5, and on the 6th landed and marched to Adrian barracks in the mud at Base Camp No. 1.

Our ten days stay at Saint-Nazaire gave us our first experience of the discomforts of "Sunny France," at least of Brittany. We were quartered in old, leaky Adrian barracks without floors. It rained almost continuously and was very cold. The mud was deep and slippery. Often shelter tents had to be set up inside the barracks where the roofs leaked.

Gun crew loading French 75 mm artillery on the recoil. In this picture note the blast from the muzzle as the piece fires and the barrel in recoil. When the lanyard was pulled and the piece fired, in one smooth motion a man ejected the spent shell and another man rammed a live round into the breach of the recoiled gun barrel and slammed the breach shut. By the time the barrel had finished recoiling, another man was ready to pull the lanyard to fire the piece again. So rapid was the coordinated fire from the French 75s that captured German prisoners asked about the 75 mm machine guns. www.worldwar1.nl

"Detail forward!" French artillery battery repositioning light artillery. www.worldwar1.nl

We were cold and uncomfortable and we had to send large working parties to unload the ship and construct a reservoir.

Then came our first experience with French railroad cars, the "40 Hommes-8 Chevaux," [Named so because it was stenciled on the side of the rail car that the capacity of the rail car was 40 men (hommes) or 8 horses (chevaux)] or "side-door Pullmans" as they were also called, and on October 17, 1917, we arrived late in the night at Guer and were transported in French camions [trucks] in the rain to the training camp at Coetquidan.

The infantry training camp was at Neufchateau, in eastern France, while the artillery units were stationed at Coetquidan near Rennes in Brittany, an ancient artillery training camp established by Napoleon. The work was severe, relentless, but the results showed the wisdom of the hard, well directed training, in which French officers played important parts as instructors.

The regiment arrived at Coetquidan on 17 October 1917, and they would remain in training at Coetquidan for four months, until the end of January 1918. For most, including my father, it would be the first time away from home over Thanksgiving and Christmas. The holidays were celebrated at the crude facility at Coetquidan shivering around tiny French wood burning stoves with a traditional Thanksgiving turkey dinner provided by the Army's supply department and other goodies provided by the battery funds. Then there would be packages sent from home at Christmas. A band played seasonal songs and there were church services, but nothing could replace the longing to be with loved ones at home. During the holidays even the hardest of hearts needed time alone and dealt with an inevitable lump in the throat, a quickly wiped tear from the eye, and a very visceral reminder of what they really were fighting for.

Away from home for the first time also gave way to trying new things, things that probably would not have been tried at home, including my father's attempt at growing a mustache. It didn't last and there were no pictures, but I always thought he would have looked good with one.

A newspaper reporter for The Boston Globe traveling with the 26th Division, Frank P. Sibley, observed that the first impression that the regiment got of France was of cold, more cold, mud and rain, and more rain which made more mud. It was a miserable spate of fall weather that greeted the newly arrived A.E.F. troops.

Sibley also noted that the second impression was of smiling people; extraordinarily hospitable and kind-hearted people with ways of living that were entirely strange to the soldiers; the acceptance as natural and comfortable the condition of cold and sparse creature comforts; the economy of fuel; the openness in performing certain "functions" in life which Americans discreetly conceal; and French money.

Sibley also wrote, "…in the beginning we seemed to be liked better than the English…"

As the eager, fresh, just-landed American soldiers marched through the French villages, they sang "Mademoiselle from Armentieres" making up their own bawdy verses as they went along. The last verse usually went like this:

Mademoiselle from Armentieres
Parlay-vous
Mademoiselle from Armentieres

Parlay-vous
Mademoiselle from Armentieres
You didn't have to know her long
To know the reason men go wrong
Hinky-dinky parlay-vous.

The SS Finland delivered the 26th Division's 102nd Field Artillery Regiment to Saint-Nazaire and almost immediately began steaming back to the United States. On her return voyage, one hundred-fifty miles from the French coast, the SS Finland was torpedoed by a German U-boat. She was not sunk. She returned to Saint-Nazaire and was repaired. After the war the SS Finland returned to passenger service until 1928, when she was finally scrapped at Blyth.

However, when torpedoed, the SS Finland was carrying a large quantity of mail destined for the United States, including many letters that had been written home by the soldiers of the 102nd Field Artillery Regiment on the voyage to France and initially upon arrival in France. These incidents explain the delay, and in some cases complete absence, in the delivery of my father's initial letters.

Dearest Sister

The first mail arrived from the States last night and with it came your letters. Never before did your handwriting look so good to me as it did last evening when Al Houle handed me your letter, while the news that all was fine at home was a God send straight from heaven. Your letters were the first that either Everett or I had received since we left Boxford just one month ago this afternoon and sister dear having been a whole month without hearing home news I don't suppose you know what those letters meant to us. The news may have been a month old and it may seem funny to hear you talking about going through the Boxford station, but they certainly gave two boys of Battery A a thrill that they won't forget in a hurry. I have read and reread your letter about a hundred times and I take it out of my pocket every little while just to look at the writing. Anything from home sweet home means more than you will ever realize to me now that I am a few thousand miles away. Don't get the idea from all that I have said that I am homesick because I am in the best of spirits, but I merely want you to appreciate what your letters meant. They certainly meant a lot. Well now for the news.

First of all I am well, in fact, I never in my life felt better than I do right now. Everett says I am looking much better than I did when I left the States except when I have to go for a couple of days without a wash as is the case once in a while.

This life I am now leading is some different than home life all right. I must confess I miss the home comforts at times, but by degrees I am getting used to the Army's way of living and find it easier to do without some of the things I have never been without. Take a common article as a chair. Why I have not seen a real true chair for so long that I doubt if I should know one. I know blame well that I have forgotten how to use one. Well it will be up to you to show me how to use one when I get back.

Up to date we have not had any real hardships to go through although little discomforts are many. For instance, at one place there was very little water and we were forced to save every drop we could. The shower bath did not have individual places for the water to come out, but holes had been made in a pipe which ran around the room; hence every time the water was turned on eight or more men had to be ready to jump in so that no water would be wasted. It may sound funny to save water, but we had to. Another thing which was scarce was wood. No food could be cooked which required more than two hours cooking. We did not suffer from lack of food nevertheless, but got all we could eat without being pigs. War bread is being used all over the country and I personally like it. In fact, fully as well as American bread the taste of which I have long since forgotten, so really should not try to judge.

The trains over here, sister, are the queerest things I ever saw and maybe they are not rough riding. They remind me of the toy trains Buster got last Xmas, and which Art and I enjoyed so much. How these little cars ever stay on the track is beyond me, but somehow they do. I saw a first class sleeping car in the freight yard yesterday, and it doesn't look any more like ours than black looks like white. The day coaches have four wheels and the Pullmans six.

The French people are very nice to the American soldiers and we are greeted with a smile wherever we go. Cheering is not the style over here but hand waving and a look of welcome greet us and keep the spirits well up as we march through the town. After all this country has been through I shouldn't think she would ever want to cheer again until the war is over. Black is to be seen on a great many women and a look of heart felt suffering marks their faces. There are almost no men to be seen who are not in uniform and those who are not are either unfit or too young. I saw a very impressive sight yesterday - a little boy not much bigger than Phil out plowing with a yoke of oxen in a field while a woman, whom I took to be his mother, was hoeing. The women seem to be filling the men's places around here and seem to be glad to do it to serve France.

The French children are very much like American children - they even want you to give them pennies as a certain one of our family does every now and then. The girls I have seen over here up to date cannot come half up to the American girl in my opinion. Some are not bad looking, but they lack the up and coming look, which the girls in the States have. The French soldier boys are very friendly to us and we have a great time exchanging smokes and trying to make each other understand what we mean. They are very fond of the "hard tack" we get every few meals and what we can't eat we give to them. You ought to see them smile and say "thanks" in English. [Hard Tack is a type of biscuit made from flour, water and salt. "Tack" is a British sailor's slang for food. Hard tack has been used for centuries for sustenance instead of perishable foods. As long as it is kept dry, it will last for years.] Some of them are fine looking and very young. One fellow I was trying to talk with this morning was only eighteen.

Well dear I guess I had better close now and make my way over to mess.

Remember I am well and happy and think of you often and wonder what you all are doing. Anything no matter how small or unimportant it may be to you folks means a whole lot to me so please write me all the news. I of course cannot write all or even half of what happens to me, but you can so please do.

Give my love to everyone and keep lots for yourself.
Jack Hobson - American Expeditionary Force

Dearest Dad

Having written both Mother and Sister a letter since I arrived on French soil I now think it's your turn to receive a letter from me. Having had a nice cool wash in some French water I feel clean and since I have no work to do I am going to drop you just a few lines.

Well Dad you ought to see the boys of Battery A now. They are all in wonderful condition, happy, and really doing some work. I swear if I keep on gaining in health and weight the way I have since I landed over here you folks will not know your own son when he comes marching home. Just think this over, I go to bed at nine o'clock and what is more to the point I go right to sleep. Stay awake - great guns I couldn't. Last night I had charge of quarters and had to stay up until half past ten and I never had such a job keeping awake before in my life. I never thought that I would ever be able to go to bed and to sleep at nine o'clock. I doubt if I am ever able to go to another dance, unless it gets over by nine o'clock. Well it is the best thing in the world that ever happened to me. A good night's sleep won't hurt any man. You tell Dr. Bryant the next time you see him that he was just right when he told me all I needed to build me up was plenty of fresh air and above all things eight or nine hours of sleep a night. I didn't believe him at the time, but I do now. Plenty of hard work and regular hours certainly has made a new man out of me and you folks will say so when you see Johnny march proudly in the front door of 129 Arlington Street. Now for some news about what we have been doing.

---Censored---

[Whoever censored this letter used a razor and actually cut this portion right out of the letter. Apparently, they took no chances with simply crossing something out. This was the only letter my father sent that was ever censored, so he must have learned his lesson early on.]

There's one thing Dad which I want to know - when am I going to get some news from home? My but it does seem strange not to have heard from you folks but once for over a month. I suppose that the next boat that pulls in will bring news from the States and I wish she would pull in blame soon. I am trying to get one letter a week off to you folks and I suppose you are writing more than that to me. I bet all my letters get there together and I suppose yours will over here.

Well Daddy Dear I guess I have told you all there is to tell and after all the chief news that you folks want to know just now is that I am well and happy.

Please remember me to the men in the office and tell them that their wishes of good luck to me has been fulfilled up to date.

Give my love to both grandparents and the family.

Lots of love for yourself,
Jack Hobson - American Expeditionary Forces

Dearest Mother

This is just a short note to let you know that I am OK both in health and in spirits. Those two things seem to be the only real news I can tell you, but I know that they will be very welcome.

No more mail has arrived from the old U.S.A. as yet, but we are all looking forward to some in the very near future. Mother, dear, a letter from one of you will be a very welcome sight to me. I am just crazy to hear what news is at home and what you all are doing. A letter from home never meant so much to me before in my life as it does now and I guess it is the same with you folks at home.

Everett and I have been together a great deal especially at night. The more I see of him the better I like him and we are really comforts for each other. Neither of us have been homesick, but we love to get together at night and talk over home things. I have lived over and over again in my dreams some of those wonderful times we all have had together and expect to live over hundreds of more times before I get back.

Yesterday three of us took a long walk out through the country, in fact it is all country around here, and pretty is no name for some of the sights we saw. Oh Mother, you would love it here only the roads are kind of muddy to walk on most of the time. I see now why these heavy trench boots were given to us.

I saw Don Appleton last night and also Morris Baker. I have run into three or four Exeter men who are with the 101st Regiment. Morris was looking fine in spite of his sad affair last summer. Don was with three other officers, one of whom was an Exeter man, so I did not have a chance to speak with him.

Well Mother dearest remember that song entitled "Keep The Home Fires Burning Till The Boys Come Home" and remember you have a son coming with them who thinks of you by day and dreams of you at night and is trying his best to be true to all you have taught him.

Lots of love to all and lots for yourself.
Jack Hobson - American Expeditionary Forces

Somewhere in France
October 28, 1917

Dearest Dad

Your letter arrived last night along with one from Mother and Sister. Those three letters meant an awful lot to me in fact more than any of you will ever realize. Just a few lines from any of you makes me feel like a new man and makes it much easier to put on that smile and say, "They're all behind you old man so what do you care about a few little discomforts." Your own handwriting Daddy always makes me feel that you are writing to me as your son and not just a business friend whom you type a letter to. It always makes me want to just grit my teeth and play the game right up to the limit for your sake if for no one else's every time I look at that letter. It certainly means a lot to me and the rest of the family for that matter when you yourself write us. This life over here is not all sunshine although we do have some wonderful times and it is just what may seem small to you - a letter from your own father - that makes me as well as many of the boys buck up and do things and put up with things they never believed they could. I'm not saying all this to fill up the pages but I really feel it Dad and without a doubt you have felt the same way back in your boyhood days when grandpa wrote you a letter. I doubt if you ever felt a letter any deeper than I did yours because you never were in the same circumstances as I am but guess you know all right what a father's letter means to a son.

I am in the very best of health as I told you in my last letter and my spirits seem to go higher as the weather grows colder which is every day. Of course there are times when I would like to be with you and the rest of the family in front of the fire in your den smoking and fooling with you but I realize that there is big and serious work to be done before I do that again and so I try to forget it and get busy. All the boys are the same way. Just as happy as they can be but they all long for home at times. It's only natural. You should have heard them chew over the news last night after reading their letters. A few who did not receive letters would come up to a more fortunate comrade and ask him if Main Street was still there and if the clock on the city hall was still running. Home sweet home was the subject around here last night. A crowd of us went down to one of the cafes to supper and to hear us rip it up you would have thought we were in Haverhill.

Dad those cigarettes you are having sent to Everett and I certainly will be a welcome gift. These that we buy over here are very poor side of ours. Even the French soldiers say so and will almost do anything to get a hold of an American cigarette. I still have a box left which I am saving for Thanksgiving. Just as quick as your first lot arrive I will start in on this box I am saving. Both Everett and I were very much pleased when we read that smokes were on the way.

Isn't that funny about Hosford Brackett. I admire him though even if he ran away to try to enlist. If you happen to see him please remember me to him and tell him he will have his chance someday but to wait until he is fully over that operation. The Army life is a great one for the boy who can stand but he is not strong enough yet.

I am awfully sorry to hear of Uncle Charlie's death and wish that either you or Mother would extend my sympathy to the Greenmans. It must have been very hard indeed for poor Grandma Gale but from Mother's letter I should judge she is standing it very well. How she ever stands up the way she does is a wonder to me.

Yes I understand that another big loan is being floated in the States. We had a chance to buy the bonds over here but as you said when a man gives his life up for his country that is all anyone can expect. Several men who did not take out bonds on the first loan took one this time.

Dad I am sorry to say that I have not had time to write grandma and grandpa Hobson a letter. I hope to find time in the near future but we are kept fairly busy. Will you please give them my love and explain to them why they have not heard from me.

Well Dad I guess I have told you all I can except what I have already written so will close.

Give my love to all the family and remember me to Mr. Bailey and Mr. Atkinson as well as the rest of the men.

Love to yourself,
Jack Hobson - American Expeditionary Forces

Dearest Grandma

I am sorry to say that I have had very little time to write letters over here or you would have heard from me long ago. Well, "better late than never", you know the old saying goes and I hope it is just as good now as it was when it started.

Grandma, this Army life is doing me just worlds of good and I am gaining in both health and knowledge every day. Things, of course, are so much different over here than they are in America that there is an awful lot to learn and see every day.

I have had lots of fun trying to learn French. I cannot say that I am making very great progress but, if we stay here long enough, I may get somewheres with it.

The French soldiers have taken a great liking to our boys and every Sunday, or any other time we get off, they come around and try to carry on a conversation with us. They will give almost any-thing they possess for a button off one of our coats or one of those which we wear on our collar with "MASS" written on it. Yes, our boys are the same way and exchanges of buttons takes place every day.

The other day three of us went walking out in the country and, during the course of the morning, ran out of matches so dropped into a farmhouse to borrow some. Having got the matches one of the party, who could talk French, started a conversation with the lady of the house. We wanted to find out something about the country around. But, alas, she was too interested in America to tell us about this place. She had never heard of New York but she had heard of Boston. She was very interested in our trip across and said, over and over again, what brave boys we were to leave our homes to come away over here to fight.

At one place when we stopped for a drink we helped hang out a newly killed pig and the thanks we received cannot be described.

All the French seem to welcome us. I shall never forget the fare-well a lady gave us one time when we had been camped there for several days. A bunch from our Battery used to go down there to her café and have big feeds three or four times a week. When we told her that our regiment was to move on she broke down crying. We told her that another lot was coming, but she said that "The Dirty Dozen", as we call ourselves, had won her heart in our short stay and that no one could take our places. She wished us the best of luck and said she would look in the papers for news of our regiment. She certainly was nice to us and I doubt if any of "The Dirty Dozen" ever forgot her.

The work we are now doing is hard at times but very interesting. I wish I could tell you all about it but I believe we are not allowed to tell of our training. Well, you all shall hear about it when I get home.

We are now in fine quarters and getting three good meals a day which is a very important factor in my life. The war bread which we get is really good, in fact, I have become very fond of it. The French candy is not quite as good as ours, but I manage to put away much more than is good for me, as usual.

Well, Grandma dear, along with the news I have written home I guess I have told you all. Please give my love to Grandpa, also Aunt Mary and Uncle Clinton. Lots of Love for yourself.

Your oldest Grandson,
Jack - American Expeditionary Forces

Dearest Mother

I have got just a few minutes to myself and so will drop you a few lines just to let you know that on October 30, 1917 your boy was well and happy.

Mother dear your letters have been a great comfort to me since they arrived and I have read them more times than I have toes on my feet. I have said so much about the pleasure that all of your letters have brought me that you must be getting sick of hearing it but I certainly have enjoyed every one. Grandpa Gale wrote me a fine letter as I guess you know while Dad's letter put the heart right into me. As far as I can make out you all have written me and what one may miss the other gets. Both Everett and I enjoyed dear little "Buster's" note and I told Everett that I would give a good deal to be rough housing the little fellow around the front room or trying to make him stop yelling "Mother" at night once again. I suppose he is all over his yelling by now but I'll bet he is still after a rough house with someone.

Yesterday being Sunday we had no work and I enjoyed a very nice little walk followed by a fine lunch at one of these French cafes. No Mother dear it was nothing like a Sunday dinner you give me at home but the mere fact that I could sling my long legs under a real table with a cloth on it and have the food brought to me made it go to the right spot. The whole meal cost four francs or about 80 cents in American money. They serve us cider in place of water but it was far from being our cider.

Speaking of cider makes me think of Thanksgiving and maybe I don't dread that day. A bunch of us are going to try to get a pass and go to the nearest real town and have lunch but I tell you little Jackie is going to really long for home that day. Well we will all think of each other and remember we have a lot to be thankful for. I will be through supper when you folks are eating your lunch.

Oh great guns but it was cold here last night and our stoves are not working yet. We also had a frost which put a thin layer of ice on the water in some places near here. Everett and I spent the evening together and believe me when I say we longed for that fire in Dad's den. Everett read a letter from his father in which he said he was toasting his shins in front of the open fire. Oh my kingdom for that fire last night.

We are now pulling our lazy bodies out of bed before the sun even starts to get up. Yes every morning when we roll out the stars are shining and the old moon is still throwing its rays across the hills. It is the same hour that we got up at Boxford 5:30 but my what a change in the light and air. Great Scott when I get home and can sleep in the morning until 6:30 or later I don't know what I will do.

Have you folks received any mail from us yet? Everett and I were trying to figure out about when you would receive the first lot of letters we wrote over here so if you can remember please let me know. More mail came yesterday which makes the third bunch we have received. Some men have got as many as eighteen letters from the States.

Oh yes Mother, will you ask Dad to send me some matches. We can buy all the French matches we want but they are poor. I can't very well explain what the trouble with them is but I do know that they spoil a smoke for me.

From what sister and you wrote I should judge that a good many rumors had been going around as to where we were. Oh Mother I should think you folks would have been wrecks waiting to hear from us. Tell sister that I very much doubt if Mrs. Pitman knew where we were going any more than she did so not to feel discouraged because she did not tell her.

Lunch is ready so I must go eat but will write more afterwards.

Well mess is over and I now I have a few minutes before drill in which to continue my letter.

Gee Mother I am all excited. I have a registered letter waiting for me at the post office but I can't get it until tonight. I wonder what it is. Well there is nothing to do but wait until the post office opens and then we will find out.

You remember that sweater you gave me which I had such a hard time taking because I thought I was not going to have room for it. Well Mother darling I wouldn't be without that sweater now for anything. The one Marj made me is also a priceless little gift and many a night I have gone to bed with it on. It is just the thing from ten a.m. up to four p.m. then yours goes on. Every time I look at it I always think of the hard time you had getting me to take it and then I laugh at myself for being foolish enough to even try to turn it down. Trust your judgment Mother and I guess I won't go far wrong.

Karl told me this morning that he had received a post card from you and was very pleased. He has been made mess Sergeant in Coyle's place and is certainly making good. It is Sergeant Pitcher now not Corporal. This change took place some little time ago but I swear I have forgotten to tell you about it although I have meant to every time I wrote.

Hobby is the same old boy - always smiling and ready to eat all the time per usual. Some of the boys claim I eat him to stand still with ease but personally I feel that he puts away more food than I do. At any rate we both eat like pigs both day and night.

That paper cutting you sent me "When Johnny comes marching home" is a peach and has caused more than one smile to break forth on a comrade's face when I showed it to him. "When will it be Corp", one fellow asked me but I am sorry to say I was unable to answer him.

Everett misses sister very much indeed and more than once has sat down and just gazed at her picture. I guess he will be one mighty happy boy when the time comes to return home to her. I miss Marjorie more than I expected to but of course in a different way. We four did have such wonderful times together that it is little wonder that I miss her. I guess from all sister writes that the two of them are sticking right together while their brothers are doing the same thing.

I have not written Arthur since my arrival over here but know that you will read him all my letters when he comes down to the house for lunch some Sunday. I shall try nevertheless to get a letter off to him at Exeter sometime in the near future. Gee I'd like to see the old boy right now for a few hours. I'm looking forward to his with a great deal of pleasure as I'm very anxious to hear the news from Exeter as well as his own personal news. Be sure and let me know about the Exeter vs. Andover game. I may be miles away but my heart and hopes are all with the boys in red just the same and Johnny intends to have a celebration all of his own over here if the good old school comes through with another victory.

Three cheers. I have got my letter and it was from Art. All the news from school and two school papers. Those papers used to find their way to the wastebasket pretty fast when I was there but I have read every word of these - yes even the ads. Oh Mother but it did seem good. What wouldn't I give for one of Wetherell's ice cream fudges now. Well it won't be long before I'll be back at it again.

Well dearest I guess I had better close now as I have some washing to do.

Keep your spirits up and tell Dad that his boy prays every night for two of the best and dearest friends a boy ever had - his father and mother. You both are very, very dear to me and I'm looking forward to the day when I may return to you both - a better man than when I left and a real comforter to you two dear people.

Love to all and lots for yourself and Daddy.

Your soldier boy,
Jack Hobson

Dear Dad

Well I suppose by this time you folks have received my first letter mailed from "Somewhere in France". It was written on the transport on the way over and sent to Mother. Oh I wonder if that letter has reached home yet! Mother's letter written on September 23rd did not reach me until yesterday so you see there must have been a delay somewhere as I have received some with much later dates. That letter dated the 23rd was the first to bring a lump in my throat. All went well until I read about dear little "Buster" crying for his big brother and I must confess that touched a very tender place in my heart. It's those little things that soften the hearts of the hardest and make the wanderer long for home. The lump did not last more than five minutes, but it was mighty hard swallowing while it was there. It would be very funny if it hadn't touched me a little. Now I don't want Mother to stop writing me about those little things because I want to hear about them but I want to let you know that my heart is in the right place and with you. I am going to do my best to save that letter as there are many little things in it that I am very proud of indeed. You very likely read the letter from Mother and know just how I felt. I wasn't in France when I was reading that - I was at 129 Arlington Street.

News of the second war loan reached our camp a few days ago and when we heard it had gone over five billion dollars it made us feel pretty good. It just goes to prove that the people of America are behind us and that's all we ask. We'll deliver the goods over here when called upon to do so if we get a backing like that right through to the end. It's wonderful and certainly has put the heart into us.

I guess I forgot to tell you in my last letter that we had received our second pay. It was in the form of French money and after we had received it we had to sit down and figure out how much it was worth in American money. I got about $36.00 - twenty of which I put into my money belt for future use. I find that we can send money home in the form of a money order and if I find I can save a little each month I think I shall send some to you to put in the bank for me. I am planning to live on my pay not touching the money you gave me until really needed. If you should receive a money order from me in the course of three months you will know what it is for and won't be surprised. My savings plan may not work out so don't be disappointed if that money order doesn't come. I would like to save a little if it can be done without depriving me of too many pleasures over here, and I think with a little planning it can be done. Speaking of money Dad, how does it seem not to have me yelling for cash all the time to throw away on a Copley dance or to take some girl to the theater? Yes Daddy I can hear you answer just as if you were right here with me, "Johnny you can have all you want within reason" and your within reason was always large. You certainly were generous to me and my pleasures seemed to be yours. Well I'll be back yelling again for it before long and know only too well that it is going to be a pleasure for you to give me what I need.

Mess call has just blown so I guess I will go and eat, but will write more later.

Mess is over and there is just about enough time to finish this letter before afternoon drill.

Last night Everett, Joe Tuttle and I went out to supper and I wish you could have seen the funny little place we went. It was a wet black night out, but in that was dry (in one sense of the word) and dimly lighted. Three hungry boys sat down there and really ate. After supper we stayed right there and just watched the different people and smoked our pipes. That is one thing I wish I could do in the States - smoke pipes in cafes. When we arrived back at camp about 8:30 we found one of our boys very sick with a high temperature so we all changed ourselves from "sports" into nurses. I rubbed the poor boy's head for over half an hour until he found relief in the sweet land of dreams. He was feeling much better this morning, but he surely was sick last night. I guess he had a bad case of the grip.

I hope my letters are not too dry reading, but remember I cannot tell anywhere near all I want to, but when I get home and are gathered around the fire you shall hear all about it from start to finish.

Please give my love to all the family and remember me to all who ask for me.

I am well and happy, Daddy, so don't worry about me or feel bad every time you look at that vacant chair. Let's all live for the day when I shall come back home ready to take up my work beside you a better and a broader thinking man because of my experiences over here.

With lots of love for yourself,
Jack

Dearest Mother

Another week has passed quickly by and Sunday is here again. I have washed, made my bed, had breakfast, and now sit down to write you my Sunday letter. I wonder if this letter will ever reach home. That is the thought that goes through my mind every time I write. Well all I can do is write and then pray that nothing will prevent my letters from reaching you. I have written one of you every week so you should get some of my letters.

In your letter written September 23rd you said you wondered if my thoughts had been especially with you all. Yes Mother dear they have and every night after I get into bed I lay awake a few minutes and just think of you dear ones at home and wonder what you are doing. In my mind's eye I can picture you all going about your afternoon's tasks, you see it is afternoon in the States when we are going to bed, and I can even hear the children playing out in the yard. Oh yes Mother I certainly do think of you and some of the happiest moments of the day are spent thinking of you at home.

What you said about my picture, darling, made me very happy indeed and if I can only live up to it I will feel that my life has been one to be proud of. Those few words "All that is noble, loving and true" mean a great deal Mother and no son would ask a mother to say more about him or think higher of him than you have said and thought of me. I have many strong temptations over here, but with those words being spoken about me I don't see how I can yield to any, even the smallest and still be worthy of having you say what you have about me.

Both of the watches you gave me that night at Boxford are going fine. I am still wearing the one you put on my wrist by that nice big fire and shall continue to wear it until it is broken. The other one I keep in my mess kit bag which is always by my bed. I am glad Daddy is wearing the one I had at Boxford as I am anxious to keep it. If you remember that was on my wrist when I got the lightening shock the first night at Boxford.*

George Croston arrived in camp a few nights ago and Everett and I went out to supper with him last night. He left Boxford after us you know and hence had some very interesting town news to tell us.

As I guess I told you in one of my other letters Everett misses sister a great deal and his love for her is far from dying. He certainly is a fine boy and I hope that sister does not change her mind before he returns because in my eyes she could not possibly find a better man. I know that sis will be true to him and Everett has more than proven to me that he will be true to her. I wonder if any girl is longing and praying for my return as she must be for his? Alas, I fear not.

Mother dear life never meant so much to me as it does now - I am really living and not just existing. To be sure the future looks kind of dark at times, but we are all trying to live in the present - forgetting that awful outlook towards spring as far as possible when life will be one hill after another. I hope that none of our boys will be forced to lose their lives over here and somehow I feel they won't. Life is all together too sweet to give up at twenty, but if it will help save the world we are all willing. I will not dwell on this subject, but it is one which we are all forced to think of at times over here.

Well darling my thoughts seem to be roaming a bit this a.m. and there is a crowd here so I guess I had better close.

Please give my love to all the family.

Lots of love and kisses for yourself.
Your soldier boy,
John

* The wristwatches referred to here were something relatively new in 1917 - 1918. Pocket watches were the norm of the day. A gentleman of the time considered the shirt an undergarment and always wore a jacket and vest over a shirt. A gentleman carried or wore his pocket watch in his vest pocket or in a small pocket at the waistband of his trousers specifically designed for a watch, or he simply carried it in the side pocket of his trousers. The watch could also be carried in the breast pocket of the jacket, attached to a chain that was attached to the lapel button hole. Watch chains of various lengths to suit the purpose with decorative fobs attached were used to prevent the watch from being dropped or lost.

The first wristwatches weren't very durable and were somewhat of a novelty. They were like pocket watches strapped on the wrist. Wrist watches were initially used primarily by the military. It was impractical for a military man to be fumbling in layers of clothing to get to his timepiece or have it fly out of his pocket if he was running. Even with a glass crystal that easily broke and not being water resistant or anti-magnetic, a timepiece that was securely attached to the wrist and was smaller and easily accessible was more practical and functional than a watch carried in the pocket.

During the First World War, Omega supplied the U.S. Army with wristwatches that had a protective grid over the glass. It probably was an Omega watch that my father had kept in his army trunk. Omega and the British company, Breitling, supplied watches to the military during the Second World War.

The wristwatch became an acceptable fashion to be worn in civilian life after the First World War, accompanying the changing clothing fashions of the times.

Dearest Mother

No mail has arrived from the U.S. for almost two weeks now and I have been anxiously waiting for some every night. It surely is hard work going two weeks or more without mail. The last letter I wrote home was dated November 4th. Did you receive it? I certainly will be glad to hear from you that some of my letters have been received and you know that I am well and happy. I was talking with Ben Pitman yesterday and he has received over thirty letters since he arrived here, but like myself he received none for two weeks.

Well at last Everett has his commission or I should say it is on its way across. He has been taken away from Battery A and is now training with the officers. I am awfully glad it went through, but believe me I miss him. I will be able to see some of him until his commission gets here and then only land knows when we will get together. He is assigned to another battery in this regiment so we will go along together when we move, but not in the same car as has been the case. I always felt that one of the family was here with me when he was around, but with him gone I feel alone so to speak. Sergeant Hughs was telling one of the officers that I wandered around like a lost sheep the first night he was gone so you see how much he will be missed by Corporal Hobson. Ben Pitman also has a commission on its way and I understand that he is to be assigned to our battery. Oh I tell you great changes are taking place over here. I am still a Corporal, nevertheless, and there I want to stay until I see a much better position than I have got now in the ranks. I think it will be pretty hard. I am satisfied right where I am for a while.

The work is getting harder every day and from the time we get up until retreat we are kept very busy. We certainly are getting a good training. The sound of the guns means nothing to us now and I would really feel lost if I didn't hear them barking. It's a big game Mother and Battery A is only a small unit which goes to make up the team. It's fun when the shells are all going away from you, but what will it be when they start coming our way.

Lieutenant Root was asking for you all yesterday and wanted to know how I would like to be back in Haverhill. I informed him that the last time I heard from you you all were well and added that I would not object in the least to seeing you all. He thinks I am looking four times as well as when I left Boxford. Several of the boys have made the same remark and so I guess I must be.

I should judge that this letter would reach you just about Thanksgiving and I can already picture you over to Maple Avenue [John L. Hobson Sr.'s home] for dinner. Be sure Mother to write me all about it. We never had big plans for that day, but we managed to have a good time. I believe we get a big dinner over here but there is no place like home on Thanksgiving. As you all gather around the table please give your soldier boy an extra thought and let us all pray that I will be with you next year. I certainly will long for home that day and will think of you all.

It is getting colder over here every day and our over coats feel mighty good. It has rained almost every day this week and the mud is awful. I have given up trying to keep my leggings clean. We now have stoves and so when we are not on duty we are able to keep warm. The wood over here is green and wet so at times we have trouble keeping our fires going, but somehow or other we have done so.

Well Mother dear I guess I had better close and wash up for lunch.

Lots of love to all the family and lots for yourself.
Jack

Dearest Sister

I haven't written you for a perfect age and I ought to hang my head in shame after the nice long letter you sent me. Well, dear, I know that you have gotten the news from those I have written Mother and Dad, and I have been very busy. I know you will forgive me this once.

Well Sis, brother in law and I are to be separated and it has gone pretty hard with me. Everett's commission is on its way across. Yes for his sake I am glad, but I certainly do miss him. He was and is just like an older brother to me and I feel sort of lost without him. You certainly have a prize coming home to you some day and it goes without saying that he has one of the dearest and truest girls I know waiting for him. I suppose in the course of time I will get used to not having him where I can see him any minute, but just now I really feel lost.

Here is something funny for you and ought to bring a smile if not a laugh to your face - It did to mine. A crowd of us were having supper at our hang out, as I call it, the other night and among the merry little crowd gathered around the table sat George Croston. He being the last one of the crowd to leave the States and the last one in Haverhill was telling us the town news. Suddenly he turned to Everett and I and said, "I understand that you two gentlemen are to be congratulated." Both Everett and I looked at each other and laughed, then asked why we were to be congratulated. Well to make a long story short George had heard a rumor around that you and Everett were engaged and that I was engaged to Elouise Bixby. Sister I nearly fell flat and I laughed until my sides were almost as sore as they were after our party at the Andover Country Club. I could very easily understand about you and Everett, but Elouise and I got me. If it had been Marjorie I could have understood it better, but where Haverhill ever got Elouise and I is beyond me. There is a little more of the story but I will not take the time to write about it as it is not of importance. Everett was forced to admit that he was interested in you but I denied my end. It ended up by everyone drinking to your happiness and then to Everett's. Now I would like to know how that rumor ever got started about me.

Great Scott as far as Everett and I can figure out you girls are well taken care of and not very short of men. We both thought that after the Battery left that men would be few and far between, but I guess we flattered ourselves a bit. How about it kid? Are these parties anywhere near as good as the "Big Four" used to have back in the States in the dim past? I know they are not better, but are they as good?

Well sister I wish you could see your brother at night after a good days work. Mud from head to foot - tired and sleepy - hungry as a bear - but oh so happy. Every place you go you must wade in more or less mud or water. Oh it's a great life for those who do not want ease and comfort all the time. When I get back you will never, no never, hear me kick no matter what happens. If there aren't enough chairs to go around stick me on the floor and I will be comfortable. Put me on the lawn or down in the coal bin to sleep and Johnny will be right at home. Oh sis when I get out of this outfit I will be fit for anything which may come no matter what it is.

Gee it has been funny how I have run into old friends and men whom I never expected to see again. Four or five days ago this man came up to me and said, "I have seen you somewhere before, but I can't seem to place you." He turned out to be a boy I knew at Nobles named Cobb. We were both on the same work so I see him every day. I also met a man out on the field this afternoon who knew B. Ware, but I can't remember his name to save my life. It sure makes me feel good to talk with someone from Boston who knows some people I do. It makes me feel right at home. As I guess I told Mother in one of my letters there are several Exeter men over here so you see I am not without friends.

Well, dear, some of the fellows are going out tonight and as I am to be one of the party I must close.

Please give my love to all the family and keep lots for yourself.
Jack

Dearest Dad

I am on guard tonight and as there is no ink in the guard house I am forced to use a pencil. Just as long as you hear from me I guess it doesn't matter what I write with so here goes. I have just posted my 1:30 relief and as there are no lights in the guard house except candles I am writing by them. Oh it's a very striking picture - Johnny with his own gun writing home in the dear night by candle light. Whoever would have thought a year ago that I would be doing it - not I.

Well Daddy Dear this place where we are now stationed is becoming a real home to me. Not like the happy comfortable home I left last July of course, but a home as far as such a place could be. I feel as if I had lived here at least half of my life and the land and country around have won a warm place in my heart.

I shall really be sorry when the order comes to pack up and leave unless of course we were to move back to the States. I am very, very happy in my work, which every day brings me more responsibilities some of which are of great importance. Twice a week I have the entire charge of the telephone and men at the B.C. station. Should anything go wrong it would mean the firing would have to stop until it was fixed. It's easy when everything goes ok but like everything else in life that is worthwhile it is blame hard to make everything go ok. All the time little things go wrong here and there which gets my goat and when he gets away things move as some of the boys under me will tell you. If everything went right all the time it wouldn't be any fun and we wouldn't have a chance to learn. The last time the battery fired our detail worked from eight a.m. until six p.m. eating lunch, two sandwiches, while at work. There was never a word said but what was pleasant and as we went back to camp that evening just as the sun was sinking behind a big hill we all decided that life was well worth living. It certainly is a pleasure to work with a bunch of men like we have over here with us. I am so used to being with real men now - I mean men who may be rough in their ways but can give and take all with a smile - that I never want to fool with the other class at all - those who cannot smile and laugh no matter what the conditions may be.

Three cheers!! Payday tomorrow and Johnny will be rich again at least for a few days. Money goes fast over here but I am still working on my saving plan. Speaking about money tell sister that I am going out to supper with John Converse Thursday night. He roomed with Lory at Andover and knows Hope. He is on guard too. We have talked Exeter and Andover all over and decided from all reports that Exeter should win the football game this year.

One thing Daddy in the Haverhill paper amused our boys very much and has caused much laughter. It spoke about the poor drafted boys having to march three whole miles in the mud and seemed to pity them. "Poor little dears I wonder if they got their shoes muddy," is a remark heard daily ever since we read about it. We fellows have just about lived in the stuff ever since we hit here so three short miles and pity amused us all. Then it spoke about their night gowns being delayed and everyone yells, "Oh, the sweet little things haven't had their nighties come." If you happen to meet any drafted soldier on the street just stop him and give him a word of advice from me - put them nighties right away and get used to sleeping in your clothes or a full pack because when you reach here you will find nighties are not in style. I would also recommend a course in mud plowing there then set foot on French soil. They may have more comforts over there than we have here, but I'll bet tomorrow's pay they are not half so happy as we are. More mail arrived last night and I received Mother's letter of October 22nd. Some poor fellows did not get any mail and more than one returned to his barrack with tears in his eyes. It is pretty hard to go three weeks without a letter and then have some come in and you not get any. More arrived tonight I understand so those who were disappointed last night may get some tonight. Let's hope so for their sakes. Well Daddy Dear I have now got to wake Converse up and try to get some sleep myself while his relief is on duty so will say goodnight.

Please give my love to the family and of course keep lots for yourself.

Johnny
OK Lieut. Pitman
[The censor]

Somewhere in France
November 15, 1917

Dearest Buster

I suppose by this time you think your big brother is never going to answer that nice letter you wrote him some time ago. Well I do not blame you much because it was a long time ago that you wrote me. I am very busy or this letter would have been answered long ago.

Mother wrote in one of her letters that you missed your big brother a great deal, in fact, she said you cried for me one or two nights. Well I miss you just as much and have often wished that I was back again playing around the front room with you or trying to get you to bed. I suppose by this time you only have to be told once and then there is no calling for Mother. Remember you are the only boy Mother has home this winter and you must be the little man of the house. I guess you are by this time.

How are all your girlfriends, Buster? Remember I am a long way off and you have a fine chance to cut me out with Miss Adams.

Buster, I wish you had been with me this morning. I saw the dearest little dog I ever laid eyes on. He was so fat that he fell into a ditch when he tried to jump over it and some of us had to pick him out. He would have been a great pet for you.

I want you to write me again very soon. Your letters are just as welcome as the rest and I love to receive them.

I believe you asked Mother when I would be home again. Well, Buster dear, we all hope that it will not be long. Just as quick as this awful war is over all those brave boys you saw at Boxford that night you were down are coming back and I will be with them. While I am away I want you to be making a little soldier out of yourself.

Lots of love,
John

Dearest Mother

Well the unexpected has happened - we have really received some more mail. It started last night about seven o'clock and has been pouring in ever since. Not only letters but boxes. I swear I never saw so much stuff coming into one place before in my life. Box after box was handed out and letter after letter. It would have done the senders good if they could have seen the beaming faces of the receivers. War has been almost forgotten for the past twenty-four hours and we all have been living back in God's own country, the USA once again. Everyone is pulling on a real American cigar and acting like kids back in first grade. One man said to me this afternoon as we sat smoking a cigar and eating real true American candy, "Hobby old man I never was so happy in my life before." I felt the same way. I got eleven letters and four boxes. Grandma and Grandpa's box of candy, two boxes of smoking material from dear Dad plus one big box of the same good from Webber. Great Scott I've got enough to last me for more than a year it seems, but of course it will be quickly used up. Share and share alike is Battery A's motto, so some who were not so fortunate as myself will be personally looked out for by me. It is a real pleasure to share what you have with these men as they appreciate it and that's what I like to have them do. Oh the whole camp is singing today. Now for a few words about Thanksgiving.

It was fine Mother and I never felt the least bit blue until I rolled into my little cot that night and my thoughts began to roam to all you dear ones at home. I thought of what Dad told me the first night he left me at Fessenden, and I tried pretty hard. "Keep a stiff upper lip Johnny no matter what happens." I have thought of it many times and often wonder if he remembers it. It's been my watchword for all times and I consider it a good one. After praying for all of you I fought off my blue feeling and by degrees went to sleep. Thursday morning early we watered our horses as usual and after grooming the beasts we marched all in a body to the athletic field where we had all kinds of sports. I ran on the Battery relay team, but alas one of our men fell and we lost. We, however, came out on top in the tug of war and a few other events. Lunch, or I should say dinner, was served at twelve o'clock and lordy, lordy what a dinner. Turkey, white and sweet potatoes, pudding, figs, nuts, and other things which go to make up a Thanksgiving dinner. I missed Grandma H's mince pie, but aside from that I wouldn't ask for a better meal. If you folks had only been with me, Johnny would have been the happiest boy alive. Well darling as I said in my last letter next year is coming and I hope to be with you all.

The spirit of the boys is way up and I certainly enjoy being with them. This crowd certainly takes the cake. You sure are going to see a fine bunch of men march up Main Street sometime in the sweet by and by.

The romance and thrills of being a soldier have all worn off and we now feel as if we had been in it all our lives. Army life in war-time and under war conditions is far from the rosy dreams it may seem outside. I never could understand why a man must be so strong to stand it, but having lived under them I realize only too well the value of health. We boys are living in a climate somewhat different than we have been used to and believe me a man must be in mighty good health to stand it. We have had very little heavy rain of late, but these drizzles come very often. Just enough to make the ground slippery. This is a clay soil over here and once you start to slide it is good night. It's just like skim ice in the States. Dampness is another thing we have our share of, but up to date all have stood up under the weather conditions fine. Oh yes colds are around, but those are to be expected at this time of year. I am feeling fine so you need not worry.

Everett and I see very little of each other these days, but when anything of interest comes up he finds his way down to my bar-racks and I to his room. He was around asking for news and I shall head for his place tomorrow night. He's a great man Mother and we should all feel proud to have our sister engaged to such a man. The best is none to good for her, but she certainly has got one of the very best. Of course we shall all miss her, but it will be all for her happi-ness. Remember Mother dear what I told you about sister one night last summer, and I should judge from what you said in your letter that she had come up to more than I said she would.

I took a nice horseback ride in the country the other P.M. and had a fine chance to take it all in as it was a pleasure ride. Just picture holly growing wild by the roadside and farmers plowing the ground at this time of year. I understand that they have two crops here, one in the summer and another in the winter. I am sorry to say that I cannot speak very well of most of the towns around here. They are very interesting to ride through, but I would not like to live in them. Everyone makes cider at home and if you get a few miles out into the country where very few soldiers go you can get all you want free. The farmer even seemed insulted when Sergt. Tuttle and I offered to pay for some in the course of our ride.

On the road from the stables to where we water the horses is a small town and we see some very funny sights there sometimes as we pass through. On our way back tonight I saw a Frenchman trying to make love to a French girl who seemed to resent his caresses. We often see one or more children going to school and I always wonder if they enjoy going as much as Buster does.

Mother dear there is one thing which I feel very deeply and that is that I shall be unable to send all a Xmas gift this year. You all have done so much and I want to send something, but alas I am unable to find anything worth sending up to this date. I do, however, send all the love in the world to you all. I fear this will be a very lonely Xmas in many homes, but don't let my absence mar your Xmas day in any way. Being my first one away from home I fear I shall be a little homesick, but I shall do all in my power to keep busy, the best cure for that disease. Be sure darling to write your boy all about the doings at home - yes even your thoughts and the merry sayings of the rest. I want all the details. Don't worry the home details are far from tiresome and the more you write the better I like it. Well dearest even if there isn't a present on the tree marked "'From John" he wishes you all a merry Xmas and a happy New Year. Next year will make up for what we lost this.

Yes, I imagine the butterfly girl of the past has flown and I for one am very glad to hear it. There are a lot of things in life worth doing besides dancing, etc. but up to now we young people have been too busy with the latter to find them. This war will make a great difference in the social life of the American people. All the men who have been over here will realize what home really means, and it is up to the girl to do her share, the girl who does not will be very much out of place. I for one realize fully what home and all its comforts mean now that it has been taken away from me for a while, and I guess there are others too who realize it. We never realize our blessings until we are deprived of them, do we Mother? You and Dad have certainly made a real home for your children and someday when the right time comes and I am worthy of her I hope to find a girl who will make the home for me which you have made for Dad.

I am sorry to say that none of my letters will be the right kind to be printed in the papers. I had rather talk with you in my letters than write them for the public.

Oh, yes, I had a fine letter from Mr. Jordan a few days ago. He certainly has been nice to me and I shall try to write him a few lines in a day or so. Please ask Dad to tell him that I received his letter and enjoyed it very much.

I have seen quite a bit of George Croston of late, and we have many pleasant minutes together chewing over our horseback rides. We are going out to supper together tonight, but I got charge of quarters so am unable to leave.

I had a short talk with Ben Pitman this a.m. and he asked for all of you. He certainly makes a fine looking officer and is very much liked by his men.

We all were very much surprised to hear that sugar was so scarce in Haverhill. Marj Stover wrote me that they had cut down on the food at Westover and it took me right off my feet. I guess you folks are feeling this war fully as much as we only in a different way. Karl Pitcher has our food problem in fine shape and I don't think that there is a single man in the Battery who can find any fault or any that he has not had enough to eat.

Well darling it is time for me to go around and see that all the lights are out, so I must close.

Remember my thoughts are with you dear ones at home much of the time and I am writing every chance I get. You people certainly have done a whole lot to keep my spirits up by your letters and I thank you from the bottom of my heart.

Good night Mother dear. Love to all and loads for yourself.

John Hobson - 102 FA

[The following is a note inserted into this letter by Lieut. Langdon who censored this letter:]

I wish we had more of the same kind of real men in our Battery. We would all be better off. Christmas greetings to all the family.

Yours sincerely,
G.W.L.

Dearest Dad

I am on guard once again and hence have an excellent opportunity to write you just a few hasty lines. Everyone else is lost in the sweet land of dreams and Johnny is all soul alone and trying his best to keep awake until four a.m. A nice coal fire is burning away in a stove beside me and 'tis well that it is because all the windows in the guard house by one means or another have been broken and it is none too hot outside.

First of all, Dad, I want to thank you for the box of tobacco you sent me. I didn't have so much as a pipe full left when it arrived and I'll be hanged if I can get away with this French stuff. Strong is no name for it. Some of the other men were out also and I gave them enough of mine to tide them over until their box came. Well, we are all set now thanks to you and can have our good night pipe every night.

Mother's cablegram reached me last Friday and certainly was a great surprise. When it was handed to me I didn't know just what to expect but soon found out that it brought welcome news "all well". Two or three of the other men received one yesterday, but mine was the first one in our battery I believe. Direct news like that makes me seem very near home and not thousands of miles away.

Everett has left us, as bad luck will have it, as has also Lieut. Root. Their departure makes me feel as if Karl and I were the only ones left of the bunch who formed the battery, Hobby having left some little time ago. I was telling Karl the other night that if he ever pulled up anchor and left I should feel like a boat at sea without a pilot and no wireless to send an S.O.S. with. Men leaving certainly does make a hole just as it does at home when one of the family goes away. We are all just like so many brothers now anyhow, and know each other's weaknesses and strong points just like an open book. I do not know when I shall see Everett again, but I hope luck will send him back to this regiment again before many months go by. If it doesn't however, we will have a mighty happy meeting back in the U.S.A. sometime. Lieut. Root, when I went up to say good-bye, wanted me to give you all his best the next time I wrote and said to be sure to tell sister that he would see that nothing happened to Everett. He certainly hated to leave all the boys. The Battery is fast being whipped into shape, for the big day when it will be called upon to do the task it was sent over here to do. The men, as a whole, are certainly taking right hold. The future looks pretty black at times and, now that the cold weather is coming on, many of the men long for home comforts, but when one bunch is away down in the mouth the other bunch is away up, so by helping each other we manage to get along fine. Rumors fly around here about twice as fast as they did at Boxford and therefore four times more. I wish I could tell you some of them but I know it would be a waste of time as they would never reach you alive. Some put the heart right into us while others make us feel pretty down. I have long since ceased to believe anything I hear - they must show me. After it is past and gone then I am willing to consider it true, but until - nothing doing. No matter what the future may hold out for our boys over here we are all praying that it won't be long before we will all be back to our own sweet homes again; alive and well.

Mother asked me in one of her letters to let you folks know what I wanted that you could send me. Up to date I have been able to think of nothing but, knowing how things are, I have something in mind; candy, and be sure to spell it with a big "C". Outside of tobacco, candy will be more than welcome. You would be surprised to see the condition it reaches us in. That lot Grandma and Grandpa Gale sent to me tasted as if it had just been bought. Some of the boys have even received homemade fudge in very good condition. The candy over here as a whole, that is where you are, is very poor although, if you are real lucky, you may get a hold of some that is fairly good but you have to be in luck. I certainly would like more real, true, American candy so, if you happen to have a few spare minutes in Boston or Haverhill, just slip me a little.

Dad, you ought to see the horse Johnny is riding around here. Nothing handsome to gaze at to be sure, but, oh, what an easy rider. Yesterday the detail was in the saddle all day, and we were up before daylight, through breakfast and grooming this morning, in order to get off to work before seven o'clock. When it comes to cleaning a horse by moonlight I am the candy kid. I don't know which was the more sleepy, the horse or I. I do know this, however, that we both were yawning to the limit. This clay soil plus a little rain makes it very slippery and the poor beasts are all shod flat, hence they resemble an amateur on roller skates at times, and causes the rider to be ever awake least he find himself in the mud with the horse on top. Many a good man has fallen off, including Johnny. Another amusing sight is to see the detail going out to work under pack. Two or three things on a man's back and a big, awkward, plotting board under his arm. Handle the horse with one hand and trust to good luck that the horse won't fall or run away. "Fighting Lizy of the Detail" as I call my animal. "Fighty Liz" for short, stepped into a nice big hole the other night as we were coming home by moonlight, but the weight I was carrying kept me in the saddle, yes, that was the only thing. Side Issue - We had to break ice in order to water the horses this morning, so you see it is getting cold. I've made up my mind to be a coachman when I get home, so if Grandma Hobson needs one tell her I'll take the job.

Please remember me to the men at the office, not forgetting Jim at Young's Hotel. Tell him I'll be back eating at his table again before long.

Lots of love to all the family and heaps for yourself.
Johnny

On Active Service with the American Expeditionary Force
December 24, 1917

Dearest Family

It's the night before Xmas but oh what a change in surrounding from other years. No merry voices of home are to be heard tonight and no stockings are to be hung up by the fireplace with the hopes that Saint Nick will visit them during the night and leave some little gift in them. Instead it is cold and damp and Johnny is sitting on the edge of his cot writing to those he loves most dearly by candlelight. Up to now the homesick feeling has stayed miles away but tonight I must confess I am just a wee bit home sick. Home with its wonderful love and comforts, home with its cheery voices and happy hearth seems a very long ways off just now and the thousands of miles between us all seem doubled. Yes folks I certainly do miss you all this evening as I have never before. You younger members of the family who have never spent a Xmas Eve away from home may not realize how your older brother feels tonight but I guess Mother and Dad will. I hope none of you will ever be forced to experience the lonely feeling I have tonight. You have one of the most beautiful homes God ever gave young people to live in and if you don't believe it just walk out and try to find a better one. My experience away from it has been very small but I realize as I never did before what that simple little word of four letters means. The great big world is a fine place to roam around in but I'll bet my last cent that when Xmas Eve comes around you would all long for home - if not before. Make the best of it, kids, while you have it and don't let a single chance go by to strengthen yourselves for the world that lies just outside the home doors into which you all must step someday. It's a great place but none of you will ever realize what it is until you step into it alone. I don't want to preach a sermon to you but mark my word, home at any time is a mighty fine place and especially on Xmas Eve.

Well some of my boxes have arrived but from different letters I have received I know there are still some to come. The post offices have found it almost impossible to handle all the boxes which have been sent to the boys in khaki from friends in the States.

Transportation is not so easy to get as in the U.S. but in spite of all the drawbacks boxes have been pouring into camp by the truckload. Up to date I have received the following: A nice big box of eats, candy and the like, from Grandma Hobson. I am going to tell you something about that box which may interest you all. It arrived yesterday and as it happened I was going to a café where we have been going for several weeks and where we are all very well known by the two very nice French girls who run the place. I took some candy and crackers along with me out of that box to enjoy with our supper and of course gave some to my two little French girls. One taste and Johnny owned the house. Nothing was too good for us and I was king with all the fixings. They surely did like American candy. Don't worry Dad I haven't lost my head or mind over them - I'm going to save both for some good American girl like dear Mother.

A fine box of eats came from cousin Kittie which was enjoyed by several other men who were here when I opened it. A box containing gum came from the Rogers plus a Yale record from my old roommate Holliday.

Now last and far from least came a box from Dad and when I looked inside and saw all it had inside the tears just rolled down my face and I couldn't hold them back. Socks - just what I need. Shoes to put inside of my rubber boots and a nice book of poetry from Marj. I couldn't have asked for more and when I found that skin vest which Mr. True had made for me I just couldn't speak. Daddy that is wonderful. The old wind blows pretty hard here but once I get that on it can blow for all its worth and Johnny won't even feel it. You ought to see the other boys look at it while I stood there so pleased. I couldn't even tell them who it was from for several minutes. The very idea that one of your business friends had it made especially for me meant more than I can ever tell you with a mere pen. Believe me that vest goes right on tomorrow morning plus two pair of my new sox. More boxes are coming so if I have not got all you folks sent, but I wouldn't ask for more, they are merely held up somewhere.

I'm sorry dear ones that all I could do was send you a cablegram but another year is coming and Johnny will make up for lost time then. Mother's cablegram on Thanksgiving cheered me up a whole lot and I hope mine will do the same to you all.

Tomorrow night four of us go down to our café to eat a real true Xmas supper ordered ahead. This will be my Xmas celebration this year. The other boys are all merry lads and we are looking forward to a pleasant evening.

Well dear ones I thank you all for all you have done to help make this a merry Xmas for me and in closing I will say from the bottom of my heart I hope you all have a merry Xmas as we have had in years gone by.

Lots of love to all.
Johnny

Dearest Sister

Dinner is over and we are all resting around on our cots waiting for watering. The horses must not be forgotten even on Xmas day. My pony had an extra amount of oats for lunch this noon so I feel that I have done my share to look out for her pleasure.

Sister you would never know that it was Xmas over here as far as the weather goes. It's far from cold and the ground is covered with a nice thick coating of mud instead of snow. We have had a few snow showers during the morning the last of which was followed by a wonderful rainbow. We ate our Xmas dinner outdoors as we do all our meals except when we get heavy rain and then and only then are we allowed to eat inside. This weather certainly gets my goat - One day is colder than Greenland and the next will be warm. Our dinner consisted of turkey, potatoes (mashed), gravy and pudding plus nuts, figs and dates. The band played and except for the mud around my feet I could have very easily thought I was eating at the dear old Copley. Now when I get that wonderful supper inside of me tonight which I told you about in my letter to the family I will be all set for a good night's sleep. Oh yes I knew I had forgotten one thing I did this morning which will please Mother I am sure - I went to church. Services were held at 8:30 under a group of pine trees and they were very fine - even if one of those showers did blow up in the middle. I saw tears come into more than one man's eyes when Lieut. Stackpole spoke of the dear ones at home and how they would miss us today just as much as we did them. We sang some hymns which we so often sing at the North Church and for the time I was right back there with all of you. Well I guess I have told you about all the excitement there is today so will continue.

Great Scott yes - Mushy - he ought to have a few lines in this letter now that he is old enough to mention. I am growing a mustache and in about another month if luck is with me I ought to have a real one. I call it "Mushy" and George Croston plus many others take great delight in asking me what that shadow is on my upper lip. George condescended to say that it was coming along fine and looked very nice the other night but aside from that poor "mushy" has been a joke to all who saw it. Don't worry sister I will have it taken off before I come home.

Now to turn to a rather sad subject for a few minutes but one which I think should be mentioned. Have you heard of Hick Whittmore's death? It came like a blow out of a clear sky to me when I saw his name around the killed in action list in a French paper. It must have been an awful shock to his sister as well as all of Haverhill. Well death must call all of us away sooner or later and no man could have passed out of this world into the next in a more nobler way than he did - fighting for America and the Stars And Stripes. I always did admire him but I do even more so now. He was a real true man and an American through and through. Everyone in the Battery spoke very highly of him who knew him even in the slightest way and his death was felt by many of his friends.

Sister dear your last letter in which you spoke of your love for Everett growing stronger was a peach. This separation dear may seem very hard for the time but take it from me he also is not having an easy time of it. He certainly is a man to be proud of and my only hope and prayer is that it will not be many months before he will be able to return to you. Trust him dear he will be back just as soon as possible and you can rest assured that 129 Arlington Street will be the first place he will head for. I have had one bully letter from him since he left here in which he told me all about his experience in flying up to date. It may be of some comfort to you if I tell you that he is just as safe if not safer in his new work than he was in his old. This comes from someone higher up than I so it's not bull. I hope that we both may return home together and not one before the other. We left together and both of us want to return together.

By the way darling there is something I wish you would do for me the very first chance you get. That is write Jeanne Schroers a letter and thank her for the box she sent me. We are only allowed to write two letters and are so blame busy that we are lucky if we get those written. I feel that home mail should be written first and find that that is just about all I can attend to with the amount of work we are doing so if you will please write and explain conditions it will help me a whole lot. I hope to be able to show my appreciation for all my friends are doing when I get back but for the time being I am almost helpless. No doubt you people wonder what we do at night and say why can't they write then. Well sister dear most of us are too tired and if we are not we usually seek some amusement different from the day's work. Supper at a café or a quiet evening doing nothing are two things of real importance over here. They rest us and for the time take our minds off of the humdrum of drills and the little unpleasant things of being a soldier. This work is far different and in many ways far harder than anything I ever undertook and anything that can be done to ease off on the strain or brighten the dark hours I feel that I deserve. Half the fight is keeping your spirits up and your body rested so I am doing very little work outside of training. Home letters are a real pleasure to write at any time but my outside mail is not so easy. Just tell Jeanne that I enjoyed her box very much and when I get a chance I will try to drop her a few lines myself.

Many of the boys have spoken of our homecoming today and we have pictured it in a hundred different ways - from a slow grave and sad march up Main Street to a dashing parade with horses, guns and the band. I wonder what it will really be like. I do know this for sure however that it will be a very glad day for every boy over here when he does really see his home lights burning once again. Bets are now going on as to how soon the War will be over and almost every evening you can get into an argument on the subject. We surely do have a great time joking about it sometimes but at others it is far from funny.

A week ago Saturday I got a twenty-four hour pass to visit a city near here. Four of us went together and didn't we enjoy ourselves. We spent the night in a real true hotel - slept in a real true honest to God bed and had a nice hot bath. Breakfast served in our room at 10:30 a.m. and sitting around in a kind of winter garden at five p.m. drinking coffee and smoking real true American cigars took me right back to my good time in Boston last winter. The trip did me the world of good as I was very tired and needed a few hours of just that kind of rest. We went into the city by the toy train which goes fast downhill - almost stops going up and moves fairly fast on level ground. We came back in style however in a hired French auto taxi cab. It was a nice big open car but every time we hit a little upgrade we had to change gears. Within six miles of camp we had a blow out and my poor feet nearly froze off while that slow working Frenchman was changing tires.

Well darling there goes the whistle to fall in to water the ponies so I must close.

Please give my love to all the family - including Marj and of course keep a lot for yourself.

More love and kisses for you all on this my first Xmas away from home and you dear ones.

Johnny

[The following is a letter from Everett Bradley to his future mother-in law, Alice Cary (Gale) Hobson. When you read it, it is no wonder that my grandmother saved it with my father's letters and it is included in this work.]

Somewhere in France
December 30, 1917

Dearest "Mother"

You could not possibly have done more to make my Christmas a most happy one than you did in writing the sweet, loving, and understanding letter I read the evening of the twenty-fourth. To receive such a message from the mother of the girl you love is just cause for rejoicing, and it's not surprising, therefore, that after perusing it and those from Alice, Mother and Father, I was "primed" to love my neighbor as never before. Yours is my deep gratitude for such love and thoughtfulness, and I appreciate, more than ever how very fortunate I am in having you, Mother-to-be, as warm friend and confidante.

We've been very close to one another during the past few months, but that's only the beginning, for, just as Alice is already considered a member of the Bradley family, I, too, regard myself as your son and look forward with keen anticipation to the many happy years of intimate relationship before us. You may easily comprehend with what supreme joy I'm inspired when I read the letter from home which tells of the bond of affection which exists between our two families, and how I revel in thoughts of the glorious future. That the war may be speedily brought to a victorious conclusion in order that Alice and I may soon start our journey on "the long, long trail" is my constant prayer. I want so much to be Alice's husband and your son in fact as well as in thought that the months I must be separated from all my dear ones seem sometimes to loom interminably long, but then the cheery confidence and the unflagging devotion to the cause expressed in the letters from those back home, on whose patience the strain is incomparably greater, sink into my soul and I'm ready to "carry on" indefinitely.

Your interest in the "pictured home" where, as you say, love will be in great measure, is a source of satisfaction and gratification, for, inexperienced as I am in household matters, I know that the inner man must be catered to in order to have the outer man at his best. Though I have no anxiety whatever concerning Alice's adaptability to the new life, I'm glad that she is receiving instruction from so competent and accomplished a housekeeper, and appreciate the zeal and care you are displaying in the preparation of another home like your own.

Alice, in her love and devotion, has progressed far beyond my fondest dreams. Last July I told her, a girl, sweet, lovable, and true, that if her heart permitted she might make me that happiest of men, and now, six months later, I'm receiving letters that thrill me through and through from a woman matured and made noble and devoted beyond words by the experiences of a short half year. Her love is my rarest possession, one I shall ever strive to merit, for such affection, loyalty, and trust cause me to realize what responsibilities I shall assume when she is mine "for better or worse." That I shall always love her is a certainty but, just as she will have the comfort of the home in her hands, I must return prepared to assure for that home the evidences of material wellbeing so necessary in our social life. My courage is high, and, with such backing as I boast, I'm sure that success must attend my efforts.

As you know, I was sent from the 102nd Regiment a month ago and now over five hundred miles lie between John and the boys of Battery A and myself. The exigencies of war have no regard for personal feelings so it was useless to moan over the new twist of fate, and I bade cheery good-byes to the men with whom I've been associated the last four months. John spent an hour with me just before I left and we both took the rapture in our intimate relations philosophically.

John, too, has matured remarkably since leaving the States and you'll find him, on his return, a keen and well-balanced young man. The life has agreed with him wonderfully and he has stood up to every test with the best in the outfit. His powers of endurance sur-prised me who feared a bit at the first for his ability to overcome the hardships which I knew were in store for us, not for lack of courage, he has the heart of a lion, but because of his constitution might not stand the grueling test of life in the open. We haven't been forced to that manner of living yet, but there have been times when we've been mighty close to it, and I assure you that you need not have the slightest doubt that John will not pull through the campaign with colors flying.

His lovable and affable nature has made him a great favorite with the boys of [Battery] A, and he has never complained or signified in any way that he is not entirely satisfied with his present lot. Of course he wants to get ahead and he's "plugging away" and biding his time with admirable spirit. When I left I asked George Langdon to keep a brotherly eye on him and I'm confident they'll become firm friends, as both are the best of "brothers."

John is bound to go up as soon as the right opportunity presents itself, his age being the only drawback to a chance for a commission during the next few months. He's a "regular feller," a man in every sense, and I congratulate you and "Dad" for having such a son to bear the Hobson standard in France.

The life I'm now leading is that of a summer tourist and state fair headliner combined and, though I, selfishly enough, always desire it, you need waste no sympathy on me whatever. Give it all to the boys of A Battery who really deserve it. I'm but the pampered pet of Fortune.

My heart speaks only gratitude and affection to you and those you love. Kiss Alice for me, then let her return it, for, as she possesses all of me, I may thus give her more than written evidence of my true feelings toward you.

Most affectionately,
Everett

Dearest Mother

Many things have happened since I last wrote home. In fact events have been taking place so fast in the past two weeks that I can hardly keep up with them. Joy, sorrow, hardships and pleasures have all come together and seem to continue to come. Life is just like a story book these days - full of excitement and adventure. One thing is lacking however in my novel - a girl. Well she may turn up in the last chapter which will be when I return to the U.S.A. I guess the author of my book does not know how to write of love and home comforts, but still I have a feeling that he is going to lead his hero (Johnny) through many hard and thrilling adventures and then take him to a love which is tender, true and never failing - his mother's. Oh darling just to let our hopes and prayers wander into the future for a few minutes. Won't that homecoming be wonderful? Sunshine and joy at the end of months of separation. You, Dad, and the rest of the family and I all gathered in Dad's room. That picture comes into my mind very often and always makes life seem more worthwhile. Well that wonderful picture is only a dream now; it's the end of my story book and I must read it chapter by chapter and word by word until I reach the chapter where it tells about that picture. We must not read ahead as that is apt to take the interest out of it but when I do get a few minutes to myself which is very seldom I love to look at that picture in the last chapter of my book. Now you very likely want to know what is going on in the chapter I am in now so we will come down to facts and news.

First the weather - we are having the first real snow storm today. Up to now we have had only one of two little falls which have only lasted a few hours. This storm started last night and has been going ever since. It is not a heavy storm like we get in the States but just a gentle falling of white flakes. The ground is all covered and from the feeling of things I guess it will remain so. However I should not be a bit surprised to see it as warm as spring tomorrow. Funny weather all right.

Mother dear your cablegram bearing the Xmas cheer and the sad news of Grandma Gale's death reached me last week. It came as more or less of a surprise to me as I had received a letter just a few days before saying that she was about the same and was enjoying her night nurse. I did not allow myself to get depressed because high spirits go a long way over here and I did not see what could be gained by sitting down and turning it over in my mind. The wording of the cablegram "Grandma free from pain. Left us Dec. 11, at 5:30 p.m." was a great comfort to me. It made me feel that you realized that it was all for the best and were taking it as you take all your sorrows - as cheerfully as possible. I know it must have been hard for you dear, but remember she is as you said, "free from pain" and think darling what a blessing that is to her after all her years of suffering. I know how hard it must have gone with grandpa as they were more than devoted to each other, but the two must realize how welcome death was to her. I am not going to write long on this sad subject as it makes a depressed feeling come over me but Mother dear I do want to say that I feel her death very deeply even if this letter does sound cold. Death is a very grave subject and one which now especially I would rather not dwell on. Someday I shall tell you just how I felt on receiving the news but for now I have said all I can.

Lots more Xmas boxes have arrived since I last wrote you and from people I never thought would remember me this year since I am so far away. I really wish I could write them all letters but as I told sister in my last letter it is out of the question. I certainly owe a lot of people a lot of thanks for the pleasure their boxes brought me. Here is a list of the people from whom I received boxes:

Grandma & Grandpa Gale
Aunt Rachel
Marjorie Stover
Miss Sara Stover
Josephine Drake
Another wonderful box from home
Cablegram from Webber
The little girls on the Highlands
Five boxes of cigarettes from Dad
Mr. Ready
Dick Thompson

These plus those I told you about in my last letter are the ones I owe a load of thanks to.

I never saw so many cigarettes before in my life as I got and I can use them all. Eats were plentiful but did not last a very long time once the lid was taken off. The warm clothes you people sent were more than welcome. With two vests and three sweaters I certainly ought to keep warm some way. These two vests have certainly made a great hit with all the fellows. I guess I was the only fellow who was lucky enough to get them in our battery. You folks certainly did look after your soldier boy in fine style and he sends back some heartfelt thanks for all you have done. I am now anxiously waiting for the letters which will tell me all about your happy Xmas at home.

I developed a slight cold last week which brought along a little temperature of 101 so I went over to sick call. The doctors are sending all the men with fever no matter how slight it is to the hospital as they do not want to take any chances of the men taking more cold in the barracks. Hence I am now enjoying a few days of real comfort between nice white sheets and in a warm dry place. I expect to be back at work again by the end of the week as I feel OK now, but the doctor does not want to hurry me. "Wait until you are more than OK before you leave," is the doctor's motto and under the conditions I most certainly agree with him. Lieut. Pitman was in to see me yesterday and George Croston has been in at least once a day. He has kept me well supplied with reading matter as well as news from the Battery. To read that you might think I had been here for weeks, but the truth is I have only been here five days. This is the first real rest I have had since I landed here and it is doing me the world of good.

I had a real nice letter from Everett a short time ago and also one from Lieut. Root. Root wanted to be remembered to all of you the next time I wrote.

Where tell me where did that rumor ever get started that I had been transferred to Headquarters? I had not heard a thing about it until Sister's letter arrived with the thrilling news. No, it is not true for I am still one of the boys of Battery A right from Haverhill. I certainly would like to know where some of those wild rumors start from.

And now in closing this rambling letter let me tell you something which you may have heard before but not from me. Another stripe has been added to my sleeve and your soldier boy now has the rank of Sergeant. I now have charge of the signal detail and Sergt. Haseltine has taken over the instrument detail. These two ranks, Instrument Sergeant and Signal Sergeant, are no longer the free easy going jobs they were at Boxford, but both carry with them a great deal of responsibility. My only hope now is that I can hold this place down and in order to do so I have to work very hard. It is easy to follow but to lead and lead through thick and thin is not so easy. Well, darling if others can do it I can. There were times when I thought I was always to be a follower but now I have my chance to be a leader of men and I hope I make a good one.

Well sweetheart I have written quite a bit so I guess I had better close before I tire you.

I feel that success is coming my way, but remember dear that in success or failure I am your son and I owe all to you and Dad if it be success - If failure it is my own fault because you two have taught me what is right and by following your advice success must come.

Lots of love for all and heaps for your dear little self.
Johnny

Somewhere in France
January 10, 1918

Dearest Sister

Just a few more lines from over the seas to let you know that your big brother is feeling much better and is now up and dressed. I went out for about an hour this afternoon and hope to be back with the battery by Saturday. This laying around is all right when you feel a little under the weather, but just as quick as I get feeling as well as I do now I long to get back with the boys.

I went over to the battery in the course of my walk this afternoon to find out news and see if there was any mail for me. Sure enough I found a letter from you dated November 26th. I also received your letter written December 10th, so you see there must have been some hold up on the November 26th letter. How is my mail reaching you folks - all in a bunch or strung out?

I was very glad indeed to hear the news of Art's bid or coming bid to Alpha Nu and I hope he accepts it. In many ways I have regretted that I was unable to make a frat while at Exeter but somehow I didn't have the qualifications for it. I am more than glad Art is to have the chance because it will mean a great deal to him after he gets to college aside from the pleasure he can get out of it while at Exeter. I'm more than pleased and mighty proud of him.

Now dear just a few words about your hospital desire. It is splendid to want to do all you spoke of and I approve of all but your coming across. You can serve your country just as well dear right over there in the States as you can over here, besides being a great help to Mother. In several of Mother's letters she has spoken of the fine way in which you have taken hold of things at home and of what a big help you were to her. She needs you Sister right there more than you realize it and by her side is where you belong during this struggle. Keep right on with your interest in hospital work, but please dear don't ask the folks to let you come over here - not for another year at least.

Yes, I knew Jack Birchman very well while at Exeter. I must confess I have kind of forgotten what he is like, but it seems to me that he was very nice. How does he know Marj?

You sister dear are not the only one who often wonders what the future has in store for us all. I too have pictured many things in my mind and must say I enjoy doing it at times. One week over here it looks as if many of our brave boys would never see home again and the next week the whole situation is changed and home seems very near. When Everett was here we used to picture and dream together, but since he has gone I have to dream alone. I'm willing to bet my last cent however that he is dreaming too and even planning for the future just as much as we are. Oh won't it be a happy day for us when your two soldier boys come marching home. The world won't be large enough to hold us will it dear? Well that day is coming even if God himself alone knows when so keep on smiling and live for it.

I have visited the city you spoke of just once up to date. It's a great place to rest up in and I believe in one of my letters I told you about my experiences at one of the hotels there.

Great Scott just fancy you being a chaperone for Hope. Yes, you are right it made me laugh when I read about it but when you stop to think of it why aren't you a pretty good little chaperone? I may have to engage you when I get back to aid me although just now I must admit I wouldn't know how to act around girls. Be prepared, Sis, you will have a lot to teach me upon my return. I can just hear you blowing both Everett and I sky high for some bonehead play we let slip. Well don't be too hard on us at first will you.

Well darling I have an idea that supper is nearly ready so I guess I had better close. Please give my love to everyone of the family (that includes Marj) and remember me to all who may ask for me. Will try to write again in a few days.

Lots of love for yourself.
Johnny

Somewhere in France
January 19, 1918

Dearest Dad

There isn't much news to tell you but just to let you know I am well,
I am going to drop you a few lines. I have been out of the hospital for
over a week now and must say that I feel like a new man. The rest
was just what I needed and I now can do my days work much better
than before I went in. All the men say I look better whereas just
before I went to the hospital every one was saying I looked pretty
tired and all in. I had to work very hard when I first took the signal
detail over and I guess the extra strain was the last straw. Now things
are coming better but there is yet a whole lot to be done before I
have things going the way I want them to. Horses, signal property,
twelve men plus planning how the days work which is laid out for
me to do keeps me right on the jump. I have two corporals to help
me one of which I am breaking into the detail game but even with
their help Johnny must move and think fast every minute. I like this
work much better than my old as it gives me a chance to really use
my brains and also a chance to lead men as well as study each one
under me. Lieut. Pitman has quite a bit to do with the detail hence I
have come to know him very well.

Everett and Lieut. Root returned to camp a couple of nights ago
and wasn't I glad to see them. Everett was just as glad to see me as
I was to see him I think. I felt almost the same as if one of you had
suddenly dropped in on me when I first saw him. I have not had
a chance to have a real heart to heart talk with him as yet but we
expect to get together tomorrow some time. I hope to goodness he
stays with us now.

I received the card you had sent me giving me the privileges
of the Old Colony Club and Dad I most certainly thank you for it.
Things like that mean so much to me now that I am thousands of
miles away from home. Just now I can't use it but I expect the day
to come in the near future when that card will come in very handy.
Dad you certainly have been awfully good to me and I more than
appreciate it. Some day when I return I hope that I can help you as

much in business as you have me while I have been over here. You will never know I fear how much you and the rest of the family have helped to make the rough edges of wartime Army life smooth. Your letters alone are enough proof that you all are behind me and these alone cheer me say nothing of the hundreds of little things you have sent me. I'm just lost in my work heart and soul and often feel that I don't take half enough time to write but you all are with me in mind day and night. I often long to be back home but I know that my duty is right here and I must forget all thoughts of returning to you until that duty is done - When it is however believe me no boat or train can take me back to America and the family too fast.

Those of us who knew each other before we entered the service make it a point to compare letters that would interest each other. From all I can gather all the young men in the States are beginning to feel the strain of being an outsider and are looking around for a chance to get into something. Oh how I wish I could talk with some of them and tell them what this life has done for me. Why Dad I'm a new man in every way. Of course there is danger connected with it all but that should be forgotten just as I told Mother before I enlisted. We need men over here in the worst possible way but mark my word before a man sets sail for over here he wants to make up his mind once and for all that he will be a man through and through no matter what happens. It's no child's play and with spring fast coming on we who are here realize it more than ever. Those who do come from Haverhill must play the game to the very limit if they ever expect to come up to the standard we boys have set.

The clippings taken from the paper telling all about Johnny and his letters very much amused me. You people certainly must have had some job picking just the right parts out of my letters to print but you certainly did it in fine style. Now the question is where oh where did they ever get the idea into their heads that I was a poet? Several of the boys saw it and said that they did not realize that they had a poet among them. Everett has had a fine time kidding me about it and all in all it has made a lot of fun and been a great success.

By the way did you happen to see the cablegram Mrs. and Mr. Bradley sent Ev at Xmas? He sent it on to me and I think the thought and wording is wonderful. Here it is, "With you in spirit - Back of you in purpose - Surround you with love - Merry Xmas to you, George and John". I thought it was pretty fine.

Last Friday the battery went out to fire a long problem and we stayed out all day. Karl had the "soup gun" or cooking wagon along and we all enjoyed a bully good dinner. Dad that is one of the many sights I wish you could see - a battery moving out and going into position for action. Of course it has now become an everyday sight with me but just the same my heart seems to beat faster with the thrill of the whole thing every time we go out. Six horses pulling the gun driven by three men all working their heads off to keep moving through the mud. The detail in front of all with their phones on their backs. Then comes the command "Detail forward!" and we all ride forward on the dead run following the Captain - mud flying all over us and other details joining us as we pass along the columns. Once unlimbered the horses are put in the woods on a picket line in the care of the drivers. I have two horse holders to whom I turn my horses over to. I shall never forget the first time I saw and experienced these things. It certainly does thrill you and I would pay big money to see some of these things in the movies. The two details go out this afternoon to lay out the plan of tomorrow's wire work and look the ground over. Two or more officers go along with us to show us what is to be done and then we figure how we shall do it.

Two more boxes have arrived since I last wrote. One from Aunt Mary and one from Grandpa Hobson. Will you please tell them that I received them OK and tell them both I will write just as soon as I get a chance. I have enjoyed both boxes very much indeed.

Well Dad I must go down to the stables and saddle up "Kid". I changed her name some little time ago, for the afternoons work. We have a fairly long ride before us so I want to be all set for it.

Please give my love to Grandma and Grandpa Hobson as well as to the family.

Lots of love for yourself.
Johnny

Dearest Mother

More mail from the home which mean more minutes of pleasure for your boy in France.

The letters telling me all about your Xmas and those written at cousin Kitty's were the ones I received plus your box. You old dear you had your mind made up to get those belly bands to me somehow and you did. Well darling they may come in very handy some day in the future and I now have room for to carry them.

I have already read parts of the book How To Live At The Front and find it very interesting. Of course as yet I have not seen or experienced all he writes but many of the others have. His short chapter on The Folks At Home is mighty good and many of the boys would not be any the worse if they read it. We all try to write home as often as possible but I fear many of us fail to in our desire for good times. The funny book I have not as yet had time to enjoy but will before today is over. My but mail and boxes from you all does help to cheer me up and make the dark minutes bright.

I have seen a great deal of Ev since he returned to camp. He's the same old Ev always smiling and ready for a good time. I never in all my life saw him looking better while he says I look fine as far as health goes but aside from that I look more like a tramp or a railway bum than the Johnny Hobson he used to know.

In fact I guess he sees a change in the whole battery. The trouble is right here - we had about one week of rain and that rain made the ground a soup of mud. Of course rain or no rain, mud or no mud, our work had to go on and our clothes were just a mess. Mud in your hair, mud on your face, mud all over your overcoat and even on your hat. I would clean up every night best I could but after a fast ride the next morning I'd be just as bad as before I washed. We had to wear rubber boots all the time and of course my once small feet got swollen and when I came to put shoes on again found I had to change my little nines for elevens in order to get any comfort. Read that to Sister and see what she says. More than once Ev has said oh if your sister and mother could only see you now. Well I guess we all are a pretty hard looking bunch but believe me we're just as happy as we are muddy. I love to hear Ev kid me about my looks and we certainly have enjoyed some good laughs about it.

I should judge from Sister's letters that she had been one mighty busy girl this winter between her Red Cross war work and good times in Boston. Well I'm glad to hear it. All of her letters speak as if she was happy and enjoying everything she is doing. Gee but I wish I were there to enjoy some of those Boston parties at the Copley once more. We boys have had some mighty good ones over here but alas no dancing. With boots size eleven on I fear I would have some trouble so it may be just as well.

You said in your last letter that you wondered if I had been sent to some school because my letters had not been written while on guard. No dear I am still with the Battery and school and such things are a long way off for some little time yet. Those are for the boys who are to be officers and a commission for me is out of the question just now. If we are over here long enough and I become of age while here I hope to come back to you with a gold hat cord on my hat but remember darling I am very young as yet for a position of that kind. My position is none too easy and if I can make a success of it then we will look higher and move our stakes on a little further. As Dad told me last winter the world wasn't made in a minute and you can't expect to take a big or small position until you are ready for it and to quote you own words dear wait and something will turn up which you do not expect - just keep going about your daily work - preparing yourself to take advantage of the chance when it comes. My time is coming and until it does I have forgotten the future but am lost heart and soul in the work I am in now.

I have changed my horse's name to Kid. Yes, she is named after Sis and is just as good a horse in the field as Sister is at home and in social life. I only have one kick against her - she is gun shy. Oh ye gods and little fishes how she does carry on if I try to hold her near the battery when it is in action. Last night when I went to take her to water bareback as usual I was only half on when she starts to run for dear life. I tried to pull myself on and in doing caught her a peach with my spur. For about two minutes it looked as if Johnny was in for a mud bath but luck was with me and I escaped. I tell you when Kid and I get leading the detail on a road hike or out to work we are in our glory. She steps right along and when the mad gallop comes she is right there and would be ahead of the Captain if she had her way.

Say what in the name of heavens has hit all the fair girls in the States? Why it seems as if every lot of mail brings news of a new engagement or marriage. We often wonder what the men are like but I suppose that there are still a lot of mighty fine young fellows still left. Wait till this crew gets back and the ministers will be kept busy and there will be lots of last bachelor dinners to attend. There is going to be a mighty big one in our family just as quick as two boys get back. That certainly is going to be a big and yet sad day for us all. Gee but I'll miss that dear Sister of mine but just think of the wonderful man she is to marry.

Great Scott, another box has arrived for me. No I have not received it yet but it is here at the Chaplain's office. I wonder what pleasant surprise it contains for me.

Well darling it is time for me to close and get busy.

Give my love to all the family and keep a lot for your own dear little self.
John

CHAPTER EIGHT

Chemin des Dames Sector
Baptism to Fire

"We have experienced the incommunicable experience of war."

OLIVER WENDELL HOMES

*"We'd charge into the jaws of Hell behind
a barrage from our batteries."*

26TH DIVISION INFANTRY: COMMENTING ON
THE PROFICIENCY OF THEIR ARTILLERY.

*"...I was in a seventh heaven of excitement and adventure.
The land I had read so much about...stood before me,
not as a dream but as real."*

2ND LIEUTENANT JOHN LAMBERT HOBSON II:
REFLECTING ON SEEING HIS FIRST FRONT.

By the fall of 1917, just as the American troops were landing in France, the Allied Powers were becoming worn down.

On the other side, things weren't going well either. Kaiser Wilhelm's power had diminished and a military dictatorship had emerged in Germany as the controlling government power. Militarily, the Central Powers were stretched thin fighting on two fronts, an Eastern and Western Front, and with sea ports blocked there were shortages of supplies and food in Germany.

Then Vladimir Lenin's communist revolution appealed to the war-weary Russian peasants and led to an armistice between Eastern Front's Russia and Germany, the Treaty of Brest-Litovsk, which was signed in March of 1918. Russia had sacrificed greatly, more than any other Allied Power nation, sending 12 million of her sons into the slaughter of the early stages of the Great War. Nine million, 76% of the Russian troops, would become casualties; 1.7 million Russian soldiers would be killed.

With the armistice between Russia and Germany in place, one million-plus German troops were no longer needed on the Eastern Front. Weary from fighting a stalemated war along the Hindenburg Line for several years, the elite Western Front German storm troopers, the sturmtruppen, referred to by the Allied soldiers as Hindenburg's Traveling Circus, were becoming a spent force. Germany immediately seized the opportunity and redeployed the Eastern Front army to the west and then in desperation resorted to the murderous tactic of mass assault along the Western Front. German troops now outnumbered the Allied troops on the Western Front. In the coming months, Germany would launch five major assaults on the Western Front. Germany, now becoming desperate and with America now entering the war, was caught between collapse at home and possible victory in the field.

The first German offensive would begin on 31 March 1918. It was an offensive designed by General Erich Ludendorff, one of the chief engineers managing the German war effort, with an attack near St. Quentin, France, north of Soissons. It was the biggest breakthrough in three years. The fifth, and final, offensive would come in mid-July 1918 at Chateau-Thierry.

In the late fall of 1917, the American Expeditionary Forces that landed on French soil totaled a mere 86,000 with many more on the way to bolster Great Britain's 8.9 million and France's 8.4 million forces already mobilized. It would take time to train and transport more American troops to the battlefields of France.

On 3 November 1917, a platoon of the U.S. Army's 1st Division was hit by a German raiding party of 250 German storm troopers at Bathelemont les Bauzemont in the Lorraine region, east of Nancy. Here, the first Americans of this war were killed in combat: Corp. James Gresham of Evansville, Indiana, Pvt. Thomas Enright of Pittsburgh, Pennsylvania, and Pvt. Merle Hay of Ellston, Iowa. They were initially buried near where they died. Their tombstones were inscribed: "Here lie the first soldiers of the illustrious Republic of the United States who fell on French soil for justice and liberty."

During the first months of 1918, the gathering but inexperienced American troops of the A.E.F. were immediately pulled from their training period and thrust into the breach to stop the German drive on the Western Front that would begin in March. The capital of France, Paris, was in jeopardy of being overrun for the second time during this war. If Paris was taken, all of France would certainly fall. During the First Battle of the Marne and at Verdun in 1916, the Allied army had successfully repulsed the German's offensive attack. It was a horrible, costly struggle. But now, two years later, the war-weary and weakened Allied force might not be able to repulse the offensive again without the help of the Americans.

With the idea of moving this regiment and as many trained American troops as he could up to the front lines as quickly as possible to meet the upcoming German offensive, in mid-January of 1918 General Pershing, who was headquartered in the town of Chaumont, inspected the 102nd Field Artillery Regiment at Coetquidan. The Regiment's History described the situation:

26th Division's departure from training camps to the Chemin des Dames front - February 1917. 26th Division, A.E.F. Division Histories, Vol. 2

The brigade and the regiment "made the grade." We did not know it at the time but the way in which we passed that inspection determined in a large measure the early date of our going to the front.

As January wore away we began to feel that our deliverance was at hand and that we would soon go up "into the line" for our period of training at the front. G.H.Q.'s [General Headquarters] scheme of training for artillery units arriving in France consisted of a period at a training camp such as Coetquidan devoted to intensive training, etc. After that the units were to go into the line for a month or so in a quiet sector. They would then be assembled in a back area with the rest of their division, or other higher unit, for a combined training, and after that the whole outfit was to take its place at the front as a combat organization. This scheme was never carried out completely for our regiment.

The March drive of the enemy made it necessary to put us and our whole division into the line without going through the combined training period. As far as can be learned, nobody in the regiment ever regretted it. Maneuvers have the same thrill compared with real war that penny-ante poker has to table stakes - only more so.

The artillery had won a name for itself for rapidity and accuracy of fire even before it left Coetquidan. As most people know, the American army guns had been left at home, and the task was to master the French 75s and the heavier 155s, and to equal the French standard of fire. The artillery of the 26th won high encomiums from the officers of all their allied armies with which they fought, but best of all from their own infantry, whose saying was: "We'd charge into the jaws of Hell behind a barrage from our batteries."

Finally at the front, my father was faced with the reality that someone could get killed in his adventure story.

Before Father is "baptized" and sends and receives his first shots fired in anger, this is probably a good place in this work to digress and describe the battlefields and the weapons of war during this time.

Early in the Great War, when the Central Powers were first sweeping across Belgium and northeastern France, traditional, archaic thinking French and British troops actually conducted horse cavalry charges wielding swords into opposing, technically advanced German massed armies who were equipped with machine guns and artillery. The Allies had a very romantic notion of warfare. The Germans did not. The French and British actually used crossbows! Sir Winston Churchill said that it was illogical to attack machine guns with the chests of soldiers. From a human life standpoint, it was very inefficient warfare.

Following the initial sweep across eastern France, the Central Powers, fighting a two-front war and stressing available resources, were unable to sustain advances and the war's progress on the Western Front mired down to a trench war. The innovation of weapons and equipment and more sophisticated battle tactics took hold to break the stalemate. The First World War became a laboratory for destructive modern armament. It was the dark side of the Industrial Revolution. Many of the weapons that were conceived during this period came into perfection during what many would call a continuation of the unresolved issues of the First World War, the Second World War.

Trench Warfare

Trench warfare was nothing new. It has been a battlefield strategy since medieval times. Trench warfare of the First World War involved infantry shooting at each other with bolt action, bayoneted rifles and machine guns at close range from mazes of serpentine trenches dug below the ground level - as opposed to breastworks that were fortifications above ground - on opposite sides of an artillery-torn piece of real estate called No Man's Land, the space between the opposing lines of trenches. The distance between opposing trenches varied but was sometimes as close as 50 yards. No Man's Land was usually festooned with barbed wire - another innovation introduced by the Germans to warfare - and other obstacles.

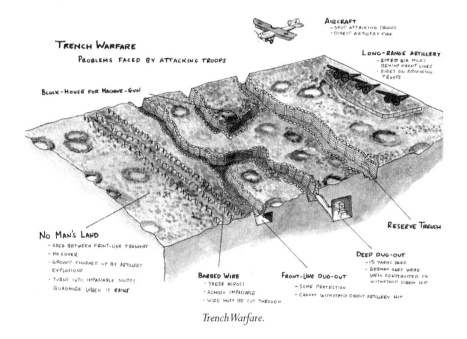

Trench Warfare.

Allied trench. www.worldwar1.nl

Aprons of barbed wire were placed far enough in front of the trench to prevent the enemy from a number of actions including their approaching closely enough to lob a grenade into the trench, and impeding their progress across No Man's Land. Barbed wire also was used to channel the advancing enemy into a convenient line of fire, making easy targets for machine gunners.

Setting up the barbed wire in front of the trench was dangerous work. The work crew was fully exposed to enemy fire while they were carrying rolls of wire and the six-foot steel pickets used to stake the wire to the ground. Sometimes they used a corkscrew picket, or queue de cochon (pigtail) as the French called them, which was screwed into the ground instead of being hammered, which was noisy and attracted attention. The barbed wire was then hung by curls in the pickets.

More often than not, No Man's Land was covered in deep shell holes with heavier-than-air poison gas lurking in the bottom of the shell hole. Shell holes were not safe havens in which to hide.

No Man's Land also had slippery mud, debris and the uncollected bodies of dead soldiers often caught on the barbed wire and left hanging there because it was too dangerous to expose a man to enemy fire to cut them out.

The worst existence of this war was life in the trenches. The primary occupants of the trenches were the infantry soldiers. Everybody did their bit, but the infantry soldier bore the brunt of the hardship. From a human life viewpoint, improving one's position in trench warfare was generally a slow and costly process.

There were several types of trenches. A firing trench was on the front line and used for firing at the enemy. Cover trenches were a backup in case the firing trenches were overrun. Behind them, supply and support trenches were used for resting troops and storage of supplies. Communication trenches were dug at an angle to the front line trench and were used to transport men, equipment and supplies within the trench system. Shorter trenches, called "saps", extended forward of the front line trench by 30 or so yards and were used for advancing on the enemy or as listening posts that were used to overhear the enemy's conversations and plans.

The trenches varied in construction. Some trenches were dug in the dirt just deep enough to provide cover for a few men lying or crouching down. The front line trenches were often of elaborate construction and were on average about seven feet deep and six feet wide and long enough so that hundreds of men could stand upright and maneuver around in them.

The deep, front line trenches had wooden planks or logs supporting high earthen walls that were topped off with sandbags piled several feet high, adding more cover with height above the ground. The front side of the trench facing the enemy, the forward wall, was called the parapet and the wall facing the rear was called the parados. On the parapet, either a step up or fire step platform was dug into the earthen wall, or planks were mounted halfway up the wall so riflemen and machine gunners in the firing trenches, which was, of course, the trench closest to the enemy, could stand on the step and shoot over the top of the trench, or they used the step to climb out of the trench when they went "over the top" for an attack.

Trenches were generally cut in a zig-zag pattern with fire-bays and traverses so that, should the enemy invade one end of the trench, a clear shot could not be taken completely reaching from one end of the trench to the other. The trenches had separate sections used for cooking, medical facilities and a latrine, and another for headquarters.

Life in the trenches and in dugouts or funk holes (caves and holes off the trench used for protection from the weather) was accompanied by constant death even when there was no charge, raid or attack going on. Artillery shellfire lobbed randomly into trenches from mortars or Howitzers killed or buried many men lounging in a trench or dugout. It was estimated that one third of the Allied casualties on the Western Front were sustained in the trenches.

At Verdun in June 1916, members of France's 137th Infantry Regiment were buried alive by an exploding artillery shell while they were in their trench. The trench was later discovered by the line of bayoneted rifles sticking up through the ground with a body buried beneath each. Left as it was found, today it is a moving monument at Verdun, the Tranchee des Baionettes (Trench of Bayonets).

Friendly fire, artillery from one's own guns mistakenly fired into the trench from behind, also killed many. It is estimated that 75,000 British infantry soldiers were killed in their own trenches from friendly artillery fire coming in over the parados.

Many soldiers were also killed, shot in the head by an alert sniper, while curiously peering over the parapet of a trench into No Man's Land. Periscopes were developed for safely looking over the top of the trench without exposure.

Aside from artillery-caused injuries, disease also took a heavy toll. Brown and black rats, breeding at a rate of 800 or more offspring each year and growing fat, the size of cats, fed on the dead bodies of humans and animals, spreading infection and contaminating food. The rats were so large and bold that they would eat a wounded man while he was still alive if he couldn't defend himself, and a pack of rats could strip a corpse of all flesh, beginning with the eyes, in a short time. Bodies that were unattended for a day seemed to move about on the ground from the rats feasting on the body inside the victim's greatcoat.

Dysentery, an inflammation of the large intestine caused by contaminated water, caused stomach pains and diarrhea and was commonplace. There was also trench nephritis, an inflammation of the kidneys.

Lice, called pants rabbits or cooties, breeding in the seams of filthy clothing were a problem and caused the men to itch unceasingly. Lice generated painful trench fever or pyrexia, an infection caused from louse feces. Recovery from trench fever took up to twelve weeks away from the trenches.

Nits were also plentiful, causing many soldiers to shave their heads entirely to avoid that scourge.

Almost certainly the trenches were filled with mud and water. Most of the trenches didn't have duckboards, planks of wood on the trench floor to keep the soldiers standing out of the water. Frogs, slugs and horned beetles thrived in the environment. With prolonged exposure to the wet mire, soldiers' leather boots were soaked through to the skin, causing rheumatism or a mildew-type foot disease known as trench foot. With trench foot, the feet become numb, the skin turns blue and gangrenous and the condition can result in amputation. Gum rubber boots and dry socks were valuable items to those serving in the trenches.

The smell in the trenches was appalling. The malodorous cocktail was emitted from a mixture of stagnant water and mud; rotting human corpses hastily buried in shallow graves in the trenches and the wafting stench of rotting bodies lying about nearby above ground unable to be collected in No Man's Land; infected human wounds and discarded bandages; overflowing latrines; dried sweat - bacteria odor from bodies that had not been bathed in weeks; rotting feet; rotting sandbags; tobacco smoke; cooking food; creosol and lime spread about to stave off the threat of disease; cordite from firearms; and the smell from lingering poison gas. Quite a perfume! Until they got used to it, the initial impact of the smell often made soldiers fresh into the trenches vomit, which only added to the overall stench.

Leonard Thompson, as quoted in Ronald Blythe's, "Akenfield", described the macabre scene in the trenches.

> We set to work to bury people. We pushed them into the sides of the trenches but bits of them kept getting uncovered and sticking out, like people in a badly made bed. Hands were the worst; they would escape from the sand, pointing, begging - even waving! There was one which we all shook when we passed saying, 'Good morning,' in a posh voice. Everybody did it. The bottom of the trench was springy like a mattress because of all the bodies underneath...

The enemy's trenches were often close enough in proximity that conversations between opposing trenches took place. Shouting insults is probably closer to the truth.

In 1914, only five months into the Great War, there was an unofficial Christmas truce on the Western Front in Belgium. On that Christmas Eve, opposing trench-bound British and German infantry troops greeted each other across No Man's Land and sang carols together, one side in English, the other in German. It was a nice and romantic image around the holiday time when the spirit of goodwill to your fellow man is prevalent. But, by the time 1917 rolled around and the Americans got into the war, it was considered an act of treason and a violation of the military code of conduct for a soldier, any soldier, to communicate in any way with the enemy. Allied officers worried that, should these friendly gatherings persist, their troops would become soft on their enemy and not maintain their fighting edge; they could realize that they were killing another human being who celebrated the same holidays and had feelings and families just like theirs. Instead, the Allied PR of the day portrayed the German soldier as a vicious barbarian: a gorilla baring fangs, an ignorant brute wearing jack boots and a Bismarck helmet, raping women and bayoneting babies. There was a psychological advantage to maintaining that image.

In order to advance position on the battlefield and overrun the enemy's trenches, the infantry, often carrying 70 pounds of equipment in a pack on their back, would, at a predetermined time and at the blowing of a whistle, swarm out over the parapet of their trenches - going "over the top" or "jumping the bags" they called it - with bayonets fixed on their rifles in a massive, frontal charge.

Before going over the top, British infantry soldiers were given a drink of rum from the 300-gallon supply of rum that was issued to each British division and that they carried with them when they moved from positions and fronts. When the charge was completed, the survivors would be issued another cupful of rum. Honestly. You have to love the British and their wonderful traditions. Tally ho, ol' chaps!

Small Guns, Rifles and Bayonets

The weapons used in WWI were as varied as the field conditions on the front lines. Rifles played a big role. The rifle issued to the American infantry was the Springfield M1903, a 30.06 caliber, bolt-action rifle that actually was adapted prior to the First World War from a German rifle, the Mauser Gewehr. Because of the American Springfield's accuracy, it was prized and used by snipers requiring exceptional accuracy as late as the Korean War in the 1950s.

The charge across No Man's Land by American infantry was led by whistle-blowing officers brandishing in one hand a Colt 45 Model 1911 U.S.

Army 45 caliber semiautomatic pistol. The pistol, designed for military use, was originally used as a cavalry weapon and became a staple for use by officers, aviators and others who worked in cramped conditions where carrying a rifle was impractical.

In their other hand the officers often wielded a trench knife. A trench knife was a nasty tool designed for hand-to-hand combat to be used when inside the enemy's trench. It was a knife blade with brass knuckles on the handle. The trench knife was effective in close combat where discharging a pistol could miss or the bullet could pass through its victim and kill a friendly fighting nearby.

In the United States Army, sidearms were issued only to commissioned and non-commissioned officers. The famous U.S. Army-issue Colt 45, which was standard military issue until the 1990s, was known for its powerful, broad, slow-moving 45 caliber projectile and its "knock down" quality. Being an American Army officer, my father carried the Colt 45.

On those previously mentioned trips to the family's home attic and viewing of the contents of his Army trunk, if encouraged, Father would demonstrate, very safely I should add, to us kids the art of keeping the Colt 45 pistol ready to fire. In combat conditions the pistol was kept at the ready in the leather flap-topped holster with the hammer halfcocked and the safety on. The holster's flap was not buttoned while in combat, of course. As a boy observing Father's full demonstration, I was always in awe at the proficiency and ease with which my father - my sweet daddy, this kind and gentle, soft-spoken man - handled his pistol forty years after the war. In the blink of your eye and in one smooth motion he could draw that awkward, boxy pistol from its holster quick-draw style and, with a few flicks of his "educated thumb," he could fully cock the hammer, remove the safety and be ready to fire. Just like that! Bang! I'll tell you, Hopalong Cassidy, my favorite 1950s cowboy TV star, had nothing on my Dad!

An integral enhancement to the rifle, the bayonet was developed in Bayonne, France, in the early 17th century as a long knife adapted to affix to the barrel of a rifle and used to stick the enemy in close quarters. The drawback was that when a man was stabbed with a bayonet, the victim reflexively would grab the long blade, or the blade would jam into bone and get stuck, a particular problem when the bayonet was thrust into the breastbone or groin. This made it problematic to withdraw the bayonet from the victim's body without detaching it from the rifle in order to continue the charge. A swift kick or push to the skewered man with a foot sometimes dislodged a stuck bayonet.

Technical advances in defensive warfare had outstripped those of offensive warfare, and infantrymen advancing with bayonets affixed to rifles were invariably mown down by machine gunfire long before they reached enemy trenches. Thus the opportunity to use the bayonet was restricted. Bayonets were more for a psychological effect, but were also still effective in fighting once inside the enemy's trench. Many joked that the bayonet was used primarily as a "splendid means of toasting bread, opening cans, and scraping mud off uniforms and in the preparation of latrines."

Artillery

Of course there was the artillery. The artillery used during the First World War ("artillery" defined as large, mounted weaponry and heavy firearms as opposed to small, portable arms like pistols, rifles and machine guns) had progressed from the muzzle loaded, smooth bore, short range cannon and round ball projectiles used during the American Civil War. Allied artillerymen of the First World War were, however, still referred to as "cannoneers."

The modern concept of artillery used breach loaded, rifle barreled - spiraled groves tapering down the inside of the barrel that spun the pointed projectile as it was shot out of the barrel giving it accuracy like the throwing of a football - long-range guns firing with relatively accurate, cylindrical, explosive projectiles that tore buildings, men, horses, trucks, earth, trees and barbed wire into piles of rubble. Artillery was also used with a fuse set to explode the projectile in flight (fragmentation shells) throwing shrapnel - shards of metal - raining down from above into trenches and onto advancing infantry. Artillery was also used to deliver poisonous gas.

French Battery of French 75 mm artillery. The American Heritage History of World War I

The size of the artillery used during the First World War ranged from small trench mortars with a 1.5-inch to 4-inch diameter projectile and the 3-inch French 75s all the way up to the Germans' huge, famous 43-ton gun, "Big Bertha." Big Bertha was a 420 mm (16-½ inch projectile) Howitzer that fired a 2,100-pound projectile a distance of almost eight miles. The projectile weighed about half as much as an American mid-sized automobile. The term Howitzer is generally used to describe large caliber artillery with a short barrel that fires a heavy projectile in a high trajectory, sort of a lobbed artillery bomb. Howitzers were considered ideal for assaults on trenches and fortifications and more commonly were smaller, 200-400 mm (8 - 16 inch), than the legendary Big Bertha, and typically could hurl a 1,000- to 2,000-pound projectile about 11 miles.

The Germans developed a long-range artillery piece called the Paris Gun or the Kaiser Wilhelm Geschutz. These bizarre artillery pieces were used to send 367 shells into the city of Paris from March through August of 1918 with the hope of pounding the French capital into submission. The Paris Gun was a 210 mm gun with a 131-foot long barrel and a range of 75 miles. The Paris Gun fired a 120 kg (264-pound) shell that took 180 kg (396 pounds) of powder charge and the shell actually went into the stratosphere! Once fired, the shell took 170 seconds - 10 seconds less than three minutes - to reach its target.

Barrages

Extensive artillery fire against enemy positions was referred to as a barrage. The intensity of a barrage fell into one of three categories: light, which was six to seven shells every minute; moderate, 30 shells a minute; and heavy, 50-60 shells a minute.

There were different types of offensive barrages. A box barrage was artillery fire aimed around a target, like a town, to either contain within or prevent the enemy from sending in reinforcements. A pin-point barrage was a barrage directed at a specific target like a trench, machine gun nest or sniper's position. A search barrage was used on important targets found by reports generated from aerial observers and spies. A counter-battery barrage was a barrage directed at enemy artillery guns. Rolling or creeping barrages were lines of coordinated exploding artillery fire that systematically progressed across No Man's Land often drenched with gas, usually rolling along just ahead of the attacking infantry. The idea was that the rolling barrage would tear up the barbed wire and any other obstructions and make a path for the attack. It was very intimidating to see one of these coming at you. The rolling or creeping artillery barrage was designed to leave nothing - not a man, tree or animal - standing or alive to oppose the advancing infantry troops.

The French 75 - Light, Mobile Artillery

Coming at the charging enemy soldiers across a No Man's Land's maze of massed rifle fire, barbed wire, and battlefield debris and shell holes was machine gunfire and defensive artillery barrages. Defensive artillery often used short-fused, exploding, shrapnel projectiles fired from small caliber, mounted guns, like the French 75s, that were positioned behind the infantry's trenches. The guns' barrels were adjusted to zero elevation, and the fuses set to explode the projectile into shrapnel immediately upon clearing the friendly trench. Each gun, if it was a French 75 mm, could be fired directly into the line of the advancing enemy infantry like an enormous shotgun.

The artillery piece issued to the 102nd Field Artillery Regiment by the French military was officially known as the French 75 mm L.36.3 Field Gun, Model of 1897. The French called it Cannon de Campagne de 75 mm MLE 1897. It was manufactured at the arsenal located at Bourges, France. The gun weighed 2,500 pounds and was mounted on large wheels and could easily and efficiently be repositioned by horse teams. There were 24 "French 75s" in the 102nd Field Artillery Regiment.

The French 75s could fire several types of shells - high explosive, fragmentation, tracing, flare and incendiary - and had a range of 8.5 km, or 5.3 miles.

In the hands of a skilled gun crew loading on the recoil, this remarkable mobile artillery piece with its 106-inch barrel and its recoil system could hurl 75-millimeter (three inches in diameter) projectiles at the rate of 20 - 30 rounds per minute. The innovative development allowing for this performance was its recoil system consisting of two hydraulic cylinders, a floating piston, a connected piston, a head of gas and a reservoir of oil. This made for a soft, smooth operation.

So rapid was the fire from the French 75s in the hands of a good gun crew, that captured German officers inquired about the three-inch "machine guns" being used on them.

In intense battle situations with sustained, rapid firing for any period of time, the barrel of a French 75 often became so heated that the steel would actually warp throwing the trajectory off target or, worst case, the projectile would jam as it exited the barrel and the barrel would burst. Wet horse blankets were often thrown over the heated barrels in an attempt to keep them cool.

There were 17,000 French 75s manufactured. Testimony to this artillery piece: they were used by the military as late as 1941 in World War II in the Philippines and North Africa.

Flamethrowers

During the early stages of the war in October 1914, the Germans were the first to use flamethrowers, or flammenwerfer. Eventually the weapon was adopted for use by both sides. The terror that a flamethrower attack would bring on the enemy was substantial. The thought of being burned alive was as terrible as the thought of being gassed.

There is nothing new about the concept of a flamethrower, spreading fire on your enemy by launching burning fuel. In some form, flamethrowers have been around since the 5th century B.C. The Germans, however, developed a smaller, lighter version of a flamethrower called a kleinflammenwerfer that could be carried by a single person, as well as a heavier model, the grossflammenwerfer. Both used pressurized air, carbon dioxide or nitrogen that belched forth a stream of burning oil at a distance of approximately

18 to 36 meters (60 - 120 feet) for 40 seconds. The Germans went on to develop a self-igniting flamethrower, the Wex.

The British developed a fixed flamethrower that was of great size, weighing two tons, that was built directly into a forward trench on the Western Front. It had a range of 90 yards. The French also had a portable one-man flamethrower, the Schilt flamethrower.

The drawback to the 1914 version flamethrower device was that the flammable liquid was in a backpack canister under pressure and would explode when punctured by, let's say, a bullet or shrapnel, which whizzed around the battlefield in pretty good numbers. When attacked by flame-throwers, the defending infantry poured rifle fire into the area of the flame-thrower attack in the hope that they would hit one of the fuel cylinders and explode the canister into a large fireball killing all nearby. Flamethrower operators had a short life expectancy, and I don't imagine the flamethrower guy was a person you wanted to be standing near when the shooting started.

Grenades

The hand grenade, named after the French word pomegranate and nick-named "pineapple" because of its serrated shell, is a small bomb detonated by impact or a timed fuse (preferred). It was deployed on the ground in close proximity to the enemy by being thrown by hand or launched by a rifle. The hand grenade was designed to break defenses in close combat warfare; it is a niche weapon perfectly designed for trench warfare. The grenade is not a precise weapon. Upon detonation, a grenade scatters destruction in all directions through fragmentation, throwing fragments of shrapnel all around it.

Grenades go back to the hand-to-hand combat days of the 15th century but were all but abandoned after 1750 with the decline of that close method of fighting. Napoleon's armies had a professional elite force of grenade throwers called grenadiers who had strong arms capable of hurling the little bomb a long way.

The hand grenade came again into its own during the First World War and, like most weaponry of this war, the Germans were very advanced, developing sophisticated grenades early in the war while the British and French were still throwing jars containing gasoline and lit rags and home-made "jam-tin" bombs.

The British and French eventually did develop hand grenades, the most notable the British Mills bomb and, when the Americans came to the

Western Front in 1917, they brought with them their own brand of hand grenade.

Machine Guns

Perhaps the most pivotal weapon used in WWI was the machine gun. The machine gun, first used by the British Army in the Matabelle War (1893-1894), was invented by Maine-born Hiram Maxim who also invented, incongruous as it may be, the hair-curling iron. He developed the machine gun in 1884. Unable to market his invention to the Americans, Hiram Maxim moved to London, England and founded the Maxim Gun Company. The Maxim Gun Company was eventually taken over by Vickers, Ltd. (Vickers machine guns became famous and the iconic machine gun of the American, French and British air forces and infantries.)

Because early machine guns were heavy and mounted on tripods, during the early stages of the First World War, the machine gun was initially viewed primarily as a defensive weapon. It wasn't very mobile and it took a squad of six men to operate a single gun.

Besides its rapid firing capability, the machine gun had a traversing elevation pod which allowed the gun to sweep its hail of bullets from side-to-side and up-and-down. The machine gun of 1914 could fire 400 - 600 small caliber rounds per minute. By the end of the war, the development of fabric or metal belts to carry the rounds into the breach doubled the machine gun's firepower. With that rate of fire, overheating barrels were a problem that was initially solved by firing in short bursts and later with the development and use of air- and water-cooled jackets around the barrel. When water became in short supply, the soldiers would urinate into the machine gun's water jacket.

By the end of the war, a lighter and more portable machine gun was developed. It eventually became as much of an offensive weapon as a defensive one.

Aircraft

Probably the most adventurous and romantically perceived services of the First World War were the air forces. At the beginning of the war, the airplane was not much more than a motorized kite, but it ultimately became one of the biggest technology advances of the war. However, France's General Foch said of the early airplane, "Airplanes are interesting toys, but of no military value."

In the first three years of the Great War, the Germans had superior air power; the German air force outnumbered the Allied air force four planes to one.

The use of aircraft was initially recognized as an effective defensive military strategy for observation, reconnaissance, scouting enemy positions (eyes in the sky) from a safe distance and occasionally dropping things - bombs, grenades and even heavy rocks - on the enemy infantry in trenches below them. With the addition of a machine gun mounted at the rear seat of observation air craft and used for strafing infantry, observation balloons, troop trains, artillery positions and troop truck convoys, the airplane became an offensive weapon.

Reconnaissance aircraft eventually were equipped with wireless communications so that two-seater spotter airplanes could relay enemy infantry and artillery battery positions instantly to command headquarters. Prior to the wireless, the pilot would make his observation and then have to wait to communicate vital information upon landing, or via a handwritten message which was stuffed into a canister and dropped from the plane to artillery and infantry command positions.

By 1915, the Germans perfected interrupter equipment that timed the firing of a machine gun mounted on the cowling through the revolving propeller blades of the aircraft. It wasn't a big step from there to the development of aerial combat (dogfights) between smaller, highly maneuverable, single-seated aircraft - fighter planes that flew at 100 mph - armed with machine guns flown by dare-devil pilots who flew with no parachutes.

The most famous fighter aircraft, probably because of one of its famous pilots, the Red Baron, was the German Fokker Dr 1. The Dr stood for Dreidecker or three wings. Reinhold Platz designed this single-seat dogfighter aircraft and Tony Fokker built 320 of them in response to the success of the triple-winged British Sopwith Triplane.

The Fokker Dr 1 had a 110 hp rotary engine, and a 23-foot, 7-inch wingspan. It was 18 feet, 11 inches in length, flew at 14,000 feet and had a flying time of 90 minutes. It was armed with two machine guns, each a 7.92 mm Spandau LMG 08/15, mounted on the front cowling with interrupter gear that allowed both guns to fire through the revolving propeller blade.

The Fokker Dr 1 aircraft first appeared on the Western Front in August 1917. Tony Fokker personally delivered the first one to Richthofen who said of the little plane, "It climbed like a monkey and maneuvered like a devil."

The German air force became so effective in air combat tactics and the creation of Richthofen's famous Flying Circus squadron that Allied aircraft became known as "Fokker Fodder." During one week in April of 1917, a time that would become known as "Bloody April," the Royal Air Corps lost 75 aircraft to the German fliers known as "The Hun in the Sun."

When the United States entered the war in April of 1917, America's fledgling military air power was struggling for recognition as a military tool in the United States. The Americans weren't credited with actually voicing Foch's opinion about the doubtful future value of the airplane for military use, but the feeling was the same. Before the declaration of war, the United States' entire air force was comprised of eight planes, the Curtis Jenny JN-4 type. All of them were sent to Mexico with Pershing's troops in 1916 to help with the expedition to arrest Pancho Villa. After that expedition, all eight planes were scrapped. The famous Curtis Jenny, which was later used as a standard training aircraft for the United States' air force, was 27 feet long, had a wingspan of 43 feet, 7-1/8 inches, a 90hp engine and flew at 75 mph. The Jenny had a maximum altitude of 6,500 feet and it could sustain flight for two hours and 18 minutes.

When the United States declared war, good numbers of American-trained pilots went to fight in France without American aircraft. The adventurous Americans flew the advanced European biplanes: the British Sopwith Pup, the SE5A, the Bristol and the famous and most successful Allied aircraft of the war, the Sopwith Camel. American fighter pilots in the skies over the Western Front also flew the Nieuport 17C and the French Spad XIII.

Many American pilots distinguished themselves and became Air Aces, those pilots credited with shooting down five or more enemy aircraft.

By early 1917, aviation had advanced and there were dogfights in the skies over the Western Front where 60 or more aircraft would engage in a terrifying dance of death that encompassed a square mile or more of airspace.

Alistair Horne, in "The Price of Glory", eloquently described the fascination with the war in the air.

Never since the Middle Ages and the invention of the long bow had the battlefields of Europe seen this kind of single combat. When the champions of either side met to fight spectacular duels in and out of the clouds, the rest of the war seemed to be forgotten; even the man in the trenches paused to watch, as the hosts of Greece and Troy stood by when Hector and Achilles fought.

By 1918, American funding of the Allied war effort increased production of aircraft and the availability of trained Allied pilots; attrition eventually took its toll and Germany lost its superiority in the air.

In April of 1918, Germany's famous Ace, Richthofen, the Red Baron, was killed, supposedly by Canadian pilot Roy Brown who was flying a Sopwith Camel. When Richthofen was shot down, he was engaged in the pursuit of his 81st kill and was violating one of his own cardinal rules of air combat tactics: flying close to the ground in pursuit of his fleeing prey. In this case his prey was rookie Allied pilot Lieutenant Wilfred May.

There is some controversy over whether Richthofen was hit from the ground by a machine gun burst fired by Australian infantry gunner Cedric Popkin as Richthofen's plane hopped over the Somme Valley terrain, or if the fatal bullet came from a short burst fired from the machine gun on Brown's aircraft as he closed in on Richthofen's plane from behind. Both Popkin's and Brown's machine guns used the same caliber bullets, 303 caliber, so ballistics could not settle the controversy. Many prefer to believe that the Red Knight of Germany died without ever losing a dogfight and the single bullet that tore into his chest and killed him was fired from the ground by the Aussie.

The mortally wounded Richthofen managed to land his plane behind the Allied lines. After landing, he lived for only a few minutes. Immediately upon touching down, his plane was surrounded by Allied ground troops. It was reported that Richthofen managed to utter a few undecipherable words and he died still strapped into the cockpit of his aircraft.

Richthofen's flying helmet, flying suit, gloves, scarf and his personal effects were subsequently dropped on his home aerodrome or airfield in a daring flyover by an Allied pilot, effectively notifying the Germans of his death. The Allies subsequently buried Richthofen's body in a great ceremony and with full military honors. He was 26 years old. The entire event proved that this was, indeed, a different, more chivalrous and romantic time.

Personal Protection

Military equipment also evolved during the war, sometimes humorously. The well recognized Prussian Bismarck helmets used by German soldiers early in the Great War were ineffective as a protective device, being made out of leather with that ornamental spike on top. They were abandoned in 1916 when the German infantry complained that during lulls in the fighting the British and French infantry sharpshooters were amusing themselves by taking target practice at the spikes that stuck up above the German trench's forward wall.

A more practical and protective bucket type of headgear, the M16, also called the Stahlhelm, that resembled a medieval warrior's helmet or a coals-cuttle, replaced the Bismarck helmet. The Germans eventually developed a similarly designed helmet that was used by the German Army through the Second World War. The design, construction and all around protection was thought to be superior to the Allied forces' helmets.

Intelligence

Communication during this war was enabled through telephone wire strung between units that were in close proximity to each other; between units spread out over longer distances, runners or motorcycle riders carried written messages. Written messages were also sent by carrier pigeon.

The United States sent 15,000 trained carrier pigeons to France with the A.E.F. and proudly stated that 95 percent of the messages carried by American pigeons in combat were delivered, including one that read: "Take it away. I'm tired of carrying this damn bird."

One carrier pigeon became famous. One hundred ninety-four of the original force of 550 men of the 77th "Liberty" Division's infantry from New York had been trapped behind enemy lines for many days. This particular bird delivered the message from what become known as the "Lost Battalion" in October of 1918 from the Argonne Forest to the Division's headquarters informing them that, even after repeated charges from the enemy and being hit repeatedly by mistaken friendly artillery barrages, the remaining men of the 77th infantry were still alive. That heroic bird, wounded in its flight, was mounted and is on display in the Smithsonian Museum.

Intelligence information was obtained through interrogating prisoners or from documents taken from captured officers. Listening posts were set up. A man would work his way close enough to enemy lines so that he could actually overhear the enemy's conversations. Sometimes they didn't have a convenient prisoner to talk to so they would go out at night on a patrol with the specific purpose of capturing an enemy soldier, regardless of rank, and bringing him back to their line for an "examination." The "interview" of the captured man was described by The Boston Globe reporter Frank Sibley in his book as going something like this:

"...some prisoners were being examined one day when word was telephoned in from the line that the Boche was chucking over some big shells from his minenwerfer. [A minenwerfer - or mine thrower - was an artillery piece that would lob a huge shell and make a crater the size of a small cellar.]

'Where are the minenwerfer in your line?' asked the [26th Division] captain, turning to the prisoner then being questioned.

'I don't know,' said the Boche.

'How many have you?'

'None.'

'Did you ever see a minenwerfer?' asked the captain with his blue eyes beginning to shed sparks. Anybody but a Boche would have known that the storm signal was up.

'No,' said the Boche.

Smack! The Irish fist met the German jaw.

'How many mienwerfer did you say you have got?' asked the captain again.

'Six.'

'Where are they on this map?'

"The prisoner indicated with a dirty forefinger; the telephone jingled and five minutes later those minenwerfer were being plastered by our artillery."

Not to leave the reader with the impression that the Allies or the Germans were complete brutes, an incident also relayed in Mr. Sibley's story was that one German prisoner came to Division Headquarters wearing a tag in his buttonhole. The tag read, "This man when captured was giving water to a wounded American soldier." The prisoner was respectfully interviewed, and then given food, water and American cigarettes.

And, so went intelligence gathering during the First World War.

Some of the best sources of intelligence came from the balloon observers who sat high over the lines in their gray, hydrogen gas-filled "sausages", spotting and reporting through a telegraph line connection to the ground the position of enemy artillery and troops from as far as 14 miles away.

These young balloon observers relished the chance to make a parachute jump, one of the occasional necessities of being a balloon observer as the highly flammable balloons tethered to a cable wound around a drum on the ground were easy targets for passing enemy planes that would quickly shoot them down. When one prepares for duty in the "sausage", he is clothed in a fur-lined "Teddy-bear suit" for warmth at the high altitude and then is buckled into a harness of webbing. In the middle of the back of the webbing is a ring to which is attached a short line that is attached to a parachute stowed on the outside of the balloon basket. When the man jumps out of the balloon basket, in the course of his free fall it is assumed that the parachute will be pulled out of the bag and open when the end of the line is reached, and the man will safely float to the ground. If all went well, the ride ended with a "Wheee!" If not, it ended with a sickening thump!

German POWs. Dichotomy of German prisoners captured by the Yankee Division. The one on the left is an infantry elite storm trooper, the one on the right an ordinary infantry soldier who was a college professor. Yankee Division photograph

The cowardly and brutal act of pilots or ground troops firing at the parachuting enemy floating defenselessly through the air, dangling helplessly from an open parachute, hadn't been accepted, although I couldn't say it never happened during this time. However, shooting down the balloons was fair game for pilots and often the objective of an entire mission.

The Germans had very effective intelligence systems, often recruiting the local citizens as spies. There was a story that when the division went into the Chemin des Dames sector there was a sign on one of the abandoned German trenches that read, "Welcome 26th Division." It impressed every-one with the need for the utmost secrecy and security.

Tanks

In the final analysis, the tank probably is the one weapon, besides the fighting spirit, determination and know-how of the American soldier - and American money - that ultimately changed the outcome of the war and broke the stalemate of trench warfare.

In 1889 Fredrick Simms designed what he termed a "motor-war car" that had a Daimler engine, a bulletproof casing and two revolving machine guns developed by Hiram Maxim. It was first offered as the Killen-Strait Armoured Tractor to the British, but everyone initially immediately dis-missed it as a mechanical toy. Everyone, that is, except for British Army officer Colonel Ernest Swinton who remained enthusiastic about what he believed to be the potential of the tank in breaking through enemy trench defenses, barbed wire and rifle and machine gunfire.

Swinton arranged a demonstration of the tank to then First Lord of the Admiralty Winston Churchill, and soon-to-become Prime Minister David Lloyd George. The demonstration was a success and Churchill established the Landships Committee to further investigate the vehicle's potential. The name of the committee was derived from the fact that initially the tank was seen as an extension of sea-going warships - hence, a landship - yet because it resembled a water carrier, it was assigned the name "tank", which, in 1915, stuck.

The first tank was named "Little Willie" and was soon followed by "Big Willie." Big Willie had a Daimler engine, weighed 14 tons, was 12 feet long, could carry three people and its top speed was three miles per hour on level ground, two on rough terrain or battlefield conditions. The first combat tank was ready by January 1916. History was made on 15 September 1916 when Captain H. W. Mortimore guided the first tank - a D1 British tank - into action on the Western Front. The Germans' first tank came on in April 1918.

In 1916, the British produced 150 tanks. In 1917, they produced 1,277. In 1918, they produced 1,391 tanks. The United States did not produce any tanks until 1918 when they produced 84 of them, none of which made it to the Western Front. In 1918, the French produced 4,000 tanks. It wouldn't be until the Second World War that the tank would be further developed and perfected, completely replacing the horse as cavalry.

It was not pleasant to be inside a World War I vintage tank. It could be compared to riding in your car while seated under the hood. The temperature inside the tank reached over 100 degrees and the smell of oil and gas was overwhelming.

By means of these descriptions of the various defenses and tools of trench warfare, one can see why the development and use of the tank was so significant in breaking the stalemate of the trench war by enabling a safer means of infiltration into enemy territory.

I found it interesting that for almost every weapon, the Germans were more advanced in their technology and further in their development than the Allies and, almost 100 years hence, their technology has survived over any other. For example, the design of the German soldier's helmet, the coalscuttle kind, is the type that has survived and is used by almost all NATO and United States armed forces today. The 9 mm automatic pistol, originally the caliber used by only the Germans in World War I, has become the standard caliber for NATO armed forces' pistols.

Gas

The most terrible weapon of the First World War was gas. Poison gas was developed by Fritz Haber of the Kaiser Wilhelm Institute. The Germans first used gas on a large scale against the French and Algerians on the Western Front on 22 April 1915 at the second battle of Ypres in Belgium. The Germans released a five-mile wide cloud of chlorine gas from 520 cylinders (168 tons of chemical) that day where it drifted over the enemy with the prevailing wind and caused widespread panic and death. The age of chemical warfare had begun.

Arial photograph of gas being released from canisters and delivered by the wind over enemy trenches. www.worldwar1.nl

British Troops preparing for gas attack wearing gauze pad gas masks, 1915. www.worldwar1.nl

Canister gas mask. www.worldwar1.nl

British mustard gas casualties. www.worldwar1.nl

The use of gas by the Allies soon followed, as well as its eventual delivery by artillery. By the end of the war, approximately 17 types of gas of the lachrymator (tearing agent) and asphyxiate (suffocating agent) type had been developed and were being used by both sides. During the last of the fighting, late in 1918, it was estimated that one in every four artillery rounds fired by both sides contained some type of gas, with chlorine and phosgene gases being the most widely used.

Lachrymator and asphyxiate were the types of gases that suffocated a person or caused eye, nose and throat irritation and violent coughing and choking. The victim often died by drowning in his own fluids. Gas instantly reduced the effectiveness of the enemy. Just seeing gas shells exploding and the gas fog advancing on the battlefield created terror, panic and confusion among the targeted troops.

The effect of lachrymator and asphyxiate type gases could be thwarted by the use of a gas mask. Early gas masks were little more than a gauze bandage or chamois dipped in a solution of bicarbonate of soda and tied around the nose and mouth with string. Canister gas masks, filter respirators using charcoal or antidote chemicals, were eventually developed. It was difficult to fire a rifle or work while wearing a gas mask, but the mask was mandatory equipment for soldiers and was carried in an easily accessible bag worn around the neck or from the shoulder. The gas masks were inspected frequently by the officers for correct operation and were ready to be put on at a moment's notice.

War, being the efficient mother of nasty inventions that she is, brought forth a more terrible gas, a blistering agent gas called mustard gas that would burn all exposed skin. This gas was subsequently developed with the idea and design of providing a more terrible agent, thereby further raising the stakes in the effort to break the stalemate of trench warfare.

Dichlorethyl sulfide/sulfur mustard, or mustard gas, proved to be the most effective and lethal of all the poisonous chemicals used during the war. It was first used in September 1917.

Mustard gas was easy to deliver by artillery, usually a 75 mm to 155 mm piece. It would form an oily fog, blowing with the wind, and sinking into low lying areas and hanging in trenches and shell holes, maintaining its crippling and killing ability for days after delivery. It got its name "mustard" from its garlic-like smell.

Mustard gas was unique…and terrible. It blinded, suffocated and burned its victims. Being a caustic chemical, it was attracted to the moist areas of the body, the eyes, respiratory tract, groin, armpits and face. It penetrated clothing, so protective, waterproof suits that were hot to wear and cumbersome to work in were developed. A person receiving even mild exposure to mustard gas quickly became incapacitated; heavy exposure would kill or, almost certainly, would maim the person for life.

The effect of mustard gas on the skin was blistering that would start several hours or even several days after exposure…the longer the initial exposure to the gas, the more severe the effect.

On the respiratory system, mustard gas caused irritation of the bronchial tubes, stripping off the mucous membrane, which initially resulted in bronchitis; coughing; difficulty swallowing, talking and shortness of breath; and then eventual blocking of the airways, which suffocated the victim.

In contact with mustard gas, the eyes would initially become irritated, as if there was some foreign body in them, and then the eyelids would burn, swell and close shut. The cornea of the eye eventually formed an ulcer resulting in blindness.

Mustard gas is nasty stuff. Unlike being blown up from explosive artillery shells or hit with shrapnel or bombs dropped from planes, shot with rifle or machine gun bullets, or stabbed with a bayonet, gas didn't kill its victim outright. It crippled him and killed in a hideously slow, horrible way. One can imagine men wearing gas masks fighting in the trenches or firing artillery with a fog of gas wafting around creating a surreal image of Hell.

There are grim pictures from the First World War of long lines of men having been exposed to mustard gas at the front lines marching to rear positions with bandages over their burned eyes, each man being led with his hand on the shoulder of the man in front.

In round numbers, by the end of the war there were 56,000 Russians, 9,000 Germans, 8,100 British, 8,000 French and 1,500 Americans killed by gas. The total casualties from gas, both fatal and non-fatal, were staggering figures, in the millions, and these figures of people killed and wounded by gas did not include those who died after the war from the lingering effects of gas poisoning.

Let's go back to the front lines and Father's baptism to fire at Chemin des Dames.

The first sector that the 102nd Field Artillery Regiment would go into was located north of Soissons, the Chemin des Dames.

In the 18th century this 45 km (29 mile) route that ran east and west between Laon and Reims was followed by the daughters of Louis XV - Adelaide and Victoire - known as the Dames de France. So they would have a good road to travel from Paris to Vauclair to visit their governess in the Chateau de La Bove and to make the ride easier on the royal carriage, the route was cobbled and later bore the princesses' name, Chemin des Dames, the road of the ladies.

Because the Chemin des Dames ridge rises 200 meters (656 feet), it forms a natural barrier in this sector between the north and the south and it dominates the valley of the Ailette. The Aisne River is to the south and the L'Aisne Canal is to the north. It has always been coveted for its strategic military position from the time of Caesar (57 BC) to Clovis (486 AD) to Napoleon (1814) and finally during the First World War (1914 - 1918).

During the First World War, the Germans initially took control of the ridge in September 1914, and held it and Laon until 1917. The Germans made the ridge and the chalk caves around it an impregnable fortress.

In the spring of 1917, the French forces under Commander-in-Chief General Robert Nivelle launched a large scale offensive to retake the ridge. The attack was a disaster, costing considerable lives and Nivelle his command. As a result, the morale of French troops weakened. General Nivelle was replaced by General Henri-Philippe Petain. By November of 1917, under the command of General Petain, the French had retaken the ridge and the Chemin des Dames. At this stage of the fighting, the ridge was in a state of general destruction and void of anything of beauty. Just to the north was occupied Laon, its cathedral's spire very visible from the Chemin des Dames ridge.

When the Yankee Division took up a position in this sector, it was still fairly quiet.

On 3 February, the 1st Battalion of the 102nd Field Artillery Regiment, Batteries A, B, C and D, comprised of 45 officers, 751 enlisted men and 644 animals, ended their training at Coetquidan. They entrained at Guer and detrained at Soissons and Mercin-Pommiers. It was reported in "The History of the 26th Division" that when the 26th Division Yankees arrived in this sector, their first front, they rolled out of their trains, loaded their wagons, and swung through Soissons…singing! They were finally at the front, and they were excited.

Visible signs of war were all around them. Every house in every village they passed through was in ruin. Every wood was a dump for ammunition or barbed wire or endless miles of narrow-gauge railroad track. Every road was a long procession of army transportation and French staff cars whizzing about. The roadsides were filled with machine gun pill boxes, trenches that led off here and there and piled stone barricades that all offered evidence that there had been some close up fighting on this ground. The winter roads were muddy with a cream-colored paste, thick mud over broken stone that made for hard marching and transportation.

It was said by observers that there was something very impressive about the way the Yankees went into this front line. They were so excited, so interested, so happy over it, and yet completely unconcerned about the danger. It was like school was over and they were on a camping trip or picnic. If a plane buzzed overhead, every man gazed at it as long as it could be seen. At each distant noise of artillery firing the men remarked, "Hey! There's one!" And then they would search the horizon for the puff of smoke that marked the landing of the artillery shell.

The battle-hardened French soldiers were at first amused at the naive curiosity of the green Yankees. Then, realizing they would fight alongside of them, they became concerned, privately wondering, "Notre allie?" (Our ally?).

As the Yankees moved up to the front lines, the guns were speaking, always nearer and nearer. But in this training sector and just ahead of the launching of Ludendorff's offensive, the guns were not speaking too intently just now. It was as if they were just giving the new arrivals notice that they were there.

Upon arrival (They arrived ahead of the infantry!), the 1st Battalion artillery batteries were billeted at Bucy le Long on the north bank of the Aisne River, northeast of Soissons. Bucy le Long would be the echelon (Post of Command or PC) or Postes de Commandement Headquarters (HQ) for the 1st Battalion. A few days after their arrival, under the tutelage of the 11th French Army Corps, French Commandant de Groupe - the French Groupe Commanders - along with the artillery of the 61st French Division of Infantry and the 251st French Field Artillery, the regiment was positioned on the front between Soissons and Laon. The artillery batteries would take up positions on the heights northeast of Soissons.

According to the prescribed training plan, the entire 26th Division went into this sector with every unit paired with a corresponding French unit. They were first sent into a "quiet sector," an area where there wasn't full scale fighting. But that didn't mean that it wasn't serious business and nobody could get killed. This was routine practice, a set pattern for all the arriving divisions, both regular Army and National Guard. American troops acted under the instruction from French Groupe Commanders officers; higher ranking American officers, e.g. majors and above, were only gradually given tactical direction of their units after 5 March.

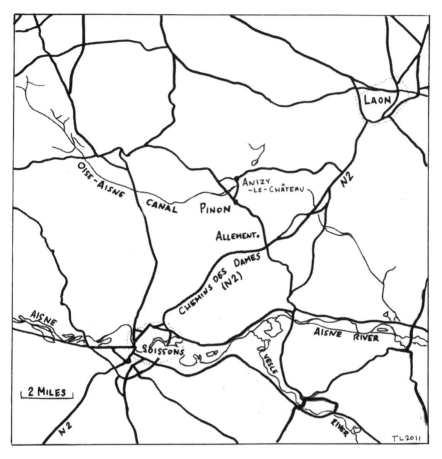

The Chemin des Dames Sector.

Photograph of Chemin des Dames as it runs along its ridge - October 2004.
It was once a cobbled road. For the army that held it, it was a fortress.
Stephen G. Hobson Collection - Stephen G. Hobson photograph

Photograph taken looking into Battery A's position on the St. Gobineaux Ridge - October 2004.
Photograph was taken looking across from the fields in back of the Vaurain Farm.
Artillery was positioned in camouflaged casements on the side of the ridge and
projectiles were fired over the top. Incoming rounds would fall into the valley behind them.
Stephen G. Hobson Collection - Stephen G. Hobson photograph

For the infantry, it was only to get harder as they went from the quarries into the trenches. Because of past fighting, the landscape was battle scarred. The entire ground was churned by shell fire. Shell holes, some the size of a barrel and others the size of a cellar, impinged on each other and a footpath wound its way on the ridges between. It was particularly difficult to navigate at night.

Battery A's position, established on 10 February, was on the edge of the ravine of St. Gobineaux, north of the Paris-Maubeuge road. While in this sector there were few changes in any of the battery's positions. It was from this position that Battery A would be for the first time "at the war," receive their baptism to fire and send and receive their first shots fired in anger.

The battery's position was a good one in that it was on the back side of a steep ridge and, aside from the fear that the gun's recoil could send the guns, which were in casements (shelter), tumbling down the steep ridge, any incoming artillery and gas shells fell over the battery and away from and below them into the ravine and the field behind them.

For some of the men in the PCs (Post of Command), there were the large caves for concealment that had been quarried from France's legendary soft chalkstone that hardens when it is exposed to the air. However, the acetylene lamps in the caves gave off fumes and made bad air in the caves. Battery A did not enjoy the luxury of cave existence.

And so it was in this fashion that the first regiments of the first National Guard division took up their positions on the battle line.

The Germans occupied the area to the north, the heights above the Valley Massif de Gobain, the Fox Salient (prominent projection), eastward to Monampteuil and Laon. The ground between the opposing forces was the area called No Man's Land. Most of the raids and patrols across No Man's Land would happen at night.

While in this sector, the 26th Division was under the command of General Louis Ernest de Maud'huy's XI Corps of the 6th French Army. According to the Regiment's History:

> While in this sector the Yankee Division was associated with the 11th [XI] French Army Corps and Gen. Edwards issued an order stating that he was pleased to consider the 11th Corps the godfather of the 26th Division. Genl de Maud'huy, [French] commander of the fortress of Metz, wrote in reply, "The 11th Corps feels proud

of the marked honor, being sure that, whatever he may be sent, the godson shall do credit to the godfather."

On the afternoon of February 5, Battery A, 101 Field Artillery took position on the line, and at 3:45 o'clock the number one piece of its 75s barked forth for the [26th] Division the first shot fired by the National Guard in the war. The shell case is at the Massachusetts State House as a memento of that event. That night the 101st Infantry went through the artillery lines and was the first National Guard contingent to enter the trenches. There was plenty of fighting at Chemin des Dames, though none on a large scale.

Battery A of the 102nd Field Artillery received its baptism to fire at 3:00 o'clock on the morning of 9 February, four days after the historic firing of the Division's 101st Regiment's guns.

The baptismal event for the 102nd Regiment was described in a letter sent home by one of the battery's gun crew ammunition handlers, Sergeant Robert Hurley, and reported in the Haverhill Gazette. Sergeant Hurley wrote:

Everywhere on our left, on our right, in back of us, in front of us, the flames and flashes of the hidden batteries cleaved the night, the shrill whistle of the 75 mm guns, the deep roar of the big ones [larger artillery] and the infernal clack, clacking of machine guns just to our front deafened our ears, but minds intent on our task we never stopped, but just jammed the shells home in the gun and sent them screaming hate to the Boche. The Prussians charging our infantry shouted in English, 'Surrender, you Yankee Sons' and the Yankee Sons never spoke but rammed their bayonets in the bellies of the Prussians and the shells that arrived in time exploded in their midst, and the barbed wire of No Man's Land is hung with big things in black coats that were once the Prussian Guards. You have probably heard a lot about 'Gas.' Well, we have experienced it. It crept upon us unawares, our eyes ran water, our throats burned, we choked and coughed and sneezed, then our gas masks went on, and the dirty tactics of the Hun were foiled, and our guns barked on. The range lengthened as the [Allied] infantry advanced. 'Send 'em home boys, our boys are giving 'em hell,' and the gun crews dead for want of sleep, sweating, dirty, sick from the smell of powder, toil on and finally the blessed moment arrives to cease fire and the men, haggard and worn, drop anywhere they can and sleep, ready for the next call if Fritz gets fresh.

Pen sketch made by C. LeRoy Baldridge of historic firing of the first artillery round by the National Guard, 26th Division's 101st Regiment, Battery A, at 3:45 pm on 5 February 1918. A Brief History of the Fighting Yankee Division

While serving in this sector, every day there was shooting of some sort by the regiment: fire for registration (firing enough shots on a given target in the daytime to establish exactly at what range and elevation and direction one must fire in the night to land a shell directly on the target), harassing fire, and, occasionally, a call for a barrage to repel a full infantry charge - a "coup de main".

On 9 March, Battery A was heavily shelled with German artillery, 77s and 210s. In all, Battery A took about 300 incoming rounds that day and Sergeant Walter C. Hughes was slightly wounded.

But other than a bad case of mange contracted by the horses that would plague the poor animals until spring when they could be "dipped," Sergeant

Hughes was the only casualty the regiment would have while serving in this sector.

The first front line fatality of the war for the 26th Division occurred the third night on the line in this sector. The man was killed by friendly fire, not a German bullet. He was an infantry lad from Winthrop, Massachusetts, who was on patrol. He disobeyed instructions to stay put in the safety of a shell hole and went out chasing what he thought was an enemy patrol. He got turned around, lost his sense of direction and wandered back into his own line. As he approached his line in the dark, he failed to answer the challenge from the forward positions and he was taken out by his own machine gunners.

While serving in this sector, in the entire 26th Division there was a total of 77 casualties: 22 deaths and 55 wounded. With a population in the Division of nearly twenty-five thousand, it was observed that this was a far healthier condition than any American city could show in peacetime.

While in the Chemin des Dames sector, Battery A fired 1,231 rounds and the entire regiment fired 12,864 rounds. Upon at least one occasion later in the war, the regiment fired more than this total in a single 24-hour period.

But, the regiment had done something to annoy the Boche. It had shown the French it could shoot, and it had gained the necessary confidence and experience to work its own sector, which was the next thing to come.

When they left the Chemin des Dames sector after six weeks, the Division had a new swing. They may have lacked some of the bravado they arrived with, but it was only replaced with a smooth and confident conservation of energy, a confidence that they could handle anything the enemy might throw at them, and that steady look in their eyes of men who have been through battle. They had death brush by them and they experienced the horror of war. They also had developed a respect for the ability of the French soldier.

Dearest Dad

Last night, much to the surprise of all of us, more mail came from the States. I was lucky enough to get six letters plus two papers. These helped to pass away the evening as well as telling me news of home doings. Now to tell you some news.

First of all about my money. I wrote Mother about it last week, but in case that letter does not reach home I am going to write you about it also. I have taken out a $10,000 insurance policy which I am paying for out of my monthly pay. I guess you have already heard of this new plan for insuring the lives of our soldiers so I will not take the time to go all over it. It sounded very good to me and you people at home should have something to help out, if Johnny is either hurt or killed while serving his country. If you do not know just what this insurance covers I wish you would look it up because in my opinion it is one of the finest things the government ever did to protect her boys. Now about my allotment. I have allotted to you $15.00 a month which will be taken out of my pay as well as the insurance and Liberty Bond. You should receive this money every month from Washington and if it does not come I wish you would let me know so that I can look into the matter. Will you please put this money in the bank for me or do whatever you may think is best with it. So much for money.

Now I want to say just a few words about this boy who has just returned to Haverhill. I understand that he has started to tell the Haverhill people all kinds of things about the condition over here as well as about the men. Just in case you folks have not got on to it yet or heard about it I will warn you that he is a very heavy user of dope. He certainly can throw out a heavy line of fish stories once he gets started and from all reports I should judge he was well underway. He may be telling you the truth or he may be under the influence of his drug and having one of his wild dreams so, for heaven's sake, don't take too much stock in what he has to tell you. I knew he was to go back and thought some of warning you then but decided to let things take their own course and I guess you all will catch on quick enough to the truth. Please keep this under your hat. Lots of the boys are to write home about him now that they have heard what he is up to so I guess the news will spread fast.

Lieut. Langdon showed me a cablegram several days ago from Marj stating that she had announced their engagement. Mother said something about Sister announcing hers and I now am just waiting for the cablegram to arrive with the good news that my sister is engaged to Lieut. Bradley. As far as I can figure it all out I am just about the only one who has not got to spend $1,000.00, more or less, on an engagement ring. Dad, maybe I'm not going to have some swell old time attending all these weddings. If I ever decide to pull off the trick I ought to have some pretty good ideas as to how it should be done. Poor Mr. and Mrs. Bradley will feel lost I should think when both Ev and Marj have to make their own homes. I offered to hold up the reputation of all three families if George and Ev could fix it up to return to their waiting brides and George approved but now the question is how they can fix it up to get back. Love and war don't go together at all in my judgment - I'm playing the war game now and will try the love game when I get home. If the latter is as interesting and as full of thrills as the former it must be lots of fun.

One of our boys back of the lines sent word up to me the other night that he saw Paul Woodman in a town near our horse line and that he asked for me. When I return from the front I am going to try and find him.

Oh yes, I must say just a few words about the weather here. What do you know, we have snow on the ground. It came last night but looks as if it would turn to slush and mud before this evening. The French say March is the worst month here but once over we will have good weather.

The candy you sent arrived in fine condition and you can bet your bottom dollar it tasted good. We had not been paid for some time and I, as well as the rest, was broke and could not buy sweets and had not had any for two weeks. The night it came Johnny just fell to and ate, ate, ate. Just fancy it - here I am at the front fighting and yet I can eat good candy and smoke good cigarettes right from

America. Well Dad, if it was not for you dear ones at home life over here would not be so easy and I would not be able to enjoy all those little comforts. Thank you, Dad, a thousand times.

Lieut. Wendell is with us for a few days and told me this morning that he had seen Ev a few days before. Percy is looking fine and wanted to be remembered to all of you.

We are all looking forward to a few weeks in a rest camp before long and we certainly deserve a rest. This life works on your nerves in fine style in the course of time and a few weeks rest will not hurt any of us. I am hoping that some of us will get a furlough of seven or eight days but the outlook for it is not very bright just now. A few days of real pleasure away from the Army routine would certainly go good. Just think I have had almost a year of it now. I love it, yes virtually love it and especially now that we are up where there is something doing but just the same a few days off on my own hook with no one to please but my own self won't go half bad.

I have not seen Mr. Brown's son for a long time but he must be around here somewhere.

By the way - why don't you people get out a camera and take a few pictures of each other and send them to me. I would love to see how you all look just as you really are - not posing but natural. Even the house would look good, so some Sunday when you are all there just please your six-foot son and have someone snap a few pictures. Mother knows the kind that will appeal to me so let her be the "chief cook and bottle washer." Home scenes certainly would look good.

Mother writes that dear little Buster still misses his big brother a great deal. You know I never realized until I left that the little fellow would miss me so much but I guess he is pretty fond of me even if I did jump on him at times.

Say, you people ought to see the dear little pets we boys have up here. They usually keep out of sight during the day but at night they all come to life. Yes, they are those famous animals called rats and mark my word, they are big ones. They take great delight in dashing across our faces at night and thus waking us from our peaceful slumbers but we have no trouble in returning again once they have passed.

We have started a paper known as "The Cave Rumor" which a few of us write up each week. It is full of knocks at each other and always causes much laughter when posted up to be read. Here is one extract which caused much laughing, "Where was Pleasure (Hobson) when the Boche opened fire last night?" Pleasure is my new name. I was out working on some wire at the time and was seen to disappear head first in a very muddy shell hole - hence the remark in the paper. You people may not appreciate the funny side of it nor did I for a short while but it was very funny for those who were in a safe place.*

Well, Dad, I guess both the censor and you will get tired of reading this so I will close.

Please give my love to all the family including the grandparents.

With love,
Johnny

---

* This is one of the stories my father would tell about himself. When he would tell this particular story, he made light of it. But, when the facts are known, it was a very courageous act.

When enemy artillery barrages broke communication wires that connected observation posts to firing batteries and the infantry's trenches, critical communication directing the battery's fire would be severed. A broken wire had to be repaired immediately and at any cost. The method of doing this was to find a volunteer whose mission was to repair the wire, which required him to run or crawl in front of his lines through No Man's Land with the wire in his hand, fully exposing himself to the enemy's artillery, machine gunfire and sharp shooters. The volunteer would have to trace the wire to the break, repair and test the wire, and then follow the wire back to his own lines. It was a suicide mission.

One night, during a heavy artillery barrage, Battery A's wire was cut and my father did his duty. Out he went wearing clumsy, heavy, rubber boots and a long, wool greatcoat with the wire in his hand, running as fast as he could, sloshing and sliding through the slippery mud. He was running bent over with his helmeted head down. He was jumping over the battlefield's debris and working his way around barbed wire and shell holes. He was going just as fast as his legs would carry him, literally running for his life dodging exploding artillery shells that were sending geysers of dirt into the air and shrapnel whizzing about his head. In his dash, long, tall, gangly Johnny Hobson, the pride of Phillips Exeter's track team, suddenly pitched over headfirst, tripping and plunging into an unseen, very large and deep, water- and mud-filled shell hole.

He accomplished his mission, though, and the broken wire was repaired. He returned to his lines unharmed. As Father said in his letter, "…it was very funny, for those who were watching from a safe place."

Upon returning from France after the war, Private Adalarde Douchette of Haverhill who served with the 102nd Field Artillery's Battery A, told of this feat. The story appeared in the 1 February 1919 edition of the Haverhill Evening Gazette under the headline, "Hobson Dares Death For His Comrades."

The article stated:

"Private Douchette, in speaking of the heroism displayed by the members of the battery while under fire…stated that Sergeant John L. Hobson did the bravest deed he had ever witnessed. When the commanding officer asked for a volunteer to repair some communication lines, Hobson was the first to answer, and without asking any aid, went out under the heaviest shell fire, repaired the lines and returned. Private Douchette said that he could see nothing but instant death for Sergeant Hobson in his undertaking, but that he did it without saying a word about it."

Cablegram

Somewhere in France

February 21, 1918

Am feeling just as fine as ever and enjoying my work. Expect more mail from the States very soon. Everett and I have seen a lot of each other this past week, in fact, we have had supper together twice. My, but it does seem good to have him back once again. We are very busy indeed just now so the only chance I get to see him is at night. Please give my love to all the family.

Dearest Mother

I am sorry to say that almost two weeks have gone by since I last wrote to you dear ones at home. Many changes have taken place and I have passed through many very interesting experiences since my last letter left France for the U.S. In fact, Mother dear, I have been so busy and interested in the day's doings that my time has been more than taken up. Well, darling, my thoughts have been with you many, many times both day and night, only they have not been written down and sent to you. Remember, "No news is good news."

Well, I suppose you know by this time that we are really at the front. Those dreams of last April have really come true at last and Battery A has fired more than one death message to the Boche and received more than one in return. I know that you and Dad are apt to feel a little more anxious now that you know that you have a son on the firing line but there is no need of it, dearest. I also know that it will make you both feel very proud to know that your boy is no longer miles behind the lines but has taken his place "On the Field of Honor" with hundreds of other men in whose veins the true red blood of an American is flowing. Don't give it a minute's thought, Mother, because God is with me and He alone can send me back to you and the rest or call me to His home above as he sees best. I have said over and over again that I am going to return safe and well and believe it more and more every day. I'm not worrying in the least so please don't you and Dad. I'm happy and never felt any better so let's all be happy and forget to worry.

Now about the Y.M.C.A. work of which you wanted to know. Yes, they certainly are doing a great work over here and are the real friend of the American soldier. At one place where we were they had a fine hut where they sold everything you can think of. A concert was held there every so often and the boys had a show. Those post cards I sent to several people in Haverhill were given by the Y.M.C.A. as has been a lot of writing paper. They always have a lot of books and magazines for us to read and everything is done for our comfort when off duty. That is all I can think of to tell you about their work.

I am sorry to hear that everyone is having such a hard time over this coal question. As far as I can figure out all the businessmen are pretty near at a stand still. How has it affected you, Dad? Every letter the boys get seems to speak of it, so I guess you must have been hit along with the rest.

I had a fine letter from Marj last night but am sorry to say that I shall be unable to answer it for some little time as we can only write once a week now. Will you please give her my love and tell her that "Little Brother" often thinks of "Big Sister." You might also add that she had better start to save her money if she intends to pay me that bet we made about Battery A going on to the firing line. I could put away a mighty big meal right now.

I have not seen Ev for over two weeks but understand that he is within a few miles of here. I hope that we float into each other again before long. I certainly do admire that man from the bottom of his feet to the top of his head. His family surely have a boy to be mighty proud of. He certainly has been mighty devoted to Sister and she to him.

I have found it out of the question to save any money over here just so long as I have it with me. I feel also that when I return I may need a little on which to take a few weeks vacation with you and some of the rest so I have made a $15.00 allotment to Dad. He should receive this every month and I wish you would ask him to put it in the bank with the rest of my small savings. Money of my own is going to come in very handy upon my return and I do not want to ask Dad to give me all my good times. I'll bet he misses having Johnny ask him for money at the breakfast table every few days. Well, Dad, I have learned the value of money now and realize that it does not grow on trees in one's back yard. What little I can save now will mean that I will not be forced to call on you so often and that is what I am trying for. I want to see just how near I can come to being self-supporting upon my return.

Mother dear, you certainly hit a soft spot in my heart when you spoke of next summer and how you were trying to find something to keep Art interested. I imagine he is very anxious to get over here and do something but tell him for me to wait. He is young and wants to complete his work at Exeter first - then if we are still mixed up in war is the time for him to come to the help of this shell torn country. If he has an auto to run around in tell him to give all the girls a ride for me.

Speaking about Art reminds me that tomorrow is February 22nd and a big day at Exeter, unless the war has interfered. What girl did he have up to the dance? I want to hear all about it, Art. It will never do for you to pull one over on your older brother while he is dancing around shell holes instead of the posts in the gym. The former is good fun but give me the latter every time as I like the music better than the whizzing of a shell through the air.

Mother, darling, there are two members of the family that I would very much like to see right now. Of course I want to see you all but these two must have changed a lot since my departure last September - Buster and "K". I imagine they both have grown a lot this winter and by now must be quite grown up. Tell them not to change too much while I am gone or I shall never know them when I walk in the front door but will have to be introduced.

Sis, the dear girl, could never change so much that I would not know her. She may have grown older and more womanly but under it all she could never hide from me the laughing and merry girl she was when I left. She will always be the same old Kid to me no matter what changes months may make.

In one of my letters some little time ago I spoke about sending me some candy. If that letter ever reached home I don't doubt but what that there is some on the way to me now but in case it did not I thought I would speak of it again. You know I have a great tooth for sweets and we don't get any too many here. That cake grandma Hobson sent me went fine and I wish you would thank her for it.

Two more things which may be of interest to you. One wrist watch has gone to the happy hunting ground where all good watches go. It was the little one. That one you put on my wrist, Mother, that last night at Boxford by the fire, still ticks out the minutes and hours of my separation from home and comforts. It started that night and has not stopped once since. The other thing of interest is the pipe Dad gave me. That pipe has gone everywhere with me and right now is purring away in my face. If I ever lost that I don't know what would happen. Sometimes I even think I care more for that pipe than my food and that is going some because we are being mighty well fed. She is a peach, Dad, and oh so sweet.

Well, darling, I have written more now than I intended to so will close with a good night kiss.

I can't tell you about our life and experiences here at the front or I would and you never would finish the letter it would be so long and interesting but this will let you know that your boy is well and happy and the rest will follow in the days to come.

Give my love to all the family including the grandparents.

Lots of love and kisses for yourself.
Johnny

Dear Dad

Just a few more lines to let you know that Johnny is still well and happy. No I am sorry to say that I cannot report all ok as my knee has been causing me quite a bit of pain and does not seem to get any better. The doctor wants to take me off the front for a week and send me back to the horse lines so that I can give it a rest for a few days. The Lieut. was going to do this but the Sergeant who was to relieve me got called away yesterday so it kind of looks as if Mr. Knee would have to get well right here. I have evidently wrenched it in good shape and you know how nice those feel. The last three or four days have certainly been dead ones around here and time has hung rather heavy on our hands. They have been those wonderful spring days when one wants to get out of doors and roam around or sit in the sun and sleep. But alas we have to stay under cover unless it is absolutely necessary to go out. These are the kind of days when the enemy can pick out our positions from balloons if we are out and around much.

I have had quite a bit of telephone trouble on my hands of late and honest sometimes it seems as if I never would get the fool things to work right. All seems ok until you want to use them and then just as sure as I'm a foot high one is bound to go out on you. If our phone at home does not break down at least forty times a day when I get home so that I can fiddle around with it I will be lonesome I know. And lines - oh yes for heaven's sake teach Buster how to cut them so I can have the pleasure of finding the break. He must be taught to do this late at night or very early in the morning so that my night's rest will be broken. Well it's all in the game but I'll be glad when we get things straightened out once again.

Another pet arrived at the position before breakfast this morning - a big dog - hungry and looking for a place to sleep. Of course our cat got her back up in the air for awhile but they are fairly good friends now but I notice the pup gives way to the cat when entering or leaving the dugout.

I was down in one of the nearby towns the other day on business and much to my surprise and amusement I saw Copley Plaza written in big letters over the door of one of the houses and a little further down the street Winter Garden. Needless to say both of these houses even if they did bear the names of places of pleasure were in ruins but the signs made me laugh and think backwards. You will often see written over a dugout door Villa of - blank - being some funny name.

Flap jacks for breakfast this morning with butter and sugar on them. Oh but they did go to the right place for sure. They have opened up a little store in this nearby town and we are all planning to put in a few francs and buy a few extras. You know they will taste pretty good these days.

The doctor was just here and gave my knee the once over again. He now thinks I have a touch of rheumatism which is fairly common among men living under these conditions. The fellows say it is a slight case of rum-atism with the accent on the rum. He has given me some tablets to take and wants it bathed with hot water twice a day.

Well, Dad, there goes the yell welcome to every soldier's ear - "Come and get it", which means mess is ready so I must close.

Give my love to all the family and keep a lot for yourself.
Johnny

The following letter, or part of a letter, was found detached from the rest of the collection of my father's letters.

I cannot tell who wrote the letter, when it was written or even to whom it was written, but apparently it was sent home by someone in the regiment to someone's parents in Haverhill and it mentioned my father so the letter was passed along to the Hobson family and was saved along with his other letters.

Because of this letter's reference to chalk caves, electric lights and no casualties, I assume it may have been written while in the Chemin des Dames sector. The letter reads as follows:

The horse lines where I am now are some 10 - 20 miles behind the lines. The battery is then taken up to the front lines, and the rest of the men and horses stay back. This does away with all unnecessary transportation of food, etc.

We left yesterday to go up to the battery at 4:00 and after passing within view of the German line for some little way, arrived at about 6:00. It is a very secure position built into the chalk caves and in a few days we will have electric lights. I wish I could say more but I can't. I saw all the men in the battery and they all are well, no casualties or wounds of any sort (even if you hear rumors of them).

John Hobson is looking like a young giant. His eye is just as bright and his courage is gaining day by day. He was showing me over the position and one or two shells whistled overhead. I wanted to duck but John said, 'Oh! They are not coming this way.' And he was right. John bade me goodnight and said he was off to an observation post for 48 hours with two men to adjust, if need be, the battery's fire and what's more he went underground [through trenches] for all of the two and one-half miles and in perfect safety.

Haverhill will have cause to be proud of her men when they get back and they'll be men and not boys, believe me. Men who can hold responsible positions.

According to the Regiment's History,

On March 9 considerable firing was demanded of the regiment. There was great hostile air activity between 21 and 23 o'clock. The hostile air activity which has been mentioned as occurring on March 9 continued for several days. It was accompanied by considerable night bombing. On March 12 the brigade headquarters in Crouy were subjected to a severe attack by German bombers. As a matter of fact, the Boche airmen bombed Soissons and its vicinity quite steadily during our stay there.

Dearest Sister

There is much work to be done today but there is no use in starting in to do it until I drop you a few lines. The war can either go on without me or stop until I finish this letter to my happy, engaged sister.

Your letter and Mother's arrived in the same mail telling me of the announcement and for the past four days I have done nothing but live with you and Marj in your new happiness. I have read and reread both of those letters, telling of the dinner, more times than any other two I ever received. Why, Sis, the night I got them I was just as happy as I would have been had it been my own engagement which was announced. Gee, Kid, for a while that evening all of France with its war could not down my joy. Happy was no name for me but strange as it may seem all through all my happiness ran a little stream of loneliness. Yes, dear, I must confess I felt a bit lonesome. Every time I read one of those letters I just let my fancies go and in my mind's eye I could picture the whole thing - yes, even to seeing you and Marj. One thing, however, was lacking, I could not taste the eats. Instead of eating all that nice fancy food which I used to enjoy so much, Johnny on the night he heard of his sister's engagement ate baked beans. Well, Sis, those good old Army beans tasted just as good to me that night as the rich food would only there was not table or decorations. I wish Ev and George had been with me and I would have given them a party neither one would have forgotten in a hurry. When I do see them again I'm going to, if we are in a place where we can. Oh why, oh why, aren't you girls over here to have it with us. Well, I'll give another when I get home. My only prayer and hope now is that your two lucky men may return very soon.

There was another thing in those letters which set me right up on my high horse and that was Art's making a frat at Exeter. It seems almost too good to be true. That boy certainly is making good at the old school. My only hope is that his success does not turn his head as it has so many men who have made frats and done great things at an early stage of life. Well, Kid, I guess you will soon take it out of him if it does, just the way you did out of another young man I have in mind. Why shouldn't I have felt happy over those letters? I guess old long legs will have to move some to keep up to his brothers and sisters who certainly are moving right along. Now for what I have been up to. I almost dare not tell you after all your interesting experiences. Well, dear, my experiences, whereas they are of a very different nature than yours, nevertheless, hold out a great charm for the young man who seeks adventure and thrills of a far different type than social doings.

A few days ago, as luck would have it, I had occasion to visit a city near here on business. Pleasure and business, of course, go hand in hand when you're interested in your work and especially when the surroundings are new. The city was somewhat down but nevertheless, there was much of interest to see. I was with another sergeant who knew the place and we sure did do that place up right. There was a private who talked French we took along with us to do the talking for us. Lunch, now there is something that will interest you all. It costs too blame much to eat at a hotel so we went out and bought our own food and took it into a very nice French woman who cooked it for us. Now for what we bought, and we ate it all or rather, all we could before we had to leave which was at one o'clock as the place closed then. Gee, but it did hurt me to leave those last few mouthfuls of food we had left when one o'clock came. Dinner for three, not civil people but Uncle Sam's fighting boys, who certainly can eat. Don't call us pigs now but say, "Well, the boys must have enjoyed themselves."

3 lbs of steak
6 lamb chops
6 big orders of French fries
12 boiled eggs
1 lb of butter
2 orders of bread
2 bottles of wine

That was the lunch that three of us ate. Just imagine eating one pound of steak each. We went into the city on horseback and left the animals in a knocked down churchyard while we went around. Now, for heaven's sake, don't have that menu put in the paper or they will think we have gone nuts over here.

I must tell you about the weather we are now enjoying. It reminds me of some of those wonderful days we used to have at Rye the first of September. The boys can now work in their shirtsleeves and we are turning in one of our sleeping blankets. Just imagine March weather like that.

Mail has been coming in by the wholesale for the past three days and the reports are that there is a lot more still to be given out.

Well, darling, I guess if I ever intend to get any work done this morning that I had better close and get to it.

There is no need to say that I am feeling fine after telling you all I ate a few days ago but I will say that I am very happy and your joy and Art's has made me even more so.

Lots of love to all and heaps for yourself.
Johnny

P.S. Saw Kid [the horse] last night for the first time since I have been up to the front. She's looking fine. Gave her Mother's message.

Somewhere in France
March 17, 1918

Dear Art

Most of my Sunday letters go direct to 129 Arlington Street, as I feel that that is the most central point, but this Sunday I am going to change my range a bit and shoot one up to Exeter. You can take it home with you the first Saturday you go, or send it so that the rest of the family may read the weekly news. I wish I could write to each of you every week but my Uncle Sam says "No" and since his word is law you people will have to abide by it as well.

Well, old man, Mother and Sister write me that you were the lucky receiver of two frat bids this winter. Let me congratulate you and say that you did something your older brother couldn't do in his three years at Exeter. He didn't even get one say nothing of two. Frats are for the chosen few and I am mighty proud to hear that my brother is one of them. I have also heard about some of the other things you have been up to and, judging from all reports, I should say that you were making quite a name for yourself at the dear old Academy. It's just great, Art, and pleases me more than you realize to hear that you are doing so well. You surely have good cause to be proud but don't let pride turn to conceit. Stay with it, old boy, and remember that whatever you do pleases me as well as the rest of the family.

Now for a little bit of advice, which is so easy to give but not so easy to follow, especially during these days. I have heard from several people that the war spirit, which is so fast spreading over America, has taken quite a grip on a good many of the men at Exeter. You, yourself, must have felt a lot of it and felt just like throwing up your schoolwork and joining the khaki clad boys in France. I don't blame you one bit, Art, and know very well if I were not already here I should want to do the same thing but, remember, you are only sixteen and, whereas you are large for your age, I want you to wait until you are at least eighteen before you even try to enlist. We all hope by that time, if not long before, that the war will be over but if it isn't, you will have plenty of time then to serve your country over here. Lots of us have the mistaken idea that war is all fame and glory and, so it is for some, but the road is a hard one and you want to let at least two more years creep away before you try to walk down it. Please now, Art, for my sake, if not for your own, wait. Let life take its own course. You're making more than good at home so just forget war and live a peaceful life where you are for two years.

This is the funniest game I ever tried to play in my life. I had the idea that war was fighting, day and night, until you dropped but, thank goodness, I find it is not, at least not where we are. Why, I have seen two wonderful spring days roll by and not so much as twenty rounds fired. We just sat around and enjoyed ourselves the same as we would at home. Then we will get a few days of Hell when we have to keep ducking every few minutes. Oh, it surely is funny and I have often tried to figure out just what the big idea is, but have given it up as a bad job.

There is one sight I wish every one of you at home could see, from Mother and Dad right down to Buster if he could stand the noise, and that's a barrage at night. Art, it is wonderful and the first one I saw I shall NEVER forget as I was lucky enough to take part in it. Everything outside is still with the possible rattle of the cartwheels on the road and the machine guns popping away every little while in the trenches. Then all of a sudden, as if the door to Hell had been opened, every hill for miles around seems to be alive. One flash of a gun is followed by another and, during these flashes you can see men hurrying to their posts, each one eager to be the first there. While it lasts you can hardly think straight until you get used to it but just as suddenly as it started, it stops and peace and quiet prevail again. It is during one of those that a man realizes what a small part of Uncle Sam's great Army he and his outfit really is. When fun like that starts your old heart just seems to beat a mile a minute, your hand itches to kill and your teeth come together in grim determination and you don't care what happens to you, just so long as the banging keeps up. Oh, it's wonderful, Art, but an awful strain on your nerves. I have been through more than one and I LOVE it.

I have not seen Ev for ages nor heard a word from him except through Percy over a week ago. I wrote him a letter some little time ago, however, and am expecting an answer very soon.

Well, Art, I have some work to do so must close and get busy. There is no Sunday in the Army you know, we work eight days a week.

Please remember me to all the boys I may happen to know at school as well as the profs.

Love to all the family.
Johnny

March 18, 1918

Dear Mrs. Hobson:

I have intended writing you so many times about your boy and to tell you what an older man thinks of John. I have waited until he had traveled the entire distance and had been at the front.

He has never faltered. Many times doing the work of a comrade in addition to his own therefore I feel great pride in calling your boy one of my best friends.

Everett is here with me and is one of our best observers. When this war is all over you are going to be very happy for returning to you will be two sons who have been proven pure gold.

My best wishes to you and your family, especially your Father.

Sincerely Yours,

William H. Root
1st LT 102nd F.A.

OVER THE PARAPET
Robert Service

All day long when the shells sail over
I stand at the sandbags and take my chance;
But at night, at night I'm a reckless rover,
And over the parapet gleams Romance.
Romance! Romance! How I've dreamed it writing
Dreary old records of money and mart,
Me with my head chuckful of fighting
And the blood of Vikings to thrill my heart.

But little I thought that my time was coming,
Sudden and splendid, supreme and soon;
And here I am with the bullets humming
As I crawl and I curse the light of the moon.
Out alone, for adventure thirsting,
Out in mysterious No Man's Land;
Prone with the dead when a star-shell, bursting
Flares on the horrors on every hand.

There are ruby stars and they drip and wiggle;
And the grasses gleam in a light blood-red;
There are emerald stars, and their tails the wriggle,
And ghastly they glare on the face of the dead.
But the worst of all are the stars of whiteness,
That spill in a pool of pearly flame,
Pretty as gem in their silver brightness,
And etching a man for a bullet's aim.

Yet oh, it's great to be here with danger,
Here in the weird, death-pregnant dark,
In the devil's pasture a stealthy ranger,
When the moon is decently hiding. Hark!

What was that? Was it just a shiver
Of an eerie wind or a clammy hand?
The rustle of grass, or the passing quiver
Of one of the ghosts of No Man's Land?

It's only at night when the ghosts awaken,
And gibber and whisper horrible things;
For every foot of this God-forsaken
Zone of jeopardy some horror clings.
Ugh! What was that? It felt like a jelly,
That flattish mound in the noisome grass;
You three big rats running free if its belly,
Out my way and let me pass!

But if there's horror, there's beauty, wonder;
The trench lights gleam and the rockets play.
That flood of magnificent orange yonder
Is a battery blazing miles away.
With a rush and a singing a great shell passes;
The rifles resentfully bicker and brawl,
And here I crouch in the dew-drenched grasses,
And look and listen and love it all.

God! What a life! But I must make haste now,
Before the shadow of night be spent.
It's little the time there is to waste now,
If I'd do the job for which I was sent.
My bombs are right and my clipper ready,
And I wriggle out to the chosen place,
When I hear a rustle...Steady!...Steady!
Who am I staring slap in the face?

There in the dark I can hear him breathing,
A foot away, and as still as death;
And my heart beats hard, and my brain is seething,
And I know he's a Hun by the smell of his breath.
Then: "Will you surrender?" I whister hoarsey,
For it's death, swift death to utter a cry.
"English schwein-hund!" he murmers coarsely.
"Then we'll fight it out in the dark," Say I.

So we grip and we slip and we trip and wrestle
There in the gutter of No Man's Land;
And I feel my nails in his wind-pipe nestle,
And he tries to gouge, but I bite his hand.
And he tries to squeal, but I squeeze him tighter:
"Now," I say, "I can kill you fine;
But tell me first, you Teutonic blighter!
Have you any children?" He answers: "Nein."

Nine! Well I cannot kill such a father,
So I tie his hands and leave him there.
Do I finish my little job? Well, rather:
And I get home safe with some light to spare.
Heigh-ho! By day it's just prosy duty,
Doing the same old song and dance;
But oh! With the night- joy, glory, beauty:
Over the parapet- Life, Romance!

CHAPTER NINE

Toul Sector
The Battle of Seicheprey

"The trouble with the American people is that they are not mad clean through and through. It isn't in most of us to kill in cold blood until we experience as individuals some situation such as I passed through that morning."

SERGEANT JOHN L. HOBSON II

"They just plumb saved our lives."

DIVISION INFANTRY LIEUTENANT REFERRING TO THE ARTILLERY'S ROLE IN STOPPING THE ADVANCE

"Thiers is the honor and theirs the glory."

SERGEANT JOHN L. HOBSON II REFERRING TO THE AMERICAN DEAD FOLLOWING THE BATTLE OF SEICHEPREY

Father did not write any letters home for almost a month, from 17 March until 15 April. During that time, the regiment was being transported a distance of more than 125 miles (201 km) via train plus an extensive march from Soissons to the Toul sector. In this sector, they would experience their first major fight and one of the most intense battles in the Allied defense of the German offensive drive. Much of the fighting would take place on 20 and 21 April during a battle thwarting the German raid on the village of Seicheprey. Also while in this sector, there would be three more brushes with death for my father; one being caught in an artillery barrage aimed at a truck convoy he was on, another where he was blown up by artillery in an observation tower, and the third when lightning struck a communication wire while Father was filling in on switchboard duty during a thunderstorm. The resulting shock, as he described it, sent father "clean across the dugout." Thinking back to him getting hit with lightning back at Camp Curtis Guild in Boxford makes me wonder, what is it with my father and lightning?

Relief troops in the form of seasoned French soldiers were sent into the Chemin des Dames to replace the 26th Division, but the enemy did not let the 26th leave that sector easily. Whether it was the beginning stages of the German offensive that actually came in full force a few days later or the enemy just wanting to harass the division's departure or greet the arriving French relief troops, the Germans sent over a gas bombardment of significant proportion described as being in "suffocating intensity". More than five thousand shells were dropped on the Allies around the Chemin des Dames, mostly containing mustard, hyperite and phosgene gases.

After the intense bombardment of the departing 26th Division's troops, the Germans turned their guns on the city of Soissons itself and they hammered that city day and night for a week. Soissons was destroyed.

Whether the 26th Division was taken out of the Chemin des Dames sector because the offensive was expected and they were thought not experienced enough to stem it or whether their talent was needed in another critical sector is a question that has been the subject of conjecture. Either way, they were not about to become "kanonenfutter" (cannon fodder).

To get to the next front, the 102nd Field Artillery Regiment had 15 days of transport ahead of them, initially by train and then five days of a hard march in cold, raw conditions with constant rain. According to the Regiment's History:

We had spent about six weeks in the Soissons sector when the orders were received relieving us from duty there. On the night of March 19-20 Batteries A, B, D, and E vacated their battery positions and withdrew to their echelons [a rear formation arranged in parallel lines with each line extending to the right or left of the one in front so that the whole presents the appearance of steps], followed on the night of March 20-21 by Batteries C and F, all this preparatory to entrain - again "for parts unknown." The storm which the Allies had been experiencing broke, as we know, on March 21 when Ludendorff began his great offensive near St. Quentin. The Germans, as part of their attack program, shelled heavily at various places along the front and Soissons sector got its share to such an extent that long-range bombardment of the depot at Soissons and Mercin-Pommiers forced the entrainment of our last batteries at Amblenie some 8 kilometers [5 miles] to the west. The entrainment was very well performed and our brigade received commendations from the division commander for the condition in which billets, battery positions and echelons were left upon departure.

The great German drive of March 21 had just started, sweeping over the very positions that the 26th had just vacated, and which the Hun might not have taken quite so easily had the Y.D. [Yankee Division] been there to help their French comrades to receive them. Orders came to proceed to the Toul sector to relieve a French division, which, it was understood, was needed to help stem the German advance. The Toul sector was comparatively quiet but vitally important. Good troops were required to hold it against the possibility of serious attack.

On the battle line north of Toul the Division took over a sector of 18 kilometers [11 miles], the longest that has been held by an

American division on the Western front. The Huns gave them a warm welcome; the arrival was marked by a terrific bombardment which compelled a quick shifting of artillery positions, for the Germans in those days had a very capable lot of airplanes for observation purposes. There followed a long series of actions, some of them battles of considerable proportions. Of these were Bois Brule at Apremont and Seicheprey, the first real battles in which American troops were engaged. The 26th never failed; the Germans had their first real taste of the kind of fighters which the United States breeds and, when aroused, sends to war.

On 19, 20 and 21 March, the regiment entrained at Soissons in 40 hommes-8 chevaux Pullmans heading south.

On 22 March the regiment detrained at Bar-sur-Aube and marched to and billeted in the outlying villages of Saulcy, Colombey-la Fosse and Arrentieres.

On 23 and 24 March, the regiment marched through Ailleveille and Colombey la Fosse where they rested, washed gun carriages and wagons, cleaned harnesses and cleaned up and reshod the animals. Soldiers mended clothes, bathed and shaved.

On 25 March, Battery A marched to and billeted at Marbeville.

On 26 March, they marched to Gudmart via Vignory-Provencheres.

On 27 March, Battery A marched to Doulaincourt via Donjeux and Saucourt. They remained in Doulaincourt for several days.

On 30 March, the columns of the regiment began their march of 30 kilometers (18 miles) to Toul in a cold, drizzling rain. Progress was hampered by steep heights on which the horses struggled.

On 31 March, they marched to Burley la Cote. They passed by Joan of Arc's birthplace, Doremey la Purcelle. That night, Easter night, they arrived at Ansauville where they were welcomed by a mustard gas barrage.

On 1 April, the 1st Battalion marched to Pagny la Blanche Cote where they remained until 2 April awaiting orders.

On 3 April, to expedite movement of artillery directly to the battery positions at the front, certain artillery pieces were pushed ahead to the battery positions on trucks. Sergeant John L. Hobson II accompanied this advance movement in the trucks. The truck convoy was caught in an artillery barrage that night. While the truck convoy raced ahead, the rest of the regiment continued its soggy march to Pagny derriere Borine through the villages of Vannes les Chalet, Blenod les Toul, Mont le Vignoble and Donger.

A year later, on 20 April 1919, after the war was over, my father wrote a letter to his mother reflecting on his experience during the ride in the truck convoy that night of 3 April and the artillery shelling they received while en route. It's okay to fast forward to the Spur Camp chapter and read this letter dated 20 April, 1919. In fact, I recommend it because the letter gives a good account of the action without being hampered by a censor and it tells of another brush with death for my father. But, please come back!

On 4 April, the regiment marched to their echelon positions at Sanzy. Sanzy was located six miles behind the artillery's positions. Sanzy was to be the position of the echelon and wagon lines during the regiment's entire stay in the Toul sector.

On 5 April at 8 o'clock in the morning, command was passed and the regiment relieved the 6th Field Artillery of the 1st Division. The 102nd Field Artillery Regiment would remain in the Toul sector in these positions until 27 June.

During this campaign the 102nd Field Artillery Regiment would be joined by the 2nd Battalion of the 101st Field Artillery, two batteries of the 40th Field Artillery French (Commandant Dieudon) and five batteries of the 247th French Regiment Field Artillery (Commandant Jamet); the 1st Battalion of the 147th

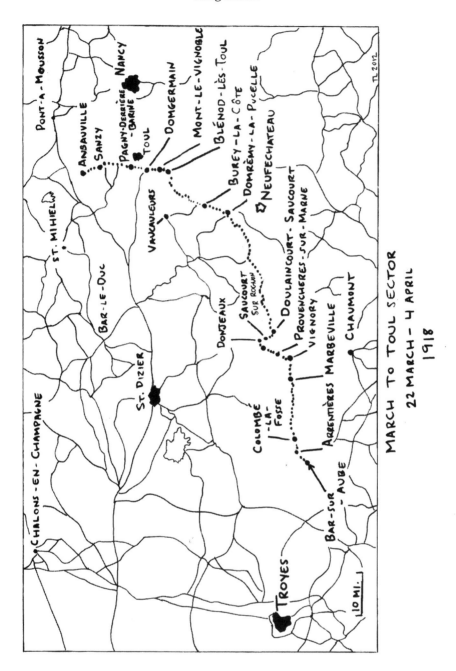

MARCH TO TOUL SECTOR
22 MARCH – 4 APRIL
1918

10 MI.

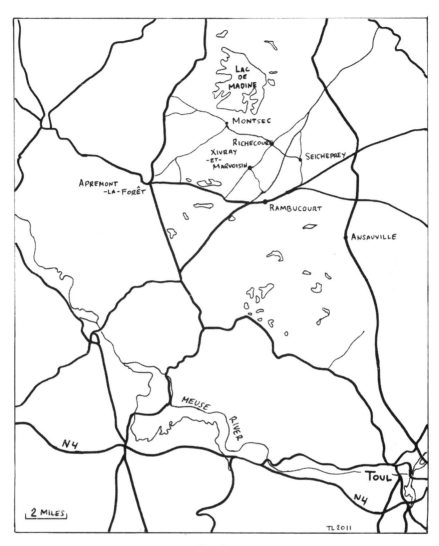

Toul Sector

*Looking across the valley Rupt de Mad from Allied occupied Rambucourt and the Beaumont Ridge,
October 2004. Stephen G. Hobson Collection - Stephen G. Hobson photograph
Across the valley, the Germans occupied the heights of the Cote de Pate (left) and Montsec (right).
It was said that from those positions "the Germans could look into our minds." The villages of
Xivray and Seicheprey lay in the valley between the two heights and the ridge.*

Yankee Division marching to the Toul Sector. 26th Division, A.E.F. Division Histories, Vol. 2

Dead Man's Curve, Beaumont Ridge, April 1918. 26th Division, A.E.F. Division Histories, Vol. 2

Dead Man's Curve, Beaumont Ridge, October 2004. Stephen G. Hobson Collection - Stephen G. Hobson photograph

Battery A positions from behind the west end of Rambucourt, October 2004. The church, destroyed in 1918, was rebuilt. Stephen G. Hobson Collection - Stephen G. Hobson photograph

German artillery shell "breaking" on the church at Rambucourt as seen from artillery positions behind the town - April 1918. 26th Division, A.E.F. Division Histories, Vol. 2

American Air Ace Capt. Eddie Rickenbacker was assigned to the 26th Division's Pursuit Group - Toul Sector, 1918. While there, the Division's Pursuit Group fought Richthofen's famous Flying Circus in the sky over the valley of Rupt de Mad, but the Baron himself had been killed a few months before. Wikipedia

102nd Field Artillery Regiment 75 mm gun crew concealed under fish net camouflage, 1918. History of the 102nd Field Artillery

Field Artillery was brought in for its front-line training, just as the 102nd Field Artillery Regiment had been paired earlier with the French at the Chemin des Dames sector. The artillery units would support the 51st Infantry Brigade.

Aside from the one constant - mud - this sector that had been exclusively occupied by the Allied forces for almost four years was the opposite of the cliffs and chalk quarries of the Chemin des Dames. The whole front was in marshy ground in the lowlands of the lake, Lac de Madine. In many cases, trenches had to be built up rather than dug into the ground. The sector was at the foot of the great plain of the Woevre. To the left were hills that went away in a series of bold shoulders and standing out from the range by itself is the peaked mountain of Montsec.

The Allied position in this sector, across the plain from Montsec, ran along a ridge called the Beaumont Ridge that was south of the valley of the Rupt de Mad. The ridge began to the west at St. Mihiel and extended east through the villages of Apremont, Rambucourt, Beaumont and Flirey.

On the opposite side, to the north of the valley of the Rupt de Mad, was the German's position that faced south and occupied the heights of Cote de Pate and Montsec. It was the dominant position. According to the History of the Regiment, it was said that from that position "The Boche could look down into our minds." In between the lines lay the valley of Rupt de Mad, and in the valley lay the villages of Seicheprey, Xivray and Marvoisin on the Allied side, and Richecourt and Lahayville on the German side. Seicheprey would become the focal point of the battle.

This sector was primarily an area of trench warfare.

The Paris-Metz road ran along the crest of Allied-held Beaumont Ridge. Allied munitions and supplies would come across this road coming up from rear supply positions at the village of Mandres through an intersection just east of Rambucourt that was fully exposed to the eyes and guns of German artillery batteries high on Montsec and the Cote de Pate. The intersection was known as "Dead Man's Curve." This section of the road received considerable harassment by remarkably precise enemy artillery fire. Transporting munitions and material to the batteries over this artillery shell-swept road was precarious.

Battery A was positioned on the Beaumont Ridge in the heavily shelled town of Rambucourt that lay across the valley of the Rupt de Mad directly across from German occupied Montsec.

The Battery's gun positions were set up behind the wrecked town. They had front (active) and rear (silent) positions between which they alternated in order to confuse enemy spotters, conceal gun positions, give the impression of new gun positions in action and simulate a heavier concentration of artillery than was actually present. This roving artillery piece tactic was an ideal use for the mobile French 75s and would be used in future fights for the same purpose.

There were substantial casements built for the forward battery positions located along the Beaumont Ridge which were left by old French artillery positions that had previously occupied this sector. The rear positions, generally in the fields behind the town which didn't have as much activity, were hidden under fishnet camouflage.

In addition to the regiment's 24 French 75s, while operating in this sector the regiment also manned three batteries of 90-millimeter French materiel. The 90s were not as efficient as the 75s but, according to the History of the Regiment, the 90s "…added to the noise, merriment and firepower of the defensive line."

There were "air stunts," dog fights, of Allied and German planes over the valley of the Rupt de Mad that stretched out before them. The aero-acrobatics must have made fine viewing for both sides looking across the valley. Iconic American Air Ace Capt. Eddie Rickenbacker flying a Nieuport or a Spad (Societe pour L'Aviation et ses Derives) aircraft was assigned to the 26th Division's Pursuit Group while in the Toul sector. The Allied pilots in this sector went up against the seasoned pilots of Richthofen's squadron, the Flying Circus. By this time Richthofen himself had been recently killed, but his squadron remained intact and proudly fought on.

To add to the "enjoyment," upon the regiment's arrival the spring thaw had begun and the dugouts had water flowing into them, requiring them to be constantly pumped out just to keep bunks from floating around.

It was in this sector that my father had another brush with death. He and an unidentified First Lieutenant were, from an observation tower believed to have been a grain silo on the Beaumont Ridge in Rambucourt, observing German movements. The observation post was systematically bracketed by German artillery firing for registration and then was directly hit by artillery firing from Montsec. Both men were badly shaken and my father got shell shocked, but both men survived.

The Toul sector was also the regiment's first encounter with mustard gas. They had experienced having other types of gas dropped on them re, but at Ansauville on 31 March, Easter Sunday night, Battery A had its first mustard gas barrage dropped on them.

On 12 April, Private Robert H. Andrews of Battery D was killed at his gun position. He was the first man in the 102nd Field Artillery Regiment killed in action.

The first casualties of the 26th Division in France did not die at the hand of the enemy. As already stated, the first 26th Division soldier to become a casualty of this war was an infantryman killed by friendly fire in the Chemin des Dames sector. The second man killed in the division was an infantryman killed in a gun accident. The third was an accidental bayonet stabbing in an exhibition by a drill sergeant on how to deflect a bayonet thrust. Apparently the infantry drill sergeant ordered a man to charge him with a rifle fixed with a naked bayonet and the sergeant missed deflecting the thrust bayonet with his arm and was fatally stabbed in the abdomen and bled to death. The sergeant's demonstration was not a success. In thinking about this, one might clinically deduct from this the disastrous consistency throughout history of the general behavior of the male of the species when given new toys, especially dangerous ones!

While in the Toul sector, in spite of its periodic relocation, the regimental headquarters was directly hit several times by enemy artillery. On 10 April, the enemy "touched up" Ansauville and put the first shot directly into the Regimental P.C. and a third into the P.C. of the commanding general of the 51st Infantry Brigade. The coincidence led to the suspicion that there was espionage directing hostile artillery fire from villages within the regiment's lines. All were on alert for spies and German sympathizers.

In one instance, a peasant from one of the villages came under suspicion when day after day he repeatedly insisted on sweeping and cleaning one observation post. This man was subsequently caught in the observation post going through maps and was summarily shot in his escape attempt by the man that discovered him, Sergeant John L. Hobson II.

In another instance, upon observing that the hands of the clock in the church steeple in Rambucourt had been swinging in a mysterious fashion, another officer climbed the steeple and had them lashed fast for fear that sympathizers were positioning the hands of the clock to give away strategic artillery positions. During the time in this sector, the regiment also devised a telephone code to prevent the enemy from listening in on conversations at "listening posts."

According to documents that were obtained after the war, the Germans had assembled artillery for this drive in large proportion. With this they intended to teach the American troops new to the Western Front a lesson in terror, or "frightfulness" as the German's referred to it when they terrorized French citizenry, attempting to paralyze them with a fear of their power.

The first signs of the American effort were becoming apparent to the German General Staff. American troops were already located in two or three quiet sectors and they had a sector of their own in the line. It was extremely desirable that "Die Amerikaner" should be given a lesson in the doctrine of frightfulness early in the game. In other words, the Germans thought it would be a good plan to throw a scare into the American troops. They picked out the Toul sector for the purpose and with the German thoughtfulness proceeded to mount an elaborate and powerful raid. This raid was by far the largest and the most serious action in which American troops had participated to date. ... [The Germans] assembled for this lesson in the doctrine of frightfulness, 236 guns, or 16 more guns than the total number of guns used by the Union Army at the Battle of Gettysburg and of far greater power and rapidity of fire. This does not include the 108 trench mortars which brought the total amount of artillery up to 344 pieces or only 48 guns less than the total number of guns in both the Federal and Confederate armies at Gettysburg.

The comparison here to a battle that had taken place during the American Civil War may seem odd, but one has to remember that the Battle of Gettysburg of the American Civil War had taken place only 52 years prior to this time and was still a comparable memory for many living Americans. Battlefield tactics and military strategy used during the early stages of the First World War actually hadn't changed much since the American Civil War.

The operation contemplated an attack over a front of approximately 2,000 meters [1.2 miles] and upon this narrow front the bulk of this powerful artillery was to place its fire. With such a mass of guns opposed to us, we were the recipients of as violent and sustained an artillery bombardment as happened to us during the course of the whole war. At the time we asked ourselves the questions, "Where did he get all those guns?" and "Where in the world does he get all the ammunition for them?" In addition to the box barrage which he put around Seicheprey and along Beaumont Ridge and the edge of Jury Wood his fire fell steadily on the advance battery positions, upon the towns, and swept the roads leading up to the front.

While some of the action started immediately upon the regiment's arrival at the sector, the Germans observing the relief operation and not knowing what the change meant or what to make of it made them uneasy and so they shot up all the roads for good measure. The action gradually intensified and culminated with the massed raid on Seicheprey on the morning of 20 April.

The German raid, operation code name Cherry Blossom, under the German command of Major General von Stolzmann, started on the morning of 20 April and lasted for approximately 24 hours, through the morning of 21 April.

The Seicheprey raid involved hostile artillery in large proportion - as already described - which supported massive infantry attacks by stosstruppen (shock troops) on Remieres Wood and Seicheprey from Lahayville. The attack was led by approximately 3,300 soldiers of the German 259th Reserve Infantry Regiment. Joining them were three companies of the 258th Reserve Infantry Regiment, two assault companies, one machine gun company and minenwerfers of the 14th Assault Battalion with flamethrowers. Additional German forces were the air forces of the 298th Air Detachment (Les Baraques), 64th Pursuit Squad (Mars la Tour) and the 123rd, 214th and 215th Balloon Sections.

At 3:08 a.m., recognizing that the enemy's attack was coming because the Germans had started their artillery "preparations" in the form of a rolling barrage across the valley ahead of their attack, the Allied observation officers signaled to begin their barrage. The enemy also concentrated artillery fire on key Allied positions. Among the places heavily shelled and gassed were the artillery positions in and around the village of Rambucourt. At 5:00 a.m., the German infantry attack came over on the heels of the barrage, following it so closely that many of the stosstruppen became casualties of their own artillery. The initial attacking force was estimated to be 1,200 strong. The stosstruppen were flanked by a battalion of infantry on each side. The mission track of the attack was to go between Remieres Wood and Seicheprey.

Following horrific artillery barrages being dropped on them by the Allies, the Germans finally withdrew from Seicheprey, being ultimately ejected by subsequent hand-to-hand fighting with infantry in the streets.

While there was sufficient ammunition initially placed at all the artillery gun positions, with the sustained intensity of fire, eventual replenishment of the ammunition was necessary in broad daylight over shell-swept roads. The first man from Battery A to be killed in action, Pvt. Melvin F. Rice of Haverhill, and four horses met their fates at the Dead Man's Curve intersection while replenishing the regiment's ammunition-hungry artillery batteries.

When the fighting stopped on the morning of 21 April, the ground in front of the American positions was a killing field and, as is witnessed in the letter dated 26 April that follows, the slaughter apparently made an impression on my father. Dead and wounded Germans were scattered all the way from their own trenches to the American front lines. With the exception of only a few minutes rest, the regiment's guns had fired continuously for seven hours manned by men wearing gas masks, as a considerable amount of gas fell on the forward positions.

In praise of what the well-trained French artillery batteries with almost four years of combat experience could accomplish, it was recorded in "The History of the 102nd Field Artillery" (hereafter referred to as the Regiment's History) that in the thick of the Seicheprey raid, a Groupe of French 75s, after a forced march of over 40 kilometers (24 miles) from a sector east of Pont a Mousson, reported to the regiment as reinforcements.

The French Groupe Commandant, accompanied by his lieutenants, stepped into the regiment's P.C., saluted smartly and asked just four questions: "Les positions? Les missions? Les munitions? L'echelon?" (The positions? The missions? The ammunition? Who's in charge?) The answers received, he left at once and telephoned within the hour that his Groupe was ready to fire!

According to the regiment's journal, at this particular demonstration of efficiency the American artillery officers present, who had just six weeks of combat experience, looked at each other and silently wondered how much practice it took to reach such ability to "shoot the works" with such short preparation time. By July they would know, and they would be doing it themselves.

At 4:45 on the morning of 21 April, the regiment provided a rolling barrage for the infantry's counterattack. The enemy withdrew to its lines and by 6:35 that morning the regiment was notified that the old positions had been reoccupied and to cease fire. The German's offensive raid had been repulsed.

During the raid on Seicheprey, in a little over 24 hours the regiment fired 13,998 rounds of artillery, including the 90s. That's an average of 583 rounds fired per hour. And that was just one regiment's firing statistics. The Germans suffered 1,200 - 1,500 casualties. The 102nd Field Artillery Regiment casualties were four men killed, one officer and 18 men wounded and four men missing who were a liaison detachment in the front line trenches that were captured. The 26th Division's total casualties were 634, which included 150 taken prisoner; 85 men were killed.

It was said by an observer that, after the battle of Seicheprey, a deep calm fell upon the sector. The Germans seemed to have decided that the American troops, whose mettle they had been trying out, were worth leaving alone. Every time they had come up against the Yankee Division, they had been repulsed with larger losses than they inflicted. Also, they had on their mind preparation for the next great offensive, the Second Battle of the Marne, and apparently were now quite content to leave this sector alone.

Sergeant John Lambert Hobson II, along with many other officers and enlisted men of the 26th Division, was cited and congratulated for gallant conduct in this engagement by Major General C. R. Edwards. In part, the citation issued on 13 May 1918 said: The American units "...held their ground; some died in their tracks, but none fell back."

HEADQUARTERS 26th DIVISION
AMERICAN EXPEDITIONARY FORCE

France, May 13, 1918.

GENERAL ORDERS

No. 40.

E x t r a c t

*

*

*

2. At 3:00 o'clock on the morning of April 20, 1918, the enemy opened on our sector in the neighborhood of Seicheprey a violent artillery bombardment from concentrated artillery, which involved all the rear area as well as the trenches and dugouts. Shortly thereafter, under the protection of a heavy barrage and dense fog, he launched a determined and vigorous attack preceded by a force of storm troops estimated at least 1,200, and two infantry Battalions with machine guns, sappers, and pioneer troops accompanied by much material. The enemy made a bold and determined attempt to gain a permanent foothold in that part of our sector.

The engagement lasted well on into the 21st, when the enemy, after a particularly desperate struggle at close quarters was forced to retire without having attained his objective and after being severely punished. The fight, by the very necessities of the case, under the smothering artillery bombardment of shrapnel and high explosives, and a drenching of gas shells, became a struggle of resistance by platoons and smaller units, individuals, and machine gun squads. These units - officers and men - held their ground; some died in their tracks, but none fell back.

The troops engaged in repelling this attack and throughout the battle proved themselves a stout-hearted lot of lads, true to their traditions. On behalf of the 26th Division, I congratulate the following named officers and enlisted men on their gallant conduct in this engagement:

*

*

*

Sergeant John E. Hobson, Battery A, 102nd Field Artillery

*

*

*

By command of Major General Edwards:

DUNCAN K. MAJOR,
Lieutenant Colonel,
Chief of Staff

OFFICIAL:

O. A. STEVENS
Adjutant General
Adjutant

Stephen G. Hobson collection.

Somewhere in France
April 15, 1918

I hope you can read this but candlelight is not the best and the pencil is none too good.

Dear Dad

Once again I am sorry to say that I have let several weeks go by without writing to any of you. Somehow time just seems to fly by with me and a week passes away like a day. I have been on the move every minute for the past month and the time I have had to myself has been very little. You will realize how much I have been kept on the jump when I tell you that about two weeks ago I went forty eight hours without closing my eyes or sitting down for a rest. Oh those were two busy days for me. The last three hours of those forty-eight will never be forgotten either, as it was during then that I passed through my first gas attack. That was Easter Sunday night and, instead of putting on a new bonnet and going to church with Mother, I put on a gas mask and lay in a dugout. That was a night which certainly will never be forgotten. This gas, Dad, certainly is awful stuff if it catches you without your mask with you and ready to put on in a second's notice. All of the men here at the front have to carry them everywhere they go and one of the officers inspects them every few days to make sure they are in good working order. I must confess I am more afraid of the gas shells than high explosives. A high explosive can't hurt you unless you are fairly near where it lands, but these gas babies can get you quite a ways off. It is bad enough to get a piece of shrapnel in you, but the agony you suffer when really gassed is beyond all belief. I do not speak from experience but from what I have been told by men who have suffered both. This mustard gas you have very likely read about, in my opinion is just about the worst. The darn stuff hangs to the ground for hours after the attack is over and still has strength enough to make a man feel pretty mean if he is near where one of the shells hit. If it is God's will that I get laid out in this war I hope that it is not from that hellish gas. I am afraid of it and I am not ashamed to admit it, and the man who does not is trying to fool himself.

The front we are on is a bit more active than the one we came off from and the boys are kept more on the jump. We are all fast learning the greatest game of the world and a few more months ought to see us pretty near experts at it, if there is such a thing. No longer do we duck every time we hear the moaning and whistling of a shell in the air. Our ears have become used to the sound and trained so that we can tell just about how near us that shell is going to land. An aeroplane is no longer gazed at with open eyed interest, and the bark of our own dear little 75s would be greatly missed should they fail to speak to us a few times at least during the day and night. We are getting hardened to it. The newness has rolled away and war has become our business. The louder the noise, the better we like it, and we hate like anything to sleep through a good barrage or miss a good duel.

You may wonder how we do sleep when for miles around the country is alive with noise, but we do, and think no more of it than you folks do of sleeping with the "Arlington Street Flyer" [local passenger train] going by. Why, Dad, we can sleep anywhere and under almost any conditions. A barn with or without hay, a wooden bed with no mattress but lay right on a slat. The floor of a house or any other place we lay our heads at night, spells sleep and rest to us. I know from experience because I have myself slept in all the above mentioned places and enjoyed my night's rest just as much as if I was in my own little white bed at home. No, a year ago I couldn't have done it, and couldn't now very likely if it was not a case of have to. Dry or wet, dirty or clean, Johnny is just as happy. This great game has got me heart and soul and whereas I have suffered a few hardships, yet I love it. It may seem strange to you folks and yet I guess you will understand what I mean when I say that any place I hang my hat is home sweet home to me these days.

My work on this front is a little harder than it was on the other as we have not enough men to do all the things there are to be done. Outside of my regular work of running my detail I am personally taking an eight-hour shift on the switchboard along with two of my men who also do eight hours each. I go on at 6 p.m. and come off at 2:00 a.m. By taking these night hours I am able to attend to most of my daily work and still get a fair amount of sleep. Work on the board is very interesting when there is something going on and the calls are coming in thick and fast, but oh, how dry when all is quiet. The man on the switchboard is at the center of everything and all phone connections of course have to pass through his board if they are for the battery and also some which are not. Last night we had a thunderstorm while I was on duty and Johnny got a shock which sent him clean across the dugout. No harm done thank goodness. We have had quite a lot of trouble with our lines here and my poor linemen certainly are getting their share of work. I have a fine Corporal in charge of all the lines and he has taken a lot of that responsibility off my hands. A trained man surely is a great help around here.

Speaking about lines makes me think of Mother's dream. The night she had that dream all was O.K. but the night I got her letter telling me about it I was having my troubles with the blame thing for fair. Gee that was an awful night too. Now for the big laugh.

Johnny has fleas or body lice whichever you wish to call the little animals. All the detail has them and if there is any member of the gun crew who has not, I want to see him so that I can loan him a few of my family. I hate to see any one left out you know. The following ditty has been made up about our dear little pets. Sister will know the tune to sing it to if you don't.

"They run wild, simply wild over me
Those funny little things they call French fleas
Every time I take a nap
They get drunk on cognac
They run wild, simply wild over me."

There are other poems dedicated to them but I don't remember just how they go so I will not try to write them. It's funny but the joke is not easily seen at night when we want to sleep and they start having races up and down our backs. Even the officers have them just to keep up with the styles.

About having a picture taken of the battery as Mother wants, I am sorry to say that it is out of the question for the present anyhow. In the first place we are rarely all together and if we were there would be no one around this Godforsaken part of France to take it. If the chance ever presents itself however, I will try to have it done.

The only officer we have with us now who left Boxford with the Battery is Lieut. Langdon. Lieut. Pitman is with us but of course did not leave the States as one of us. The rest are all new men. I wish I could tell you just how things were run and explain what I mean when I say that the Battery is rarely all together, but I fear I would be treading on military matters about which we cannot write.

Well, Dad, the calls are beginning to come fast and I have to stop so often to answer them that I guess I had better stop altogether. Please give my love to the grandparents, as well as all the family.

Lots of love for yourself.
Johnny

Dearest Mother

There really isn't any news to tell you but as I have a few minutes to myself I guess I will have a little chat with you by mail. Several weeks went by a short time ago when I didn't have a chance to drop you people even a post card, so now we must make up for lost time. Life still flows along in the same old way, full of excitement and interest but, curse the luck, we are not allowed to write about many of those things. I should think my letters would be pretty dry reading but I always try to get something into each one which will interest you all. I don't know what that something is going to be in this letter but it may come to me as I write.

First of all I want to tell you how my thoughts have wandered towards home of late. You would naturally think that as time goes on my thoughts of home would become less and less as I become accustomed to it. Such is far from the case, however, and now more than ever before I find myself lying awake for a few minutes every night dreaming of you and home. Those certainly are happy minutes too, Mother dear. Spring somehow seems to make me long to get back to you all once again and yet at the same time, as I wrote Dad, I love this game. The picture of the family I brought with me I had to leave in my barrack bag when we left from the front and I have only had one chance to look at it since and that was only for a few seconds. I did, however, see your picture in the paper a few nights ago dressed up in your cooking clothes. Mother dear, you look just about twenty years old there, and were you not my own mother I could fall in love with you just as Dad did.

You folks are always interested in my health so I guess I had better say just a few brief words about it. I'm feeling fine but find that this life is telling somewhat on my nerves. There is nothing to worry about because no man can go through all I have and not feel some strain on his nerves. I love the noise, I love the excitement of the front and must say that when I leave it all for a day of business behind the lines I miss it. A few days ago I was forced to take a trip back a ways on some wiring work we are doing and dropped into a barn, where the Salvation Army has a store, for a cup of hot chocolate. Well Mother, all was quiet, I only had one of my men with me and I believe that for the first time since I was sick I relaxed. Every care in the world seemed to vanish, there was no one wanting to know this, that or the other thing and what few brains I have got seemed to stop whizzing and figuring and I felt as carefree as a school boy. Of course it couldn't last long as I was working on a fairly big job, which had to be done in about two days whereas it would take anybody but Uncle Sam at least five days to do it and it was up to me to make every move and minute count. I surely can appreciate now what a quiet house and room must mean to dad at night after a busy day. Up to the time I was made Sergeant I never had anybody to figure for but my sweet self but since then I have often wondered if anybody in the U.S. Army ever figures things out but Johnny. They do, of course, but they never fail to give me my full share of it.

Yes, I understand Paul Woodman was very near us at one time, that is to say the place where our horses were and most of the Battery. Several men told me he asked for me but I was at the front with the firing battery at the time and could not get away. When I returned to the horse line it was late at night and we pulled out for another place early the next morning. I wish I had seen him and will keep my eyes open.

Speaking about a rest as you did in one of your letters caused me to smile. It has got to be almost a joke with all of us now and anyone who has the nerve to mention such a thing at once gets the ha, ha. Here we have been in the service over a year and in France eight months but no signs of a rest nor even a day off. The chances have looked pretty good once or twice but some hurry call always seems to come and rest vanishes from sight. We are all working like dogs both day and night and I must say that I shall be very much surprised if they do not give us all a good day off when we come off this front. We certainly deserve it. There is a rumor around that the whole 26th Division has one big surprise in store for it next month and real rest would certainly be a surprise. We're over here to work, not rest anyhow but you know that old saying "All work and no play makes Jack a dull boy." Well, put two and two together and I fear we will get dull. When we are trying to figure out what else it might be I take the joy out of life for some by laughing and telling them we're going to another front where we are to catch the worst hell we ever got and the surprise is that wine is to be served with each meal. Naturally no one believes me but I do love to see the expression on some of their faces and hear the arguments which follow.

I had a nice talk with Lieut. Langdon yesterday and he told me some interesting home news which Marj had written in her letters. No one thing especially but news which had not been in your letters and interested me. I told him what I had heard from Haverhill and we then talked the war situation over a little enjoying a good laugh at each other for being so muddy and dirty looking. He looked like a king side of me but not the way he did when at Boxford. Neither of us know just where Ev is nor have we heard from him for some little time. I hope to find time to write him before long. I suppose I'll meet him some one of these fine days when I least expect it.

Here's a little bit of news that I wish you folks would keep right in the family as I do not know how it is going to turn out and until things do happen I had rather the public should know nothing about it. Every so often, as I guess perhaps you know, one or more men are picked from each battery to attend some school, where, if they complete the course successfully they receive a commission. Well, dear, last month I was to be recommended for the man to go from Battery A but, alas, I would not be twenty one when the course was up hence could not be commissioned. One of the other Sergeants went. More men are to be sent again, however, and one of the Lieuts. said that by then I would be old enough and the Sergeant who would probably be sent. This is only a dream which seems almost too good to be true. Lots of things can happen between now and the time that next bunch goes, but if all is O.K. I guess I will have my chance. I have not even got my hopes up but it is kind of nice to know that your work has been noticed and that you are considered good enough for advancement. That made the second time I have been forced to wait just on account of my age. I certainly would like to come marching back to you as a commissioned officer. These schools are mighty hard I understand and I might not be able to pass once I got there but I surely would make one awful try. Don't expect anything but, at the same time don't be surprised if something like that does happen. Please now keep that right in the family.

I have looked all around to try to find a place to send you a cable but have had no luck. Every town anywhere near us is, of course, pretty shot up and the only people you see in them are Uncle Sam's fighting boys. If I ever get into a whole town again, however, I will try to get one off to you.

Just imagine it, Mother, I have not seen a woman for land only knows how long. If I ever saw one around these parts I swear I would run a mile, thinking she was some angel sent from heaven. Someone tried to tell me the other night that girls are taking pies, etc. to the "dough boys" in the front line trenches and it may be true but they stay away from the artillery. The girls themselves would look pretty good to me, but bring me, oh bring me those pies. I swear, Mother, I'm going to be a regular joke when I get home every time I go to a dance. Honest, I won't have any idea how to act.

I am very much interested in these "get together meetings" the families of the Battery are having. I would like to walk in on you all some night and just say "hello" and tell you all how things were going over here. I believe you are reading each other's letters from the different boys so you ought to be getting about all the news.

That's right - I knew there was one thing which I wanted to be sure and remark on in this letter and that is the three wonderful letters I received from Art a few days ago. Talk about fine, well they surely were beyond words, and the English he used made me think he was at least twenty two - twenty three years old. It was great. If Exeter ever taught me to write English like that it surely did something for me. That boy certainly is coming right along.

Well, darling, I guess I have written about enough for this time so I will close.

Please give my love to all the family and keep a lot for yourself.
Johnny

Dearest Mother

I have a few more spare minutes to myself this afternoon and not feeling like sleeping have decided to have another short chat with you folks at home. There is more news to tell you today than there has been since my arrival in France but, curse the luck, I can only tell you about one half of it. Well, half is better than none, so here goes.

First of all, right off the reel, I am going to try to answer your question about my looks these days. It is no easy job for a man to describe himself and especially one in my position who has not seen his own face in a mirror for ages.

I do know this, however, that I am still the same old awkward six footer that left home last September. Yes, I think I have put on a little more flesh but as to weight I cannot say. You see there are no scales around these parts to jump on whenever you want to. My hair is running wild, this I know as I forget to comb it except on rare occasions and my steel helmet raises cane with it. My face is fast clearing up, however, and this to me is a godsend. Of course the old trouble is not all gone but is so much better that I doubt if you would know me. Mud and dirt are to be seen on me at almost all times but they never hurt a man yet. Now for a bit of news that will interest "K".

As I sit here writing there is the dearest little kitten I have ever seen on my shoulder purring away as if all the world were at peace and she had nothing to worry about. This cat we found at the position when we pulled in and ever since has been a friend to us all. She sleeps at the foot of our beds, eats the same mess we do and is just as good a fighter as any of us. She has no fear at all of shells but like all the rest of us seeks shelter when they come too fast. Why, the little animal even has fleas like us and joins right into our scratching parties. She differs in just one way and that is a serious one. Uncle Sam failed to issue her a gas mask and the other morning we got caught in an awful gas attack. Ever since she has been coughing badly but continues to live and seems to be getting over it. We were going to use her for our air tester, but when this attack did not kill her we decided we were out of luck and would have to test the air ourselves. When we leave here I am going to try to pack Miss Pussy in my saddlebag or stuff her into my English gas mask.

Good old Mary, how I wish I could see her right now and ask her to bring me another plate of oatmeal. She certainly did look after my many wants when I was home and I will not forget all of her little kindnesses in a hurry. Please remember me to her and tell her that I shall expect to see her cheerful smile around the house when I return. I guess I won't be quite as fussy about little things at the table as I was before I left. [Mary was the family's cook]

Now, Mother dear, I want to turn from the light and gay side to the dark side of this war which must be faced by all of us. You and Dad have a boy "over there" and he does not want to write home letters that are going to worry you but the truth must come out and very likely will have been rung all over the city by the time this letter reaches you. There is no more cause to worry than there ever was, only facts were brought a bit nearer to home and your son last week. As you very likely know by this time, darling, the battery has taken part in her first BIG battle and I might say right here has covered herself with glory which will go down in history. Luck has been with us up that never-to-be-forgotten morning and we had lost no men. That day some of our brave lads had to fall and they did so fighting for a wonderful cause. I know the news of their death must have caused worry among all who have sons over here with the battery, and it is only natural that it should but, darling, I want you and Dad to forget that there is such a word as worry. It's hard I know but it's the only way we live happily these days. It was one awful fight, dear, and the things that I saw as dawn broke and the feelings that I experienced are things that I hope no other member of our family will ever have to pass through. The feelings I couldn't describe while the sights are too awful to write about. Every one of us who passed through that fight are changed men and the hell and awfulness of it will go through life with me. You who are at home can never realize it and after it was all over I threw myself on my cot and thanked God that you never would. The trouble with the American people is that they are not mad clean through and through. It isn't in most of us to kill in cold blood until we experience as individuals some situation such as I passed through that morning. I was so mad that the tears just rolled right out of my eyes and had duty not held me with the Battery I fear I would have been with the "dough boys" cutting men down with cold steel. I can't write any more about it as I begin to boil over every time I think of it but I do want to ask you all at home to bow your heads and offer up a very humble prayer for those brave lads who lost their lives that morning. Theirs is the honor and theirs the glory. We who are here must fight on and on to the final victory and when it is over we will pay our respects to them but for the time being we must push on and forget.

I suppose by this time Dad has started to think of his fishing trip. How many rods have you got stored away in your closet this year? I wish you could send over some of your fish but I fear they would not keep.

Well, Mother, I guess supper is ready so I had better make my way to the kitchen.

Please keep what I have said about the fight right in the family as those few lines are personal and I had rather they would not go outside.

Give my love to all the family not forgetting Mary. Lots of love for yourself.

Johnny

P.S.
Your Necco candy arrived O.K. but I have forgotten to thank you in my letters. Please send some more if you can get them.

FAITH
Robert Service

Since all that is was ever bound to be
Since grim, eternal laws our Being blind;
And both the riddle and the answer find,
And both the carnage and the calm decree;
Since plain within the Book of Destiny
Is written all the journey of mankind
Inexorably to the end; since blind
And mortal puppets playing parts are we:

Then let's have faith; good cometh out of ill;
The power that shaped the strife shall end the strife;
Then let's bow down before the Unknown Will;
Fight on, believing all is well with life;
Seeing within the worst of War's red rage
The gleam, the glory of the Golden Age.

FUNK
Robert Service

When your marrer bone seems 'oller,
And you're glad you ain't no taller,
And you're all a-shakin' like you 'ad the chills;
When your skin creeps like a pullet's,
And you're duckin all the bullets,
And your green as gorgonzola round the gills;
When your legs seem made of jelly,
And you're squeamish in the belly,
And you want to turn about and do a bunk:
For Gawd's sake kid, don't show it!
Don't let your mateys know it-
You're just sufferin' from funk, funk, funk.

Of course there's no denyin'
That it ain't so easy tryin'
To grin and grip your rifle by the butt,
When the 'ole world rips a-sunder,
And you sees yer pal go under,
As a bunch of schrapnel sprays 'im on the nut;
I admit it's 'ard contivin,
When you 'ears the shells arrivin',
To discover you're a bloomin' bit o' spunk;
But my lad, you've got to do it,
And your God will see you through it,
For wot "E "ates is funk, funk, funk.

So stand up, son; look gritty,
And just 'um a lively ditty,
And only be afraid to be afraid;
Just 'old your rifle steady,

And 'ave your bay'nit ready,
For that's the way good soldier-men is made.
And if you 'as to die,
As it sometimes 'appens, why,
Far better die a 'ero than a skunk,
A-doin' of yer bit,
And so- to 'ell with it,
There ain't no bloomin' funk, funk, funk.

Somewhere in France
April 28, 1918

Dear Dad

Just a few hasty lines this morning to let you know that your boy is still well and happy. There is not much news but I know a few pages of writing from the front will please you even if news is lacking to some extent. I understand that you are very anxious for me to send a few cables every now and then. Just as quick as I get off of the front, Dad, I surely will make it a point to get one off to you, if there is a place anywhere around where we go to do so. Up here on the lines it is of course impossible but we are going back for a rest before long I believe, and then will be my chance.

We have had a lot of these dark half rainy days of late and the ground is covered with that slippery coating of thin mud. It is really quite an art for one to stand up and of course Johnny had to lose that art last night as he was crossing a ditch and fell head over heels into the mud. No serious harm done, however, except I managed to give my left knee one awful bang.

Water has become another very important factor around here. It flows into some of our dugouts like a river and the only way the gun crew has been able to sleep at all is to have a man work on the pump all night to keep it from running into their bunks. This was bad enough but when the one and only pump we have here broke they found themselves out of luck for fair. They now have to use a pail which makes it slow, hard work. The dugout I am in has very little water in it but a plentiful supply of mud. Those who have been to the front line trenches with messages say we are the lucky side of the "dough boys" who are living in three times worse places than we are. Well, it's all in the game, so why worry?

Rumors are flying around this part of the country so blame fast these days that I find it hard to keep up with them. "Where do we go from here, boys?" is the question before the house every night. A two months trip followed by a long sea trip is the latest and is growing stronger every day. Home is being talked of daily, while every night after mess a crowd of us gather in the kitchen and talk over by-gone days and try to picture Haverhill and the changes which must have taken place since we left. Yes, I must admit the whole Battery is tired and the strain on our nerves is beginning to tell. The whole division has done some wonderful work and now we all long for a few weeks of quiet rest and a chance to clean up. No one is kicking however, and we all have a smile for every day.

There is one little item about the awful battle which took place here, which I referred to in Mother's letter, which I forgot to mention and may be of interest to you all. Johnny, along with his whole detail, and the gun crew got cited that morning by the commanding officer for extreme bravery under heavy artillery fire of the enemy. Our names were all sent to the general and he is to act upon them as he sees best. What he will do we have not as yet found out but we will all get honorable mentions at least if not more. We did no more than our duty but that in itself was no easy matter to perform that morning with instant death staring you right in the face at any minute. It was a wonderful morning, Dad, for our battery to show just what kind of boys she was made up of and her boys proved to be real honest men with a fear for nothing but God himself.

I have had an awfully hard time to get that paper you sent me some time ago, about Grandma Gale's Will, registered as we have been on the move or on the front ever since I received it. I did, however, manage to get it off a few nights ago by one of the drivers who brought supplies up to us and received a note from the battery clerk last night saying that it had gone. I am sorry the delay was so long but under the conditions it could not be helped. If you do not receive it within a reasonable length of time please let me know and I will look into it.

By the way, Dad, has my money which I allotted to you been arriving all right? You should be getting fifteen dollars ($15.00) from Washington every month and if you are not I should like to know it so that I can have the pleasure of jumping on someone over here. Since that money is coming out of my monthly pay, I want to be sure that it is going where I told them to send it and not anywheres else.

Listen, Dad, when you get a few more spare minutes in Boston I wish you would send me over some more candy. We long for sweets almost as much as we do cigarettes and they are hard to get at times, especially at the front. I have to run into the kitchen every day or so and tell the cook what a hell of a good scout he is and how much I enjoy eating his meals so that he will give me a piece of bread THICKLY covered with sugar to feed my sweet tooth with. He always gives it to me and if my line of soft stuff is good enough he puts a little butter on also. I claim a man is pretty badly off when he has to do this to get a taste of sweets. I am hoping the box Grandma Hobson sent me will arrive before long as I know that will contain candy or cake.

I should judge from some of the letters I have received from Mother that you and she were getting quite sporty in the absence of your oldest son. A week at the Touraine with theaters in the evening sounds good to me. I wonder if I ever will be roaming around in the gay lights again with some nice little girl hung on my arm the way I used to a year ago last winter. If those girls could only see me now - mud from head to foot and a pair of rubber boots on. I fear they would say, "He may come out alive but he'll never look the same." Well, Dad, I'll fool them all someday, I'll go in one door looking like a bum and come out the other looking like a gentleman. I don't suppose Sister has dragged you to many tea dances at the Copley this winter, has she? Dear old Dad, how you did hate those.

Summer is fast approaching but as yet none of you have said what your plans were. I suppose it is a bit early yet but be sure and let me know what you are planning on, when you start.

I have not seen Lieut. Langdon for some time but hear his voice over the phone every day. He is just a little ways from here, still with the battery. George Croston seems to have disappeared off the map and I have neither seen nor heard from him for over two months. I suppose we shall all meet again in some rest camp. Maybe there won't be some swell parties pulled off if we do ever all get together again. I swear, Dad, if I ever see Ev again it will take more than one café to hold me.

Oh, Yes, I have got a most pleasing afternoon coming to me today. A few pleasing moments with the dentist. I have got a couple of teeth which need filling and one which he wants to pull out. He has just about as much chance to pull that one out as he has of winning the war. I know he can fix it if he wants to and I'll be hanged is Johnny if going to lose a tooth just because a dentist is too lazy to fix it. I told him words to that effect yesterday when he looked at it and he said, "Well, we'll see." You just bet he will see.

I received a fine lot of cigarettes from Mr. Atkinson yesterday and shall write him a letter the very first chance I get. Your business friends, Dad, certainly have been good to me since I have been over here and I certainly appreciate it. It will be a very happy day for me when I can sit down to lunch with you and a few of your friends at Young's again. I certainly did enjoy those hours as well as the meals we used to eat at that hotel together and they cannot come back any too soon for me. Please remember me to Mr. Bailey and Jim when you see them again which I trust will be very soon if you have not changed your habits.

Well, Dad, I guess I have bored you about enough for this trip so will close.

Give my love to all the family and keep a lot for yourself.
Johnny

On The Wire
Robert Service

Oh God, take the sun from the sky!
It's burning me, scorching me up.
God, can't You hear my cry?
Water! A poor, little cup!
It's laughing, the cursed sun!
See how it swells and swells
Fierce as a hundred hells!
God, will it ever have done?
It's searing the flesh on my bones;
It's beating with hammers red
My eyeballs into my head;
It's parching my very moans.
See! It's the size of the sky,
And the sky is a torrent of fire,
Foaming on me as I lie
Here on the wire…the wire…

Of the thousands that wheeze and hum
Heedlessly over my head,
Why can't a bullet come,
Pierce to my brain instead;
Blacken forever my brain,
Finnish forever my pain?
Here in the hellish glare
Why must I suffer so?
Is it God doesn't care?
Is it God doesn't know?
Oh, to be killed outright,
Clean in the clash of the fight!
That is a golden death,

That is a boon; but the...
Drawing an anguished breath
Under a hot abyss,
Under a stooping sky
Of seething, sulphurous fire,
Scorching me up as I lie
Here on the wire... the wire...

Hasten, O God, Thy night!
Hide from my eyes the sight
Of the body I stare and see
Shattered so hideously.
I can't believe that it's mine.
My body was white and sweet,
Flawless and fair and fine,
Shapeless, from head to feet;
Oh no, I can never be
The thing of horror I see
Under the rifle fire,
Trussed on the wire... the wire...

Of night and of death I dream;
Night that will bring me peace,
Coolness and starrys gleam,
Stillness and death's release:
Ages and ages have passed-
Lo! It is night at last.
Night! But the guns roar out.
Night! But the hosts attack.
Red and yellow and black

Geysers of doom upspout.
Silver and green and red
Stare-shells hover and spread.
Yonder off to the right
Fiercely kindles the fight;
Roaring near and more near,
Thundering now in my ear;
Close to me ,close... Oh, hark!
Someone moans in the dark.
I hear, but I cannot see,
I hear as the rest retire,
Someone is caught like me,
Caught on the wire... the wire...

Again the shuddering dawn,
Weird and wicked and wan;
Again, and I've not yet gone.
The man whom I heard is dead.
Now I can understand:
A bullet hole in his head,
A pistol gripped in his hand.
Well, he knew what to do,-
Yes, and now I know too...

Hark the resentful guns!
Oh, how thankful am I
To think my beloved ones
Will never know how I die!
I've suffered more than my share;

I'm shattered beyond repair;
I've fought like a man the fight,
And now I demand the right
(God! How his fingers cling!)
To do without shame this thing.
Good! I'm ready to fire;
Blame me, God if you will,
Here on the wire… the wire…

Dear Art

We have just finished giving the Huns one of our early morning barrages and all is peaceful along the front once again. The boys have all gone back to bed and I sit here alone with my thoughts waiting for more calls to come in over the wires. I guess I will wait too because there is rarely anything going on much before eight and I turn in at six. Well, we were pretty busy for about an hour so will call the morning's work done and turn our thoughts toward home.

So you and Sister are really going to have an auto to fool around with this summer when Mother does not want to use it. Well, Art, I am glad to hear it. It will do Mother a lot of good to be able to get out for a ride afternoons and will give you something really worthwhile doing in keeping the car in good running order and driving for her. Sister ought to get her share of fun out of it and it certainly will be a help to Dad to have one of you drive him to the station every morning and meet him at night during the summer months. I wish I was going to be there to take my turn at the wheel but there is lots of time coming. Be careful now, Art. Remember a fellow with a car is very apt to break some nice little girl's heart. I won't say a word if it is only one girl's heart you break but if I ever return and find you have them all after you and have not left even one for me there is going to be war right away. Be sure and send me a picture of the car when you get it and I want to see you all in it.

You spoke in your letter of April 13 how small and valueless the work you were now doing seemed beside the tasks which might be put before you were you a little older. I refer to your desire to come over here and drive an ambulance. Well, Art, the further you go in life the stronger that feeling will get until you yourself overcome it. We all think the other fellow has the best most important job and feel that ours is small and useless side of his. I have been the same way myself and often feel now that the gun Sergeants are better off than I am and that their work is far more important than mine. But such is not the case at all by any means. They are helpless to fire unless I keep my lines open and it does me no good to keep them open if the gun Sergeant has not his crew and gun ready when the order comes to fire. They go hand in hand. We cannot all be sergeants nor can we all be over here fighting. Some must remain at home and keep that end of things up and it is just as important, so don't think for a single minute that your work either on the crew or as next year's hockey manager is useless. If you were here your work would seem just as small side of what others are doing and so it would be in one way but remember old man that we cannot expect to take the big positions until we have shown to those higher up that we can handle the smaller ones. It is better to start low and work up than to start high and fall. Your work has pleased me to such an extent that I have told several of my personal friends about it with a great deal of pride. Stay with it and remember your older brother is heart and soul behind you.

Gee it seems as if we fellows never would get a rest but that we were booked to stay right on the lines until the end of the war. We hear that we are to be relieved on such and such a date but those dates come and go but we remain in the same place. Well we can not stay here forever that's sure and we are all hoping that our roaming will start again before long.

These wonderful spring days we are now having make us all long for Boxford once again and life in an open tent instead of a dugout. Dances, suppers by the pond and happy Sundays spent at Rye with the folks returning to the tent at night for a good sleep in the open air are a few of the things I long for these days. Dugouts are all right for a while but they are small and the air is poor.

Well, Art there really is no news to tell you except what I have written Mother and Dad and of course you will read their letters so I will close.

Please remember me to all the boys and profs I know.

Lots of love,
Johnny

The following was sent by Benjamin Pitman, 2nd Lieutenant of the 102nd FA, to Arthur Hobson, Sr. as an explanation of the handling of the Battery Fund.

Somewhere in France
May 9, 1918

My Dear Mr. Hobson

Your cablegram to George Langdon did not arrive until after he had left the organization on his return trip to America. It was forwarded to me, and I have followed the instructions contained therein, and in a cablegram to the Mayor of Haverhill have repeated the request made a week ago in my wire to Mrs. Pitman.

Just at present there is not a single officer with the battery that has any connection with Haverhill. I am with the Bicycle Headquarters and near enough to get to their "echelon" every few days, so I think that the best plan will be for me to handle it for them. The present Battery Commander, 1st Lieutenant Harold Morrison, has the remains of the original Battery Fund and the Haverhill Fund in his possession. There is still quite a little left of these, but not enough so that we have dared to spend it as we felt that it was needed, lest we run into a really serious situation and be caught without enough to pull out with. We talked it all over and decided to ask for more, knowing that the people of Haverhill would gladly give many times the figure we named if they could know how much it meant to the men. I will try to give you an idea of some of the situations that we run into and of the uses to which the money will be put.

When we are on the march, for example, we often arrive at our billets late, and leave at a very early hour next morning. The animals are usually terribly tired and hungry. Once in a while the forage fails to arrive, or we get a short ration of it. Then the battery that can dig down and buy enough hay and grain in the village to give the animals a feed is in a far different and happier position next day than the battery that starts off with the beasts still all in and weak from hunger.

Again, when on the line, the operation of the guns and their crews with the telephonists in positions up front, the horses, caissons and wagons in the echelon are effected. The work is grueling, as John has probably told you. The hours are uncertain and there is always two men's work for every man to do. Under these conditions food assumes an importance that we should have been amused at in civil life. The issue food is mighty good, no complaints from the artillery as to quantity or quality, but the lack of variety makes it sometimes tiresome. Then if we feel that we can buy eggs, and jam and cereals, and cocoa, and other things like that, it just about adds 100% to the men's mess, and reacts on the spirits of the men in about the same degree. All the armies have discovered that this is true.

Then there are many, many things that we cannot get from the QM or the Ordnance Dept. when we need them. Over and over again the officers have chipped in and bought things that we simply had to have at once, candles, rope, flash lights, batteries, ordinary things that you never think of until you're up against it, good and hard, and can't get along without them.

These are examples picked at random from various phases of our existence, but I believe that they will serve as illustrations.

A cablegram from my mother says that $800 has been sent already and that the remainder is being raised. Up to date I have not heard of its arrival in Paris, but have written to Salen and Schroeder, our agents, to see if they have received it. They are also helping us in the Regimental Fund, and I believe that it will be more convenient to use them as agents for the Battery Fund than anyone else. I have suggested that the money be cabled to them and deposited in the Bank of France, or the Guarantee Trust Co., and that arrangements be made so that the Battery Commander, or one of the other officers, can draw on the fund by check as it is needed. If the officer in question becomes a casualty or is ordered away, I believe that we can arrange it from here to have another take his place, by doing it through Salen & Schroeder, who will be personally known to the bank. Please let us know how you feel about this and what arrangements are made.

I wish I could write you about all the boys in the battery and let all the people back home know what a magnificent change has come over the whole organization since we have been really in the thick of things. It is making men and soldiers out of us all. Paddy Hughes is the best "Top" in the regiment, and is one old timer who has come through for 100% in this show. Hazeltine is invaluable, a fiend for work and simply full of snap and efficiency. Cronin is doing a mighty good job and so is little Bob Hurley. John has done splendidly with the special detail, and they have done some very fine work under pretty stiff conditions. It is not easy to go out and repair lines at night with gas and flying metal in the air. Back at the echelon they have had some wild times too. Every night rations and ammunition goes up and the drivers, out on the open roads, have the roughest job of anybody in the battery. I shall never forget the night of the battle of Seicheprey when we rode over 65 kilometers and got gassed and shelled until we were almost too exhausted to notice either, nor again the night when poor little Rice was killed. It is all very thrilling and wonderful, but it seems horribly unnecessary. Let us hope it will soon be over.

With kindest regards to all your family, and a message to the auxiliary that we appreciate thoroughly the way in which they have responded to our call.

Very sincerely yours,

Benjamin Pitman
2nd Lieut. 102nd F.A.

Somewhere in France
ON ACTIVE SERVICE WITH THE
AMERICAN EXPEDITIONARY FORCES
May 12, 1918

Dearest Mother

Your long and interesting letter of April 21st arrived this evening along with two from Sister, one written on the 16th and the other on the 22nd. Also one from Art dated the 19th. Needless to say all of these were more than welcome to your soldier boy who at all times longs for news from those near and dear to him at home.

Arthur's letter contained a picture cut out of the paper showing some "Mass. men resting on way to Aisne Front." That was the rear end of our battery and several of the faces of our boys are very plain. Had the picture man only moved back a little ways you would have seen Johnny proudly standing at his horse's head with the detail lined up two and two behind him. Mrs. Houle sent Sergt. Houle a picture which she cut out of some Sunday paper which shows the battery on the march with Al riding along as big as life. Get her to show it to you if she has not already done so. Many pictures were taken of the battery that day including a movie. If this is ever sent to Haverhill be sure and see it as I was caught by the camera several times. It shows the battery detraining and Art's picture shows us on the way to the Abby where we spent our first night in what is known as the first zone or the war zone. I hope that movie comes to Haverhill as it shows almost all the men as well as the guns, horses and ruined buildings.

Speaking about horses. News was brought up to me by one of the drivers a few nights ago that they had to shoot my horse - Kid. I'm glad I was at the front and not back at the horse lines because I never could have stood by and seen her shot. I thought the world of her and she would follow me around like a dog and would throw her head around in a playful way every time I came near her in the picket line. I took a great deal of pride in her and if you could only have seen her hold her head up and dance when I was on her you would think she was proud of her rider. Not only did I ride her all winter and care for her but she carried me throughout a road hike last March on which the whole regiment made a record yet to be beat for covering the greatest number of miles in the fewest days. All the detail were crazy over her and many a night I have had one of them come up and ask if they might not ride her to water. I always cleaned her myself if possible even if the rule is that no sergeant shall clean his own horse but detail one of his men to do it for him and when I was too busy to do it myself lord help the man who did if he failed to do a good job. Well the old girl's gone now so I will have to look up another one but - there's no love like your first love. We never owned a saddle horse like her and I never expect to find another her equal. Any child could ride her at times and at others she was a handful for any man. I have used up a lot of space writing you about her but I've spent some of my happiest hours over there with her and believe me I shall miss her when I return to the horse line.

Your description of the parade in which you all took part was of great interest to me, especially where you spoke of the people saluting the Red Cross flag and your realizing the sacredness of your work. Mother dear you only realize half of it. You cannot realize it all until you have seen some of their work over here. It's too wonderful for words. I have talked with men who have been wounded and taken to the large base hospitals where women working for the Red Cross have cared for them as only a woman can. Doing all in their power to take the place of a mother during the soldiers suffering without the least thought of themselves. One boy was telling me of an "Angel of Mercy", as we call the nurses, who cried and even knelt down and prayed by the bedside of one of her patients who died from shell wounds. We who must face these shells and cold steel can do so with much lighter hearts when we realize that the flag with the Red Cross on it is behind us to care for our wounds when the battle is over. The work starts at home and grows greater and greater as it pushes its way forward on the "Field of Honor."

It also doubly pleased me to hear that dad has found time or I guess I ought to say made time to take a personal interest in all this military work. His work and yours along these lines are coming over here to me in almost every lot of mail that arrives. After reading their letters almost every time someone will come up to me and say, "So and so writes me that Mr. or Mrs. or both Mr. and Mrs. Hobson have done this or that" and oh how my chest swells and grit to do what is right takes a hold of me every time I hear these things. A pride I never knew I had before comes to the surface. Mother dear you and Dad have found your way not only onto the hearts of the battery boys' friends at home but into the hearts of many of the boys themselves whom you have merely seen at Boxford but have never met. Just for an example of what I mean let me tell you briefly what took place tonight. Three or four of us were sitting around in a dugout with water over our ankles reading our mail by the soft light of a candle which was before the switchboard. All was still except for the drip of water coming in the door and we were all busy reading our letters and smoking one of dad's cigarettes when one fellow says, "Listen to this boys" and read the following from a young lady friend of his in Haverhill. "Mrs. Hobson whose son is a sergeant in your Battery came up and spoke to me the other night at a meeting. She certainly is one of the most pleasing women I ever hope to meet and if her son is like her and doing the work in the battery she and Mr. Hobson are doing here he must be doing more than his share and a credit to the battery." I do not know the young lady nor did you up to that time but your work darling is known throughout the city and even beyond to the shell torn fields of France. Proud, why dearest it makes me throw my head in the air just to think I am your son.

Now a few words about your dreams of what you referred to in your letter as hearing in your slumbers. We have heard the same thing talked about and retalked about it by candle light and the dying ashes of the field range but - how much there is in it remains to be told by the beautiful future. Many things point that way just now and before this letter reaches you I imagine you all will have seen and talked with Lieut. Langdon and perhaps Capt. Morse. But many things point the other way also so there is nothing to do but live and hope. We have done wonderful work over here and the 26th Division is well known throughout France and should be by the Boche.

Many of the boys are wearing service stripes now which are gold and look something like this... After six months of foreign service you are entitled to one and one every four months after I believe. I have not got mine yet nor have any of us who are in the firing line.

Mud and gold do not go well together so we are waiting until we come off the front before we get ours.

Oh yes, Mrs. Pitcher wanted to know about Karl. I have not seen him for over a month as his work is at the horse lines sending food up to the front but I will send a note to him tomorrow night by one of the drivers and ask him about mail. He brought the ration cart up one night himself but I was out on the lines when it arrived so did not see him. He is all OK and happy from all reports.

I am awfully sorry to hear of Herman's disappearance. Keep up your hopes as he still may be alive and only a prisoner.

My knee is much better and I can now walk as I used to before I fell that night. It looked bad for a time and a hospital looked pretty near but luck was with me and I pulled it back into shape right here without losing a day's work.

I wrote sister a short time ago and asked her to be sure and send Hope some flowers for me on graduation day - also enclose a card. I hope that letter reaches her in time but if it does not please send the flowers and explain their delay.

I am very tired due to lack of sleep and the conditions we are living under. My sleep is broken and has to be taken any old time work will allow. We have not had our rest camp yet but are still hoping. That's the place where Johnny will make up for lost time as well as all the rest of the battery.

Well darling I must close and pump some water out before the men on the lower bunks float away.

Love to all and lots for yourself.
Johnny

Dearest Mother

At last after almost two solid months of service on this front I find myself back at our horse lines. My but it does seem good to be away from the roar of the guns and the strain of being on the firing lines. We are only about five miles back of the lines but living conditions are far better and there is some chance for pleasure such as band concerts etc. I never realized I was so tired but now I must confess I am having a reaction after all I have been through. I feel well but oh so tired and worn out. My nerves have relaxed and after a few more days of half rest I hope to feel like my old self again. One poor boy came back last night and went to the hospital this morning ready to drop from work but Johnny is far from that stage yet.

Last night five real true American girls right from the U.S. came to town and gave us a show consisting of songs and funny stories. Another lot are due Saturday night. The band plays almost every night and I would not miss hearing it for the world. I just lay under some tree with a few other men smoking my pipe, watching the sunset and dreaming of home. War seems thousands of miles away at these times but all one has to do I raise his eyes and look out across the fields to the road and he will come out of his dreams and realize there is still a war going. Slowly winding along that road he sees the long line of teams drawn by mules and horses on their way to the front with food and ammunition for the boys. There they go standing out like a picture against the setting sun but you can rest assured that it will be Mr. Moon and the stars who will guide them when they reach the true front. Those who have never gone down that road cannot realize what waits behind those hills nor the romance and thrills that those drivers will experience before they return early the next morning. I have only been back here four days but every time I see that line going out a funny feeling seems to creep around my heart and it seems to say "Take me back to the lines again." Strange as it may seem I am really homesick for the firing lines with its lure of adventure for all who have been there. When I watch that line going out and one by one sinking from sight behind a hill that poem written by Service often comes to my mind which I like so well "The Lone Trail". Read it Mother if you have not already done so and at the same time picture those wagons passing by on their way forward. Every noon when the drivers of our Battery get up they are asked a thousand and one questions about the health and welfare of the boys up front. This never wears off although our teams go up every night yet every morning those questions are asked and re-asked. It's the same at the front. Every night when the team arrives a small crowd will gather about it and inquire what the news is at the horse lines. The men's love and interest in each other cannot be appreciated except by those who have seen it.

I shall never forget my first afternoon back here. I slept until ten not having left the front until eleven and arriving here about two a.m. Questions came so fast I could not answer them while some new men who had just arrived over here and been sent to the battery looked at me as much as to say "Oh if I had only had his experiences." Nothing seemed too good for me and men I had not seen since I went forward greeted me with warm and hearty handshakes especially Jim the cook. It seems the boys had been kidding him for several days that I had been taken prisoner and he had believed it and was quite upset. When he saw me appear in the mess line that noon his face bore one big smile and he asked how I got away. I had heard of the joke before but didn't have the heart to carry it on. Poor Jim surely does get made the goat of about every joke going.

Well I suppose by this time you all have seen Lieut. Langdon and heard some of his experiences over here. He wrote me a fine letter from Paris bidding me good-bye. My knee was troubling then a great deal so I could not get over to say good-bye. I'm so glad for his sake as well as Marjorie's that this chance came and now my only prayer is that "Ev" may get the same before long. I have not seen the old boy for almost four months now but am mighty anxious as I have lots of things to talk over with him and want his advice on one or two matters. Capt. Root is expected to visit us before long and he may be able to advise me as to what steps to take on certain things but "Ev" is the man I should like to see first. Things have changed in the battery since we left home as I guess Lieut. Langdon has told you and the future looks rather funny to me. We all are studying it, especially the sergeant, and with politics and pulls working both for and against you it is up to us to keep awake and see that nothing is pulled over our eyes while we slumber. Hence I have been up on my toes and keeping my eyes wide open for a long time. I know now what I want and find that in order to get it I have got to fight for it or I'll never get it while conditions are as they are now. It's all in the game and Johnny can play it just as well as the rest and intends to. George does not know my plans I don't think but he does know the conditions. If he has not told you what they are all this will sound like Greek but I guess he has. It's a wonderful life and I have learned a lot I never knew before.

My hay fever has not troubled me a bit as yet and I rather doubt if it does just so long as we are around these parts as it is fairly wet.

Oh yes, Mrs. Pitcher was telling sister that she had not heard from Karl for a long time. The very first thing I did when I arrived was to ask him if he had been writing home regularly. He said he had - in fact he said he wrote every week so the trouble must be in the mail service somewhere. He is in fine condition and looking better than I have ever seen him look before. Please tell Mrs. Pitcher that she does not need to worry about him as all of his work is back here and there is no danger here unless an awful attack is pulled off and there is not much danger of that.

By the way Mother, do you folks take or buy the Saturday Evening Post? If not for heaven's sake do so. There are some wonderful articles in them about this war and they are true. In the last one I received was an article entitled "Dirty Work on the Cross Roads" and oh how true and vivid that brought out the feelings of the drivers and what they have to face at times. I have spent many happy minutes reading these stories and living them at the same time.

The Citation I wrote dad about a little time ago resulted in all of us who were at the forward position receiving a very fine letter from the General. I wish I could send mine home as I am very anxious to keep it but there are things in it which are not allowed to go through the mail.

Oh yes, oh yes, the pictures you and sister sent me. Mother they were foods for a heart hungry for home and those he loves. Sister has changed or else that funny little hat she had on made her look different. She looks older but just as pretty as ever. In the one where she and Mary are together I didn't know which was which for a minute. They look enough alike to be sisters if two girls ever did. I see that Mary still has that loving smile of hers. The pictures of myself were mighty good but I think the one where I have my hat off and holding my pipe flatters me. The dear old street at Boxford brought back fond memories of happy hours while the one of Dad and I even if I could not see his face brought back to my mind a day I shall never forget. It was taken the last Sunday I was home just as I was starting off to say good-bye to grandma and grandpa Gale. Dad went with me and that walk down to 112 Main Street with him was a glad one and yet a sad one. I remember neither of us said a great deal but somehow I could feel his heart reaching out for mine and mine for his in a way neither of them had ever done before. Then came the good-bye to dear grandma and as I leaned to kiss her I realized only too well that it was for the last time. Oh how often my thoughts have turned towards her since then and that good-bye. She seemed to understand. I often feel now that she is looking down at me from those heavenly gates above and wonder if my deeds are pleasing to those eyes which wet with tears looked up into mine that day. I now am anxious to receive some pictures of the rest of you so please hurry them.

I have not had a letter from Dad personally for a long, long time and am wondering if his letters have been lost or if he has been too busy to write. If the latter please tell him that he must take the time as I am anxious to hear from him. I know I have been over here a long time but my love for home and mail has not died a bit but grows stronger as the days go by.

Well darling I guess I have written about enough for this time so will close.

Please give my love to all the family and keep a lot for yourself.
Johnny

CHAPTER TEN

The Million Dollar Raid

*"The 'captives' consisted of one small, undersized
German who apparently did not have wit enough to find
his way home with the others when they
withdrew from their trenches."*

HISTORY OF THE 102ND FIELD ARTILLERY

This action was described in the Regiment's History as:

The next event of special interest to us was the "Million Dollar
Raid," so called because of the large amount of ammunition which
was expended on that occasion. This raid was planned to take place
in the vicinity of Richecourt [Located northeast of Seicheprey],
with the objective of wrecking the Boche trenches and dugouts and
capturing prisoners. The artillery plan included a short but very
violent preparation, a box barrage around the raided area and certain other gas shoots and fires of neutralization. Two hundred and
four guns were assembled in the sector for this purpose. Five batteries of French 75 portees of the 247 French Field Artillery, some

batteries of the 103rd Field Artillery (the 155-howitzer regiment of our brigade) and some French 120s, were the additional guns which were put into our regimental grouping. H hour was at 2:30 on May 31.

On the nights of May 24 and May 25 and May 25 and May 26, Battery A changed position, putting two guns in the forward position 372 and two guns in the silent position of 376. This brought all of the 1st Battalion into one group.

The raid was well planned and was pulled off exactly according to plan. The Boche was too alert, however. He had learned from past experiences in the war that if men are left in the trenches when a well planned raid is sent against them with good artillery support it is almost certain they will be penned in by the box barrage and many will be killed or captured. His plan of action evidently was that at the first signs indicative of a serious raid against any portion of his line his advance troops were to immediately withdraw from their trenches, leaving the raiders to romp in them as they pleased.

This was exactly what happened. The trenches were found deserted. The "captives" consisted of one small, undersized German who apparently did not have wit enough to find his way home with the others when they withdrew from their trenches.

On June 16, the enemy attempted his last raid while we were in the sector. It was directed against the village of Xivray. [Xivray is a village located north of the position of Battery A and Rambucourt.] The raid was repulsed with heavy loss to the enemy. In this action our regiment had a chance to do some very effective shooting, most of it being done by the 1st Battalion as the raid occurred in its zone of action. The Boche tried to duplicate the Seicheprey business in the town of Xivray. He attempted to come from the east and went into Xivray with an assaulting force of about 500. Meanwhile, he put a box barrage about the village to hold off any counter attacks.

A strong artillery preparation, although not as heavy as the Seicheprey one, began at 3:05. The fire fell on all known battery positions, much of it being gas. Our batteries were not neutralized for an instant. The guns were served by the men in gas masks and, although our telephone wires were repeatedly cut, they were rapidly repaired during the course of the action. Our barrage came down promptly and cut up the enemy very badly as he attempted to follow his own barrage into the town.

The attacking enemy party on Xivray consisted of 399 Landwehr troops, 200 Bavarians, 80 storm troops, 40 pioneers and 20 men carrying flammenwerfer.

On 19 June, at 2:30 in the afternoon the regiment participated in a "gas operation" with the purpose of an attack in the Bois Sonnard. The result was not known but it must have done something to annoy the Germans because they responded with a concentration of explosives and gas (not mustard) up and down the line. Apparently the gas operation had an unintended result of disrupting a hostile raiding party of 60 Germans who had planned a raid between Beaumont and Jury Wood. Two officers were killed and 21 prisoners taken. Obviously peeved, that afternoon German artillery fired for registration on Rambucourt in anticipation of a larger "show" they planned for that night. After firing several bracketing rounds, at 3:43pm they landed an artillery shell directly on the observation post (OP21) in Rambucourt that was manned by Sergeant John L. Hobson II and a Lieutenant. Having identified the location of the muzzle blast of the German artillery that was firing from across the plain, the regiment's 90 mm batteries on the Beaumont Road in Rambucourt answered and opened up on that German artillery position that fired the shot from Montsec and the German artillery position went up in a flash and smoke.

The Million Dollar POW, Richecourt, 31 May 1918. "The small, undersized captured German without wit enough to find his way home with the others." 26th Division, A.E.F. Division Histories, Vol. 2

1914 drawing of the silo that was OP21 in Rambucourt that was hit by German artillery.
Stephen G. Hobson Collection - Colette and Bernard Carle Photograph

Where OP21 once stood in Rambucourt on the Beaumont Ridge, October 2004. Note the view
from the silo's position across the Rupt de Mad at German positions on Montsec and
Cote de Pate. Leaning up against what was in 1918 a stone wall in front of the observation tower
(OP21) and is now a cinder block wall is where my father wrote his letter of 30 May to his
father. Stephen G. Hobson Collection - Stephen G. Hobson photograph

MY FOE
Robert Service

A Belgian Priest- Soldier Speaks:
Gurr! You cochon! Stand and fight!
Show your mettle! Snarl and bite!
Spawn of an accursed race,
Turn and meet me face to face!
Here amid the wreck and rout
Let us grip and have it out!
Here where ruins rock and reel
Let us settle, steel to steel.
Look! Our houses, how they spit
Sparks from brands your friends have lit.
See! Our gutters running red,
Bright with blood your friends have shed.
Hark! Amid your drunken brawl
How our maidens shriek and call.
Why have you come here alone,
To this hearth's blood-spattered stone?
Come to play the ghoulish brute.

Ah, indeed! We well are met,
Bayonet to bayonet.
God! I never killed a man:
Now I'll do the best I can.
Rip you to the evil heart,
Laugh to see the life-blood start.
Bah! You swine! I hate you so.
Show you mercy? No! ... and no!

There! I've done it. See! He lies
Death a-staring from his eyes;
Glazing eyeballs, panting breath,

How it's horrible, is Death!
Plucking at his bloody lips
With his trembling finger-tips:
Choking in a dreadful way
As if he would something say
In that uncouth tongue of his...
Oh, how horrible Death is!

How I wish that he would die!
So unnerved, unmanned am I.
See! His twitching face is white!
See! His bubbling blood is bright.

Why do I not shout with glee?
What strange spell is over me?
There he lies; the fight was fair;
Let me toss my cap in air.
Why am I so silent? Why
Do I pray for him to die?
Where is all my vengeful joy?
Ugh! My foe is but a boy.

I'd a brother of his age
Perished in a war's red rage;
Perished in the Ypress hell;
Oh, I loved my brother well.
And though I be hard and grim,
How it makes me think of him!
He had just such flaxen hair
As the lad that's lying there.
Just such frank blue eyes were his ...

God! How horrible war is!

I have reason to be gay:
There is one less foe to slay.
I have reason to be glad:
Yet - my foe is such a lad.

So I watch in dull amaze,
See his dying eyes a-glaze,
See his face grow glorified,
See his hands outstretched and wide
To that bit of ruined wall
Where the flames have ceased to crawl,
Where amid the crumbling bricks
Hangs a blackened crucifix.

Now, oh now I understand.
Quick I press it in his hand,
Close his feeble finger-tips,
Hold it to his faltering lips.
As I watch his welling blood
I would stem it if I could.
God of Pity, let him live!
God of Love, forgive, forgive.
His face looked strangely, as he died,
Like that of One they crucified.
And in the pocket of his coat
I found a letter; thus he wrote:
The things I've seen! Oh Mother, dear,
I'm wondering can God be here?

To-night amid the drunken brawl
I saw a Cross hung on a wall;
I'll seek it out, and there alone
Perhaps I may atone, atone...
Ah no! 'Tis I who must atone.

No other saw but God alone;
Yet how can I forget the sight
Of that face so woeful white?
Dead I kissed him as he lay,
Knelt by him and tried to pray;
Left him lying there at rest,
Crucifix upon his breast.
Not for him the pity be.

Ye who pity, pity me,
Crawling now the ways I trod,
Blood-guilty in the sight of God.

Dear Dad

You never know where you are going to be sent is a sure thing in this Army game. Here I was back at the horse lines when I last wrote Mother figuring on ten days or two weeks change from the lines but I had only been there five days when down comes the order for me to return to the front for observation work. Orders were orders so tired as I still was Johnny had to roll up his roll and set out for the land of romance and adventure once again. Just what was in store for me I did not know but it was with a light heart and half closed eyes from lack of sleep that I rode back to the firing battery. There was a Corporal with me and there being no extra bunks when we arrived at the position the Corporal and I found a bed on the ground in an empty ammunition arbi [shelter]. There I slept from one a.m. until about two thirty when the Boche drove both of us out with a few well-placed shots. We found a safer place in the kitchen for half an hour then returned to the arbi again where we slept until ten a.m. After storing away a breakfast of rice, karo, coffee and bread we made our way to the other end of town where the observation is. Oh, oh, what a life I have been leading since - lots of rest in the way of sleep and plenty of shells but mighty interesting work. Three hours a day Johnny looks through a pair of powerful glasses out across No Man's Land and into the land of the Huns. It is the duty of the observer to watch the roads of the enemy, keep tabs on the balloons and locate any Batteries he can. Dad the sights I have seen through those glasses is worth my trip over here. I have seen the enemy moving about and this afternoon was called up to direct by phone the fire of one of our Batteries. For half an hour or more I watched their shots fall and ordered what changes I saw fit. I wanted to see the problem through as I had one direct hit to my credit and was getting the fire under control but a lieutenant came in so I turned it over to him. He said my shots were well placed which pleased me very much as I had never directed a Battery's fire before and had been firing on what I had picked up from those higher up. I have learned a lot about this old Army game since I have been over here and now am anxious to get a chance to go off to some school over here and get the fine points. Odds seem to be against me just now on account of my age and one or two other reasons I will not go into here. Well I will be of age before many more months and then my turn may come.

I had a fine long letter from "Ev" a couple of nights ago and he seems happy in his work but anxious to get back from the rear to the front. I saw Capt. Root Sunday and he said "Ev" was looking fine. Capt. Root himself never looked better and seems much happier in his new work. He always keeps a fatherly eye over the battery and often sends up cigarettes.

Right now I am sitting by the side of the road in front of an observation house with my back against a high stone wall. All is peaceful but from all reports I should judge that there was a little party on for tonight. You would never suspect it though to see the boys fooling in the street.

I spoke in one of my letters about the wonderful sight it is to see a barrage at night. Well there is an evening barrage of a bit different nature which is also interesting and funny. The boys are the guns, rocks are the shells and rats are the enemy. Every time we see one someone yells barrage and everyone grabs a rock and lets go at Mr. Rat. Up to date we have killed two and injured five. Not bad for our human battery - hey what? The rats in this dugout have no fear of human beings and even before the last candle is blown out at night they start in to run around. They are large enough to use for draft horses and the other night hitched one up to one of my boots and pulled it half way across the room. They keep some of the boys awake but I'll tell you right here it will take more than rats running across my feet to disturb my slumbers or keep me from going to sleep.

Oh yes - I had my first real bath for two months about a week ago. All of my clothes were put through a steam process at the same time which killed all the coo-coos. Just imagine two or three hundred men running around a town square nude and you will have a picture of the way it looked while these coo-coo baths were going on. Yes I will admit female faces were not to be seen as this town was on the front. Now I am wondering when I will get my next chance to really take a bath.

Say Dad you ought to see the raid the American boys make on the beer cases every time any comes to town. Three or four wagon loads come to one place and in half an hour you can't buy any for love nor money. The water here is none too good and the boys sure do go for that beer. I have seen the day when we couldn't get water and had to buy light wine to drink. These towns around here have overdrawn their supply of hops by a good deal so you can imagine what a great demand there is for beer.

I wrote Mother about the death of Kid, my horse, but think the letter got lost. Yes the poor old girl is gone and I am sorry. She died of lockjaw caused from being fed while hot. It seems one of the boys at the horse lines rode her up to the front one afternoon and fed her just as quick as she got in. I never hope to get another horse her equal but let's hope I land a good one when we leave here. There was one horse who was a real pet and I took a lot of pride in her. She would follow me like a dog and when she turned those big eyes of hers on me a feeling went around my heart like no girl has ever sent - as yet.

We are all anxious to hear what kind of a reception Lieut. Langdon received upon his return. Of course it was a peach but I want the detail of it. "Ev" wondered, aside from Marj, which family was the most eager to see him and also added that he wished he and I might steal in upon you all for a few hours. Well Dad this war can't last forever and someday we'll enjoy that grand and glorious feeling of meeting again after months of separation. I guess we both will have enough to tell each other over our after supper pipes while the smoke carries all cares away and we are happy with each other again. I long for that day just as much if not more than you do and I know it cannot come too soon for you. It was pretty hard on all of you when I left but you will be doubly repaid for your sacrifice when Johnny comes marching home. And even if God should claim my soul while fighting for those I love you will have your reward. Just read some of Service's poems and see the pride a father feels whose son gave up his life for his country. Death means nothing Dad if after you are gone the world is forced to say, "There was a man. He saw his duty and he did it forgetful of self and the price." It's being disabled for life from gas or wounds that we fear. Well Dad as you told me one of those last nights at Boxford, "You're coming through it all right, but I hate to think of what you have got to go through." And now you must forget what I am passing through because it is not as bad as you and Mother may picture. It is Hell at times but those stages I just look forward to my home coming and the "H" seems to be knocked out of Hell. We are all living for that day and it is bound to come.

Dad, the interest you have shown this past winter in the war work around Haverhill has pleased me an awful lot. It must have taken a lot of your time and thought but it was more than worthwhile. We may have guns and all that over here but the boys cannot fire them unless you are all behind us. Your work has put new life and hope into me and I face battle knowing that my father is behind me in both actions and words to the very last.

I suppose when you receive this letter the gay summer season will be just about opening. The golf links will be filled with a different set of men I guess this year as most of the younger men will be over here but I hope there are still a few left to give Jean, Josey and Marj a good time at the dances. Step off a few with them yourself for me. Maybe I wouldn't like to drop in for one evening of dancing. Well let's hope and pray I'll be there next summer if not before.

There goes my call "come and get it" so Johnny must close and eat.

Please drop me a few lines Dad as I am anxious to hear from you.

Lots of love to all and lots for yourself.
Johnny

Dearest Mother

Just a few lines from your boy this morning with the hopes that they may reach you on or about your birthday and may help as best they can to make the day a happy one. Gifts from me are out of vogue just now but all the love and kisses in the world go across the deep blue ocean to you from your soldier boy on your birthday especially.

Somehow I never can remember the others of the family as dates and months do not stay with me long but yours does stay. Another year has been added to your sweet life and changes we never thought could take place have been brought about. After the day is over darling just stop and think of all that really has taken place and do not fail to look over the great and noble work you yourself have done since last July. Let us all hope and pray that next year as you sit down to eat your cake that you may have your whole family about you including your future son in law.

Things over here are rolling along in the same old way day in and day out. After these past eight months experience I have become so hardened to it all, that lack of sleep, a hard bed or dirty hands and face are just a part of the week's work. A group of us will sit out in front of the observation in the evening talking and smoking when a shell lands perhaps fifty yards or less up the street from us. No notice is paid to it, the talk goes on just the same as if nothing had happened. Just charge it all up to the day's work and let it go at that. Last night as I was writing "Ev" a few lines we had a gas attack but that did not worry us in the least. Just put on your mask and write away. There was one hitch last night however. I had just lit a cigarette when the shells started to fall and when I was forced to put my false face on I had to throw it away as the inventor of gas masks left no hole through which to smoke. Naturally that's the time you want to smoke worst. So you see, I was out of luck.

Sergeant Hurley's account of April 20 [battle of Seicheprey] was fine and very little over done. I was mighty glad when I heard we had been able to get it by as I knew it would be of great interest to you at home. I said very little about it in my letters feeling that a little would go a long ways. I shall never forget it. You can bet that.

The picture of Katherine pleased me very much. She has grown prettier since I left. I guess by the time I get back she will have all the boys after her if she has not already. Well tell her to save a little place in her heart for me and not to make too many dates in advance as I shall want the pleasure of taking her to a few parties myself. I certainly have got two mighty fine sisters as well as brothers. I suppose Art is now the proud owner of an E with crossed oars. I read in the papers some little time ago that the schools and colleges were to stop giving sweaters to their athletes until after the war is over but I hope Art gets his before this rule goes into effect.

Tell Art for me that he wants to go light on the sweet stuff this summer so that he will keep in prime shape for crew next fall. I don't suppose he is smoking yet but if he is ask him to stop that altogether. I am a great one to preach on smoking but I do see him making good at crew and know that he cannot if he smokes very much.

How is my friend old Dick this year or isn't he at Rye this summer? I have been intending to write him all winter but somehow have never gotten around to it.

The Grip got started in the regiment a couple of weeks ago and has been passed from one to the other just like it does in our family. I was so darn sick for two days with it that I thought for sure I was going to die and didn't care if I did. My fever was well up and I had to lay in a closed dug out half conscious for about thirty six hours. The doctors all knew what it was as most of them had a touch of it themselves and hence weren't sending men to the hospital until the third day. If you were not much better then, off you went. It came quick and left quick but while that fever was up I certainly was a sick man if ever I was. I was laid flat on my back for two days and felt ok the third except weak from not eating. That was less than a week ago and you'd never know I had a sick day in my life to look at me this morning full of pep and life with my color all back. Just charge those two days to [Kaiser] Bill and forget about them.

Oh yes, I must tell you about Betty. Betty is my pet rat, and a finer rat you never did see. She eats my candles, nibbles at my matches and just loves the cigarettes I smoke. Like all other girls she has to know all that is going on so she reads all my letters and leaves them on the floor. Last night, however, I gave her a run for her money and I doubt if she comes back. I woke up about one o'clock, all was dark and I felt Betty walking peacefully over my chest. I waited until she got on my leg and then I tossed her clean across the room against the room stove. Just as I did so her mate made a flying leap from the bunk above onto my head and went after her. I was troubled no more. When these rats jump from a table or bunk to the floor you would think a ton of bricks had landed, so you can imagine their size. I thought a cat had hit me when that one landed on my head. Be sure to have a few in my room when I get home or I will be lonesome and won't sleep. Funny isn't it how a man will get used to these things and they will not trouble his night's rest at all and yet run all over him.

I do remember giving someone some money for a picture while at Boxford but just who I have forgotten. I think however it was for that big picture of camp which we got. If I can find out anything about the other I will let you know.

I am sorry to say I have not had a chance to send you folks a cablegram yet. I intended to ask Captain Root to do it for me but we got talking about Ev and other things and I forgot all about it. I was so glad to see one of the old bunch again that everything but getting news went out of my head. I don't see Captain Root very often these days and have not seen Ev for four months. Just think. Wait until we two meet again and I won't even know my own name. If we are very lucky and get permission I am going to try to get where Ev is as I am very anxious to see him again. I'll make the old boy take that bar off his shoulder and eat and drink just as we used to when he was a sergeant like myself. Oh Mother dear, those were happy days. Ev never will forget some of those parties nor will I. I guess we both have had some mighty good ones since but I always wish he were along. You'll hear more of these good times when we get home.

I received Grandma Hobson's nice letter but her boxes seemed to be held up somewhere along the line. Keep up hope they will come someday. Your information about mail not being taken from the front is wrong I am glad to say. We surely are allowed to write and send our letters back to the horse line on the wagon at night. All mail for the Haverhill boys comes to the horse line first. Then they send it up to those of us who are on the firing line by the ration cart at night. Oh yes, dear, mail comes and goes just the same as when we were at our training camp.

I guess poor Bessie and Myrtle will kind of be in the shade this summer won't they with two autos in the family? Poor old horses. Here they have stood by us for all these years and now they are to be more or less forgotten. I wish Kid was still living so I could ship her over to you for Dad and Art to play around with. They both would have their hands full at times but would have a real mare. She was a real mare, Mother, if there ever was one. I think Dad and Art would fall in love with her just as I did after taking a few good falls as I had to before I learned how to handle her. She'd keep Art in trim for crew if he took her out in some field and rode her bare back all summer. I swear I could ride that horse anywhere, saddle or no saddle, and enjoy it. I can plainly see however that I am behind the times so when I get home have decided to buy an auto and catch up to the times. I'll let you know when I'm going so you folks can have it all ready for me along with the bill.

Who is at the beach anyhow this summer? I suppose all the girls are there and perhaps some new ones but how is your stock of boys this season. I guess most of the real live ones who are worth much are over here fussing or fusing shells, as it were, instead of bothering the fair sex much. I guess and certainly hope that the girls are busy also with war work of a bit different nature but just as important. My, but I would like to look in on you all someday about eleven o'clock. You can tell everyone that I am thinking of you all and wish that I might enjoy a morning dip followed by an ice cream, which, by the way, I have not tasted since leaving the States. And then that air - Oh ye Gods but I would like to fill my lungs with it once more. A few good dances wouldn't go bad either but these things must all wait until my duty over here is done.

I suppose Jeane is wondering how I ever get along without the girls but I do. Please assure her for me that I am getting used to being without them and the strain is not so bad at all.

I suppose Marjorie Stover has changed a whole lot this past winter but is still driving her Buick around the beach. Has Josey grown any? Between Dick Thompson, Dick Stover and Art most of the fair ones ought to have a pretty good summer out of it after all.

Things along our sector of this front have been very quiet for some little time now. Of course we get more or less shelling every day but we do not count that. Gas comes our way every so often but not very heavy, thank goodness. When things are like this life gets very monotonous and just at present everyone is hoping for a little excitement. One of our observers discovered a pick and shovel gang at work the other afternoon so we had a little fun for about ten minutes firing on them. From the way they came back at us it looks as if we killed some of them. Well, that's what we are here for.

I have not heard a word from Karl since my return to the front. I guess he is all ok however - perhaps a bit lazy like all the rest of us but that can't be helped these days.

There is no sign of a rest camp in sight yet and our hopes of a few weeks ago have faded. Where we are going or what we are to do when we come off this front still remains a mystery. I often think we are anchored here for the duration of the war. I for one am ready for a change any time even if we move to another front.

The poor Y.M.C.A. is having hard work here to keep in enough supplies for us. A load comes up about every night between eleven and one o'clock and they are all sold out before nine the next morning. Cigarettes last but sweet stuff goes like the wind on a March day. Hot tea is the style just now and almost every night a crowd of us goes over and have a cup of tea as beer is scarce just now.

Listen Mother, be sure and tell me all about the entrance Lieut. Langdon made. Did you know he was coming or did he just walk in on you all as a surprise?

Also, what are the plans for the wedding or are they going to wait until Ev gets home? He certainly was a happy man to get back and yet how he did hate to leave the boys over here.

I have a little hay fever after all. You remember I thought the dampness here would keep it away but it hasn't. It isn't bad yet and here's hoping it doesn't get so.

Well darling, I have raved on and on here until I notice I am onto my fourteenth page so guess it is about time to ring off.

Please give my love to all the family and remember me to Mr. and Mrs. Stover as well as the rest.

A little extra love and a few extra kisses for you on your birthday. Just think - I'll be of age in August. It doesn't seem possible does it Mother!

Lots of love and kisses.
Johnny

Dearest Sister

I have just come down from the observation room where I have been for the past three hours trying to pick up some movements on the part of the Huns but with no luck. It is just 9:15 a.m. and I have nothing more to do until six tonight when I observe again so guess I will take a few minutes and drop you a few lines of news from the front.

Things still remain quiet and peaceful around these parts with the exception of a couple of nights ago when we had a small argument with the Boche. It looked for about half an hour as if it might be another affair like we had April 20 but it all passed over after about an hour's fighting. We fellows at the observation have been very busy the first part of the evening for the past few nights as we have been seeing troop trains pulling in and out in the land of the enemy. We have also picked up three or four blinker stations and caught the Germans sending messages from them. All these things have to be very carefully watched of course and keep us pretty busy during certain hours. [Kaiser] Bill is a wise old cuss and has to be watched very, very carefully lest he pull something over on us.

We have two fine Lieutenants here with us and have had a chance to learn a lot about maps and firing charts from them. They are not the kind who consider themselves twice as good as anyone else and are too proud to tell you anything for fear you will know as much as they do. These two will tell you anything they can and every night one of them puts his head into our dugout after I come off duty at 9 o'clock and yells, "Well Sergeant, are you ready to start off on our nightly rat hunt?" If I happen to be in bed I just pull on my shoes and out we go both armed with rocks to kill some lazy rat who does not move fast enough to get out of our way. This hunt lasts about half an hour then we talk war for a while over our pipe or cigarette. They are two mighty fine men and it is a real pleasure to be working with them. I wish the battery could get a hold of them.

Two of the men here came down with this darn grip last night and I have had my hands full trying to run things as they should be run with two men short. They will very likely be all right tomorrow but it takes a little figuring to keep things going smooth while they are sick. This grip certainly does get you quick and you are mighty sick while it lasts.

Yesterday afternoon one of my corporals and I walked down to the next town to buy candy, jam, etc. for the bunch. The Y.M.C.A. in this town can't seem to keep a supply on hand and there is no Salvation Army hut here. In the next town, about half an hours' walk away, we found the best Y.M.C.A. I have been in, also a Salvation Army hut. The Dough Boys are stationed in this town and after buying about half of both huts we sat down and talked life over with them. It made me think of some country store to see us all sitting around on boxes and barrels chewing the fat like so many girls would at a lawn party. The adjectives were a bit different than those used by the fair sex when talking but the speed we were going was about the same. Men from every walk of life were there and first you would hear the polished talk of an educated man then broken English of a foreigner followed by a few poorly expressed thoughts of some street bum. Well we were all happy, all glad to be alive so the party flowed along fine as one of that kind usually does when a few soldiers get together. "My gal back home" had to be told about and how sad a parting it was when the speaker left for France and of course a few remarks about the wedding which was to come when he got home. Next a big Scotch fellow, a Corporal by rank, told us of his experience April 20, a tale which never grows old is the story of that morning, and his narrow escape from being captured. He was a peach and I took a liking to him right away. He has a brother in the British artillery and showed me a very interesting letter from him, parts of which I wish you could have read. Number three was a southerner and you know what that means, coon stories and a good laugh. Act four was pulled off by a farmer, by heck, and his was dry and had a strong smell of barn and horses about it. Thus it went on one man after another telling some event in his life or a funny story. Remember dear, this was not a show but just a gathering of ten or eleven soldiers in a Y.M.C.A. hut. I have written it as if it were a play but such was not the case. This is our social life at the front and it is lots of fun. Every fight has its stories and it is in this way that they are told from one outfit to another and in years to come will be told and retold to those who follow us. Men will be men when they get together and I love to be around with them. Frank, straightforward talk right from the shoulder is what I like to hear and we surely have it around these parts.

Another family has moved in. I've got those darn coo-coos again and am all bitten up from them and a bug which flies around here. Wash as I will I can't seem to get rid or stay rid of these French fleas. They just love me and sometimes I think I will go crazy with them. Well it's all in the war I suppose but...

No more news from Ev as yet but it is a little early as I only wrote him about ten days ago. I have missed him like everything ever since he left us and can imagine in a small way how you must feel with your future hubby away over here. I am hoping that some time about the end of summer that he will have the same chance George had to return home. Wouldn't that be great, Kid, if he could!

I bet Marge was the happiest girl on earth when she saw George walk in. I have no little girl waiting for me so it does not make quite so much difference when I get back just so long as I get there alive and well sometime but these men who are engaged ought to get back just as quick as possible. I suppose George came up to the house to see you and the family. Well here's hoping he did not give you all too bad an account of your older brother. The next time you see him tell him that the mud had dried up and now we are enjoying the beautiful French dust. Give him my very best and tell him the boys have missed him a whole lot and often spoken of him.

What kind of a crowd have you got at Rye this season? Or haven't you enough there to call it a crowd? I often think of you enjoying a nice cool sea breeze during the day while I roast over here in the sun. Who is down there this year and in what way have they changed during the winter?

June 10, 1918

Have been so darn busy for the past two days that I have not had time to finish my letter but will do so now.

Say, Sister, you ought to have been here last night and seen the sight I saw. Two officers came out to the observation about 7 p.m. to adjust their battery on a road leading out of a German town. They were having a little trouble as the wind was very strong and they were using what is called a long fuse. After trying to get their shots where they wanted them for half an hour with no luck and the guns firing poorly they decided to hit a house just this side of the road and then increase their range or "walk through" as it is sometimes called. It took about ten minutes to get a direct hit on the house but when they did it was some sight. Poor Mr. House was blown to bits. About an hour later I was up to the Y.M.C.A. and the Germans took revenge on the town by giving us a shower of shrapnel every two minutes for half an hour. I thought I never would get back from that Y.M.C.A. alive with all that lead flying over my head.

Are we ever going to move from here? That is the question which we all are asking each other daily. Here about a month ago I wrote to Mother that we expected to leave for a rest camp very soon but very soon never seems to come. It gets awfully monotonous staying in the same place day after day and week after week especially when there is no excitement. I love to roam and the quicker we start in again the better I will like it. Moving always means a lot of hard work when you start out but once on the road it is heaven even if you do sleep in a barn or chicken coop overnight as we usually do. I'll be worse than a dog when I get home, always wanting to roam off somewhere, anywhere just so long as I am roaming.

I heard last night that Lieut. Wendell was to return to America this month. I wish I could see him before he leaves as I have a letter I should like to send home to you folks. He has left the horse lines I understand so I guess it is too late however well I may hit up with someone going your way before the summer is over and if I do I will send it along. It is about the fight April 20 and I would not have it lost for the world because it is a citation in a way and I think a great deal of it since they are not the easiest things in the world to get.

By the way, dear, how is dad these days? You and Mother always say, "All well and happy." But it has been ages since I have heard any direct news from dad. I wish you would ask him to take a few minutes next Sunday and drop his boy a few lines. He may have written several letters but they have never reached me. I am very anxious to hear some news from him so please ask him to write even if it is only a few lines just to let me know he is all OK. I miss his merry, "Good morning, Johnny" or, "This is a fine time to be coming around" when I walked in for breakfast about eleven a.m. Sunday morning and a few lines directly from him will help a whole lot. I think a great deal of dad and I shall never forget how badly he felt when the time came for me to leave to take my place in this war. He did his best to cover up his feelings but I could look away down deep into his big heart and see it bleeding. And the last few nights when he would do his best to bid me a cheery good night I could see two big tears in those kind eyes of his and often wondered if I was doing the right thing in leaving him. You all felt badly but somehow he seemed to feel the worst. Now I often sit in front of my dugout and just long for a few lines from him to let me know he is all right. The rest of you keep me well posted and I suppose I ought not to ask dad to write too often as he is very busy but I do want a few lines from him so please ask him to write again.

Well, darling, I guess I have told you about all the news so will close.

Lots of love to all the family and lots for yourself.
Johnny

P.S.
I notice this pencil has written very light. Here's hoping you can read what I have written. Do not try too hard as there is nothing very interesting in all these ten and half pages.

Young Fellow My Lad
Robert Service

"Where are you going, Young Fellow
    My Lad,
  On this glittering morn of May?"
"I'm going to join the Colours, Dad;
  They're looking for men, they say."
"But you're only a boy, Young Fellow My Lad;
  You aren't obliged to go."
"I'm seventeen and a quarter, Dad,
  "And ever so strong, you know."

"So you're off to France, Young Fellow
    My Lad,
  And you're looking so fit and bright."
"I'm terribly sorry to leave you, Dad,
  But I feel that I'm doing right."
"God bless you and keep you, Young Fellow My Lad'
  You're all of my life, you know."
"Don't worry. I'll soon be back, dear Dad,
  And I'm awfully proud to go."

"Why don't you write, Young Fellow
    My Lad?
  I watch for the post each day;
And I miss you so, and I'm awfully sad,
  And it's months since you went away.
And I've had the fire in the parlour lit,
  And I'm keeping it burning bright
Till my boy comes home; and here I sit
  Into the quiet night."

"What is the matter, Young Fellow
My Lad?
No letter again today.
Why did the postman look so sad,
And sigh as he turned away?
I hear them tell that we've gained new ground,
But a terrible price we've paid.
God grant, my boy, that you're safe and sound;
But oh I'm afraid, afraid."

"They've told me the truth, Young Fellow
My Lad:
You'll never come back again.
(O God! The dreams and the dreams I've had,
And the hopes I've nursed in vain!)
For you proved in the cruel test
Of the screaming shell and battle hell
That my boy was one of the best."

"So you'll live, you'll live, Young Fellow
My Lad,
In the gleam of the evening star,
In the wood note wild and the laugh of the child,
In all sweet things that are.
And you'll never die, my wonderful boy,
While life is noble and true;
For all our beauty and hope and joy
We will owe to our lads like you."

From: Commanding Officer Battery A 102nd F.A.
To: Mr. A. Hobson, Haverhill, Mass.
Subject: Appreciation

1. The commanding officer Battery A desires to express to you not only his own sincere appreciation for your contribution to the Company Fund of Battery A but also the appreciation of every soldier of this organization. Not only the material benefit which comes to the organization thru having a sum on hand to purchase such little luxuries as are available at the front, but also the knowledge that the people at home are interested in the organization and are thinking of the comfort mean much to the spirit and morale of the men.

It is a privilege to me to have command of an organization where there is such an admirable spirit of comradeship and willingness, and you may be sure your gift comes to an organization that is making an excellent job of its duty.

On behalf of the entire personnel of the battery, I thank you for your gift.

H. Morrison
1St Lt. U.S.R. 102nd F.A.

[Poem sent to John Hobson on July 4, 1918, from Mrs. Bradley.]

The Stay Behinds

Ye soldiers in the trenches lined
And sailors on the perilous sea,
A hail from us who stay behind
In forge and shop reluctantly.
We formed the iron hot and red
O, sentry, at the listening post,
The night is dark the night is drear
Take heart, at home a shining host
Of factory lights are winking clear
The night shifts on a willing crew
We work for you, we pull for you.

In those who only fight to live,
Who helpless lie on beds of pain
Burns deep the wish that they might give
Home and comfort not in vain.
Good luck to you, the tried and true.
We pull for you, we pray for you.

Long is the way, and hard the fight
But who shall stay our gallant men,
We stay behinds with main and might
We'll see you through and home again.
O, lads in khaki, lads in blue,
We'll pull for you, we'll work for you.

[To Marjorie Bradley from Lieut. Langdon]

Those Who Return
Clinton Scollard

Those who return from scarred and stricken places
    Our men of valor, will they seem the same,
    Or will they wear on their beloved faces,
    Something inscrutable we may not name?

Will they take up their duties and their pleasures
    With aims and ardors that they knew of old,
    Or will they weigh all life with newer measures
    And view the past as one a tale long told?

They who have looked into the eyes of dangers
    Unsensed by us, and which we may not feel,
    Will they not be sometimes to us as strangers,
    Holding at heart what they may not reveal?

Unchanged, yet changed in this that they have seen
So near the veil that hides the Great Unseen.

CHAPTER ELEVEN

The Second Battle of the Marne
Chateau-Thierry/The Pas Fini Sector

"Ils n'ont pas passé - [They did not pass]"
INSCRIPTION ON A FRENCH BATTLEFIELD MONUMENT

*"The artillery of the 26th … must meet the onslaught
with the most intense fire possible and keep firing until
about to be engulfed in the advancing masses,
then blow up their guns and retreat"*
A BRIEF HISTORY OF THE FIGHTING YANKEE DIVISION A.E.F.

*"…on the train we passed a beautiful forest but for
me the beauty was gone, all because I had seen blood flow
in some woods that looked like them."*
SERGEANT JOHN L. HOBSON II

If there was a Second Battle of the Marne there certainly had to have been a First Battle of the Marne. The First Battle of the Marne, known as "Miracle of the Marne," was fought by British and French forces in September 1914, in the opening stages of the war before the Americans got in. That battle thwarted Germany's initial plan to sweep across France and capture Paris. The Germans were stopped then at the Marne River, around Chateau-Thierry, and their line had been stationary behind the Aisne River ever since. Thus began the characteristic siege of trench warfare in this sector. Now, almost four years later in the Second Battle of the Marne, the Germans would attempt to break out, cross the Marne and try again to push through to Paris.

In previous offensives and in late March of 1918, the German high command had ordered a major offensive along the Hindenburg Line north of Chateau-Thierry from Chemin des Dames northeast of Paris toward the Marne, threatening Paris. The 102nd Field Artillery had already participated in the defense of this move in the Soissons and Toul sectors. According to the Regiment's History:

> The end result of the [recent] Germans' effort [in March] was a rounded bulge in the line of the Western Front thirty miles wide at the base, extending south about 25 miles to its apex at Chateau-Thierry. By July it became clear that the Germans would renew their assault toward Paris along this area of the front.

> At Chateau-Thierry the Germans occupied the northern half of the city and the Allies held tenaciously in the southern half, with the Marne between them, bringing the Germans' position dangerously close to Paris.

> West of Chateau-Thierry, the German advance was halted at Vaux, a little town that lay below the railroad line, and at Belleau Wood, where the Marine Brigade of the Second Division made its historic stand against this offensive on 26 June. Vaux was No Man's Land. Neither side could stay in Vaux and neither side take it. The little town was ground to dust under the heavy artillery bombardments and the town was completely wrecked by both armies.

In anticipation of the German offensive in this sector, on the night of 24 June the battery left Rambucourt having been relieved by a battle scarred regiment of French artillery, the 266th R.A.C., Commandant Balambois fresh from fighting around Mont Kemmel in Flanders, and the regiment had withdrawn to regimental echelon in Sanzy. Their service in the "Old Home (Toul) Sector" was at an end and their fortification of Chateau-Thierry had begun.

In the evening of 28 June the regiment marched through Trondes-Pagny-Sur Meuse and on the morning of the 29th took up billets at Ugny. The time in Sanzy had given the regiment time to refit equipment and they made a smart business like appearance as they marched to Ugny.

On 30 June, the regiment entrained at Vaucouleurs heading west for a destination unknown to them. The route was roundabout because the railroad was cut along the bank of the Marne and they would have to travel west toward Paris before going east back to Chateau-Thierry. Because German bombers and strafing fighter plane attacks could be expected near the "voies de recades" (ways of bypasses), the battery's machine guns remained set up on the trains, but the ride westward was without incident. As the train rolled westward and crossed the Seine, the Eiffel Tower appeared causing great excitement in the regiment. The train's passengers received cheers from passersby and these cannoneers had fantasies of strolling the streets of Paris on the 4th of July. It was not to be. The trains swerved north leaving Paris and the fantasies behind and, pointing north, came to rest at a regulating station at Noisy le Sec. Alas, they were going to the front once more and now the response to cheers of passersby was only a slight, sad wave of the hand.

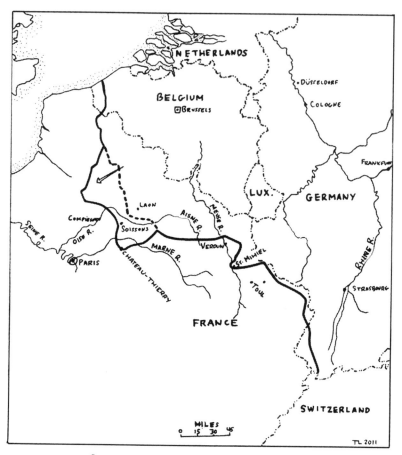

SECOND BATTLE OF THE MARNE/AISNE OFFENSIVE

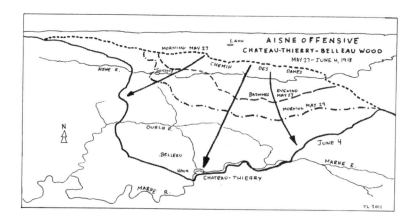

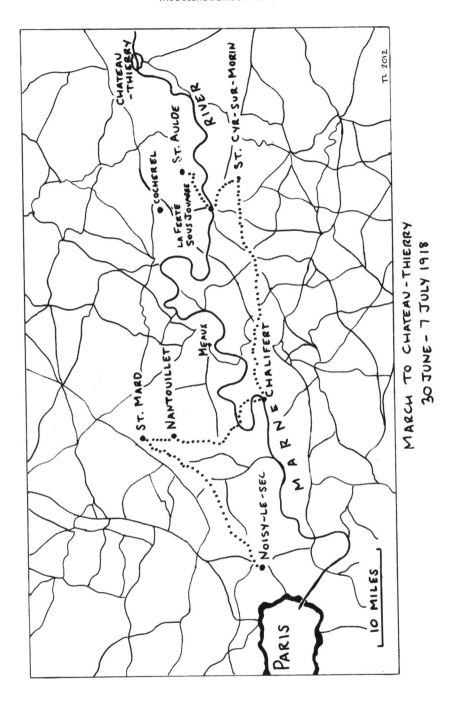

MARCH TO CHATEAU-THIERRY
30 JUNE - 7 JULY 1918

CHATEAU-THIERRY

ST. AULDE

COCHEREL

LA FERTE SOUS JOUARRE

RIVER

ST. CYR-SUR-MORIN

ST. MARD

NANTOUILLET

MEAUX

CHALIFERT

MARNE

NOISY-LE-SEC

PARIS

10 MILES

TL 2012

The regiment detrained that evening at St. Mard and marched southeast to bivouac in a chateau park near the village of Nantoullet east of Paris. The owner of the chateau there was a French artillery captain, Captain Emile Tartier, whose family had owned the chateau for 200 years. Captain Tartier, who welcomed the soldiers of the regiment, had been wounded in the Great War fighting at Charleroi in 1914, pinned under his fallen horse. He was taken prisoner by the Germans and released to return home three years later when the Germans figured that in his crippled condition he could no longer fight for his country.

The next day they marched to their billets; the 1st Battalion and Battery A billeted at Chalifert. (Chalifert is located on what today are the outskirts of Disneyland Paris.) Here they spent the first four days of July away from the front enjoying the beauty of the Marne and France in the summer. They had special dinners, played ball games and had a brief, well-earned rest after five months' continuous service on the front.

With new orders to proceed to the front at Chateau-Thierry to relieve in two days the 15th Artillery of the 2nd Division, on the afternoons of 4 and 5 July the regiment "hitched up" and marched 40 kilometers (25 miles) to billets at St. Cyr along the Petit Morin. Hostile air observations made it necessary to make all marches at night.

On 5 July, they moved west through LaFert and crossed to the north side of the Marne. They marched northwest to Faviers le Limon where command was passed to French staff officers for additional orders.

From the intense level of activity it was very apparent that a great German attack was imminent somewhere in this quarter. Allied infantry and artillery were urgently being shuttled about to establish positions. The Regiment now was sent to relieve a French artillery regiment at Cocherel-Dhuisy that was being shuttled to Chateau-Thierry. On the morning of 6 July, the French guns were gone, having been repositioned at Chateau-Thierry.

The batteries of the 102nd Field Artillery Regiment were posted north of the Cocherel-Porte Ferre road.

The situation was intense. Intelligence indicated that the Germans were planning an attack from over the heights in front. Orders were given to check the advance right there or "...serve the pieces while a man lived." In other words, there was no retreat.

In anticipation of hand-to-hand combat by the artillery units, additional pistol ammunition was issued to the battery's officers. Meals were served at the artillery gun positions and the gun crews slept in relays. In anticipation that the German offensive might overrun the regiment's position, the battery commanders were advised to distribute any monies they held in the battery fund among the officers so the money would not be in a central location.

The regiment remained in this position on 6 and 7 July. On the evening of 7 July, the regiment was repositioned and marched along the Marne to St. Aulde and to Villers-sur-Marne. They billeted that night at Boise de Villers.

On the night of 8 July and the morning of 9 July, the regiment completed its original order and relieved the 15th Field Artillery in the sector around Chateau-Thierry. It would become theirs to defend.

The 26th Division took over the entire sector from the 2nd Division on 10 July.

Nobody actually knew it, although intelligence suspected it, but the German offensive which had been stopped in June north of Chateau-Thierry was scheduled to begin again no later than 15 July. All the division knew was that they had arrived at a sector very different from the others where they had served. There were no trenches here; it was country of alternating woods and wheat fields, fields in which the crop was already golden and ready for harvest. Right in front of them lay the Eterpilly plateau. The ground had not been held long enough to be trenched to a great extent so, upon the infantry's arrival, they first set about to build defenses, an unpleasant task for the engineers.

The artillery was generally placed in the edge of the woods in hastily dug positions, with no shelter for the men except grave-like trenches with room for only one or two men. Every patch of woods sheltered a battery or two.

On a large scale, the German massive offensive plan was to attack with their First, Third, Seventh and Ninth Armies that included 52 divisions along an extended crescent-shaped, 22-mile front approximately 60 miles east of Paris. The front would extend from the north at Soissons, south to Chateau-Thierry on the Marne, and the offensive push would be to the west with the objective of taking Paris.

The position of the 26th Division was as follows: the extreme right was held by the 101st Infantry, facing north. The 102nd Infantry lay along a roll of hills, its line extending a little beyond Bouresches; the regiment faced almost east. The 104th was in the Belleau Wood facing east and northeast, and the 103rd Infantry, north of Lucy le Bocage, faced north and northeast, on our extreme left. One battalion of artillery was in position in the fields right and left of the Paris-Metz road; another out on the left flank, was on the line Champillon-Voie du Chatel. This artillery regiment had been firing steadily since its arrival in sector and gassed - for in this sector gas was used to a large extent by the Germans. The general direction of the [Allied] attack was to be northeast…

In the above, excerpted from Sibley's "With the Yankee Division in France", the "One battalion of artillery in position in the fields right and left of the Paris-Metz road…" was the 51st, the 102nd Field Artillery Regiment, Battery A…and my father.

Then came the attack described in the Regiment's History:

At 11:30 o'clock the night of July 15 the heavens to the east of us became one steady sheet of flame. Our own guns drowned the noise but we knew that the German attack had begun. At 1 o'clock a.m. we got the French wireless "L'ennemi attaque," [The enemy attacks] and his last great effort was under way.

The 1st and 2nd American and French Moroccan divisions broke the German line near Soissons and the Allied counterattack swung eastward as planned. However, south of that line, the French were forced back across the Marne.

The 26th Division, the 102nd Field Artillery Regiment and my father's Battery A were now positioned at the salient point of the German drive. They were the key to General Foch's defense and subsequent great counter-offensive plans.

Battery A was initially positioned on the edge of the Boise La Croissette woods west of Chateau-Thierry outside of the neighboring village of Domptin.

The use of roving gun positions with the nimble 75 mm artillery between active and silent positions was constant. They had successfully used this tactic in the Toul sector. In case of attack, orders were that all guns were to be withdrawn to the main or battle positions and there fought to the last. "The History of the Regiment" describes the action as follows:

Sunset of July 16 showed that the German had shot his bolt all along the front. The regiment in the next two days reconnoitered and selected its positions for our own attack which, all along the line from Soissons down to Chateau-Thierry [35 kilometers - 22 miles], was to strike him while he was yet reeling from his own frantic effort to break through. Little by little the plan was unfolded to us. We did not know its details until many days after.

The artillery of the 26th was placed with orders that an attack in force against their positions was inevitable; that they must meet the onslaught with the most intense fire possible and keep firing until about to be engulfed in the advancing masses, then blow up their guns and retreat. The attack did not come on the moment, as expected, but finally a dense body of Germans [Prussian Guards and the Bavarians] was discerned preparing to attack. Before the Huns had fairly started, the guns of the 101st and 102nd F.A., aiming with open sights at 2,000 yards [With exploding artillery shells and a short fuse, this adjustment on the guns would be tantamount to firing a 75 mm shotgun directly into the face of the advancing enemy infantry.], began a drum fire of such ferocity and accuracy that the enemy was thrown into complete confusion. It was the expiring effort of the Hun; at that moment the tide turned, and then the gallant infantry of the 26th went over the top and at them. That was on the 18th of July. From that instant to the 25th [July] the Yankee Division chased the Hun northward, licking him time and again.

The world knows what the Yankee Division did at Chateau-Thierry. It earned from the French the name of "Saviors of Paris," and, as stated in "A Brief History of the Fighting Yankee Division", praise from the famous Gen. Degoutte of the Sixth French Army: "The 26th Division alone is responsible for the whole Allied advance on the Marne. They are shock troops, par excellence!" Sweet words these must have been to those brave soldiers.

The Second Battle of the Marne, the events that took place at Chateau-Thierry and the subsequent Aisne-Marne Offensive were the turning points of the First World War. If there was a defining battle during the First World War, this was it. The Central Powers would advance no further. It was there that the Allies finally broke the stalemate of the trench warfare, stopped the German's westward advance on Paris and began the Allied offensive called "The Big Push", or the Aisne-Marne Offensive, that would drive the Germans back to the north and east across France and to their eventual surrender four months later. The fight at Aisne-Marne was the equivalent of the American Civil War's Battle of Gettysburg. It was the high water mark. Also in the Second Battle of the Marne, the United States, with nine divisions committed to French Command, suffered 30,000 casualties, which was more in alignment with the enormous losses of the other Allied nations associated with the other battles of the Great War. America had indeed shed its blood for freedom in Europe.

After the Second Battle of the Marne, the 102nd Field Artillery Regiment went on to glory and a place in history in the Aisne-Marne Offensive. After stopping the German advance, in the counteroffensive that followed they would chase the Germans 34 kilometers (21 miles) northeast toward Reims to Chery-Charteuve before resting. By 21 July and through early August, the regiment was engaged in the agreeable task of marching in pursuit of the beaten Boche.

The pursuit of the German Army was made over ground wrested from a broken enemy, and the signs of a beaten, retreating army marked the withdrawal ground: wrecked roads, new graves, unburied enemy dead, hastily abandoned wounded dressing stations and dead animals. There was abandoned equipment everywhere: guns, ammunition and wagons. The farms and villages left in the wake were destroyed and the fields torn asunder, marred by artillery shells and foxholes dug by the enemy. The ground they fought on was to become sacred, but also forever scarred. The remains of the trenches are still there today.

In its pursuit of the enemy to the northeast, on 19 July, Battery A supported, with a rolling barrage, the advance of the 101st and 102nd Infantries outside of Chateau-Thierry.

On 21 July, Battery A marched in pursuit of the beaten Boche to Lauconnois Farm.

On 22 and 23 July, they fired supporting actions in the capture of Trugny and Epieds.

On 24 July, they marched in pursuit of the enemy to Grange Marie Farm where they fought until 26 July, capturing La Croix Rouge Farm and the Wood Vente Jean Guillaume.

On 27 July, they pursued the enemy to Ourcq and Sergy where they set new positions in the vicinity of Croix Blanche Farm on the edge of a clearing in the woods southwest of Fresnes.

Battery A supported infantry until 1 August, firing artillery barrages on machine gun nests around the woods of Pelger, Planchette and Jomblets.

They then moved to positions southeast of Chery-Chartreuve where they supported the 8th Infantry Brigade of the 4th Division until 4 August, at which time the battery was finally relieved from duty and given orders to return to a rest area on the Marne.

It is not surprising that on that night they were glad to wrap themselves in blankets and go to sleep on the ground even though there was a drizzling rain. On the night of 6 August, the regiment marched to its rest billets at Saacy-sur-Marne.

On 13 August, the regiment marched back through Chateau-Thierry and entrained at Latrecy, destined for the rest and training area at Chatillon-sur-Seine.

Battery A's advance from Chateau-Thierry to Chery-Charteuve was rapid and aggressive. That was borne out by a dialogue that took place on the road to Chery-Chartreuve that was recorded in the Regiment's History.

When the battery's advanced position, which it had held for the past two hours, was approached from the rear by Allied infantry, the artillery battery was asked by the infantry commanding officer,

"What are you, the support?"

"No, Sir."

"The reserve?"

"No, Sir."

"Then, what are you?"

"We are the front lines, Sir."

The infantry proceeded to dig in behind the artillery battery.

"You're a hell of a front line! What's been out in front of these batteries?"

"Nothing, Sir, but patrols."

[Beginning 9 July,] for nine days [the 102nd Field Artillery Regiment] had been busy in a very unstable sector and then for a period of 17 days it had been constantly engaged in pursuit or battle with the enemy. In the course of its operations it had advanced in an air line over 40 kilometers [25 miles]. The actual distance marched must have been closely double this amount. It had successfully supported the infantry of four divisions, the 26th, the 42nd, the 4th, and for one engagement a battalion of the 28th, which, as fast as they were depleted and exhausted by the fighting and pursuit, were withdrawn and replaced with fresh troops. The operations had imposed a most severe strain upon both men and animals, and the greatest exertions had been extracted of the command throughout the entire campaign.

At its conclusion the horses were the principal hindrance to its further advance, as they had been constantly in use since the offensive started, bringing up additional ammunition while the guns were in action and then being called upon to move the batteries when changes of position occurred or the pursuit was resumed.

There were six complete changes of position during the offensive. The difficulties of watering horses in much of this country added to the perplexities of keeping them in condition. Our service of supply had never failed us. At no time was there any lack of ammunition or of food.

We [the regiment] had fired during this period 58,186 rounds of ammunition. This had been done without a single accident of any kind, premature burst or otherwise. Indeed the regiment had but one such throughout the entire war. Good luck may explain some of it but it is none the less true that the regiment understood and practiced the proper care of ammunition and guns.

After the strenuous efforts of the Chateau-Thierry drive, the regiment was billeted in Saacy-sur-Marne from August 7 to 13 to rest and refit. On 13 August, they retraced their steps back through Chateau-Thierry and boarded trains. They detrained at Latrecy and then marched in the warm, August haze to a training area at Chatillon-sur-Sein. Regimental headquarters were established in a chateau at Pothiers. The rest gave the soldiers their first (and last) rest billets, time to relax and clean up, to bask in the sun of the Cote d'Or and swim in the neighboring clear streams. The all-important horses were groomed and fed on green grass. While there, there were training exercises recorded in the Regiment's History as follows:

> Three days were employed in simulating direction of battery fire by airplane direction, the battery matching along and, upon the dropping of a message from the plane, going into action at once on the designated target, and receiving corrections by wireless from the aerial observer, who was Lieutenant Bradley, formerly of Battery A.

During the Aisne-Marne campaigns including the Meuse-Argonne Offensive, the Germans committed 52 divisions to this fifth and last offensive. One million two hundred thousand American troops participated. There were 50,000 Americans killed and 200,000 wounded.

The 102nd Field Artillery Regiment sustained a total of 102 casualties - killed, wounded and missing. Of the officers, two were killed, one seriously wounded and three slightly wounded. Of the enlisted men, 21 were killed, 19 seriously wounded, 38 slightly wounded, 12 men gassed, three shell-shocked and three were missing. Sergeant John L. Hobson II was part of these grim statistics.

Early in the Second Battle of the Marne, during the night of 14-15 July (there is some confusion about the date, but this was the date according to Division reports), while repairing a broken communication wire, Father and another man were caught out in a field during a mustard gas artillery barrage. Seeking cover from the barrage, the two men took safety in a shell hole and became trapped out in the wheat field for half an hour while the gas shells exploded around them. Father was drenched with mustard gas from the shells that were piled on them during the barrage. A report filed by the 26th Division's Gas Officer stated that night 1,500 77 mm gas shells landed on the Boise La Croissette.

Father was severely burned on his hands, legs and groin, and was debilitated by the gas he had inhaled into his throat and lungs. Several days after being exposed to mustard gas he became unable to perform his duties and was taken off the front line and sent to Base Hospital No. 116 at Bazoilles-sur-Meuse, located about seven kilometers (four miles) south of Neufchateau, where he would recover from his wounds and get some rest.

Western Union Telegram
[Undated]
Received at 6B
33 Collect 7:40 P
Washington D.C. via Haverhill Mass

Arthur L. Hobson

Little Boar's Head N.H.

Deeply regret to inform you that is officially reported that Sergt. John Hobson field artillery was severely wounded in action July fifteenth. Department has no further information.

McCain The Adjutant General

Post card to Arthur L. Hobson, Sr.
Somewhere in France
[Undated]

Laid up in the hospital with mustard gas burns. Nothing to worry about as I am getting along fine. Fine bed to sleep in and fine food to eat. My spirits are away up and that is more than half the battle. Have passed through much of late about which I will write later when I feel better. Love to all and lots for yourself.

Johnny

Somewhere in France
July 26, 1918

Dear Dad:

There is all kinds of news to tell you and the rest of the family as I have passed through a lot of interesting experiences since I last wrote. I am not going into many of them however in this letter as writing in bed is not a very easy job but I do want to let you all know that I am OK and will be up and around again before long.

As I guess you know by now I got mixed up in a mustard gas attack and am now laid up in the hospital with burns from the darn stuff. In brief here is what happened. One night about the 18th [July] the Huns threw over a bunch of mustard gas shells and of course had to break one of my most important lines about half a mile from our position. Well, Dad, there was nothing to do but get it fixed as quick as possible and I must confess I didn't have the heart to order two men out while I sat in a dugout so I called for one volunteer to go out with me on the line. Just the man I wanted spoke up and let me say right here it makes all the difference in the world who you have with you when under heavy fire and I had just the boy I wanted. Well we made our way out to the road and started across a big wheat field following the line. A wonderful July moon shone down on us and we talked and sang as we made our way to the edge of the woods where the big boys were breaking in a wicked way, tearing up the sod and throwing it everywhere. The nearer to those woods we got the less we talked until at last all we said was, "duck" or "down" and we both would fall flat. It seemed as if we never would reach that break and twice we had to stop to fix our test phone. One big baby broke within a few yards of us and as I lay there I would feel the hot gas hit my face. I wish I could describe to you just how a man feels when he finds himself in places like that. Somehow he does not think of home but he in a half unconscious way seems to call to God to give him courage to push on. Well, we reached the break and for ten minutes we worked fixing it right in a big hole full of gas. We made our test and then thought of going back. That's as far as we got, thinking of it, because they were landing all around and our best bet was to stay where we were so there we lay for half an hour. We got back ok but oh what a night. About two days later my voice nearly left me and I felt a fierce burning around my privates. I tried to fight it off but it got so bad that I could hardly walk so I had to give in. On the way to the base hospital on a French Red Cross train the burn broke out on my right knee and a little on both hands. I had just enough in my lungs to make me cough and talk as if I had a bad cold in my throat. I might just as well tell you now as a year from now that for about forty-eight hours I suffered as I never have before and never want to again. Once at the base I was dressed and cared for and now feel very comfortable. It takes about three weeks before they let you go but when that time is up I will be in fine shape and all rested. There is no need to worry or give it another thought because by the time you get this letter Johnny will be his old self again. The man who was with me is also laid up in some hospital but I have not been able to find out which one. I don't mind the burns half as much as the fact that I was expecting to leave for officer's school the end of this month and, of course, that is knocked in the head for a while. I'm all right however Dad, my spirits are away up and I'm happy and smiling all the time. This is just one more thing to add to my adventures in France and believe me my trip from the front here on a stretcher was an adventure in itself. I will tell you all about it someday. If you ever start to worry just say, "I'm too lucky that they can't get me" or as I told one of the men, "Why worry. I'm still all together and that's more than some can say."

Have not seen Ev yet but am still holding out hopes of seeing him one of these fine days.

Well, dad, I must close and take my afternoon nap.

Please remember me to everyone at the beach.

Lots of love for the family and lots for yourself.
Johnny

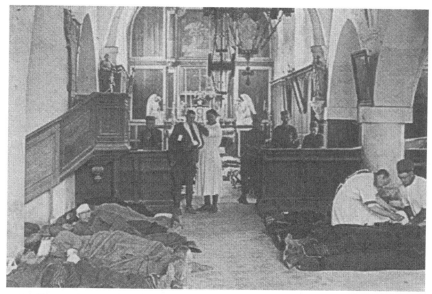

Photograph taken of the interior of and wounded being treated at the Saint Ruffin and Saint Valere church at Bezu Le Guery in June 1918 when the field hospital was used by the 2nd Division. Subsequently used by the 26th Division, this was the triage station my father was initially taken to for treatment. Stephen G. Hobson Collection - Gilles Lagin, Belleu Wood Museum Photograph

Interior of the Saint Ruffin and Saint Valere church at Bezu Le Guery, October 2004. Stephen G. Hobson Collection - Stephen G. Hobson photograph

Dearest Mother

Just a few lines from your boy this evening to let you know that he is feeling much better than I did yesterday. Last night I had my first real night's sleep since I was burned and, believe me, it was a peach. I have almost no real pain now but feel uncomfortable at times, but that is to be expected. My old time pep does not seem to come back but rest and good food will restore that. I walked around some today with my bathrobe on and ought to be up and dressed in a few days. There is no hurry and I want to make sure I am OK before I do much moving around, as this gas acts very funny on some and it is the after condition we want to watch.

It is very cool where I am and fine air. Some mornings when I wake up I could easily fancy myself at Rye on a September day if you folks were only here. I love to lay here in bed smoking a cigarette and trying to picture in my mind what you all are doing. I can see dad start off for Boston and picture the rest of you at the Club, or taking a dip in the nice, cool ocean. Those hours of dreaming are happy ones and take my mind miles away from battle talk and the thought of the trenches. The pictures you sent me of yourself and the auto, I was forced to leave behind as I left the battery rather unexpectedly and could not get them. I wish I had them with me but they are to be forwarded, so may arrive any day. You looked very young and pretty sitting on the steps, much too young, in fact, to be the mother of a boy nearly twenty-one.

Oh yes, dear, I know something that may interest you. One sergeant is to be sent home the last of every month from each battery. Sergeant Haseltine went from our battery this month. I am not saying that I shall be picked but there is a chance since I still hold out the rank of Sergeant. My chief ambition is to be sent off to school, but the outlook for that, now that I have had this set back, is rather bleak for reasons which I will tell you and dad someday. I may get there yet if I just keep going. "Don't worry about anybody or anything" is my motto. Yes, darling, I can truthfully say that at last, after almost a year away from all I love I have learned that priceless lesson you spent so many years in teaching me, "Don't worry about tomorrow it will take care of itself." That is not the only lesson by any means I have learned from my experiences in the big world alone. I have found that I knew most of them before, but, oh, how they have been impressed upon me since I started to roam. Experience IS a hard teacher at times but if a boy is not willing to learn from those who know, such as his father and mother, experience will soon teach him when he gets away from them.

The battery has done some fine work in this big drive and Haverhill certainly has an outfit to be proud of in battery A. Her memory certainly will go down in history in letters of gold. When I left the boys were all very tired due to lack of sleep and the strain on their nerves, but I understand they are off the lines now and I guess will get a good rest. We all have seen some real fighting and all we want of it. Let's all pray that it will be over before long so that we can return home and live in peace for the rest of our lives.

Well, dear, I am afraid this is kind of a dry letter but as I said before, I have no pep but want to let you know I am coming along fine.

Love to all and heaps for yourself.
Johnny

Dearest Sister

The evening shadows are falling and the last bright rays of today's sun are pouring in on me as I sit here, in bed, waiting for the evening papers to arrive with the news of how the big drive is going. We may be out of it for a while but, just like a football player, we are all eager to know how the big game is progressing. In the next building a "vic" is playing some good old time tunes, such as "My Little Girl You know I Love You" and Johnny's thoughts wander back to the days that used to be. All is quiet, and peace reigns throughout the ward. A pretty nurse hurries by every now and then throwing a cheery smile as she passes, while the patient in bed 44 (Johnny) answers it as best he can. I am not used to smiling at women and feel that I make an awful mess of it and look foolish. I guess I do. Well, I do the best I can anyhow. Now for my health.

I feel much better and the burns are fast going and my voice coming back by degrees. I am in hopes that the doctor will let me up tomorrow or the next day, as I long to get roaming again. The great question now is, will I get back to the battery? When I leave here I go to a replacement camp and land only knows where I may be sent from there. I rather like the uncertainty of it all and, believe me, nothing is sure in this game. You are here today and somewheres else tomorrow. I'll bet I have been over more than half of France already. Well, keep right on sending your mail to the battery until you get a new address from me. I rather expect to get back, but there is no telling where I may land.

I am very anxious to see Ev, as it has been six long months since our paths ran together. Just imagine, six months without seeing the only person over here who really seems like one of the family. I have written him and asked if we couldn't, someway, cook up a party together. If we can, oh joy, oh bliss, what a party it will be. Dad will get a draft on my letter for sure then. When I miss Ev the way I do I often wonder how you ever get along. He surely has won my faith and I am heart and soul with him.

What is the news at Rye, dear? I am very anxious to hear about the dances and life at the bathing beach so be sure and tell me about it. Just about a year ago Ev and I were starting our wild dashes for Rye and back to Boxford in the Stearns. Maybe those weren't the happy days.

I am glad Hope enjoyed her flowers and I am looking forward with much pleasure to her letter and the ones from the other girls you gave my address to. I hope they all write. You said you sent Hope the flowers but, darling, did you buy them with my money as requested? Please answer this question in your next letter.

Oh yes, I knew I wanted something. Will you please send me Ruth Heywood's address as I should like to drop her a few lines if I get time.

Well, here comes the papers so I must close and read them before someone else grabs them.

Remember me to everyone and tell them I often think of them.

Lots of love and kisses.
Johnny

P.S.
I almost forget to mention your hospital work. I am proud of you, Sis, and my one wish is that you were here nursing is Base 116. You certainly are doing your bit, dear, towards winning the war.

Somewhere in France
August 2, 1918

Dear Art

I am sorry to say that conditions have been such for the past month that I have been unable to write you a letter of congratulations on your being elected vice-president of your frat. The big shells were whining over my head when I read the good news in one of sister's letters, but I forgot all about them for some little time so pleased was I with your success. It's just fine, Art, and my only wish is that I were there to shake your hand and tell you, face to face, how proud I am of the record you have made for yourself at Exeter. You were very young when you went there but, believe me old-timer, you have made a name for yourself to be proud of. Your work on the crew pleased me enough but your last success surpassed my fondest dreams. I've been watching you as best I can 3,000 miles away, and you just bet you have got your older brother behind you, heart and soul. Stay with it, and make next year even better than last, if such is possible.

I suppose now you are enjoying a summer well earned and are capturing all the girls' hearts by taking them out to the teahouses in the Ford. Gee, but I would like to see you running around the beach in it. I suppose you have it one day and Sis the next, or is she too busy with her hospital work to use it? Those little cars certainly are doing great work over here and you will see them nearly every day winding their way in and out among the shell holes along the front. Your ambition to drive one of these out where the big boys break is never to be realized I fear, as those of us who are over here now intend to finish the job before another spring. Hell is popping now and from all appearances will continue to pop for a while to come. I wish I could write you all about it, as it is a story full of thrills but, cheer up, you will hear it all someday. Try driving the sedan across the hay field and through the woods and you will have a little idea what the boys who drive over here are up against. What kind of a time did you have on your trip? Now for a few lines as to how I am getting along.

I am feeling much better and the doctor told me I could get up today. I, of course, feel very weak after being in bed for nearly two weeks, but strength will come back in a few days. The skin is peeling off of the places where I was burned, and my hands look as if someone had chewed them up, while other places have turned jet black. I am in hopes that there will be no marks left but the doctor says there may be, especially where I was burned on the knee. Oh, well, I should worry, I was lucky not to get the darn stuff all over my face. I imagine I will leave here sometime next week for a rest camp, where we do light work until we are fit to be sent to a replacement camp. There are two other sergeants in here with me from different outfits, and we three are going to try to go along together. One of them, an infantry sergeant, looks just like Mr. Smith and when I first saw him I swear I thought he had left Woodland to come over here. He has that wonderful smile of Mr. Smith's and is almost as good fun. I wish you were here to bum your way along with me, Art, as I know you would enjoy it except when the roading gets rough and sleep does not come on account of "beaucoup" work. Well, tell the folks that I am almost myself again, a little the worse for wear, but still happy and going. You can't kill a slim guy no matter how hard you try. He may sink for a few minutes but will come up laughing and stronger than ever. Mother will tell you the same thing, that you can't kill a slender person.

I have not been to Paris yet but have passed very near it. So near, in fact, that we had a chance to see a few good looking girls and some real buildings from the door of our freight car. I hope someday before I return to have a chance to really see the city and enjoy a good blowout there. From all reports I guess a man can really enjoy himself there if he has a few hundred francs. I have received no pay since the last day of May and am now living on the American money dad gave me just before I left. I have saved it for some occasion such as this and believe me, but it has come in very handy when I want any extras as I do quite often. I shall use my letter of credit as soon as possible, as I shall very likely receive no money until I hit the battery again and land only knows when that will be. I shouldn't worry, I'm all set for cash, thanks to Dad.

I am going for a walk with those two sergeants now so must close as they are ready to start.

Give my love to all the family and drop me a few lines when you get time.

Johnny

Somewhere in France
August 4, 1918

Dear Dad

There really isn't a great deal of news to tell you since all I have done since I last wrote is to lay around the hospital. Not a very exciting way to spend one's time as about all we can do is eat, sleep and smoke, but such is life in the army. I have made two bold attempts to get my clothes but the doctor does not seem inclined to agree with me, that I am ready for them. We are allowed to walk all around the hospital grounds in our bath robes but I want to get my suit of brown and get moving once again. I feel fine and you know how restless I get if I have to stay still more than one day when I feel ok. There's not much I can do, however, to speed my departure up, so I am just holding my mules and telling the doctor daily that I could fire the whole battery alone I feel so good. The rest I have had here has done me the world of good, however, and I feel like a new man. When I first landed here I had not closed my eyes for 72 hours I had been so busy, and so I was ready to drop from lack of sleep. All that is made up now and I feel ready to take up my duties with new vigor.

Last night I ran into three other boys from the battery at the Y.M.C.A. One was gassed, one had a rupture and the third had a broken instep caused by a caisson passing over his foot. We four sat down at a table, lit up a cigarette and lordy, lordy, how we did talk. I had not seen any of the bunch for ages and it surely did me good to see those three. Two other men left the battery for a base hospital before I did, but up to date I have been unable to locate them, these two were from my detail and I should like to find them.

No direct news has come in from the battery but we are all trying to get some. Dame Rumor has it that they are off the lines. This is almost official and I am inclined to believe it, knowing what they have been through from paper accounts.

Lots of changes are taking place over here in the military world and I am in hopes that when I get out of here I may hit up with some good luck and move up a peg. I will be old enough this month and, if luck is with me, I ought to fall on something good. All the sergeants are hoping for some kind of advancement before fall and I guess lots of them will get it from all reports.

Speaking of age, gee, it doesn't seem possible that I will be twenty-one this month, does it? How time does fly. Almost old enough to know better I should say, Dad. How about it?

I have had the funniest dreams since I hit this place that I have ever had. Just about every other night I take a trip home, and the night before last I dreamed of Sister's wedding. I swear I could see the whole thing and Sis looked as pretty as a picture in her white dress. The only part I could not figure out was the fact that, instead of taking the train at Haverhill for their wedding trip, they got on at the Brookline depot. I woke up just as I was about to throw a slipper at Ev.

Speaking about Ev, yesterday afternoon I happened to hit up with a pilot who had both of his arms broken, and I asked him if he happened to know where the 2nd Corps Aero School was. He wasn't sure but said he thought it was in southern France which is miles away from here. Hence I guess there is no hope of Ev dropping in to see me. I have written him several letters, however, and hope to get an answer before long. Mail will do me more good than five tons of the stuff they have been putting on my burns.

Oh yes, did Mr. Atkinson ever get my letter thanking him for the cigarettes he so kindly sent me? I wrote it at the front and mailed it but have never heard if it reached him. I hope it did because I appreciated those cigarettes more than he will ever know. If he didn't get it please let me know and I most certainly shall write him again, because it was very thoughtful of him to remember me in such a nice way and I want him to know how much I appreciate it.

Well Dad, I guess you are tired of reading this poor writing so I will close for now.

Please give my love to all the family and keep a lot for yourself.
Johnny

Dearest Mother

Now that I am feeling better myself once again I am going to write you folks a real letter, telling you, as best I can with a pen, the experiences I have passed through since I was gassed. I am still in bed so the writing will not be any too good but, if you are able to make it out, I think you will find it rather interesting reading.

My first move, when I found that I was unable to perform my duties with the battery any longer, was to report to the doctor at our field hospital, or dressing station as it is more commonly called. This was located about a mile and a half from the battery position which, at that time, was only a short ways from our front line trenches on the edge of some woods. The Red Cross man, who was on duty with the battery, went down with me as I felt very weak and unsteady on my feet, due chiefly to lack of sleep. Of course this walk to the dressing station was not the most pleasant in the world as it hurt me to walk. On arriving at the station the doctor looked me over and I explained to him, as best I could with what little voice I had left, that I had been through a very heavy mustard gas attack. This was hardly necessary because one look at my hands and knee was enough to tell him what was the trouble. He wrote out a tag, very much like the kind you put on a trunk, and I was put into an ambulance, which looked very much like a police patrol, and was taken a few miles to another dressing station where I got out. There were three other men with me, all whom had gas burns. At this dressing station we were asked a few questions and given a little to eat; then put into another auto and carried about ten miles to the hospital where my troubles began.

Just as quick as I got out of the car I was laid out on a litter and told to keep very quiet. I lay there half asleep for about twenty minutes and then was carried into a tent where my clothes and all except personal belongings were taken from me. Then I was put onto a rubber litter and carried into another tent where two men, dressed in rubber and wearing rubber gloves, gave me a bath with hot water and dressed my burns. Oh joy, oh bliss, how I did suffer when the soda was put on the raw skin. But I knew it was all for my own good so I grit my teeth and said nothing. After putting a nightgown on me and wrapping me up in blankets I was carried out into a big room and set down beside another litter. I was suffering but the pain could not keep my heavy eyelids from closing and, before I knew it, I found sweet relief in the land of dreams.

How long I slept I do not know but I was waked up by a very soft female voice, the first I had heard for nearly three months, who wanted to know if I wanted a drink of coffee before I was put on the truck. I tried to say, "Yes, please," but by this time my voice was all gone so I had to nod my head. She knelt down and put her hand under my shoulders to hold me up while I drank a fine hot cup of coffee with milk and sugar in it. Then came the worst part of it all, my ride in that truck to evacuation 7. I'll bet that driver hit every rut in the road and a truck, at best, is none too easy riding. Some had shrapnel wounds, others in the car were in my boat and the groans were enough to move the heart of [Kaiser] Bill himself. I was twice as well off as some of those lads but I suffered untold pain all the way. When we reached the hospital we were at once put in different wards according to our troubles. The wards were big tents and when I rolled from my litter onto a nice, white bed, with a cool night breeze blowing over it, I thought I had hit heaven for sure. The lines were miles away, no guns were to be heard and after drinking a hot bowl of soup I went to sleep. Mother, dear, that sleep was the most beautiful thing of all. No pain could have kept me awake that night and my dreams were of you and Dad. We three were alone together in Dad's room at Rye and I could see you both just as if you were there beside my bed. I was in the middle and you and Dad were smiling at me. We were talking about something but I have forgotten what now.

The next morning my burns were dressed again and I was put on a French litter and pushed into a French ambulance with four other men. We were carried to the depot where an American Red Cross train was pulled up but, alas, it was full. We were then taken from the ambulance and laid in a freight shed along with about forty other litter cases. There we lay until eleven p.m., the hospital sending our dinner and supper down to us. At eleven a French Red Cross train pulled in and we, along with many others who had arrived during the day, were put on. Two litter cases to a compartment. We pulled out about midnight not having any idea where we were going or how long a ride we had before us. Two Frenchmen served our breakfast the next morning and it was very good. All that morning, from my litter, I watched the country roll by and really enjoyed myself as the burns felt some better. At noon the frogs were around again with soup, bread, jam and one nice, big, cool cup of red wine per man. We landed here about four o'clock that afternoon where my burns were again dressed. Here I have been ever since but expect to leave any time now.

I wish I could describe to you the feelings I had while on my trip from the front here, but I cannot do it with a pen. There, upon the lines, for six solid months I had a life full of excitement where every man must do for himself. It was second nature to me. Then, all of a sudden, you find yourself helpless, not even allowed to put your own stuff away for fear you would overdo. Could not walk but must be carried on a litter from which you were allowed to move under no conditions. Hopeless is just the word and how I hated to have people waiting on me, bring my meals and the like when I was used to doing for myself and hustling for my own food. White beds and soft voices of women all seemed so strange, so new to me at first, so used was I to the soft surface of Mother Earth for my bed and the voices of the stronger sex. I was just like a wild man coming out of the woods. On the way here on the train we passed a beautiful forest but for me the beauty was gone, all because I had seen blood flow in some woods that looked like them. The lines had left a mark on my mind and I must confess, for several days after I hit here, war talk of any kind soured me. I'd seen too much and yet not anywhere near as much as some. Now, after two weeks, all looks bright again. I feel like myself once more and all of life seems like a song. There's big work yet to be done and I am now anxious to get busy on my end of the big task. Now, I feel myself, I cannot afford to waste time here when big things are waiting for me in the world I had to leave.

Last Sunday was a red-letter day for me if I ever had one. I was taking my afternoon nap when I felt someone run their hand over my forehead. I opened my eyes and found Ev on one side of my bed and Capt. Root on the other. I was so surprised I could hardly speak at first. It has been six months since I have seen Ev and one or two since I have seen Capt. Root. Ev had all the latest news from home which did me a lot of good to get it as it has been some little time since I have received my mail from you folks. Capt. Root couldn't do too much for me. He gave me a bunch of cigarettes and then came up Monday morning with more and a box of cigars plus a lot of Boston Papers and some candy. He now is trying to arrange it so that, when I am strong enough, I can go with him, in his auto, for three or four days visiting all the big aerodromes he is in charge of. It surely would do me a lot of good being out in the air like that, and would give me a chance which very few boys have of seeing some of France from an auto. I hope he can arrange it as I would like to be with him and I will also very likely have a chance to spend one or more nights with Ev as well seeing some of his work. I am quite excited about it and hope it can be fixed. I never saw anything fall through yet that Capt. Root wanted, so I guess this won't. It surely was fine of him to ask me.

Ev looks like a king. He still wears that wonderful smile of his and is just as jolly as ever. I felt as if I had found a lost brother when I saw him. I have had a lot of happy hours in my life, and there are many more to come, but none have ever equaled or ever will equal I don't believe, those hours Ev and Capt. Root were there. I have felt away up in spirits ever since.

Capt. Root said he would be in again Thursday or Friday. I hope to see Capt. Bell also before I return to the battery. Kind of getting above my rank I should say when I have a Captain and a First Lieutenant coming to see me. Ev showed me the picture of the engagement ring Sister bought and I liked it very much. Just as you said in your letter last February, it was simple but very good looking.

To go back to the subject of hospitals again. I have said very little about Base 116 and it may be of interest to you all, especially Sister, to hear a little about how a hospital over here is run. The wards consist of one long building and contain about fifty beds.

These buildings come in sections and are put together by the engineers. I will do my best to draw you a picture of the inside of one of them. Room with two beds for extra sick.

In the rear of the Ward is a big tent which puts me in mind very much of a circus tent, in this are more beds. I was lucky and got a bunk in the wooden building. During the day there are two Nurses (women) and two hospital men on duty in the ward. The bed of every man has to be made just so each morning and you would die laughing if you could see some of the boys, who are up, taking lessons in bed making from our little New York nurses. Temperatures and pulses have to be taken and medicine given out - the nurses do all this. The hospital men do most of the dirty work, such as cleaning the place up and trying to hold the well men, who are just waiting for a chance to get out, where they belong. At night one nurse and one hospital man swing the whole thing. After you have been here two weeks, if you are up and dressed, you can get passes to visit the nearby towns. The food here is fine but not half enough of it to suit me as the more I eat the more I want - as usual. We get all we need, considering we are doing no work. Yesterday was one of the men's birthdays and right after supper he was presented with a nice big cake. He had it passed through the ward and each one of us got some. My, but it did taste good. I hope I am somewheres on my twenty-first birthday where I can have a good time. It certainly would be great if I could be with Ev and Capt. Root. I surely would give them a real party. When the nurses came around taking our ages and home addresses a few days ago, she could hardly believe me when I told her I was only twenty. "You are pretty young to be Sergeant, aren't you?" she said. I wonder what she would have thought if I had told her I intended to be a Lieutenant before I was twenty-two. I wish Sister could see a little of this work over here but I have no desire to have her take it up. Some of the sights you see as you walk through different wards just make the coldest heart go out to the poor boys who are bearing their pain so bravely and cheerfully. Some have their legs off, others their arms and yet they wear a smile and laugh. It surely is a brave lot of boys Uncle Sam has sent over here to do his work and America can well be proud of them. Those who return deserve all the nation can give them and I guess they will get it.

August 8, 1918

Capt. Root was in again to see me again this morning and brought more cigarettes with him. He is treating me just as if I were his own son and believe me, Mother, I did appreciate it. He also brought the good news that he got permission to take me off for the trip in his auto. He seemed as much pleased about it as I was, and that is going some. I got my clothes today and, unless something unforeseen turns up, will leave here with him Saturday morning. Just how long we shall be gone I do not know but one night of more or less freedom will seem like Heaven to me.

Today I am going into a town, three or four miles from the hospital, with two other Sergeants. There we can have a real feed and Johnny intends to eat eggs and French fries plus some meat just about all the time he is there.

Now, about this mail question before I close. As I have told you I have no idea when I shall return to the battery. They may, and may not, forward my mail so here is what we have decided to do so that I will be sure to get your letters. You are to send them in care of Capt. Root and he has very kindly offered to see they reach me, as I am to keep in touch with him. Do this with a few letters then start in sending them to the battery again as I shall be back by then. Here is Capt Root's address:

W.H. Root
Capt. Engrs. N.A.
A.P.O. 757

Anything you send him will be sure to reach me no matter where I am.

Well, darling, I have written quite a bit and you must be tired of reading it all, so I will close.

Please give my love to all the family and keep a lot for yourself.
Johnny

Western Union Telegram
August 5, 1918

Number 3B   Sent by: LS   Rec'd by: RX No. of words: 23
From: France
    9:25 A.M.

Mr. Arthur L. Hobson
Little Boars Head, NH
    John slightly gassed/ Base hospital one sixteen/ Excellent treatment/ Assumes rapid recovery/ No danger/ Spirits high/ Sends love.

Bradley

Western Union Telegram
August 7, 1918

Number: 11   Sent by: Rec'd by: RX No.of words: 20
From: Chatillonne
    5:50 P.M.

Mr. Arthur L. Hobson
Little Boars Head, NH
    Saw John Sunday/ Absolutely all right /Walking daily/ Month rest/ Mail letters to Root/ Battery fine.
William H. Root
Capt. Engineer Corps.
My Dear Mrs. Hobson:
    I was sorry not to have found this for you but it was in a letter I received on Tuesday instead of those I received on Wednesday. I will write it just as Henry did.

"Yesterday I saw all the Battery. They had just moved out after being in position for almost five months.

"They got to the big show and you will hear great things of them. They looked fine.

"I ate dinner right with the boys. John Hobson is well and lucky to be here for a shell broke over his dugout and he had a slight shell shock. He is some lucky. [This was an incident that happened in June at Rambucourt and is detailed in a subsequent letter sent home on 16 September 1918.]

"I saw the Colonel who by the way is most wonderful to me and he said John would be sent to school to try for a lieutenancy. Lieut. Morrison, the battery commander, is holding it up for the present, I think."

Perhaps Henry would rather not have me tell you that last sentence for it is only a supposition, so please do not repeat it.

Any time you are passing stop and I will give you any news if there is any. Let's hope you will find me a bit more presentable.

Cordially yours,
Victoria Knipe Root

PS:
Henry's address is:
William Henry Root
Capt. Engineers Corps
US APO 757
AEF
France

Captain William Root was, indeed, a good friend to my father. William Henry Root was born in Roxbury, Massachusetts, in 1879 and he was graduated from Norwalk Military Academy and St. Laurent in Canada. Following completion of his education, he moved to Haverhill as a member of the construction firm of W. A. & H. A. Root Construction Co. He was elected alderman to that city in 1916 and served without pay, setting a precedent for municipal office holders.

He married Victoria Knipe, founder of the William A. Knipe School in Ward Hill, which was named in memory of her father, a prominent Ward Hill shoe manufacturer.

William H. Root was 38 years old when the United States got involved in the Great War. When war was declared, he resigned his position as alderman, after serving only one year, to organize Battery A of the 102nd Field Artillery. When the battery was first organized he was initially commissioned as 1st Lieutenant at Camp Curtis Guild, Jr. and later promoted to Captain, serving as an observer in airplanes with Everett Bradley. He was later reassigned to the engineers where he constructed "aerodromes" and other buildings.

When the war ended he had attained the rank of Major and was made Lieutenant Colonel in 1919.

After his military career, he returned to the construction business in Boston and directed the construction of many Boston buildings: the Park

Square Boston YMCA, Boston Five Cent Saving Bank, Consolidated Gas and the Studio Building, as well as the University Club and the Hotel Bradford.

He also built many buildings in Haverhill: the Whittier Building, C.G. Ellis Building, William Knipe School in Ward Hill, the Greenleaf School addition, Bradford Academy, the Victory Building and the Essex Associates Building. The buildings still stand, but most have long since been renamed.

William Root died in 1937 at the age of 58.

After a month recuperating from his mustard gas burns behind the lines, on 17 August, Father turned twenty-one years of age. Father celebrated his twenty-first birthday in the company of First Lieutenant Everett Bradley and Captain William H. Root away from the front lines and in the peace and beauty of the French countryside southwest of Paris. There was no letter from Father describing the event. However, it was under circumstances that his grandfather, John L. Hobson, Sr., probably never imagined when he wrote that note to his grandson a year before on the occasion of Father's twentieth birthday. But, I'm sure it was a party that would have pleased his grandfather.

My father and the battery were well away from the fighting, for the time being anyway.

Every week during this time, a selected group of non-commissioned officers were ordered to attend officer training school away from the front. The regular officers were being sent home in large numbers to become instructors in the new divisions being trained in the United States. These exiting officers needed to be replaced.

Having attained the age required for becoming a commissioned officer, Father was appointed to attend Saumur Artillery School in Saumur, France. Ancient, beautiful Saumur is on the Loire and dominated by the magnificent, turreted 14th-century castle, Chateau de Saumur. Saumur is located west of Tours and 43 kilometers (27 miles) north of Pothiers where the battery was located and resting.

Dearest Mother

This has been by far the best week I have had since I have been in France. Eating, sleeping, and going all over the country with Capt. Root in his car is all I have done and it has done me the world of good. I feel like a new man now and when the Captain leaves me at the hospital Sunday night or Monday morning, I shall be all ready to start on my trip back to the battery in the very best condition to take up my work again. I will tell you as best I can, without mentioning the names of the various places I have visited, what has taken place on my trip.

Capt. Root called for me at the hospital last Saturday morning about ten o'clock and we started out for his headquarters which are about two hours ride from the hospital. There he left me in his room while he went down to the office to do some business. Lunch was brought up to me in the room as it is not customary for enlisted men to eat with officers and they had a mess downstairs. Oh, Mother, I shall never forget that meal if I live to be a hundred, three of the most wonderful meat balls I ever ate, two eggs, bread, butter, jam and a nice cup of black coffee. We were fed well enough at the hospital but nothing like that and the cooking couldn't be beat. The Capt. had more business to do after lunch so I took a walk in the garden back of the house and tried to talk French with the daughter of the landlady. We got along fairly well but, like all other girls, she tried to talk too fast and I had to ask her to put the brakes on several times as I couldn't follow her. The Capt. came back about five and we set out, along with a Lieut. to the town where Ev is, arriving there about six thirty. Ev did not know we were coming and hence was very much surprised. That night the four of us, plus two other Lieutenants Ev knew, had supper in a private room at the hotel after which we walked down to the city Club. Ev and I returned to his room about midnight and, of course, had to stay up two or three hours talking over old times and dreaming sweet dreams of the future, when we shall return home. Just think, I had not seen the old boy for SIX months and I felt just as if I had met my own brother. It was almost too good to be true. He hasn't changed a bit except, perhaps, put on flesh. After talking ourselves sleepy we both hit the nice feather bed he has and were soon off to sleep. The next morning (Sunday) we had breakfast in his room. I believe he has it there every morning. I met the French family he is staying with and when they found out I was Ev's future brother-in-law nothing was too good for me and they couldn't do enough for me. They all think the world of Ev and he has become one of the family. After breakfast we took a walk up to the field and looked the planes all over and had our picture taken which I believe Ev has sent you. It is mighty good of him but I look as if I had the whole world on my back. Such is far from being the case as I have not a care to my name these days, except to make sure I eat all I can lay my hands on. It will, however, give you an idea of how bum a line sergeant looks side of a Lieutenant. Ev and I enjoyed a quiet dinner together that noon, Capt. Root and the Lieutenant having gone off on business. That afternoon Ev took me out to see the sights of the town and, believe me, when I say he has one mighty pretty place to live in. First we went out through the park and followed the river along for a ways, then we inspected an old fortress away up on a hill from which we could look down on the town. Our next move was for a graveyard. "Not a very cheerful place for two young, spirited youths to walk", you may say "and especially one who has just returned from the front." The place may not have been cheerful but the sights were more than interesting. Ev knows just about every French person in town it seems and I was forced to smile hearing him talk to them in their own lingo. He has it down cold now and can talk French almost as well as English. Supper that night with the Captain I had to leave at seven thirty Monday morning and I certainly did hate to say good-bye to Ev as I had no idea when I should see him again. All day Monday we went from one field to another, the building of which Capt. Root has charge. It was all more than interesting to me and the country we passed through was beautiful. I do not know how many miles we made that day but it was around 120 and we did not get back to the Captain's room until nine that night, having been on the move all day. Tuesday morning, bright and early, we started off again to inspect more fields and see more of the country. That night we spent in a city at a hotel where I had a chance to get a real bath. We ran into one of the battery boys, who was transferred last April, and he had supper with us and spent the night with me. There was a wonderful moving picture place in this town where, plus the pictures, they have fine music so we went there in the evening. It was the first time I had been in a French theatre so everything was interesting beyond words. They played several American selections which sounded mighty good to me. A Frenchman came out and sang a few songs but I could not understand what he was singing about so, when the rest laughed I did, not having any idea what the joke was. We had to go to bed by candlelight with the shades down over our window, as the alarm for an air raid sounded just as we reached the hotel. As good luck would have it there was no raid or, if there was, I failed to hear it. The next morning after getting four eggs, three cups of chocolate and land only knows how much bread and butter under my belt, we started off again. I could have put away four more eggs but was afraid I would shock the hotel keeper. We had heard reports that the battery was in a nearby town so Capt. Root decided we would find it and pay the boys a visit. This we did, finding them just about noon. We got them a bunch of cigarettes plus a bag of sugar and flour. Everyone was low on smokes and you should have seen the happy look on the faces of those men when we pulled in with the back seat covered with cigarettes. The battery is only a short ways from where Ev is and are in their first rest camp. [Chatillonne-sur-Seine] I believe we are to have some more training along certain lines where we showed weakness while at the front, but I guess the work will be light and will serve to pass away the time as well as keeping the men in condition. They all look fine and you would never know that they were fresh from the front. Yesterday afternoon, after doing a little more business, we ran down to see Ev again, where I am now. I spent last night with him and, unless things change, shall be here with him until Sunday. This will mean that we shall be together over my birthday which is tomorrow. Capt. Root has gone off but is to return in time for the dinner I am to give he and Ev tomorrow night to celebrate my twenty-first birthday. Sunday I shall very likely return to the hospital, having been gone for eight days. I never shall be able to thank Capt. Root enough for all he has done for me. Fresh air, good food and plenty of sleep was just what I needed to build me up and he certainly has seen to it that I have had all three, as well as giving me a chance to see Ev. He couldn't have shown more interest in me had I been his own son and I certainly appreciated what he has done.

While I was at the battery yesterday I got my mail and had two from you, one from Sis, one from Dad plus one from Grandpa Gale. I was very much amused at what Mrs. Cooper told you about my being stationed in some large city not working very hard for a living. I wish it might come true but there is no danger of it while the war is on I fear.

Dad's letters started to arrive just after I wrote that one to Sis and since then I have received one from him with every lot of mail that has come in. I didn't think he had forgotten me but just wanted to hear from him personally as well as the rest of you.

Grandpa Gale's letter was full of interest and I shall try to write him before I leave here. Be sure, Mother, that you show all of my letters to both of the grandparents, won't you, because I do not get a chance to write them very often.

So Art has turned into a chauffeur has he? Good for him. I have got a mental picture of you getting into the big car and saying, "Home, James!" or of Art waiting outside in the yard with the car for Sister to come out of some tea house, or sitting side of the curb stone while you and Sis are in some store buying a hat. But what makes me laugh out loud is when I think of Art, in his shirtsleeves, changing a tire on that big car out in the hot sun. That's alright, I'll bet he is doing a good job of it just the same. As I wrote him, I am afraid that his dreams of driving an ambulance over here will never come true. I hate to discourage him, but I hope not for his sake as I do not want to have him, or any other member of the family exposed to shellfire. It is lots of fun to read about it and see it in the pictures but quite another thing when you are there yourself. Ev and I will do all that end of it but I hope all the rest of you will only read about it and I think that is all you will do the way things are going just now.

Luck has been with me all summer and the only time I had hay fever was last June and that was more of a slight cold than hay fever.

I have had very little work around the horses all summer and this may be one of the reasons.

Your account of the work Sister was doing at the hospital, and the courses, was of great interest to both Ev and myself. Neither one of us knew just what the course was but your letter cleared the matter up very well. I hope she did not get overtired doing it. Ten hours a day is a whole lot for a girl to be on her feet. I am proud of her and hope she follows it up but feel as Ev feels, that she ought not to undertake too much.

Dad writes that "K" makes a very good little housekeeper and I can easily imagine she would. The picture you sent me of her some little time ago has brought me many minutes of pleasure. She has grown older and much prettier since I left and she was a picture of beauty when I last saw her. It won't be long after she reaches Sister's age before she will be changing her name and leaving us to make a home of her own. My only hope is that she gets as good a man as Sis has, she can not get any better in my eyes.

I suppose Art will have his eye out for a bride before long also and, if anyone should ask you, it looks to me as if I was to be the next to last one to leave you folks. Ye Gods, I haven't even got a girl in sight yet. I think you had better consult Mrs. Cooper on this point.

Well, Dear, I guess I have written about enough for this time so will close.

Ev sends his love to all the family. Lots of love for you all from me.
Johnny

Dear Dad

For the benefit of those who so generously contributed to the Battery Fund I am going to write a few lines to let them know how much their money was appreciated by the boys and to tell them for what their money has been spent. I wish that you would please have this letter printed in the paper in order that all those who gave money to this fund will realize what it has meant to the battery boys over here.

First of all I shall take up the cases of the poor boys who have been laid up in the hospitals from one cause or another. These by the grace of God have been very few considering what the battery has been through in the last six months. The men who are taken sick or wounded on the field are of course sent at once to some large base hospital for treatment. Just as soon as they leave the battery they are left alone in the world, so to speak, and in most cases with very little or no money in their pockets. While we are in action the battery commander has no time to follow these men up and see that as many of their wants as possible are attended to. Of course the hospitals do all they can for the men, but if a sick or a wounded soldier has a few francs of his own with him he can buy many little things that will add to his comfort and pleasure while he is confined to the hospital, thus making the time pass quicker and the hours brighter. The next question is "How do we get money to these men since they are out of the reach of the battery commander?" The battery very fortunately has a man over here who is very interested in it, having been a member of the organization once himself, and still holds a great interest in it and the welfare of its men. This man is Capt. Root. He has a machine of his own and on his tour of duty passes near some of the large base hospitals where our men are sent. He very quickly has taken it upon himself to see personally that men from the battery laid up in these hospitals get a little extra money, which is taken from the fund, for any extra comforts they may be able to get. The battery commander is backing Capt. Root in this work and I feel that it is one of the greatest if not the greatest work that the fund can do. Here is just one instance that I happened to see myself and which I think will prove to you that the money you gave was given to a good cause and is being spent to a good advantage by those to whom it was entrusted. I happened to fall the victim of mustard gas and was sent to a large base hospital where I met four of the other members of the battery. As luck would have it I happened to have a little money with me but the other four men were without a red cent and longing for a little candy and some cigarettes. The battery commander did not know where we were and hence could not forward our pay to us. The battery was taking part in the big drive at the front and no one had time to find out where we were. In other words we were S.O.L. or "Sure Out Of Luck" as far as money went. Capt. Root came in one day and gave those four men enough money to buy a reasonable amount of candy and cigarettes. That night as one of the men lay on his cot eating his candy and smoking he said to me, "Sergeant, that money was a gift straight from heaven," and he meant every word of it.

Next comes the boys in the field who in this last great push covered themselves with glory and performed deeds which should make Haverhill prouder than ever of her battery. While we were driving the Huns back, there was very little time to eat or sleep. Anything we could lay our hands on was good enough for us just so long as we could keep the enemy on the run. Rations came very well, however, considering the great speed with which we were advancing and those who were not too tired to eat generally got enough. After several weeks of the hardest kind of fighting the battery was relieved from the lines and sent back, tired, dirty, and worn out from lack of sleep. They wanted good food and a change if possible from the same old Army rations. I do not say that the Army food isn't good because it is, but a change or a few extras such as pancakes and biscuits go pretty good after a strenuous few weeks on the firing lines. When the outfit arrived at their rest camp, I believe they had no sugar at all and no one dared mention a bag of flour for fear of his life. Did we go without? Not a bit of it because thanks to you people at home we had a fund that we could buy it out of and we all knew that you folks at home wanted your soldier boys to have the best money could buy or you never would have sent that money. We bought one large bag of sugar and one of flour thus enabling the men to have their pancakes and biscuits both of which they very likely would not have had for several days had it not been for the generous gift of you people at home. It would have done you all good to have seen the happy smiles on the boys' faces when they saw that bag of sugar and flour coming in and when it is put in the form of flour it will grow several inches. The boys never kick on the flour but eat what they get without saying a word but they certainly do enjoy and deserve what few extras the fund can buy for them. "All out boys! We have got pancakes for supper tonight!" is a yell I love to hear or land at the kitchen after a hard day's work and find hot biscuits with butter waiting for me. We look forward to these just as a child looks forward to Christmas or his birthday.

Last but not least comes the smokes. I don't suppose the women know what these mean to the men, and some may say we would be better off without them, but I cannot agree with them on this point. A good pipe of tobacco and a nice mellow cigarette or cigar, if you are lucky enough to get one, certainly help to pass away the time and settle your meals. Along the smoking line the men would have been out of luck for fair had it not been for the fund. Very few men had cigarettes when they came off of this last front and very few had any tobacco with which to roll their own. But the fund came to the rescue and cigarettes and tobacco were given out the second night we landed in our rest camp. All were happy now that they could have a real smoke again.

Other little things which I have not time to mention are bought out of this fund and all of you who gave toward it, no matter how large or how small the gift may have been, can rest assured that that gift has gone to a great cause and that the men who are enjoying it appreciate beyond words what the people of Haverhill have done for them and we in turn shall try to make Battery A one that Haverhill can be proud of and already have gone a long way toward doing it. I hope that before many more months this war will be over and we shall return to Haverhill to enjoy the world wide peace for which we are now fighting.

Sergt. John L. Hobson
OK
W.H. Root
Capt. Engineers C.

WESTERN UNION TELEGRAM
[Undated]

Received at: 4B   Chatillon-sur-Seine via Haverhill Mass. N F 2
Arthur Hobson
Little Boars Head N.H.
John has left for school period
Write him seven eighteen period Root

CHAPTER TWELVE

Saumur Artillery School

"…by means of good hard digging, and patience,
he is going to make good here"

SERGEANT JOHN L. HOBSON II

What was in 1918 Saumur Artillery School, October 2004.
Stephen G. Hobson Collection - Stephen G. Hobson photograph

Saumur, France, October 2004. Stephen G. Hobson Collection - Stephen G. Hobson photograph

The regiment's rest period was deserved and welcome, but short. The big drive was on to push the enemy back into Germany.

In the first days of September the regiment entrained for the St. Mihiel sector. The regiment shattered all records and loaded onto trains at Poinson in 42 minutes.

On 12 September, the 102nd Field Artillery was at war again. For seven hours, accompanied by five thousand Allied guns and eight American divisions, they pounded the enemy in the St. Mihiel sector. The 102nd Field Artillery Regiment alone fired 13,000 rounds. A brigade operations order was issued directing "…pursuit… sparing neither horse nor man." The enemy was in retreat.

The 26th of September was the beginning of the Meuse-Argonne offensive, and the regiment would participate. It was to be the greatest Allied offensive of the war.

On 9 and 10 October, the 102nd Field Artillery Regiment suffered its heaviest casualties of the war. The Meuse-Argonne offensive would be the bloodiest around Verdun and it lasted until late in October. It appeared that the war would be over soon, but there was still work to be done.

Meanwhile, at Saumur…

Dearest Mother

Things have been taking place in my life so fast for the past two weeks that I am sorry to say I have neglected one of the first duties of a good soldier, to write home. I have by no means forgotten you all, however, during these two weeks of adventure and many times each day, and especially at night, my thoughts have crossed the ocean to visit you all for a few minutes. Now the question comes up, what have I been doing that I have been unable to find time to write.

As you must know by now I have left the battery and gone back to school days once again. They are a little different from the days I spent at Exeter as the subjects are a little deeper and the reward at the end of the course of a little different nature from what one gets when he has completed the course at Exeter. If I make good here my reward will be a Sam Browne belt and two gold bars, one for each shoulder. In other words, dear, my dreams of all winter have been realized and I now find myself studying for a commission. This may at first seem to be a fairly easy job but there is an awful lot to artillery and an artillery officer must, if he is to be any good, know the game from top to bottom as far as possible. Saumur tries to give us as sound a training in all the different parts as possible in the short time we are here. Hence we have to move very fast and for me it takes quite a bit of studying to get some of it through my head. My experience in the battery has helped me a lot but here I have things to figure out which, up to now, were mere names to me. How I am going to come out remains for the future to tell us, but one of my fondest dreams will be broken if, for one reason or another, I am unable to pass the exams and miss out on my commission. My heart is set on it for the sake of you folks at home as well as my own. I've got the chance for which I have been working for months and now I have got to make good.

Dad's cablegram congratulating me on behalf of the whole family upon my appointment to school pleased me very much indeed, and I can just see the smile of pride and joy on his face, as well as the rest of you, if in two or three months you get a cable from me saying that I have made good. Now for a few lines about the course here.

First of all comes the division, which is made up of six or seven sections, each section having twenty men in it. These classes, or sections, each have an officer as instructor and in charge, so to speak. He teaches us some subjects and then there are both French and American officers who lecture on other courses. Morris Baker is my instructor in telephone work. We take up every phase of artillery that is possible and get a lot of work outside. Half the section will be privates one day while the other half play the part of officers and do the whole thing just as if they were a battery commander. They must put their battery in position, figure the date, etc. just as if they were with some outfit in the field. We have our first day at the range tomorrow and I am wondering what I shall be, an officer adjusting the fire or one of the gun crew.

Every good artillery officer must, of course, know how to ride a horse and here is where the fun comes in. There are any number of wonderful riding halls here and twice a week, under a French instructor, we go to one and try to learn to ride in French saddles in the French style. We are not allowed to use stirrups for the first month and hence some of us take some mean old falls, but the floor is sawdust and we do not get hurt but merely get a mouthful of sawdust. The French have got some of the most beautiful horses here that I have ever seen and some can give you a mighty wild ride around that hall. We all dislike this riding without stirrups but it is the ONLY way to learn to really ride and after a class is over you always hear laughing and kidding. These French saddles are very different from any I ever rode in. Later on we learn to jump and get outdoor work.

Here is a list of the courses I am taking. They may be Greek to you and some were, and still are, to me. However, they will serve to show just what I am studying and, if no one else explains them to you, I will try to when I get home.

1. B.C. (Battery Commander, firing dates, etc.)
2. Ammunition (Shells, fuses and their effects and how made.)

3. Ballistics (What happens to the shell from the time the gun is fired until it lands.)
4. Dispersion (The effect wind, air, gravity. etc. has on a shell)
5. Telephone
6. Horses
7. Material (Study of the make up and parts of 75m/m gun.)
8. Topographical Surveying (Map work, etc.)

Some of these subjects are very hard for me to get through my head but every day I am beginning to see light and when the course is over hope to really know a little something about all of them.

There are no classes on Sundays and only two calls so we are free to do just about what we like. I usually take lunch at some café and study or sleep the rest of the time. Some hire these French wheels and go out to see the sights but as yet I have not done this. We use these French wheels to go off on, to some of our field work and they are a circus to ride. One usually falls apart on every trip.

They have the most wonderful Y.M.C.A. here that I have ever seen. It is in a house that I should judge at one time was a private home and reminds me of a club more than a Y.M.C.A.

Mr. Brown's son is here as I guess you know by now. He is in the same barracks with me but not the same section. There are also several boys from the 102nd Regiment here so you see I am by no means alone. Potter Hurd, an old Exeter friend of mine, is also here. Ask Sister about him if you do not remember him. He is in the 155m/m guns, larger than the 75m/m. Well so much for school.

I received a long letter from you yesterday which Capt. Root had forwarded to me. I see that the news of my accident at the observation post * could not be kept in the dark, as I had hoped it would, but now that you have heard of it - it was a very narrow escape and, as Major Goodwin told me that evening when he came out to the post to see how much damage had been done, I was a lucky boy to be alive to tell the tale. Needless to say I was slightly shell shocked and was unable to control my hands, feet and head which thrashed around in good shape for several hours. I shall never forget Major Goodwin, now Lieutenant Colonel Goodwin in the 101st Regiment, as long as I live. I was laying on two duck boards when he arrived, two or more hours after the observation room was hit, shaking like a leaf. The very first thing he did was to ask for me, and when he came in to see a troubled look at once came over his face just as if I was his own boy. Since you know I did get laid out I will tell you a little about it, but I had hoped that it would never reach home. I had just sighted a Boche battery and the Lieutenant in charge had just come up on my call and we were getting ready to open fire on it. Several shots were passing over the O.P. [observation post] when all of a sudden one landed about 400 feet in front of us and right on line with the O.P. I turned to the Lieutenant and said, "If they only take a bracket on those shots they will land one right on us." We both laughed and began sending data to the battery we were to fire. The next thing I knew I woke up in the corner of the room, which was filled with black powder smoke, with the Lieutenant on top of me. He was groaning to beat the cars and at first I thought he had been seriously hurt. I carried him out with the aid of one of the other men and he came to fine. Whatever hit me then I don't know and probably never shall. Everything went black and I fell, as I was later told, into one of the boy's arms. They carried me to the officer's dugout and sent for a Red Cross man. He worked on me half an hour and then declared me dead. BUT I fooled them and came to life about half an hour later, cold and without the use of my eyes. I was blindfolded for ¾ of an hour but God saw me and opened my eyes. That's the whole story in a brief way. The Lieutenant was OK at the end of five or ten minutes but Johnny was not quite so lucky. Well, it's all in a lifetime so why worry. A man cannot expect to come through this war without some unpleasant experiences. If he did where would the fun come in?

Mother, I wish you would call Mrs. Stover up on the phone for me and tell her and Mr. Stover that I am all OK again and came out of the gas without a mark. There is one small one on my knee but that will wear off. Also give them my love.

I had a fine letter from Marj and also one from Hope. It certainly does seem good to hear from all my old friends and know they thought of me on my birthday even if I was miles away and on foreign soil.

I was with Everett and Capt. Root at Chatillion-sur-Seine on the 17th of August and we had a very nice little party about which I guess Ev has written you, wish you all had been there, so I will not go over it again. The French people Ev is staying with gave me a very pretty bunch of flowers which I found waiting for me in Ev's room upon our return from dinner. They pleased me very much indeed.

Well, dear, I guess I have written enough for this time so will close.

Give my love to all and keep a lot for yourself.
Johnny

*The incident my father writes about here was previously mentioned in Chapter 10 on the Million Dollar Raid. Father's description in this letter is better than if I had previously elaborated on it. The incident was accounted for in "The History of the 102nd Field Artillery" as follows:

In the afternoon [of 19 June] at 15:43 our observatory (OP21) was struck by a shell which landed just below the aperture of the observing instrument. One man was hurt and the place was badly wrecked. Shortly before this, "OP21" had reported puffs of smoke at 54.1-34.6 [map coordinates], apparently a battery in action. Our 90-mm Batteries near Rambucourt were put on it and shortly thereafter a cloud of smoke appeared at the point in question which lasted about five minutes, much to the satisfaction of the personnel of the 90's. There was no further activity from that particular point thereafter.

When I read my father's account of this incident, several things struck me: one, how lucky he was not to have been killed and, testimony to the old military saw, "You never hear the one that gets you," neither man in the observation post reported actually hearing the incoming artillery round that actually hit the observation tower. Incoming artillery shells usually whistle in flight.

Dearest Sister

As I put the date on this letter a mental picture comes into my mind and I wonder if the same one is not in your mind. I believe it must be, because what took place that night I do not think will ever be forgotten by any of the Bradley family or ours. As a matter of fact, I guess there are a good many families in the good old U.S.A. who will not forget that night in a hurry. It hardly seems possible that it was a year ago that Everett and I kissed you goodbye and then, on the following day, started off on our great adventure in the war - and yet in many ways it seems as if it must have been longer as so much has taken place since that day. Marj is married, George has been over here and back, Ev has taken his place as an instructor after months of experience and I have spent seven months on the battle field plus enjoying (?) two small lay outs. You at home have also done a lot since we boys left for the fight. You, darling, have given your time to Red Cross and are now waiting for your call, Art has made good at Exeter, Katherine has learned how to help Mother out with her house work, Buster has grown from a baby into a real little man. But Mother and Dad have done more than any of us - they have given their oldest boy to the country and, having done that, they began to work for their country, their family and their soldier boy. Giving all that was theirs to give for all three and keeping cheerful even if they knew big drives were taking place, that hundreds and even thousands were bleeding and passing on every day and that their boy might be one of them at any time. We all have learned patience and to trust in God more than ever before since that night a year ago and, whereas life may look a little bleak at times, I think, as a whole, it is brighter and better from our experiences over the past year. But the greatest day of all is to come - when the transport that brings us all home and steams into some U.S. port and, with the thanks and blessings of all the world, the Yankee boys march home. This day is not so very far off, dear, and it will come as a surprise to us all. It may be another year but what is that in our lives when we are all doing such fine work. The Boche tried twice to make me absent at the final roll call but I am too lucky and when the cheers and bells of America let loose to welcome her sons home Johnny is going to be right there. I wouldn't miss that party for anything. You will not see much change in either Ev or I except that we both look older and are a whole lot wiser than when we left. Nevertheless, you will still find that, as usual, we have a lot of crazy ideas in our heads and will be able to frame up just as good parties as we used to, with the help of you girls. Well, now for a little news.

First of all, mail. I had three bully letters handed to me a few nights ago. One from Hope, one from Marj Stover, and a nice long one from Eloise. These three letters pleased me very much and I hope they will all take the trouble to drop me a few more lines in the near future.

This week has seen a big advancement in my work and I am beginning slowly but surely, to understand a little about firing a battery, from an officer's view point. Last Wednesday we were out and on the range all the afternoon, firing. I was on the gun for a while and then did some observing. It seems like old times to be sensing shots once again. This, you know, was about 25% of my work while I was at the observation post last spring. Next week, I believe, we have two days out at the range. It is some littler distance from the town as we go out either in trucks or on the tramway, depending on which range we go to.

Last Friday they took the trouble to give us an exam in BC and I understand that we are to get one a week in this subject from now on. They are not hard for the men who can handle angles but for a thick head such as myself, they are none too soft. As I guess perhaps you know there is quite a little geometry to the artillery and I never was much good at that stuff. Well, we'll get it somehow but only land knows when. How I made out I do not yet know. Math certainly is my big handicap here but I hope to be able to master it. If, however, I can't I will have to try for a commission elsewhere, where it will not need quite so much. Things look fine now, however, so we need not worry. I have a lot of things cooking in my head, so if one fails some one of the others are bound to work.

Last night I enjoyed a fine supper downtown with one of the men in the section. Four eggs, French fried potatoes and steak made up the meal along with a little bread and butter. Bread is very hard to get in Saumur and in many places they will not serve it to you unless you have a bread ticket. The mess at the school is fine but we all like a little change once in a while so eat outside. There is no mess line here and no mess kits. We eat in a nice mess hall and use real plates which we do not have to wash ourselves. This saves a whole lot of time and trouble. The food is all put right on the table and we just walk in and fall to, the same as you would at Exeter.

Another great help here is the fact that we do not have to carry our own wash water. So many pails are put in each barrack and are filled by the women who take care of the place. In this way we lose no time in the morning and when we come in at night after a dusty ride in the trucks, the water is all ready for us and all we have to do is to wash up and head for the mess. Needless to say we are all hungry when meal time comes around. There are lots of little comforts like this which we could not have in the battery but which we must have here in order that we can put all our time on our work. This idea of not having to slave all day Sunday, as well as the other six week days, is something new for me. Another thing - when you go to bed at night you can rest assured that you will be forced to get up about three or four a.m. and fire a barrage or "stand to" for a couple of hours. These things sound small but mean a lot to me.

As I wrote to Mother, Potter Hurd is here and asked for you all. He has not changed a bit since I last saw him at Exeter.

Well, dear, there really is no news to tell you except that I am well and happy, so I will close.

Please give my love to all the family.

Lots of love for yourself.
Johnny

Dear Dad

Another week gone and my first month at Saumur completed. It does not seem as if I had been there that long and yet time seems to be going faster and faster every week and the work becoming more interesting. Lots of little points, which a week ago were not clear to me, have straightened themselves this past week and, slowly but surely, I feel that I am gaining a little ground every day.

Last week we spent two days on the range and this is where you really learn and have impressed upon your mind what has been told to you in lectures, or which you have read. I did not get a chance to conduct the fire but we all have to go in turn so my time will come. Every man here has a chance to fire two problems at least before he leaves and sometimes three. We all have to observe the fire when one of the men in our section is adjusting and you really learn just about as much this way as if you were doing it yourself. Yesterday we had a field service in which we went out in trucks and picked a battery position and then figured the firing data for it. This week we take the guns out with horses and have to put them into place.

The ways of doing lots of things here is far different from the way the battery used to do them when really on the front and so it is not all old stuff to me by any means. The more ways a man can learn of doing things the better off he is over here, because you can never tell what your conditions are going to be. Hence it has been with the greatest interest that I have read and heard lectures on all these different subjects. The object in view is always the same but the means of arriving at it may be a bit different from what I have been used to.

We had our third exam in BC last evening and, from all I can gather, I must have made an 80 or 90 on it. They are not hard any of them but there are so blame many little things to think of that, as a rule, I forget one or two and thus get the example only half right. I made 70 on my first exam and 60 on the second. That second one fooled the whole section and, out of twenty men, only three made 70 or above and yet it was easy, but full of little catches here and there. Well, such is life, just so long as there are exams to be dealt with.

We start to ride horse back outside the last of this week which I am very thankful for as I am getting a little tired of going around the ring with no change in the sights but the same stone walls looking at you where ever you go.

I had a fine birthday letter from Grandma Hobson last Wednesday as well as some cards. They were a little late in arriving to be sure but I think I enjoyed them even more than I would have if they had reached me on time as they brought back fond memories of my first birthday away from home. Mother's letter telling me all about the big party you folks had up in the barn was very interesting and the two little poems she sent me went right down deep into my heart, especially the one about the Service Flag. I am going to try to keep that, but have found it hard indeed to keep letters and the like because when I move I have no place to carry them. Well, if I get through here I intend to buy a trunk, if one can be got, and then I ought to be all set when it comes to keeping little things, such as letters and the like, which have brought many minutes of pleasure to me.

Things look brighter over here than they have ever since the War began. The Americans, as you must know from the papers, are covering themselves with glory which will never be forgotten. I was reading only last night how a bunch of our boys went over the top yelling just as if they were in a football game. The Germans can't hold out when the French and Americans open up at them and this is being proved every day. We're driving here and we're driving there, while the enemy seems to be falling before us like a child before a runaway horse. They don't know what to do and, from all reports, I should say were fairly well down in the mouth all around. Our spirits and hopes are going up every day, our boys are full of life and youth and how can men who are worn out stand up in the big test with the boys who are fresh and ready to fight until their last drop of blood is gone. I wish I could describe to you some of the sights of real manhood I have seen myself, tell you some of the stories I have been told by the dough boys and try to tell you of the wonderful work the U.S. Government has done over here. Dad, you couldn't believe them unless you were here to see it all yourself. And, yet, who has made it possible for the U.S. to carry on all this great work, both here and there? Dad, it is men like yourself who have given their own flesh to the great cause in the form of a boy who will gladly shoulder the gun while his father in turn, backs the country up with money and a spirit that can't be killed. Your lot is, in many ways, the harder one because, aside from your own worries and cares, I know that no matter how cheerful your face may look, deep down in that big heart of yours there is a longing for your boy to come home, and a constant worry for fear he will lose what you gave him - his life. The end is in sight, however, and no one, man, woman or child can tell me that it isn't because I know better. I am not fool enough to think I shall be home right away because even after the peace terms have been drawn up six months or a year from now, there will be a lot of work to be done over here and it is up to the young men to fall to just as they are now and do it. I would gladly spend a year or more over here in government work after the war is over if they would only give me a month with you folks at home first. Of late I have had a very strong desire to see every one of you once again and I hope, before many months, luck will come my way again as it has so many times in the past year. I am not homesick but just feel that I want to see you all, talk to you, hear your voices and enjoy the blessings of a father's and mother's love at home.

A new lot of men arrived here yesterday to start the course the first of October. I am in hopes that one of the Sergeants from the Battery may be with them but believe we do not send another man here until next month. Nevertheless, I am going to look around as I know the battery has seen some heavy fighting since I left them and I am very anxious for news from them. I think an awful lot of that bunch of boys and should hate like everything to hear that any one of them had been hurt or killed. I, of course, am out of the fight for a while but my heart goes out to those who are in it, as I know from experience just what it is like. I wrote one of the sergeants a few days ago and hope that I get an answer before long.

In my last letter I believe I forgot to tell you about the wonderful send off Lieutenant Morrison gave me. There is a long, long story connected to our relations with each other which I cannot very well go into now but may someday. When the order came in for me to leave he told me that he wished to see me at least three quarters of an hour before I left. After getting all set I went around to where he roomed (we were in a rest camp) and found him alone in the garden. Well, Dad, I wish you could have heard the talk he gave me, it was fine. He told me all about the school, as he was there himself, and wished me all the luck in the world, adding that any time I needed help or money, or wanted a recommendation to be sure and let him know and he would see that I had any one of the three or all of them. He also asked me to let him know, if possible, how I was getting along. He was supposed to have come down here himself last month as an instructor but order came in sending the battery back to the lines, and they would not let him leave as he is a valuable man. He is one of the best artillerymen I ever saw but he and I do not agree on some little points. He has done a lot for the battery and the men have learned a whole lot under him. I am in hopes that he will show up here before I leave but if they keep the battery at the front I am afraid he will not.

I suppose Art is back at Exeter by now, starting off on his last year at the old school. He must have a lot in store for him this winter after his wonderful success last. What wouldn't I give to be home next June when he graduates and be able to see him walk up and receive his "dip" [diploma]. I have wondered several times what he is going to do when he gets through there. I know he is anxious to come over here and no one can blame him for that these days but, no matter what the conditions may be at the time he graduates, my hopes are that he will go to Harvard and take military training there for at least one year before he leaves home to cast his lot in this country. You folks are, of course, the best judge but I hope you do all in your power to find some form of military work near home for him as he is young and you need him there while I am gone.

I suppose you all went to Marjorie's wedding the first of this month. I wish both Everett and I might have been there but, since we were not, I am awaiting eagerly for the details and know that Everett must be. I intended to send George a cablegram but was unable to at the time, so the next time you see either one of them will you please tell them I thought of them on the big day and wish them all the happiness in the world. I guess Everett would give anything to get back to Sister. I know I would if I ever had a little girl like her waiting for me upon my return.

Well, Dad, I guess I have written just about enough for this Sunday so will close. Remember, I am always anxious to hear from you so, if you get any extra time, just write a few lines and head them for France.

Give my love to all the family and keep a whole lot for yourself.
Johnny

Dearest Sister

Well, the first part of my course at Saumur is over and the marks have gone in and we are all anxiously waiting for them to be posted so that we can see about where we stand. All this past week we have been rushing along at breakneck speed, every one of us wondering how in the name of heaven we ever were going to get all the stuff. Two days we were out on the range, Wednesday we were in the field all day long up to six o'clock and then, to add to our joys, we had two exams, one in B.C. and the other in my darn friend dispersion of whom I know nothing. We have not as yet heard from these but, judging from all reports, I guess we all took a headlong dive down on the B.C. with one or two exceptions and I am not one of those. Dispersion turned out to be very easy but long, as there was a great deal of figuring to do and lots of chances to make little mistakes. I think I made somewheres about 65% and 75% on it which, whereas it is not by any means good, is better than I expected. It may interest you to know how I have made out in our weekly B.C. exams, not counting this last which I have not heard from, so here are my marks in the order in which I received them, 70%, 58%, 85%. These are only fair I know but they are a little better than the average in the section I believe. Well, cheer up, your brother was not born with brains, he was unable to get any at school he was so thick but somehow, by means of good hard digging, and patience, he is going to make good here. The worst is yet to come but we have all laid a good foundation and are ready to meet it.

More good news from the front came in this morning and was greeted with cheers and a stronger desire than ever to be back with the battery at the front, taking part in the battles which are to free the world. Sis, I do not know how much you at home can appreciate it all but let me say right here that things are taking place now that the world will never forget. Drives are being made that fairly make my blood run cold with excitement and I often long to be back with the battery from Haverhill, which is doing her bit in them. To be sure, I was in the start of all these victories, which are to lead to the downfall of Germany, but what wouldn't I give to be up in the big push now. This sounds strange to you, I know, but if you only stop and think of it as a game of football and the soldiers one of the players you will understand how those of us who have been in the game and are now out of it feel. It's hell I know and a man suffers and many fall under the strain but yet it holds a charm and a thrill for those who are real men. Of late, I have often wondered what the boys are all going to do when it is over and we come home. If the rest are like me they are going to find it pretty hard to settle down to business and a life of ease, so to speak, after going through this for a year. I'm just plain everyday wild and am so used to taking everything as a matter of course, and letting troubles and cares take care of themselves without worrying my head off about them, that, when I go into a business where I must look out for them, I fear I shall be lost. Jack Hobson is my only worry and just so long as he is cared for, eats and sleeps, and is paid once a month the rest of the world can do as it pleases. I realize I ought not to be this way but, if I had ever stopped to worry over other people's hard luck, or stopped to think of the tears that would be shed over this or that dead body I have seen, I never would be where I am today, but in some bug house or, at least, very unhappy. I hope to break myself of this selfish attitude towards life before I reach home, where everyone thinks of the welfare and happiness of the others, but since I have been gone all that seems to have left me. War makes real men out of mere boys all right but it tends, as I believe I told Mother before I left, to harden them and change their views of life and the world a great deal more than anything else could do. Justice, truth, honor, and a sense of duty, even at the cost of your own life, are learned in the battlefield as in no other place, in my opinion, but, somehow, a man seems to lose something which he had before he took his place on the fields of death. I cannot describe it but no doubt you folks at home will, and perhaps have, noticed it.

So poor Dad may get caught in the draft? Well, I do not believe that there is any chance of it but if he does, tell him to look me up just as quick as he lands over here. I know of a few of the ropes and will do all in my power to show him some good times which he will never forget. What I wouldn't give to have him with me now as my Bunkie and know that he was always near me and I could see him anytime. Or to take him into some little French café and set before him a meal of eggs, meat and French fries. Of course there would be one addition to these but that goes without saying. It might not go quite as well as the ones he gets in the first room to the right as you enter Young's by the big door but, just the same, I'll bet they would taste pretty good on a Saturday night after a busy week. If this ever came true and dad did join me over here I never would even notice the little girl who put the food on the table, but would be lost in a seventh heaven of joy. I should hate to have him leave you all but it certainly would do my heart good to see him once more. Don't worry, dad, if you ever had to soldier under me as your Lieutenant your life would be one of ease and comfort as far as I could make it. I would be forced to smile, however, if I ever had to put you through 75 mm drill or teach you detail work. It would be hard for me to imagine you in uniform but, once there, I'll bet you would make a much better soldier than your son.

Speaking about fathers coming over here. One of the lads in our section had a cablegram a few weeks ago that his father would arrive at Saumur on the one o'clock train. He was over there on business. Well, Sister, if I was ever jealous of a man in my life I was of that lad. He dressed all up to kill and met his dear dad at the depot and what happened after that I do not know but he must have spent some of the happiest hours of his young life between then and eleven P.M. Another fellow I know in the regiment just, by chance, ran into his sister in Paris a few months ago. He didn't even know she was over here as a Red Cross nurse and, as a matter of fact, she had only been here a few days. But one of the strangest cases of this kind that I have ever heard of was told to me by one of the nurses at the hospital last August who said she saw the event take place with her own eyes. They were unloading a Red Cross train and, as is always the case, a few of the nurses were there to help in any way they could and to give out cigarettes to the wounded. One nurse was lighting a cigarette for one of the litter patients when another litter was placed beside the one on which the smoker was laying. On it lay a poor lad with both legs gone and his head all done up. As she bent over to light the cigarette this weak voice from the next litter said, "Hello, Mother. How long have you been over here?" I wish my mother had been there on the station platform when I was carried out of that Red Cross train a couple of months ago. She never would have known her son I know and it would have hurt her to see him suffering, but, oh, the comfort it would have brought to have felt her hand on my head and her lips against mine. Hers would have been so cool and nice while mine were burning up. Well, I doubt if any of us ever meet over here but, if we do, I hope it will not be as it was in the case of that mother and her wounded son.

Yesterday I received a fine letter from Grandpa Gale along with the Exeter Newsletter. The letter had been forwarded to me by Capt. Root and, I should judge, had been delayed somewheres before reaching him. Will you please tell grandpa that I enjoyed his letter very much and hope before long to be able to find a few minutes in which to write him a personal letter. I also got a peach from Art with the pictures taken on his trip in the Ford last spring. He also will hear from me before long so tell him that he has by no means been forgotten.

Speaking about pictures. I should judge, from what Art said, that the photo Ev sent you all of the two of us more than pleased everyone, especially Mother. Here, as I said in the first of my letter, I fear I have thought too much of myself and hence have not forced myself to have one taken before. As I wrote Mother, it is very good of Ev but only fair of me. I look as if I had lost my last friend, whereas, if the truth were to be told, I had more real friends then than I ever knew I had before. I have made a vow to myself now, however, since I have come to life and realize how much a picture of myself means to you all, I should have realized it long ago, and that is that the very first thing I do the last of next month, if I get my commission, is to head down town and have my picture taken. This will be one really worthwhile having, because I will not look like a bum and my clothes will fit me.

And, here again, I will use the expression I have nearly worn out in this letter, "Speaking about" and will use it again. Speaking about clothes makes me laugh. In order to have a uniform ready when you get through here you have to order it several weeks in advance so, next Saturday night, another lad and I are going down and order ours. Vain is no word for either of us - we are worse than that. Every time we pass a shoe store we must stop and decide which pair of high top boots we like the best and which style we are to get. Not having seen any which hit our taste in every respect we have decided to have a pair made to order. There are several advantages in this but the chief one is that you will get a pair that really fit you and do not hurt your feet or look like hell after you have had them for a few weeks. Sam-Brown belts are easy to get and we have found "beaucoup" of them which hit us right to a "T". Overcoats are our chief worry. You can get them but to get the one we like is another matter. But, between you and me, if I can see my way through on the money end I think that, like the uniform and boots, will be made to suite my taste. If I really do get through here all right I have made up my mind that I at least will have the kind of clothes I want and not wear whatever is handed out as the poor enlisted man has to. I have a long ways to go yet, however, so let's not get our hopes too high because a heavy fall may be in store for me. I just told you about this to let you know that the laugh is on Johnny now, and not Sis and Mother, when it comes to picking out clothes.

Here is something for you to tell dad for me which I forgot to put in his letter last week. The letter I wrote him about the battery fund was written before I received his letter asking me about it. There was some trouble in regard to it among the men and I did hear something of a letter being, or going to be, written home about it. Captain Root heard of trouble along these lines, through one source or another, and asked me how much truth there was in it. I told him what I knew of the matter and he looked into it still further and found out that all was O.K. and, knowing that there still might be trouble at home, asked me to write you (Dad) and tell you just what the money was being spent for. I thought it would be still better to write a letter to the public, which I did, and which I should imagine has cleared everything up for you and the rest and so I have not written you a personal letter about it. If anything else comes up please let me know and I will try to find out all I can for you.

Well, Sister, I guess I have told you all the news and you must be tired out now, reading all this so I will close.

Please give my love to all the family and keep a lot for yourself.
Johnny

Saumur Artillery School
Saumur, France
October 20, 1918

Dearest Mother

Another week has gone by and only about four more remain before I will know the final results of my work to become an officer. We received our marks for our first five weeks work a few days ago and my average was 75%. I passed everything but one subject and missed that by four points. Those weeks were not so very hard but we are well under way on our last lap now and, I must confess, am finding things very hard. In fact, I have often wondered of late if the gold bar was really worth all the work I am now going through to get it. But there is one thing and, I can nearly say one thing only, which is keeping my shoulder to the wheel and my teeth set and that is YOU and DAD. I must make good for your sake no matter what the price may be. Glory and fame is all right for some but, if I didn't have a father who had made a high mark for his son to live up to and a mother who is praying night and day for my success, I am afraid I should be saying, "Hang my commission in the yard and send me back on the firing lines with the boys." Oh, how strong that desire to be back on the firing lines has grown since the big drives have been on and how I have longed to throw up my chances here and get back into the fight once again. I have made many friends here and met some of the best men in the world but Mother, my heart is miles away with the battery men who are pushing the Huns back onto their own ground. I am almost homesick for the shell-torn fields and the moaning of shells over my head. That's the life for me, out chasing line trouble and cursing the Boche all the evening for breaking them and pulling us out of our dugouts. Will I ever in my life enjoy the thrills and excitement of battle again, or, will all be over before I have a chance to get up there and put the last finishing touches on the job? I know, darling, you cannot understand my feelings these days and, from my letters, you may think I have gone war mad but such is not the case. I will be as glad as all the rest to see it over but, while it is on, I want to be in it and I am not alone in my desire. Lots of men who have been up into the fields of death long to get back and take part in this final victorious drive of the Allies. Well, dear, first we will try to make good here for the sake of those who desire and justly demand the best I have to give and then, if there is any fun left up front, we will head for it full speed.

Yesterday I had the pleasure of hearing one of the best Frenchmen talk I have ever heard. He took the place of our regular riding instructor who was sick. After pounding around the hall for an hour we all went outside to hear what we expected to be a talk on horses but which turned out to be a history of the school and a few stories of the early years of the war plus this French lieutenant's personal experiences. He had been wounded eight times and wore several medals. Interesting was no word for him, he was better than that and kept us all laughing for nearly an hour. He told us of his dealing with German prisoners when he was in the intelligence department and how he used to get information out of them. He tells a story of one German sergeant he was questioning who, when asked how they got information out of French prisoners, made the following answer, "We give them a bottle of wine, some cigarettes and they will tell us every general who ever commanded a French division." This struck the Frenchman very funny and, if I could tell it as he did, you would be forced to laugh as we did. He speaks French, German, and English and certainly has been through a lot of experiences in his life.

Last night there was a show given downtown by four actors and actresses from the States. "Somewhere in America" was the name of it and it was very good indeed. One joke I happen to remember ran like this, "Which had you rather be - a general with an eagle on your shoulder or a private with a chicken on you knee?" There were lots of other good ones but, as is always the case, I have forgotten them.

I received a nice long letter from you this week giving me an account of Marjorie's wedding. Gee, I wish Ev and I could have been there. I also received Sister's letter telling me about it and asking me if I could take care of one of the pictures which were taken of the bridesmaids. Well, if I make good here I surely can and if I don't I want to have it and will make a place for it so, if you have any extra ones, please send me one. Pictures certainly do bring me a lot of pleasure and, as I wrote Sister two weeks ago, must bring you the same. Well, darling, when your boy puts on the Sam-Brown you certainly shall have one of him if it takes my last cent to get it. You can have very good ones taken here but I hope to get to Paris when I get through and if I do you will have a real one of me. I have not changed a great deal, dear, but perhaps look a bit older that I did when I left.

Well, darling, lunch is ready so I guess I will close and make my way over to the mess hall.

Lots of love and kisses for you all.
Johnny

Saumur Artillery School
A.P.O. 718
October 20, 1918

Dear Dad

I have just written Mother a letter telling her about all the news there is for this week but I have a little something I want you to do for me so am going to drop you a few lines.

As you must know by now from my letters the training I am now taking to become an officer will be completed the end of next month. If everything goes as we are hoping it will I will leave the ranks of the enlisted man at that time and take my place as a second lieutenant. This, of course, means that instead of having clothes and the like issued to me I will have to buy them. The letter of credit which you so kindly gave me before I left the States has, as you know, only has been used once and that for a fairly small sum. What is left will buy my first uniform and send me out of here looking as I ought to, but with very little extra money left. I feel more than ever as you did when you gave me that letter that it is always a good thing to have a little money on the side to fall back on in case you are wounded or something happens to your pay. The gold you gave me lay in my money belt for nearly a year and I often thought when my pay money had been spent, that I would use that when I wanted a good time but I always thought of what you told me when you gave it to me, "Keep this and do not spend it in a foolish way as you may really want it someday." That day was a long time in coming but when I was gassed and sent to the base hospital dead broke that money bought me things which otherwise I would have gone without. Some still remains in the belt as I used my letter of credit to supply me with money when I left the base. After buying my first outfit a little will be left but I know of several places now where that little will be absolutely needed. Hence, Dad, I am going to ask you to send me $100.00 more when you get a chance, to be used as a safeguard or whatever else I may need it for along these lines. Your expenses have been very heavy since I left I realize and I am not going to ask you to give me this money as a gift but am enclosing a check for the $100.00 which I hope you will accept. I am in no hurry for this money so you can send it to me in any form you think best - express checks, letter of credit or cable are all O.K. to me so do as you see best. If for any reason I should fail to get a commission, let us hope this will not be the case, it will not hurt to have this money with me or I can return it.

Last week I ordered my uniform which is to be made in Paris through a firm who has an agent here. It is costing me about 315 francs including an overseas cap made out of the same goods as the suit. I have not had a chance as yet to look the overcoats over very carefully or price them but imagine they cost 150 to 200 francs.

The work here is getting deeper and deeper as the days go on and I find that I have to work pretty hard to get it. However, I hope grit and nerve plus what few brains I have will pull me through a winner.

Please remember me to all the men in the office.

Lots of love for yourself and the rest of the family.
Johnny

Saumur Artillery School
A.P.O. 718
France
November 3, 1918

Dear Art

It certainly has been a long time since I last wrote you but I trust you have got all the news of my doings such as they are from Mother's letters. There really has been very little of excitement taking place in my life since I left the battery and came down here to try for a commission so this letter may be a bit uninteresting but you will know that your brother at least has not forgotten you.

First of all I want to thank you for the pictures you sent me some little time ago. It surely did seem good to see your face again and the pictures were very clear. I showed them to Potter Herd an old Exeter man who is here and we both agreed that it seemed mighty good to see some familiar sights. I think, Art, you have grown at least a foot since I left and judging from the pictures I think you could handle both Dad and I with ease in a rough house.

Sister writes me that you broke your nose playing football. I hate to kid you about that pug of yours, Art, but if you repeat the stunt many times I fear there will be just a blot on your face. I am sorry to hear you met with this hard luck but am glad to hear you are out for the team. Please let me know how the big game [Exeter vs. Andover] comes out and be sure and tell me where you are playing.

Well, Art, you are not the only one who is fretting his head off over exams these days. I too am having my troubles along these lines and I hope to goodness you are making out better than I am. I guess you are all right because you have more of a head for that stuff than I have. I have got one of the fool things coming tomorrow and I have been studying just about all day trying to get ready for it. I nearly go wild I get so blame mad at some of these exams here and my temper is not to be fooled with for several days after. I never was cut out for a student that is a cinch.

The news from the front certainly does look good to me and I guess before the winter is over we will see the end. Then the question before the house will be how soon we all get home? I swear I pity the poor kids who follow us and have to study all about this war in history. That is one thing I guess we escaped or are you poor boys at Exeter getting some of it now?

Mother wrote me some little time ago that the boys at Exeter are very young this year and that you all are forced to take military training. How do you like it, Art, and are you an N.C.O. or an officer?

Well, old-timer, I have a dinner engagement "le soir" and it is time for me to make my way down town or I will be losing out.

Please drop me a few more lines when you get time and remember me to all my friends at Exeter not forgetting Vic.
Johnny

Dearest Mother

There is very little news to tell you today, in fact, I don't think there is any, but I have a few spare minutes so will drop you a few hasty lines to let you know that your boy is all O.K.

I am sorry to say that the real French fall has set in and we have been enjoying for the past two days just what we had last fall while we were training, mud and water. It has rained, almost without stopping, for two days now and hence just about everything we own is wet and the barracks are very damp. Yesterday we were out on field service in the pouring rain with the guns and I wish you could have seen us when we got back - muddy, wet and hungry enough to eat the mess hall down. There was a great exchanging of dry clothes and I do not own hardly a single thing I have on now as all mine are either wet or in the wash. It has also begun to turn cold which of course means that the work outside will not be quite as pleasant as it was.

One of the other sergeants from the battery arrived here last Sunday and brought with him all kinds of exciting news from the boys. They have been up in the thick of it again and the old Haverhill luck has been with them and only one man hurt and he not badly. I am sorry to say that other batteries in the regiment have not made out so well and I fear, from the reports the boys brought with them, that the losses have been pretty heavy in some outfits. Lieutenant Morrison, as perhaps you know, has been promoted to the rank of Captain still commanding the battery. Lannigan has been made a first lieutenant and one or two others whom I do not believe you know. I understand that the sergeant who took my place is slated for the States and will leave very soon, so you may have the honor of hearing another man fresh from the fight talk at one of your meetings. There is lots of other news about the boys I should like to tell but it is not well to dwell on details here.

I had one of the most wonderful letters from Ev the day before yesterday that I ever hope to receive from any man. If his letters to Sister are half as good as the one I got, and I fancy they are better, she must look forward to them. His letter to me just made my old heart beat faster and my teeth grit harder in order to make the final hill here which we have now started up. My second lot of marks came out last night and I am all O.K. with an average of 74%. The next lot we get will be the final results and they go in at the end of next week I believe.

Well, darling, it is time for work so I must close.

Please give my love to all the family and keep a lot for yourself.
Johnny

Dear Dad

Here it is Sunday again and it seems only yesterday that I sat down at one of the Y.M.C.A.'s tables to write last Sunday's letter home. Time certainly is flying and a week passes away before I know it. So much is taking place right now the world over that a man has very little time to think of himself and I guess this is one of the reasons for a week seeming like a day to all of us.

I suppose you people at home are anxiously waiting the outcome of the armistice just as we are over here. The papers are being sold like hot cakes and the little French lad, who stands by the school gate, must make a young fortune on them every night, selling them to the students as they rush by on their way to supper. The whole business seems too good to be true to me and I doubt if I can ever bring myself to think it is really over until I see PEACE written in every paper and the U.S. begins to load her troops on boats home-ward bound. Even after I did get on a boat I should have my doubt as to where I was going until I saw the big buildings of New York harbor looking me in the face. That day, Dad, will be almost a dream but I will realize it is true when I see you and Mother and hear you say, "Welcome home, our roaming boy." Gee, that will be the hap-piest moment of my life and am now praying and hoping that it is not a great ways off. I can't imagine just what home is like now and many of the sights and surroundings of Boston have been half faded out with all the new things I have been seeing over here. American customs have also been sort of half forgotten and could I talk French I should call myself a Frenchman not an American. A bunch of us were talking home around the table in a café a few nights ago and someone asked what an American telephone looked like and how it worked. Well, Dad, it's a fact that none of us could tell him for at least five minutes. We all decided thereon that we would need nurses for awhile after we got back or, at least, a few lessons on how to behave in America. I really am forced to smile every time I think of my first few days at home. Just as Sister wrote, a few weeks ago, that at times I did not feel like her real brother but more a soldier of her dreams. Those words express just my feelings. You folks seem too good to be real, home, with its sweet fires, joys and comforts surrounded by love, seems more of a sweet dream to me than anything that possibly could be true. You and Mother have grown to be people who have too much love in your hearts to be living in this world filled with war and death and human suffering. But yet, at all times, I can feel you both guiding my footsteps and I do not believe it will be so very long before you guide them to your front door and I will realize that I really have a home and am not a wandering boy any more. Let us hope God will speed that day.

Now a few lines in regard to my work which I know you are all interested in and perhaps you, Dad, a little more than the rest since some day I am to work side by side with you and of course you want to know what kind of a man you have got for a partner. Well, I report all O.K. up to date with about one more week of hard work and only two more exams. As I wrote Mother the middle of the week, my average is 74% and a few tenths up to now, and I feel that I am going to be able to hold my own. There are still several subjects I have not heard from and will not until the last thing. These of course may be just the ones which are to prevent me getting through here but I doubt it very much. Everything looks fine just now and unless something unforeseen turns up I guess the goal I have sought for will be reached about the 24th of this month. You can rest assured that I will cable you the final results just as soon as possible in order that you all may take part in my disappointment or joy as the case may be. Mr. Brown's boy is coming along about the same as I am and we both agree that, whereas our fathers have brains their poor sons have very, very few. This next week, starting in tomorrow, has some very interesting things in store for me. We have an aeroplane adjustment one morning which I have never taken part in before, since we used very little of this kind of adjustment at the front, when we did I had my hands full to keep the telephone lines open to the radio station. We also fire a bilateral problem which is very hard but which I am anxious to see worked out now that I have some idea of how they should go. Gas drills are also started this week and I believe we have a lecture on the darn stuff also. I do not know much about the contents of gas but mark my word I know how it affects a man once he gets it. No one, be he a general or private, can tell me or impress upon me any more the care which must be taken with that stuff or the pain a man suffers with it. I'm afraid of it, always was and always shall be, and I'm not shamed to confess it. Put me out in the open fields or in a dugout and shell me with high explosive shells but keep those gas shells away. Instant death or a shrapnel wound for me, if a man must be hurt, but spare me the absolute human agony a man goes through when gassed - it's wicked that's all. The hardest part of this course for me will be the week after this when we pass through the gas chambers and have gas on the field. I've seen and been through too much with that stuff.

I wrote Grandma Hobson a long letter a short time ago and I hope it reaches her all right. Mail has been held up a little I believe and so, if this one gets through first, please tell her there is one on the way.

Well, Dad, I have a try on down town this morning so must be on my way. Let's hope the uniform fits.

Lots of love to all the family and yourself.
Johnny

CHAPTER THIRTEEN

Fini la Guerre!

"If those brave lads who gave up their lives for peace could only have looked down from heaven and seen the joy they had brought to the world they would realize that they had not given their lives in vain."

SERGEANT JOHN L. HOBSON II

The final days of the First World War unfolded in late October and early November. Defeat of the Central Powers was eminent and imperial Germany, suffering under the prolonged war of attrition, began to fall apart. The Hindenburg Line had collapsed. The poorly supplied and demoralized army was in retreat. The starving 100-million population of Germany began rioting in the streets of Berlin. German sailors mutinied. The military refused to back the Kaiser any longer. In early November the Kaiser abdicated and fled to Holland in the Netherlands. After 22 years in exile, he would, ironically, die in then Nazi-occupied Holland in 1941. He is buried in Doorn.

During the last months of the war the regiment gave support with rolling barrages to advancing Allied infantry at Bois d'Haumont. On 10

November the battalion and the regiment were moved in the direction of Beaumont and into position on the Beaumont-Flabas road. When the cease-fire was declared the next day and Battery A fired its last round of the war, the battery was positioned just west of Beaumont, about halfway between Louvemont and Neuville.

According to "The History of the 102nd Field Artillery", this was how the war ended for the regiment:

At 6:15 o'clock [A.M.] on November 11 the regimental and battal-ion wireless stations reported that they had picked up the following message from FL (Eiffel Tower):

From: Marechal Foch
To: Commander-In-Chief
Hostilities will cease upon the whole front from the eleven Novem-ber, eleven o'clock [a.m.].
The allied troops will not cross until a further order the line reached on that date and that hour.
Signed, Foch.

In the 1st Battalion, firing ceased at 10:59:30. One final round was fired from the first piece of Battery A at 10:59:32. Given allowance for time of flight, it was calculated to make the shell explode in enemy territory at precisely 10:59:59.

In the 2nd Battalion, each gun was elevated to its greatest range and loaded with a shell inscribed with a message to the Kaiser. Their last shot was fired by as many men as could get a finger on a lanyard.

In the trenches, the infantry reported that just moments before 11 o'clock a German machine gunner fired off a scorching hail of bullets toward the Allied trenches and then, precisely at 11 o'clock, the German gunner stood up, made a deep bow, and walked away.

On the eleventh hour of the eleventh day of the eleventh month of the year 1918, the Great War, the World War, the First World War, the war that was supposed to end all wars, was over.

In this horrible tragedy sparked by one assassin's bullet, the combined countries of the Allied (Entente) and Central Powers had mobilized 65 mil-lion soldiers. It is nearly impossible to get complete agreement from sources on the casualties because of incomplete or destroyed records, changed borders, and subsequent deaths resulting from wounds received in battle. Generally, however, there were a total of 37.5 million casualties including military and civilian - killed (8.5 million), wounded (21.2 million) or missing (7.7 million); approximately a 58% casualty rate. Of the military dead, approximately 5.7 million were Allied soldiers and 4 million were from the Central Powers. Of the 4.2 million American armed forces mobilized, approximately 8% (321,000) became casualties - 117,000 killed and 204,000 wounded.

The last American soldier officially reported killed in action in the First World War was Henry Gunther of Baltimore, MD, of Co. A, 313 Infantry, 79th Division of the U.S. Army. Gunther was shot through the head at 11:01 A.M. while he was charging a German machine gun position with a rifle and fixed bayonet near Metz, one minute after the cease fire. Posthumously, Henry Gunther was awarded the Distinguished Service Cross.

General Pershing and several division commanders would later be investigated and their actions criticized for ordering charges on the morning of 11 November and wasting the lives of some 3,500 A.E.F. soldiers killed on that day after they knew about the pending Armistice. There was outrage and charges of murder. One could reason that that was the fault of the communications of the day. The commander's defense was that while they knew for two days prior that there was to be a cease fire on 11 November, it wasn't made official until five o'clock that morning and then subsequently communicated out to the field positions. Note that receipt of Foch's wire to the regiment and battalion was timed at 06:15. So it was that this war ended as it began - tragically.

The 26th Division was on the front line for 210 days, the second longest of all the U.S. Divisions serving in the war. The 26th was second only to the First Infantry Division - the Big Red One.

The entire 26th Division, both the infantry and the artillery brigades, captured 3,148 prisoners.

The 26th Division had 11,955 casualties; 1,730 were killed, 10,089 were wounded and 136 were taken prisoner.

Of the approximate 1,500 men in the 102nd Field Artillery Regiment, there were 348 casualties representing 22.69%; 32 were killed, 15 died of wounds, four died of disease and 297 were wounded in the line of duty.

Following the cease-fire on 11 November, the next five months for the 102nd Field Artillery Regiment and the men of Battery A were spent in France. During that time, there was celebration, sporting events and preparations made for returning battle-weary artillery soldiers to the States. Soldiers were deloused and fitted with new uniforms. Rifles were issued and those artillerymen who didn't use rifles regularly were retrained and drilled in the manual of arms. They were, after all, eventually to be reviewed by the Army's top brass - including General Pershing. The Regiment wanted to make an impressionable show of marching with shouldered rifles before leaving France, and, of course, in the big parade in Boston when they returned to the States.

On 29 March, the 102nd Field Artillery Regiment, by now clean, rested and more than anxious to go home, entrained at Mayet and the Le Mans embarkation area. Upon arrival at the port city of Brest, they boarded the steamship Mongolia for the voyage back to the States. The rest of the 26th Division boarded transports sailing about that same time. The entire Division had trickled back to Boston by the first few weeks of April. The USS Mongolia, with the soldiers of the 102nd Field Artillery aboard, sailed from France on 31 March arriving at Commonwealth Pier in Boston on 10 April. Upon arrival, the soldiers were billeted at Camp Devens, which is located about 35 miles west of Boston in Devens, Massachusetts.

Dearest Sister

Yesterday and last night were two times in my life that I wouldn't
have missed for all the world and I wish you might have been here to
enjoy them with me. A pen cannot describe them and words would
only half express the joy that filled the hearts of every man, woman
and child in this country and the world over, I guess. I am not going
to try to tell you all that took place as it would be impossible to
do so, but I shall give you a little idea of how the signing of the
armistice affected Saumur.

The news that Germany had really signed the armistice reached
us officially early yesterday morning and of course we greeted it
with loud yells and cheers. All the morning we went about our work
with broad smiles on our faces and the lectures all seemed long and
dry. In the afternoon, however, we had a field service on horseback
and then things began to pick up. I drew a great, big wheel-horse
who was slow, lazy and not very sure-footed, but all these little
drawbacks did not bother me in the least. On our way out to where
we were to take up our battery position we saw several people putting flags outside of the windows, but aside from that all seemed
very much as usual. We had our service and started home about 4:30
and then, for the first time, I really realized the fact that the war was
about over. As we approached town little boys and girls would run
along side of us yelling, "Fini la guerre!" [The war is over!] as hard
as their lungs would let them. Flags hung from nearly every building
and the streets really looked alive, there were so many out. As I rode
along on my speedy charger I couldn't help but wish that we were
riding down Tremont Street on parade for the last time, but that will
come in the course of time. The mess hall that night was more of a
mad house of joy than a mess hall. The girls were singing while the
soldiers just yelled and yelled. After supper I walked down town,
with one of the lads in my section, and there we saw things that I

never expect to see again - No New Years Eve was ever gayer than last night. The streets were just packed with people, all cheering, all yelling and all wearing a smile. Little French boys were shooting sky rockets off from the curb stone which, when well aimed, would go down the street in fine shape. Lots of them, however, hit the buildings but that didn't make much difference just so long as they made a racket. The cafes were all filled and French and American soldiers ate and drank together as if they both were from the same country. If they could not understand each other that did not matter, they could make gestures and yell just the same. The bars were down all around and each and every one just pitched in and enjoyed themselves. Oh, what a wild and glorious night it was, and it will go down in history as perhaps the best and happiest night the old world ever had. It seemed as if a heavy load had suddenly been lifted from the shoulders of everyone and they had nothing to worry them but to make merry. I never had a better time in my life and never felt so happy. What must Paris have been like - too wonderful to even imagine. A Frenchman told us that all the lights were on once again for the first time in ages. I wish you could have been over here to see it all but I guess the good old U.S. let go that night as well as France. It was worth all the pain and hardships of the past year and I thought, when I got into bed, how glad I was that I had done my little bit toward bringing it all about. I must confess that a feeling of pride came over me, that I, like millions of others, had been up on the lines in the hot of it and had fought to bring peace to the world. Those seven months of fighting seem like a dream to me now and I can hardly realize that I have heard the din of battle or shot to kill. If those brave lads who gave up their lives for peace could only have looked down from heaven and seen the joy they had brought to the world they would realize that they had not given their lives in vain. I wish the troops up on the lines now might have been able to make merry but they must have found their joy when the guns lay still and peace reigned over the battlefield. Can you imagine it, dear; doesn't it all seem too good to be true and to think that I shall be allowed to return to you all well, unhurt and happy? Let us hope that those guns never speak again and that no more will be called upon to die for freedom.

In your last letter you asked about Karl and said that his mother had not heard from him for a long time and was a little anxious. Well, I went right to the sergeant, who has just arrived here from the battery, and asked about him. What he told me took me right off my feet as I did not even know Karl had been sick or I most certainly should have written him or tried to do something for him if possible. I suppose the sad news has reached Dr. and Mrs. Pitcher by now and they know Karl is dead. It was an awful shock to me and I was speechless for nearly five minutes after I was told the facts of the case. Just before I left to come up here to school Karl had a slight swelling under both of his eyes and complained of not feeling any too good but, like all the rest, thought he was tired out from the drive with a cold hanging around. Brights disease [kidney disease] was never thought of by any of us and the afternoon I left, when I went around to say goodbye to him, he told me he was feeling much better, so I dismissed the thoughts of anything serious being the matter. It seems, however, that only a few days after I had left, while the battery was on their way to the front, that he became worse and was sent to the hospital. His legs were so badly swollen that he could not get either his shoes or leggings on and his eyes were all swollen. I understand that the doctor told some of the boys at that time that he would never live to see the States again but they could not believe it since he told them the same thing when I was sent away gassed. Karl did not live, however, many days after he reached the base. Why someone did not write me of his condition or of his death I cannot understand because everyone knew that Karl and I were very, very close friends, but I never knew a single thing about it until I was told by the sergeant. It must have been an awful blow to Mrs. Pitcher and I wish that you would extend my sympathy to her. I knew Karl like an open book, having been with him now for over a year under almost every kind of conditions. I feel his loss very deeply and the boys in the battery must also. He was just like a boy who never grew up to me and you always found him ready and willing to do his share of the work or undergo his share of the dangers. The army had made a big change in him and he had proved himself to be a real man. Many a night when I would come down from the lines for a day or so I would find Karl still up even if it was late and oh, how welcome his voice was when I heard him say, "I've saved some hot coffee for you men," and then serve us. Then he would take me to one side and say, "You'll find some bread and butter in the store room, but there isn't enough to go around but if you want some go in and help yourself." Then on other nights, we would sit under the trees and watch the rockets play upon the lines while we talked of days that used to be. Karl never said a great deal of wanting to get home, none of us did because it did no good, but I could tell, from the way he talked, he was always a little homesick for those dear little children of his. Sister, he loved them more than words can tell and he loved to talk and dream of them. I am sorry I couldn't do something for him when the end drew near but I never knew a thing about it until yesterday.

This surely is a small world after all, isn't it? No matter where you go there always seems to be someone there you know or who knows some friend of yours. The other night I was standing in the hallway of the school building, talking with some men and looking around, when my eyes fell on this lad who looked like some one I used to know at Exeter, but for the life of me I couldn't place him. He turned around and, for some reason, looked my way, and there we stood merely looking at each other for at least half a minute. Then almost at the same second we both started towards each other. He couldn't place me any more than I could him but this trouble was soon cleared up and it turned out that he was at Exeter the same time I was. It surely is funny how you run into old friends like that even away over here.

I received the two papers you folks sent me, one containing the account of Marjorie's wedding, and the other one Everett's letter and mine. You know, I think I shall give up writing and let Ev do it all hereafter because his letter had anything I could write stopped a mile. In the first place I don't have the thoughts he has and if I did I couldn't express them as well.

My uniform is all done and fits me like the paper on the wall. If the trench coat I am having made turns out as well as the uniform I ought to make a bully looking officer as far as clothes go. The next question is - am I going to get a chance to wear it? Well, we will know before very long now.

There goes the mess call and you know what means, I must close and feed my face.

Please give my love to all the family and keep just heaps for yourself. Johnny

Saumur Artillery School
Saumur, France
November 16, 1918

Dearest Mother

There is very little real news to tell you all this week but nevertheless I shall drop you a few lines just to let you know that your boy is well and happy.

Well, dear, my course at Saumur is about over, in fact you might say it is over, as the final marks have gone in and we now only have a week left in which we attend lectures, demonstration fire, etc., but are not marked. Now the question remains, how have I come out after three months training to become an officer? That question will be answered this week and I am anxiously awaiting it. Am I to be made happy beyond words because I have made good or am I to receive the greatest disappointment of my life? Thoughts which no pen or words can fully express are rushing through my head just now, but when the final reports come in I shall rest easy once more and a heavy load will be lifted from my shoulders. Let us hope all comes out as we have planned and hope it will. If it does, no cablegram can reach you folks too quick to let you know of your son's full happiness in his victory. It has been a long, hard pull from start to finish for me and failure to gain the goal I have sought for so long would go pretty hard, but it is by our failures that we win in the long race of life, so should I fail I will bear in mind that God has had me do so for some reason which, whereas we may not be able to understand it just now, will some day be made clear to us. On the other hand should victory be mine and the goal reached, I shall leave here to perform it with the best I have to give. I wish I could write my thoughts on paper at this time because, in years to come, I should like to look back and see just how I felt in my first big test to live up to the reputation of a Hobson.

I suppose all of you at home are wondering how long it will be now before your soldier boys come marching home. We, over here, are wondering the same things and home is being talked of a great deal. My own personal opinion is that you will see the battery back in the States before hot weather sets in perhaps by Easter. I am very anxious to see the old divisions, whom have seen most of the fighting and been over here the longest, sent back just as soon a possible and I think they will be. My only regret is that if I pass here I shall not be with them. There is still a lot of work to be done over here and, as I guess I have told you before, we who graduate this month, will very likely be called upon to help do it. If it were not for you dear ones at home I must confess I had rather stay here and help finish the job than return home and leave it for someone else, but, Mother, I want to see you and Dad and the rest in the worst possible way. If all of you or even one of you could only get over here to spend a few weeks with me I would feel like a new man. If the chance ever presents itself I am going to cable you and I shall expect every one of you to drop your work, yes, even dear old Dad, and come over her to pay me a visit. You and Dad will have to come regardless of how busy you are and bring as many of the family as possible. You will not hear from me for several yet but just bear in mind I am keeping my eyes open for the chance. Ev would not object in the least to seeing Sister and I swear I don't see any reason under the sun why you, Dad and Sis couldn't get over by next fall if we boys are still here. If Ev is where he is now he could take care of you if I couldn't. This may be all more or less of a dream, the kind you and I used to have together after all the rest were asleep, but some dreams do come true you know, even the ones you and I had. Let's hope this one does.

Just what is to happen to me when I leave here remains for the future to tell, in fact nothing is definite in my life just now. Dame Rumor has a lot to say as to what is to become of us would-be-seconds in this November class, but she is a bad one to believe. At any rate I have some very interesting chapters coming in my life and none of you want to be surprised if you get a letter headed "The

North Pole" or Boston, U.S.A. After this week I hope to get some idea as to where I am to be sent, either as a sergeant or lieutenant, but just now I must confess I am lost at sea without a compass. I am seeing to it that I get three meals a day, all the sleep I want and am leaving everything else up to Uncle Sam to figure out for me. He's my boss and what he says is law so why worry about it, do as you're told and you'll land home some day.

Cold weather has set in over here for good now I guess and the old wood fire, when we can get wood, feels pretty good. Nice, cool, fresh air greets us every morning and sends us all on the double quick to breakfast. Here we get a rather cool reception as there is only one small stove in the mess hall and that's not going when we eat breakfast. Outside work is not quite as pleasant as it was but there is more snap to it in many ways.

This afternoon another lad and myself went out to an old chateau, just outside of town, where, for the large sum of 5 or 10 cents, you are allowed to go all through it. It was very much like all other old chateaus over here I have been through except I enjoyed the paintings in this one better than usual. They certainly were wonderful. From one of the towers we were able to look for miles around and I never realized Saumur and nearby towns were so pretty until I saw them from this tower. We visited the dungeon and room where they used to torture their prisoners in olden days, as well as inspecting everything else. Every time I go into one of these old chateaus I cannot help but picture in my mind the people who used to live in them and I can even fancy myself in one during a war. It would have been hard work to capture a place like that in the early days and even today, with our modern artillery, I fear we should have a hard time to destroy such a fortress. How they ever built these places is beyond me and once built I fail to see how they ever found their way around in them. They have an underground passage in this one which lead under the river to a nearby town and the well they used to let people down to get to it is land only knows how many feet deep. We put some dirt in a newspaper and then lit the paper and dropped it down the well, I thought it never would reach the bottom. You can imagine the size of the place when I tell you we were nearly three hours in going through it and seeing all there was to see. Give me a cozy little home "for two or three or maybe more" every time. No Lord's and Lady's chateaus for me, they're too big.

Last evening I attended a very fine little show given by two ladies and a man at the "Salle Cornet" (I think that is the way you spell it). A couple of hours before I heard a lecture on gas in the same place, which however had no bearing whatsoever on the show. Lots of old time songs were sung and we all spent a very pleasant evening.

Speaking about gas, we have our big gas demonstration this week at the range which we are supposed to pass through just about every gas made except mustard. Having seen and been through what I have with gas I made up my mind that, if it was possible, I would get out of this stunt, realizing also that should the least little thing go wrong with my mask and I should get a little of it it would go very hard with me since I was gassed once. Hence I went to the section instructor this A.M. and told him just what I had been through and added that, were it possible, I should like to be excused. He was somewhat surprised to hear I had been laid flat on my back from the stuff and didn't blame me a bit for not wanting to run any risks out at the range, so said he would see to it that I was excused. I'll take my chances with the rest on the lines and gladly give up my life with the boys if it is necessary but, Mother, I cannot see the sense of risking my lungs and exposing myself to danger back here from gas after all I have been through. I suffered enough once from it and may God spare me from any more pain like I went through last August.

Well, I guess I had better close for this week and get to bed. The next letter you receive from me will have some real good news in it I hope.

Give my love to all the family and keep a lot for yourself.
Johnny

Saumur Artillery School
Saumur, France
November 21, 1918

Dearest Dad

The Y.M.C.A. has gotten out these green envelopes and we are supposed to write what they call "A Father's Xmas Letter" to go in them.

Instead of "A Mother's Day or Mother's Letter" this is supposed to be "Father's Day or Father's Letter". I must confess, Dad, I do not know just what to say that would be unusual but just the same I am going to try to write you today just as I did Mother on "Mother's Day". Do not expect to find anything new but just a plain, everyday letter from Johnny.

First of all, I received your cable and can easily see that you are just as glad of the big victory as we boys are and words cannot tell you how glad we were to hear that bloodshed had at last stopped and the guns were merely staying in position until the peace terms were really signed. No doubt you have read and reread in the papers how the news was received by our troops on the lines and, whereas I was not there myself, I can easily imagine from the paper account what it was like. I have watched the rockets play along the front lines many nights but they had a far different meaning than they did the night the fighting was called off, and I was there to study them, learn their meaning if possible and spread the alarm to the batteries when that deadly German barrage flare went, I did not enjoy them as those men must have a few nights ago when they all meant joy. Oh, how I wish I might have been there to see it all. Big fires burning on both sides of "No Man's Land" and cheer after cheer ringing through the night. You who read of it all rejoice, as well you should, but just think of the joy it brought to those of us who have faced the hell and death of it all. Dad, our joy knew no bounds, the future had a new outlook at once, home seemed nearer than ever before and, best of all, we realized that we would not have to face the pain, the suffering and the bloodshed of battle again. It was almost too good to be true and, as I wrote Sister, I really felt proud that I had been in the thick of it and knew what war really was. I will tell you, Dad, how I have always looked at the front. It's a hidden land full of adventure where every red-blooded American longs to go and flirt with death. You leave the horse lines after dark on the wagons and slowly wind your way into this wonderful land. Just as quick as the towns fade out of sight and you are left alone with the drivers, horses and perhaps the moon, if there be one, you have a feeling of adventure come over you and you press on with interest into "The Land Behind the Hills" as some call it. I have talked with men here, and elsewheres, who have never seen or experienced the wonders of the front and they all wish that they had had a chance to see it. Personally I talk very little of what I have seen up there and been through except to my very close friends or to men whom I know can appreciate to some extent what it is like. It is hard for those who have not seen it to believe all that I have seen take place before my very eyes and I often wonder how you are going to believe all I shall tell you some day. You and the family shall hear it from my own lips, however, and every word I tell you will be the truth with no bright painting on it. I pride myself on what I have been through and seen and there are many men today who would give money to see what I have. Dad, it is wonderful and to think I have been spared to see and do more is greater yet.

The money you so kindly sent me is here but I fear the way things look just now that I shall never use it. No, I haven't flunked the course but have passed it, as far as I know, and I should have heard before this had I missed out. I understand, however, that no more commissions are to be given. This is not official as yet but the opinion is pretty strong that way just now. There is still hope, however, and if any are given out I expect to get one. Just what is to happen none of us know. Our course is over Saturday and several hundred men stand ready to put the gold bar on if Uncle Sam gives the word. If he does not, we have passed and shall be ready for them if another war comes up, while we are still young and of fighting age. It has been a hard, wonderful course and I guess we all know a little something about artillery, we ought to anyhow after all we have been through here and on the lines. If we are not commissioned only land knows where we will go or what we will do. We certainly will make A number 1 sergeants at any rate. I received a long letter from Mother this A.M. and, judging from her letter I guess you have all been pretty busy of late.

Well, Dad, it is time to eat so I must close.

Please give my love to all the family and keep a lot for yourself.
Johnny

Dear Dad

There is all kinds of news to tell you folks today but the trouble is that I am unable to state much as real facts. However, I am going to drop you a few lines telling you what I can of the conditions here and then try to look into the future, as best I can. I have put off writing for several days with the hopes that things might settle down to facts but they do not seem to, so I am going to do the best I can under the present conditions and shall try to write you something definite later.

Well, Dad, I know it will please you all to hear that I have passed and now am a proud graduate of the Saumur Artillery School having made a final average of 74.7%. I had a little better than four points to spare which pleases me very much as I did not expect to get more than an even 70% which would just let me by. It has been a long, hard pull, Dad, for me. But, by staying with it and never giving up I have won out and proved to myself that, by hard work and long hours, I could master what three months ago looked nearly a hopeless task for me with my weakness in handling figures.

I suppose you will stand up now and salute Second Lieutenant Hobson but, please be seated and do not salute because I am not to become a second lieutenant after all but shall return to you as a sergeant when the time comes to return home. Just after our final marks went in an order comes down from General Headquarters stating that no more men would be commissioned in the A.E.F. The school put up a fight for us and has done all in its power to secure permission to commission the graduating class but of no avail. It seems that the orders come to General Headquarters from Washington and of course what the White House says goes these days more than ever. Here we are, six or more hundred young men, trained in the very best artillery school in the world, passed the course and ready to be commissioned as second lieutenants when the order came out.

Right up to the very last every man of us felt sure that they would commission this class if no more, but we were wrong.

Now the question comes up what are they going to do with us? The orders are now that every man shall be sent back to the outfit he came from with his same rank. We all have papers showing that we have completed the course here and if, at any time in the future, officers are needed they shall be taken from the men who have passed here. We have talked and retalked the thing over and wild rumors are flying about everywhere, some with a foundation and some without. There are many drawbacks to sending each man back to his own outfit which I will not go into here but which I guess you can very easily see for yourself, but those are the orders now. They may change at any minute but for the present we are just hanging around here hoping against vain hope that they will. It is of no use to tell you how it will hurt my pride to return to the battery and be forced to take orders from a top sergeant or a second lieutenant when I really outrank the former and am equal, or should be equal, to the latter. I have slaved for the right to be entitled to a salute and to pull myself from the ranks and have done it only to lose it. Needless to say I am very disappointed, as are all the rest, to have the goal right in my hand and then feel it slip through my fingers. But, as I wrote Ev yesterday, they cannot kill my spirit or knock the smile off my face and my mind is made up to accept whatever comes in the proper way, knowing that I have made the most of the chance given me. It will not hurt me to bottle that pride up in the least, in fact, I guess it will do me good, and if I am sent back to the old bunch, Dad, you can rest assured that the boys will find the same old sergeant that left them, a bit wiser as to artillery matters than when he left but ready and willing to do his part as before. My time here has not been wasted by a good deal and, whereas we all are a bit disappointed just now, we shall all be fully repaid for our work someday. My dreams have faded but, Dad, I am the gainer just the same. The war's over, I'm alive, well and happy and who could ask for more after all I've been through and seen so many of my friends called "West", some at my side, while I have come through without a mark. No siree, I have no cause to kick, have I? I should say not. All the men are taking it just fine, and now that the disappointment is wearing off to some extent we are making a joke out of it.

It may interest some of you to hear about some of the funny sights which have appeared around some of the barracks of the graduating class so I will describe them very briefly.

The sad news reached us Saturday evening and Sunday morning the following appeared on the door of one of the barracks. A bunch of flowers tied up with a black ribbon on which were pinned four or five gold bars. Above was a large piece of wood over which hung several officers' hats cords and upon which the following was written, "In memory of John K. Commission, Born September 1, 1918, passed away November, 24, 1918. Below this was written all the medals he had won in the battle of Saumur which I have forgotten off hand and which were mostly things I doubt if any of you ever heard of unless you have been studying the gentle art of firing a 75 m/m gun while I have been gone. Half the school naturally came down to see it and it was mighty clever. Next appeared a little tombstone cut out of wood which was draped with black cloth covered with gold bars and hat cords. This also bore a few lines in memory of John K. Another bunch had taken off their black braids, which all students wear on their blouses and caps, and nailed them up on the door of their barracks forming the letters S.O.L. Thus it runs and you can bet John K. Commission has many such things around to mark his death.

The two hundred dollars you sent me I shall keep for a while anyhow, until I find out for sure where I am going to land and until pay starts in regularly again. We have not been paid for two months as the school intended to give us those two months in our final statements. Now that we shall get no final statements I do not believe there will be time to make out a payroll before we leave in which case I may need the money. I am in hopes that I shall have a chance to see Paris on my way to wherever I am going and you know what that means. I would like a furlough but I fear that is out of the question for just now. Ev wrote that his did him a world of good and told me it would do the same for me if I could only get free from all military cares for a few days. It would, there's no doubt about that, but I fear I shall be back in the States before I ever get a chance to forget military stuff. I'm just like you, Dad, when it comes to vacations; I've always got my foot in the pie and up to my neck in the soup. In other words I just do not connect when vacations are handed out. I hate to get out of harness, once in, and am always busy at something when the chance does come. Well, we should worry, there's a good long one coming when I get discharged and I will tell you right here, Dad, that I am expecting you to enjoy part of it with me. I don't care where we go or what we do but we both are going to have a good time and you are going to be far enough away from the office so that you will forget business and have a good time with me. I mean it now and am looking forward to a trip with you somewheres upon my return. I'll be blowing in on you quicker than you think so you had better start thinking of some place where we can enjoy life to the limit after I have enjoyed what I have missed for so long for a couple of weeks - HOME.

I'll tell you all a little joke which may amuse you after the way I used to flit across the polished dance floor when at home. I blew into the Y.M.C.A. last Saturday night about ten o'clock and found a very fine little dance in full sway. They have these every Saturday night but I never happened to get over to one before for some reason. I found a nice easy chair by the fire, lit up an American cigar I had managed to buy and began talking war with a group of men I knew. All of a sudden the idea came to me that once upon a time I had been able to dance and, since the custom is for anyone just to cut in and have a good time, I decided I would make my first attempt at dancing for over a year. I picked out a very good-looking girl who surely was a peach of a dancer and cut in. Ye Gods, Dad, I surely did make a bad move when I left that chair by the fire. Dance, why I had no idea at all of it. Dick Thompson may have made us all laugh at times when he danced but he was a wonder side of me Saturday night. I had almost forgotten how to hold the girl and must confess I had to think twice before deciding which arm should be put around her slender waist and which hand should hold hers. She was very nice, however, but I'll bet her feet hurt worse than Sister's ever did when I got through walking on them with my big high top boots. I had to laugh on my way home that night at how much a man can forget in a year and the funny experiences I shall have when I first get home and try to break into a little society. Mother and Sister will have to be very stern with their boy at first until he has learned once again the gentle art of playing at this society game.

Well, Dad, I guess I have raved on about long enough for this time so I will close. Unless you hear otherwise from me you had better start sending my mail back to the battery.

Lots of love for all the family and a heap for yourself.
Johnny

Dearest Mother

It is Thanksgiving morning and I have just got up from the breakfast table and made my way to the Y.M.C.A. to spend about an hour with you and the family before someone grabs me and wants me to do this, that or the other thing with them.

Today marks my second Thanksgiving away from home and it will only be a matter of a few weeks before my second Xmas in France comes around. My, but the time has gone fast and, to me, it seems only yesterday that the good ship Finland put into Saint-Nazaire and landed Battery A on French soil. Then came those four months of training at the big camp on the hill only a few miles from Rheims where we learned how to handle the guns, lay wire and read the signals which every artillery man knows. Those were perhaps the best four months of my life. Everything was new, everything held out an interest for me and I had many friends around me, both officers and enlisted men. I shall never forget those days, Mother, because it was during them that I put away childish toys and fancies and entered into the first stages of manhood. We were all happy but the dark side of war was only a short ways off and it was only to be a matter of weeks before those faces, which were soft and gay, were to become hard and stern from battle. I shall not forget the night we left the training camp for the front in a hurry, nor shall I forget the thoughts which went through my brain as, at one a.m., I put the saddle on Kid and took my place at the head of my detail to march to the depot. Then as we neared the front and saw for the first time destroyed homes and towns, the excited talk of men as they gazed upon the ruins from their boxcars. I was laid up with a slight cold the night the battery moved up to take her first position on the Chemin des Dames front but was well enough to join them the second night, which I did. Will the memory of the ride from the horse lines to the cave ever die? I hope not because I was in a seventh heaven of excitement and adventure. The land I had read so much about, the sights I had tried to picture in my mind, when reading Service's poems by Dad's fire all stood before me, not as a dream but as real. Next we moved to the Toul sector where, for two or three months, we enjoyed about all the thrills and hardships which a soldier at the front can enjoy. There we had our first big fight, which I wrote you about last April, and there, for six weeks, I lived in an observation post which looked right out upon Montsec which I guess you have all read about. Then, dear, came Chateau-Thierry the battle which stemmed the great German advance on Paris and which will never be forgotten. I have read many articles written about that battle in American magazines and I certainly hope you have run across some of them because they are very true and well written. I missed out on the last part of this fight because it was up there in that death hole that I was gassed, but I was in long enough to know what it was like. A few weeks of pain followed and then came those happy days with Major Root and finally here. I claim that I have a lot to be thankful for today and I know that you folks at home have, because you have a boy in France alive, well and happy while thousands of families have lost their boys on the same ground that I have so luckily passed over. Another year will see me home and next Thanksgiving ought to be the best one we have ever had, all together and all happy.

I received the long letter you wrote from the Touraine yesterday noon and am glad to hear that at last you and Sister have found time to take a few days' rest and change from your hospital work. I wish I might have been with you to enjoy the theaters, etc. You made the remark that you would be glad when you could take Ev and I with you. Well, darling, you can mark my word that we shall be glad when the day comes that we can go with you on your good times in Boston and elsewhere. Ev writes that officers are still arriving to be trained and he is kept as busy as ever, but wishes things would let up so he can get back. It is only a matter of time now and it will go fast since the fighting is over. You know, I have an idea in my head, the way things look just now, that I shall beat Ev home. Had I been commissioned I fear he would have been the first to reach 129 [Arlington Street] but, since I am returning to the 26th Division, I kind of think you will see me walk in first. Well, we'll see.

My hour is up and one of the sergeants in the section is already on my neck telling me to show signs of life or we never will reach the town where we are going for lunch in time so I guess I had better close and get walking.

Give my love to all the family and keep just loads for you own sweet little self.
Johnny

Dearest Sister

"Nothing to do until tomorrow and less to do then" is my song these days and it is very true. I am just hanging around Saumur waiting for orders to pack up and pull out for the battery. There has been nothing to do so all the week but eat, sleep and kill time any way that is possible. I have spent most of this time at the YMCA in front of the fire reading or looking into the flames and trying to figure out when I shall be sailing for home sweet home and what the future has in store for me. There I have sat, for what seems ages, watching the smoke curl up from my cigarette and just dreaming and resting after three months of hard work. I have been off on a few long walks but must confess I have grown a bit lazy and take more pleasure in sitting in an easy chair than tramping through this fall mud which has made its appearance this past week. Some of the boys left this noon and I expect I shall receive my traveling orders either tonight or sometime tomorrow. I have no idea where the battery is so I am unable to tell you what kind of a trip I have before me but you can rest assured that it will be a gay one if it is anything like the one I had coming up here. The lad I have been bumming around with here got his orders to leave this noon and his last words to me were, "God, I hope I can arrange some way to get home by New Years." Gee, wouldn't it be great if we all could.

The last rumor concerning the battery I heard last night when one of the lads from the 101st told me that he heard both regiments were in Metz. I hope this is so as I certainly should like to see that city as well as Montsec which is only a few miles away. Last spring Montsec was almost in front of the observation post I was in and, on clear days, we were able to see the smoke curling up from Metz. That is a beautiful country up through there and it has been my heart's desire for many months to see those woods and hills which last April, when were up there, were in German hands. Montsec had many battery positions behind it and it used to be part of my work to try and locate them. Since then I have heard that the Germans had wonderful positions on the reverse slope and their guns and flashes were well camouflaged and was almost impossible to catch their flashes with glasses. We did, however, while I was there spot one big baby which got fresh one too many times. The woods in that sector and the hills for miles around just seemed to be alive with artillery at times and it was a great sight to watch them blaze away at night. I am very anxious to see some of the German towns and it is with a feeling of regret that I was not there that I read daily in the papers of the American entry into this or that town. Those boys are just enjoying the fruits of their hard fighting to the limit now and, thank goodness, Johnny will be with them before many more days. I wish I could pick up some little things to bring back to each of you but I hate to carry a single thing that is not necessary as it is in the way and adds just so much more weight to your load. I have had so many chances to get just about anything under the sun right from the battlefield that at times I have thought I was almost foolish not to grab ahold of a German boot or wrist watch for one of you but have always come to the conclusion that if I bring myself home alive that will be enough. If I can lay my hands on some small thing however, I shall most certainly bring it back. I carried a machine gun bullet, which fell at my feet last fall or rather last winter while we were on the Chemin des Dames front, in my pocket for months but lost it at last. The dear little thing was meant to hit me but merely fell biff at the edge of my boot not having the heart to kill me so young and fair (?) I guess. I have also tried to keep plans showing our wires at all the different positions but these, like the lead, have all been lost in one way or another or thrown away when there was no place to carry them. I'll even lose the papers I have received from here if I don't watch them like a mother watches a baby. Let 'em go but you can bet I won't lose my life - I watch that both night and day. No, Sister, I did not come over here to win glory and to pick up all kinds of stuff so that I could sit and look at it and tell someone how I got it. I came over here to serve my country and fight as long as she needed me. I came over here with nothing but a suit on my back, have lived for over a year with almost nothing and I'll return the same way.

Thanksgiving night I was out for supper in a little café about half a mile from town and there I saw a sight which took me right back home. A mother playing the piano while her little son, five or six years old, sang. I got homesick for Buster and, since I could not take him in my arms and play with him, took the little French boy. His father is a very well-to-do Frenchman who works for some large exporting house at Bordeaux and his mother was one of the best looking French women I ever saw. When this lad, who was with me, and I finished supper a French soldier, who was there, got out a fiddle and played good old French jigs while my friend and I tried to learn some French dance steps from this little boy's mother. It was loads of fun and having that little fellow there laughing and playing with me made me think I was at home.

To be sure Xmas is not here yet and it may be a bit early to start thinking about it but I am going to say just a few words about Xmas presents. Darling, don't give them a thought as far as I am concerned because only a few things can be sent and that money you all would spend on them can find a better use. A nice long letter from each of you, full of love and news of your doings and preparations at home for that day will please me more than anything else in the world. Dad sent me some money out of which I have bought a very fine trench coat which I can wear after I am out of the Army and which cost 264 francs made to order and I am going to call this my Xmas present from you all this year. It has pleased me a great deal and feels, oh, so good, to get something on that is really made of good stuff. The lining buttons in and can be removed in hot weather so that the coat may be used for either a raincoat or a duster when I drive that car I want to buy when I get home. Regulations may not let me use it when I get back to the battery since I am not an officer but I am certainly enjoying it now and shall store it away if not allowed to wear it until I get home. This is the first expensive thing I have bought since landing here and I never would have got that only I thought I owed John Hobson a little real personal comfort so gave his old body a treat. I suppose it seems strange to hear me talk like that but I swear I am sick of issue stuff and long for something real. It's the best Xmas present I could have and I am just as happy with it as a girl with some brand new thousand-dollar

Easter dress. There are lots of other things I should like to buy, such as a good silver cigarette case, good looking shoes, and suits but I just must hold onto my money as I may really need it someday and what's the use of spending a lot out when I am not to get my commission. I have managed to make out on my monthly pay so far, most of which goes to pass away dull evenings and to make merry when those blues come as they are bound to come once in a while. Dad, the dear man, has given me more than enough as I guess you know but I have only used that when I had to, such as when I was hurt. Not having spent much the past year I thought a long time before buying that coat but finally made up my mind it was worth every franc I paid for it and, sister dear, I surely am pleased with it so don't worry about Xmas presents as I already have one from you all.

I suppose the people in the States will be wild with joy in a few weeks when the first transport, carrying a large number of American soldiers, puts into New York. The sick and wounded are to be gotten home just as fast as they can get boats to take them and I am mighty glad to hear it. There is no place like home to get well or forget the wound you may have or the gas which is still in your lungs making you feel mean. The well ones will follow next and I really believe you will have the pleasure of seeing the good old 26th, who has done such fine work over here and is said to be equal to the best French divisions, march down Broadway by Easter at the latest. I am all right and happy over here but I shall never be contented once I hit the U.S. until I get my discharge. As soon as I hit American soil I want to catch the first train home and stay there. Yes, I know I shall want to roam again after a few months but I've had enough for one year and am ready to settle down for a few months at least. I'll bet old Ev is doing all in his power to get a pass for home and I can just hear him cuss every time a new bunch of officers comes in to be trained in observation work. Cheer up, old dear, he'll be back to you just as quick as possible and before you realize it the phone will ring and it will be Ev telling you he is in Boston and coming out on the next train. I saw in yesterday's paper where a lot of observers had left for home and it won't be long now before he is one of them.

Yes, I should think it would be rather dull for you with both Marj and Eloise gone but I suppose you and Mother both are kept busy with your Red Cross work.

What is "K" doing these days? I have not heard a word from her or about her for ages. I cannot blame her much for not writing as I have not written her for ages but tell her my thoughts are often with her and a few lines would be appreciated.

Well, darling, I guess I have dreamed on enough for now so I will close and make my way down town.

Give my love to all the family and lock a lot up in your own little heart.
Johnny

CHAPTER FOURTEEN

Rest & Relaxation

"I have no work to do but eat and sleep..."

SECOND LIEUTENANT JOHN L. HOBSON II

Montigny-le-Roi,
France
December 5, 1918

Dearest Sister

Once again I take my old pen in hand to drop you all a few lines to let you know what I have been up to the last few days. I am not writing in the fine Y.M.C.A. at Saumur this time but am in a kitchen of a French home which is right next door to the barn in which I am living. A nice big fire is burning in the stove while the old French lady who owns the place is busy preparing supper for a bunch of old, hungry American soldiers who will arrive here about six o'clock. There is also a dear little French girl about six years old running around and who keeps climbing up on the bench side of me trying to figure out what I am doing. Now I suppose you all wonder what in the name of heaven I am doing here and that is just what I have been trying to figure out myself for over forty-eight hours. Well, I will tell you what has happened and then perhaps you can dope it out.

Four of us left Saumur last Monday noon to find our batteries. Our traveling orders told us to first go to Tours which we did. There we hung around until six o'clock that night when we took a train for Long. The French railroads are all overworked these days and have a great deal more work thrown on them than is possible for them to handle, hence we were almost half a day late in reaching Long getting there about two the following afternoon. Not having ever ridden on any of these trains I know you have no idea how disagreeable it is to be on one for nearly twenty-four hours. It is almost impossible to sleep and you have to eat whatever you can lay your hands on at the stations, which is usually very little. We all knew this so armed ourselves with sandwiches before leaving Toul which is a very large city. Upon arriving at Long we found that we could get a train for Meuse at four o'clock and this was very lucky too because, whereas Long itself is a large place the depot is over a mile from the city and since there are several different schools there, the place is crowded and hence no place to enjoy life. Our train instead of pulling out at four, as it should have, decided that it might make a run on time if it did this so waited until six. When we reached Meuse we all got the surprise of our lives. It was nothing but a small country station with no houses in sight and not even a light burning in the depot. We had no idea which way to turn and, to make matters worse, two of our party, who were in another car, forgot to get off and they had the orders. We were standing there wondering what to do when a big husky lad shows up and wants to know if we were just back from permission. "Permission, Hell," my comrade said, "We're from school and had orders to report here but damned if I can see any place to report." "Cheer up," the other boy said, "divisional headquarters are only about two miles from here and that's where you fellows must be bound for." It surely was comforting to have someone know where we wanted to go because it is easy money that neither of us did. I told our big friend that I had no idea in my head of walking two miles that night in the rain and dark, carrying a roll. He told us that there was a casual camp a few minutes' walk from the station and we very likely could find a place to sleep there and could ride out on the supply trucks in the morning. That was fine but how in the name of heaven were we to find that camp, absolute strangers. I gave him a cigarette and he at once became very nice and offered to show us the way which he did. Once at the camp our troubles were over. There were all 26th Division men there and we were home once again. Hot coffee, bread and butter were served to us and all the rumors and facts of the division were poured out to our hungry ears. Gee, it was fine. The night was mean but we made merry and the funny part of it was that we didn't know any of the boys. They were 26th men and we were and that was enough. The next morning we had a good old 26th breakfast, rolled our rolls and headed for the poor little depot again to catch a truck for divisional headquarters. There I met the surprise of my life. We found 600-odd men all waiting for a train to take them off on their permissions. The first man I ran into was Cummings who used to be with the battery but is now with the divisional show. We were talking and he was telling me the latest news of the battery when I felt someone looking me over pretty carefully. Just then Cummings said, "By the way, Hobson, do you know the Kingsberry brothers from Keene, New Hampshire?" Good Lord, I thought I should fall flat. "Do I know them, well I should say so," I said, whereupon he lead me to where all three of them were sitting. I had a fine talk with them and had supper with them last night as they were unable to get transportation. After meeting a few more men, one of which was Al Houle, we jumped a truck for headquarters and here, working in the office, I ran into Arthur Henderson who used to be the battery clerk. There we got our orders. It seems that the entire 26th is forming around here. They are all here as a matter of fact but the artillery, who is somewhere turning in their guns and horses. There was no use in sending us to them because we would just have to hike right back here so I have been attached to divisional headquarters for food and quarters until the batteries arrive. Lord only knows when this will be with transportation tied up the way it is, so all I have to do is hang around here and wait until they pull in. There isn't a darn thing to do and the boys from the battery, who have just returned from permission, are stationed a good two miles from here so I am sort of alone as it were. I have no work to do but eat and sleep so you see I am enjoying a rest but must confess I am sick of hanging around. I have a fine place to sleep in, a hayloft, and the lad who is with me and myself have really made a fine little home of it. We rise about nine, go to a pump and wash up and then loaf until bedtime. We felt full of pep for some unknown reason this P.M. so decided to walk to the next town and see some of the boys from his battery who are there. It is very muddy walking and looked like rain so I did not feel like going with him. Well, here I am well and alive, with the future very unsettled.

I must tell you a funny little thing which took place just as I started this letter. A couple of dough-boys came in to get a drink and, as the cork in my ink was stuck, I wanted to borrow a knife to get it out so I turned to them and asked if they had one. After removing the cork I handed the knife back saying, "Thanks ever so much." What was my surprise when the lad says, "That's all right, Hobson, you can have anything I have." I was taken off my feet needless to say as I had never seen the lad before that I could remember so I asked him how he happened to know my name. "Well, sergeant," he said, "you were pointed out to me yesterday morning at the depot by one of your friends who made the remark that you were one of the finest men who ever breathed God's fresh air and who always gave the boys under you a good square deal." I had a long talk with him and he was a fine lad but I nearly passed away laughing to myself at his first remark. Keep that inside the family now as I should not have told you except for the fact I thought it might amuse you as it did me. Whoever pointed me out or made that remark I know not, but it was one of the battery men because he knew I was in the 102nd and had just returned from officer's school.

Well, darling, the men's supper is nearly ready and I have a little date of my own tonight with a couple of men I met this morning, so must close.

Please give my love to all the family and keep just heaps for yourself.
Johnny

Montigny-le-Roi,
France
December 7, 1918

Dearest Mother

Here it is Sunday again and again I take my pen in hand to write a few more lines home. It would not seem right these days if I did not sit down in some Y.M.C.A. barn or dugout and write home. It is a regular habit with me now and I wonder what I shall do when I get home and cannot write my weekly letter to one of you.

Well, dear, there really is very little news to tell you all because, as you must know by now from a letter I wrote Sister four or five days ago, I'm doing nothing but hanging around the little town of Montigny waiting for orders to join the battery or have them join me here. There is nothing exciting or thrilling about that, is there? I get up late every morning, take as long as possible about washing and shaving at the town wash house and then spend the rest of the day smoking and roaming around. Eight o'clock always finds me in bed in the hayloft and by nine I am lost in the land of dreams. There is a very detailed account of one of my days at Montigny.

Last evening, however, I happened to run into a little luck by chance and really spent a most enjoyable evening plus breaking my rule of going to bed at eight. Why, would you believe it I stayed out until nine o'clock? Rooming right next door to our barn in a private house is a sergeant from "F" Battery who is also stuck here. I was over talking with him about four o'clock and we got so interested chewing the fat that we forgot all about mess until it was too late to eat in the mess-line so asked the lady who owns the place if she could cook us up a bite to eat. All she had was potatoes but said if we could go out and buy some meat she would be very glad to cook it up for us and give us some French fries to go along with it. We got the meat all right and along with two large glasses of coffee we had a bully little feed. I happened to have some bread and jam which I had bought that noon as we added that to our banquet. This lady was very young and her husband was a sergeant in the famous Blue Devil Alpine Climbers you may have read about. He was not home but is expected within a few days. After supper a very nice young girl about 26 years old came over and we four sat around the old family lamp and tried to talk to each other for nearly three hours. The French are crazy about pictures so I showed them the pictures of home I have here with me, trying, as best I could, to explain them. They both thought you looked altogether too young to be my mother and had a bully old time trying to kid me that you were really my girl and not my mother at all. I doubt very much if they believe it now. Sister and "K" they gazed at for a long time and then almost together said, "Oh, what good-looking girls" or words to that effect. Art they were sure was at least twenty years old and wanted to know if he was with me. I am sorry to say that I did not have a picture of Dad and Buster to show them as the picture of the family is in my barracks bag and I know not where that is and have not seen it since away back early last spring. There were three little kids there also as well as their grandfather. He was a very fat old man who loved American cigarettes and, as I had a fairly large supply on hand, I was able to keep the old boy happy all the evening. I must tell you one thing which happened which pleased me very much. About eight o'clock one of the little kids climbed up on a chair and went sound asleep. I have often seen pictures of little fellows asleep in a chair in front of the stove but I never saw one before until last night. He was too cunning for words and I swear I would have let him sleep there until we left but was afraid he would fall so I called his mother's attention to him who put him to bed. My evenings, such as last evening, will be my pleasantest memories of France and will live on when the others are faded out with age. I love to be among these country people and my only regret is that I have not had a chance to really live with some French family while I have been over here.

Just before I left Saumur I was able to buy a small 75-m/m gun which I had sent home to you all as a Xmas present. It is really a very fine little model of the real gun and if you notice all the parts work just as they do in a real gun. If this does not reach you please let me know.

Well, darling, I fear this is a somewhat dry and uninteresting letter but we will hope I have some real news for you next Sunday.

Give my love to all the family and seal a lot up in your own little heart.
Johnny

Dear Dad

This is the life for me. Talk about your men of leisure, well that's Johnny these days. I was lucky enough to get a room last week with two other sergeants from the regiment and we three are just enjoying life to the limit. Not one darn thing to do but sleep late every morning and talk late every night with our French mother and sister. This sister lives across the street but is over most of the time. They certainly do enjoy having us around and if I am not laughing and trying to talk French every minute of the day and night the poor old lady thinks I am sick and wants to know what is the matter. For three nights running I kept the whole room roaring with laughter including the old lady's father who must be 70 if he is a day old. "Come on, Mr. Jack," he said the other night, "kid Miss Bertha some more." He's a regular old trump, Dad, and some of the remarks he makes nearly set me crazy with laughter. Last night I decided I would give them all a rest and, knowing that if I stayed in I would be called upon to perform, I made arrangements to spend the greater part of the evening out. Arthur Henderson is here, who used to be with the battery, so we took a fine long walk under a fine December moon. I blew back home about nine o'clock and just as soon as I put my foot inside the door Madame and Miss Bertha landed on me full force both talking as only women can. They talked so fast I couldn't follow them but one of the other sergeants who does understand French, said they had been cut up all the evening because I had gone out and were giving me a fine old call down. I laughed my head nearly off, which made matters worse, and then tried to explain why I had spent the evening away. Madame said that they all looked forward to having us there at night to have a good time with them and that I must always do my walking during the day and have my evenings free to spend with them. Oh, Dad, it's great to have them feel this way. We three fellows just own the house and our smallest wishes are attended to at all hours. I had a slight cold the other day and my eyes felt rotten. I was telling one of the boys about it and the Madame got wise - hot towels went right on.

Now I suppose you are interested to know how much we pay for all this. Madame will set no price, try as we have to make her do so, so we give her one franc a night for our room each and a franc each for breakfast and buy her husband cigarettes and do all we can for the three kids. She seems to think this is too much but I would gladly pay five francs a day for the chance to sleep in a warm, dry place and have a nice stove to sit around at night. These days in Montigny-le-Roi have certainly been the best I have spent in France.

I went up to see Ben Pitman at his office last Wednesday. He is looking fine and was very pleased to see me. He wanted to be remembered to all of you.

I understand from Henderson that Major Root has returned to the States. Gee, I wish I was in his shoes because I must confess I am very anxious indeed to get back now that the fun is all over. There is a great deal of talk now as to when we shall set sail but I guess that is about all it is.

The batteries are still stuck for lack of transportation but I understand they have been promised trains this week. I do not know where they are going but hope it is for the coast.

Well, Dad, I fear this letter is rather dry but there really is nothing of excitement to write about these days. I am well and happy and that is about all there is to say.

Please give my love to all the family and keep a lot for yourself.
Johnny

Dearest Mother

I am sorry to say that I was unable to write my weekly letter home last Sunday as orders came in early that morning to pack up and leave for the battery, which had pulled into the area the day before. We left Montigny about nine o'clock Sunday morning and arrived in Daremont, where the battery is billeted, about noon. Needless to say I was mighty glad to see all the old men again and hear their experiences since I left them last September for school. They have been through a lot and I guess, from all the reports I have heard from different men, that they were very lucky to escape without losing a lot of men. At times it has looked as if the entire battery would be lost but God has been with them and they have come out in fine shape. Now if we can only keep off the "flu", which is after all of us, I guess we will reach home in the course of time.

My Xmas this year was nothing like it was last year but, nevertheless, it was a very happy one. We had a fine big dinner that day including roast pig and that went a long ways towards making the day a cheerful one. That evening, when I went to bed, I placed my candle at the head of my cot and spent a good hour with you folks at home by looking at your pictures. When I blew the candle out and lay down to sleep I must confess the world took on a rather gray look and my heart longed for home. Fifteen months is a long time to be away from those whom you love and love you and all I am living for now is the day to come when that transport steams into New York or Boston Harbor. I see by the papers that we are expected home soon, in fact I believe some Boston paper said Xmas would see the 26th on U.S. soil. Xmas has passed and we are still here, but do not give up hopes, dear, because I really believe February will see us home. Transportation is all tied up over here, as I wrote you, and there are lots of little things to be done as well before we start off on the best trip of all, but we're coming sooner or later so keep the smile on your face and that undying courage in your heart that you have shown during the months of struggle. I am having the hardest fight now to hold myself in a cheerful frame of mind and to keep my interest up in the work which I am now doing. The fighting is over and all I want or care about is a passport home and that desire, whereas it is only natural, is very apt to make me feel blue as well as down and out, because the time goes so slow. This, they always say, is the hard part of war and I agree with them. You know just my feelings at this time, darling, as only a mother can so I shall not take the time to write them. I have learned in the past year to make the best of conditions as I find them and above all things to keep happy and busy so I guess we will be able to make time hurry a little.

Yesterday afternoon I was sitting in a café reading some Boston papers with another sergeant. He was looking the pretty girls over on the social page of the Sunday paper when all of a sudden he came out with "Ye gods, Jack, just take a look at this peach. How would you like to take her to a dance ce soir?" I took the paper and looked at the girl for almost half a minute and then the idea came to me that somewhere, back in the past, I had seen her so I looked at the name below. I had to read it twice before I would believe my own eyes that it said, "Miss Barbara Ware." When I told the other sergeant that I knew her he just laughed and laughed, "Why you poor bum, she's a living goddess." He said, "Where in the name of heaven did you ever meet her?" He finally half believed I knew her and started to laugh again, "If she could only see you now she wouldn't even look at you." I told him I would not blame her much but just the same I would bet my last franc she would. He cut the picture out and added that it was going up on the wall in his section house. If any of you happen to see "B" just tell her for me that her picture nearly broke a soldier's heart.

I have not heard from Ev for some time but a letter came to the battery from him for me a few days before I joined them and was sent to Saumur so it ought to be back before long.

Well, dear, I am well and happy and hope to see you all again before very many months pass by.

Please give my love to all the family and seal a lot in your own heart.
Johnny

Dear Dad

I have just come off the regimental guard and, as I feel tired due to the lack of sleep last night, have decided to stay in and do a little writing instead of playing the café as I usually do in the evening. There isn't a great deal of very exciting news to tell you but I will do my best not to make this letter too dry reading.

As you can see by the heading of this letter we have not moved since I wrote Mother ten days ago. The latest reports are that we shall pull out between the 13th and 15th but that's only tonight's rumor - tomorrow night will very likely have it that we are here until death calls us away. In other words no one really knows when we are due to move. Rumor has it that, when we do say good-bye to Daremont, we are to start for the coast making one stop of two or three weeks in which to clean up in and get rid of our dear little pets, the cooties, before going to the port to embark for home. Well, Dad, cheer up, I'm coming home sooner or later and the longer I'm gone the more glad you all will be to see me and the more I'll have to tell you. Keep smiling until I get there and then I'll extend that smile to a laugh by telling you some of the most amusing stories of my experiences over here that you have ever heard. Some are really funny.

The day before yesterday was a real red-letter day for me. A lot of little things happened to make it such but the best of all was when one of the men said, "Sergeant, there's a box waiting for you in the office." Those words were heaven to my ears and when I climbed the ladder to my hayloft and looked inside that box my joy gave way to a couple of big tears. Home had come to me and I was enjoying to the very fullest measure what loving hands had so carefully bought, packed and sent to me. I could picture the care and love with which that little box had been packed in Mother's room. I could see you all standing around and I fancied that some such thought as this was in all of your minds. "Oh, that I could do more for him but the law says, 'No,' and since conditions are such that this one little box, a poor token of my love for him, bring him all the joy in the world and carry to him my deepest love." Wasn't that very thought in the minds of each of you, Dad? Then I could see you discussing what was going in the box. There was no doubt in your mind what should be sent overseas to your son so you dropped two nice boxes of the very best cigarettes in. Mother, God bless her dear little heart, did not know what to send so she put in a handkerchief between the folds of which she placed love and kisses. Sister and the rest of the younger members of the family added candy to fill my sweet tooth and nuts to make me think I was at some big dinner party. Thus the little box was packed, kissed good-bye and sent on its way to find me. It found me and brought with it all the love that was so thought-fully put in every corner and when I opened it this love went deep down into my heart. I cannot and never shall be able to tell you all how much I have appreciated all you have done for me. You, Dad, may have been away from home for months at a time but I doubt if you ever were in a place or country where any little gift or thought from home meant more to you than it has to me since I have been gone.

It may be of interest to you to hear how I am spending the money you sent me and which I drew on my letter. It has been going for food and good times, times which will live in my memory for a long time. The last week at school was filled with banquets and, as you must know by now, I lived or nearly lived on that money in Montigny for the sake of extra comforts. Here in Daremont I am getting suppers fit for a king every few nights which means as much to me as a big dance or theater party used to. The battery is feeding good but I like to get away from the crowd every few nights with one or two fellows and eat off of a real table while some little French kid plays around reminding me of Phil. Every cent is bringing me pleasure and I would have gone dead broke ages ago if I had not had it. As it is I am set to enjoy myself for a long time yet.

Well, Dad, so much for tonight. I'm going to smoke one of your cigarettes and hit the hay for dream land.

Give my love to all the family and keep lots for your self.
Johnny

Dearest Mother

Last Sunday I was busy all day and hence was unable to write my weekly letter home. Sunday morning I went off for a long walk with another sergeant getting back to Daremont about two o'clock when we sat down to a big dinner which we had ordered a few days before. We had a fine, tender rabbit which had just been killed, potatoes, green peas, steak, egg pudding and all the milk we could drink plus, after dinner, coffee with the man and woman of the house. Needless to say we did not go to mess that night but sat around and tried to figure out how in the name of heaven two human beings could eat so much and still live. Well, I guess you will agree with me that I have a good excuse for not writing home last Sunday.

Now, dear, I have a great disappointment for you so get all set for it. This very likely will be the last letter you folks will receive from me and I am going to ask you all not to look for another one from me because, if you do, I am very much afraid that you will look in vain as I think this is the last of my book. Yes, Mother, the final chapter only it does not end by saying, "she lost herself in the arms of her lover while the white moon looked down and smiled at the happy couple," or words to the effect. This is merely the end of book one and book two will start pretty soon. Our hero has not meet the girl of his dreams yet but read on, darling, turning the pages of day and I think you will reach that part where your hero meets the girl and you see him fall in love before your very eyes while you smile and say to yourself, "God bless him, he is my boy and I am proud of him." This part of our story is coming out before we reach even that part where there is a long, long chapter coming in which you are to play a leading part. This chapter opens the later part of next month and is to open with a big transport carrying hundreds of soldiers landing at New York or Boston. One of these hundreds is to be your boy returning proudly home after 16 months of service in France. It is hard to picture just how this chapter will work out and impossible to realize or express in words the feelings which will take place within us as we read it but it will be the most wonderful of all chapters yet written for us all. Now, having broken the ice to some extent I guess you are all set for the real news.

The battery leaves here Saturday, the 19th, on its way to the coast. We are to stop at a large camp in Le Mans for a week or ten days to get cleaned up and if possible get rid of the cooties. I believe we also are to be in sort of quarantine but that is a small detail. Somewhere around the first of next month we leave Le Mans for the port of embarkation and, according to reports last night, are to set sail for home about February 10th. The exact date, of course, I do not know but, darling, I guess you can be prepared to receive a phone call or letter from me in the States, the last of February. I guess the Boston papers will tell you all when and where we are to dock so keep your eyes on them. It all seems too good to be true but it is. We do nothing in our spare time now but talk of home and I even dream of it at night and wake up with it on my mind. Time goes fairly fast but there are days that seem a whole year and hours which seem months, but we're coming home and, what pleases me most of all, is that I am to be free to enjoy the whole summer, the best part of the year, with you all. Just think of it, dear, another summer of pleasure when war with all its hardships will be forgotten and I can live and enjoy a vacation well earned. This coming summer will mean a lot to me and I shall appreciate Rye and home as I never have before. I am in hopes that it will be possible for me to have a car of my own in which I can ride for one whole summer just as much as I want and where I want but if it isn't my life will be just as happy because I am with you. My one hope has always been to have an auto and somehow I feel that now, before I start in the business world with Dad, I am going to have one in which to enjoy my first vacation since I left the U.S. Just think of it, dear, it will only be a short time now before I will be dancing with real girls, eating off a real table, sleeping in a real bed and enjoying the peace and quiet of home sweet home. This all sounds strange to you I know but to me it is real and has been merely a dream for months. All would be perfect if I only knew Ev was to be on the same boat with me but, from his last letter, I fear he will not get back so soon. It will not be long, however, before he arrives and we all start off again where we ended a year ago last September.

What camp we are to go into when we land I do not know but suppose it will be Devens. I guess here again the papers will inform you so again I say keep your eyes on them. Should we land in Boston I shall look for you the first thing but may be only able to give you a smile as I very much doubt if the boys are allowed to really see their folks until they land in camp. Look for a tall man wearing a mighty happy smile and that will be Johnny.

I understand that no more mail can be written after the 17th of this month so I guess you will not hear from me again until I land. I will let you know where we are to be stationed and if I cannot get to see you will let you know when you can come to me just as soon as possible.

Well, darling, I have got work to do so must close.

Will see you next month.

Love to all,
Johnny

POSTCARDS
(Undated)

Am off on my first leave, K, and having a fine time. Received your long letter just before I left the battery. Wish you were here to enjoy the life of a big French city with me. I am with another sergeant and we are just taking life easy.

Lots of love, dear,
Johnny

February 9, 1919

Am off on a two weeks permission including travel. Shall be here in Pau about eight days. Am enjoying lots of food and sleep. Staying in small hotel - Theater last night. The opinion is now that we shall sail March 8th.

Love,
Johnny

Mayet, France
February 24, 1919

Dearest Mother

I ought to be taken out to the nearest stone wall, stood up against it and shot at sunrise as a deserter. To think that any man 3,000 miles from home should let a whole month go by and not write home is an awful thought and the man who commits such a crime should meet death with the white handkerchief over his eyes. Well, thank goodness, there is no such law but it makes my head hang low when I think of how you all have been anxiously waiting for news from me, watching for the post man, always with the hope that he may have a letter from your boy, and he has not for a long time. There is no use in trying to explain it because no matter how busy I have been I should have written when I saw that we were not to be home as early as we expected. All I shall do is to ask forgiveness and know that you will grant it.

Well, darling, the unexpected happened the sixth of this month and for the first time in my 18 months service I was handed a pass. Another sergeant and I put in for one together to vist Pau, Basses Pyrenees and through some streak of luck landed 14 days including travel. We were never so surprised or taken back in our lives and, needless to say, happy beyond words.

We received our pay the morning of the sixth and just as we were leaving the office saw a train pull into the station. We had no idea at all as to where it was going or which direction we wanted to go but both of us wanted to get out of Mayet before they had time to recall our passes so off we started on the run just getting aboard as she pulled by the road crossing. Two o'clock that afternoon found us in Tours, the third or fourth largest city in France. I had been there twice before, once on my way to Saumur and again on the way back, so knew the ropes fairly well. We reported to the R.T.O. (Regiment Transportation Officer) and told him where we wanted to go and asked how to get there. "Take the midnight express for Bordeaux," was his snappy answer. Tours, whereas it is a big place, is one of the worst places in France to stop in because it is headquarters for the S.O.S. and the rules of the city are fierce. You cannot get a blame thing to eat outside of the station until 6:30 if you are an American soldier but here's where my two trips there before with their trying experiences came in very handy. The other sergeant had never seen the place before so we went around and saw the sights until five o'clock when we both were so hungry we just had to eat and Johnny was just the boy who knew a nice little out of the way place where we could eat without the M.P. on our necks. After supper we played the cafes for a while and as both felt pretty tired by nine o'clock decided to rest over there until noon the next day which we did.

Twelve five the next noon found us both in a second-class coach speeding towards Bordeaux. We arrived there the first part of the evening and got the cold shoulder right off the reel from our friends the M.P.s who informed us in very plain words that we could not leave the station and could not get a train for Pau until the next morning. I expected as much since I have done quite a little moving about with two or three men in a party and you certainly hit some funny places and run up against all kinds of rules. We spent that night in the Red Cross Barracks but before going there looked high and low for a way to escape but all in vain. Up to date it very likely sounds as if we were not having a good time but we were enjoying ourselves to the limit but luck was not breaking as well as it might. They have lots and lots of rules and there are just as many ways of getting around them as there are rules which I will tell you about some day. Some places are tied up so tight with M.P.s that you cannot move cross ways, but there is always a little gap somewhere if you are lucky enough to find it and through these we all go. It may mean a little head work and a flying dash down dark unknown side streets but just so long as we get where we want and what we want to when we want to all is well.

Nine o'clock the next morning we boarded the train for Pau and arrived there about four in the afternoon after a wonderful ride through beautiful country. We hit up with two "bloody" English soldiers on the way and I doubt if I ever laughed so much inside without having it show outside before in my life as I did with those two chaps. The expressions were funny in the first place and the way they pronounced their words certainly appealed to my sense of humor. I have met a lot of them but never really had a long talk with them before. They call the Germans "Jerry" and every good lad is known as a "bloke." I was taking a short catnap after we had talked about an hour when one of them leans over and said, "Oh, say American old bloke, wake up and give England a match."

Upon arriving in Pau we asked where we could get a light lunch and were told that the Hotel Davin had fine food so we went there. Both of us liked the food, and the waitress, so decided to get a room there for one night at least. We liked the place so much and they were so nice to us that we stayed there all the time. We had a nice, big double room with two beds and an open fireplace for which we paid six francs a day for both of us and three francs for wood. Breakfast, consisting of chocolate and bread, was brought to us in bed every morning which cost four francs and we paid twelve francs for dinner and supper. Mighty cheap I thought. There were several large high class hotels there but they cost too much for a soldier's pay to afford and I'll bet we could not have had such a good time in one as we did in the little old Davin where we were kings.

Next comes the act known as "the right street but the wrong hotel or the mystery of the Pomme D'Or Hotel." The first night we were in Pau we went to the movies which let out about eleven. We started for our hotel and somehow or other got in the hotel next to ours which was called the Pomme D'Or. We walked in big as life, tried to find our room and couldn't. We carefully explained that we had a room there and at the end of ten minutes had the manager plus the guests out in the aisles and halls looking for the lost room of the two American sergeants. I laughed till the tears rolled down my face at that manager running all over that place in his nightshirt trying to find our room. He finally tried to give us one and we decided we were in the wrong place so set the whole crowd, including the manager, up to a bottle of wine for their trouble and beat it. The next morning I went in and explained that it was our mistake and the old boy just yelled he laughed so hard.

Before telling you any more of the funny little experiences we had which I can assure you were many, I am going to write a few lines about Pau itself.

Pau is away down in the southern part of France very near the border of Spain. It is just outside of one of the big American leave areas and as a result has not been spoiled by the soldiers. Before the war lots of wealthy people from the States and England used to spend their summers there and many of the largest and best villas are owned even today by these people. There are very few places in France a Frenchman was telling me where the game of golf is played but that is one of the chief sports at Pau as it is an American and English game. Hare and hound chases on horseback also used to be enjoyed by the rich. Henry the Fourth has a big chateau there and we spent one whole Sunday morning going through it. I did not think it as pretty as some I have been through but well worth the time it took to look it all over. The Pyrenees Mountains stood out fine all the time we were there with the exception of one day when it rained. We walked away out in the country one afternoon and it was so hot we had to take our blouses off and yet all we had to do was turn our heads to the Pyrenees and see snow. There is a wonderful walk there which is just crowded in the afternoons and the parks are the most beautiful I have ever seen. There really isn't much use in trying to describe the place because it is impossible to realize the beauty of France until you have really seen it with your own eyes. These few lines, however, will give you a little idea of the place and we shall hope that in the years to come both you and dad may have a chance to visit the place.

When we arrived there we only had one tin of tobacco between us figuring that it was best to buy it there rather than carry it with us. But when our tin was almost gone, as it was very soon after we arrived, and we tried to buy some we found we could not get any American, French or English. This kind of put a dark cloud on the outlook as neither of us fancied the idea of staying eight days without a smoke. Well, after going twenty-four whole hours without a smoke we got to that point where a man must do something, so decided to take a flying chance and enter a city we were supposed not to enter on our pass but where we could buy cigarettes. That evening we were sitting in one of the large cafes laying our plans for the next day as to the safest and easiest way to get to this other town when two young ladies about twenty four years of age entered and sat down at our table. Ah, the plot thickens. We all got talking about one thing or another when one of the girls asked us if we had any American cigarettes. No, we were very sorry we did not and what troubled us more was that we could not buy them or any other kind. Right there the problem was solved. She banged on the table with a glass and the garcon came over on the hot foot and wanted to know what we desired to drink. We all gave our order and she said something to him which I was unable to get. All I know is that when those drinks came two packages of Spanish cigarettes came with them. I at once made friends with the garcon and from then on could buy all the cigarettes I wanted on the q.t. but I must never tell where they came from or let anyone hear me ask for them. They were smuggled over from Spain and hence the secret must not be let out. If you ever want a good smoke, Dad, try a Spanish cigarette, they are really and truly good but strong. The girls laughed at us for being so slow about catching onto the place but once onto it we did it justice all around. These two girls like American cigarettes the best as do most of the people over here but you ought to see them eat those Spanish ones up.

The next act is, 'Nero, the Ax', or South African full of vin rouge. We rose one morning at our usual hour, 10 to 10:30, and the day being extra fine decided to have an early lunch and go for a long walk. We started off about 12:30 and must have gone two or three miles when I made the remark that I felt lazy and wished someone would come along in a nice, big car and give us a ride. I had no more than got the words out of my mouth when I heard footsteps approaching in a motor at a very high rate of speed, also much yelling. Both the other sergeant and I turned around to see who the gay party might be and try to figure out whether they were returning at two in the afternoon from an all night racket or starting in on one for that night. Much to our surprise the driver stopped at the curb where we were standing to watch them pass. He was a great big coon and with him were two other men also of the dark race and all full of wine. "Where beeeee you gentlemen a'goin'?" he asked. We explained we were out for a short walk to see the country and he told us that if we would jump in he and his friends would really show us the sights. "Foolish boy, you didn't go I hope," I can hear you say, darling, but adventure was what we wanted and you can't kill a Y.D. man so in we got. We saw the country all right and also rode over every square inch of the road. First he would try one side for a few feet and then the other. He did not bother either of us at all with his speed and criss-cross stuff because I knew the worst that could happen would be a trip up a tree or in some ditch and neither one worried me at all. I just enjoyed the sights and we got the best view of the mountains we got all the time we were there. But, wait, our adventure does not end here. Nero took us to a large French Aviation School where he belonged and led us into the café there on the grounds. There were a lot of French sergeants in there who all rose to their feet and saluted as we entered with our three cloudy friends. All Nero wanted was a drink of any-thing strong so I got the barmaid, explained the situation to her in a soft tone while Nero was singing and then in a loud voice ordered the drinks. The other sergeant and I drank beer while Nero and his friends drank water with a little coloring in it like grape juice. I thought they would get wise to the fact that I had tipped that waitress off but they never did and enjoyed their drink. At this point in the game both the other sergeant and I decided it was time to part with Nero so we began talking war with the French sergeants. One took a liking to us and showed us the camp and as he was teacher there also invited us out to see his class fly. While we were walking to the field he expressed his great regret that they had no double planes there so that he could send us both up, but that all they had were single fighting machines. When I saw one student dive the nose of his plane two or more feet into the ground when making a landing I was glad there were no double planes there. Oh, how that sergeant did lecture that poor lad. We saw quite a bit of this sergeant later and met several of his friends. They certainly were nice to us and it was a pleasure to spend a few minutes with them every night or so. One came as far as Bordeaux with us on our way back. He was going to Paris to study for a commission. I hope he had better luck than I did.

Another day we took a 14-mile hike to a nearby village for lunch. Thus our eight days in Pau passed. Lots of sleep in a real bed, lots of food off a real table, plenty of walking and the gay life of the French cafes. I returned to the battery in wonderful condition and the men say I never looked better in my life. The trip home was about the same as the one up so I will not describe it now.

When I got back to the battery the very first thing I did was head for my mail and, would you believe it, I got letters written as far back as June. They had gone to the hospital, then Saumur, and Lord only knows where else. Your pictures arrived and I certainly have enjoyed them.

Darling, youth is a strange and wonderful thing but the thoughts and desires which enter the mind of a man my age are more than I can figure out. Here I have been gone from home for a whole year and a half, undergone all hardships and dangers and now, when it is only a matter of weeks before the division sails for home, a strong, undying desire to volunteer to go up into Germany grips me. At times it seems as if I just must go, the desire gets so strong. I want to see the country as it is today and take part in the work which is going on up there. I've talked with men who are in the Army Occupation and the more I hear the more I want to go. "Lots of work," they all say but I have learned long ago not to let work phase me. You and Dad both know that no man ever loved his home more than I do or is more anxious to get back and that desire is in my heart. What is, dear, the longing for adventure which all young people have or have I fallen in love with this wild life in the army? It would only mean about a year's more service over here, if all goes as planned and oh, to think of what I could get out of it. Yesterday I all but put my name in and I do believe that the only thing that stopped me from doing it was your picture. I happened to take one look at it as I was leaving my room and then did an about face and said, "Johnny, it can't be done. You've got a mother awaiting your return and it would break her heart if you didn't get there when the division does." Darling, what is it that makes youth so anxious and eager to get into places where there is danger and do things which are not wise? Ambition often leads us on wild and foolish paths I know but it can't be ambition calling this time because there is nothing up there to win fame or glory in. I lay it to adventure, the dame thing that, in this country, has lead me up high hills, over rough paths and through dangerous places just because she lead the way. I often wonder if all young men my age have the same spirit of always wanting to do that which is foolish just because there's a thrill of adventure in it. Something must be taking place every twenty-four hours of the day or I get restless and now that we have been hanging around more or less I guess the old restless bug has got working again.

Yes, darling, I know just how you folks at home must feel to see so many men returning, very few of whom have earned the right to their second service stripe while the 26th who is nearly ready for her third is still left on foreign soil. No one feels it any deeper than we do and I'm afraid there will be lots of trouble over it in the days to come as well as other matters which I will not bring up here. The truth will all come out, whereas I do not believe in telling all I know, you and Dad will hear the real facts and some things may surprise you both. It's fine when the band plays and all the people turn out to watch you pass but that band does not play all the time and when it has stopped and the cover is removed there is a lot of unpleasant things to see. Things which make the man who has seen action under fire sore and mad clean through. Just to show you one of the smaller things which in one way counts for very little and in another counts for a lot I will tell you one thing that I noticed while on leave which got me a bit up in the air. While we were in Tours, we naturally met any number of officers on the street, mostly men who have never even seen the front or heard a gun go off. They have been doing S.O.S. work and yet out of all we passed we only received two real salutes. Some kept their pipes in their mouths, others would salute with a cigarette or cigar in their right hand and I even saw one salute with his left hand. We've seen real action and yet we are called down in fine shape if we don't get our salutes off in good shape. You may not be able to understand just what I mean but I cannot make it much plainer here. Well, it's a great old life anyhow.

Well, Dear, I guess I have written about enough for this time so will close with lots of love for the whole family and your own sweet self. Sergeant Houle sends his best to you all. He is back with the battery again.

About the auto, I do not care what kind I have just so long as it is big enough for my long legs and will stand a few long trips.

More love, darling.
Johnny

CHAPTER FIFTEEN

Spur Camp
Le Mans, France

"A new world has opened before me"

SECOND LIEUTENANT JOHN L. HOBSON II

"Buddy, there's a [new] man we've got to soldier under.
He wears three service stripes and a wound stripe and I'll
bet my last franc he knows this Army game."

OVERHEARD COMMENT MADE BY A SOLDIER IN FATHER'S NEW COMMAND

Still a student when the war ended, my father subsequently was graduated from Saumur Artillery School. However, the Army decided not to award any more commissions to the last graduates. With tremendous disappointment, the class was returned to their old units at their previous rank. Father returned to the battery as a Sergeant.

After getting some rest and relaxation back with the battery, just before the 26th Division was to ship out for Boston in late March and early April of 1919, the Army decided, after all, to award commissions to the last graduating class at Saumur Artillery School and then to immediately ship home and discharge as many of those newly graduated junior officers as was practical and still maintain operations in France.

Because so many senior officers were returning to the States and being discharged, the junior officers that remained in France were being given the opportunity of a military lifetime: large commands and exceptionally large responsibilities for their junior rank. My father thought this would be an excellent opportunity to gain some experience, enjoy the French country-side at the expense of his Uncle Sam in the civilized manner of a commissioned officer, and all this...without being shot at!

The day before the USS Mongolia sailed for Boston with the regiment aboard, my father made the last-minute decision to stay in France and continue his adventure. So it was that he did not sail home with the rest of the regiment and he missed the big parade in Boston. He quickly penned a letter of explanation to the family and entrusted it to Al Houle to deliver to the family when the ship docked in Boston.

First (Top) Sergeant Albert (Al) L. Houle is first mentioned in an October 1917 letter Father wrote from Coetquidan. Sergeant Houle drifts in and out of Father's adventure from the beginning to the end. He was from Haverhill, popular and obviously a trusted friend. Sergeant Houle served in the Quartermaster Corps, Mobile Veterinary Service with the 102nd Field Artillery, Battery A. It was reported that for a while he served away from the battery on General Edwards' staff. Newspaper reports said that Sergeant Houle refused a commission twice wanting to remain serving with the battery and his friends from Haverhill. Before the war, Al Houle was with the Haverhill police force serving as a patrolman. In one of Houle's letters sent home from France, which he heads "Somewhere in This World" instead of the traditional Somewhere in France, Al Houle described the boys of the Battery as looking fine, ready to fight...or eat!

Father continued his military experience in France with a command and administrative responsibilities, as he would say, basically "acting as Captain with a 'second's' pay." He first served in the Depot Service at Le Mans and then finally at an Embarkation Camp in Saint-Nazaire.

The Spur Camp at Le Mans, his first assignment, was located about two miles outside of the city of Le Mans. Le Mans, located more than 100 kilometers (62 miles) southwest of Paris in the Loire Valley, is an ancient city

Spur Camp

with Gallo-Roman ramparts and a beautiful Gothic and Roman cathedral that overlooks the city. The River Sarth runs through the center of the town.

In view of what he had been through and how much he missed his family, his decision to remain in France was terribly difficult for him. For weeks afterward he agonized over the effect it would have on his family, especially the effect on his sister, Alice, whose wedding he would now miss. The unfortunate method of how the news of his last minute decision to remain in France reached his family didn't help matters.

When the USS Mongolia landed in Boston and Father didn't walk down the gangplank with the rest of the battery, there was some outside confusion by the public as to exactly where he was and what he was doing.

Expecting their son to be aboard, on the day the USS Mongolia sailed into Boston Harbor, the Hobson family had arranged to journey out in a reception boat to greet the arriving Mongolia and escort her to the pier. After the reception boat docked, the family went to the pier to welcome home their son where The Mongolia had docked and was discharging the troops.

In the faces of the thousands of soldiers pouring off the ship and searching in the crowd, with increasing excitement they looked for their son. One can only imagine the family's emotions going from excitement to increasing anxiety when they couldn't find him. The family was eventually approached by Al Houle who handed them the letter that father had entrusted this soldier to give to his family upon his arrival in Boston. The letter of 26 March explained everything.

Based on misinformation received from one of the officers arriving at the pier in Boston the day before, the next day the newspaper erroneously reported that Father and Philip Kerrigan had both received their commissions at the last moment (true) and they had been "honored" by being selected to remain in France and were assigned to serve as attachés of the Peace Conference (not true). It was reported that, "Their duties will include carrying important messages and documents from Paris to the different capitals of Europe." (Nice work if he could get it, but it certainly wasn't true.) Father's letter that had been hand carried to the family made no reference to such a grand assignment. But, true to form, and in spite of what must have been tremendous disappointment for them that their son was not home, his family was in complete support of him, whatever his new assignment was to be.

463

Because the war is over, censorship of letters would have then been relaxed and, being an officer, Father gets to censor his own letters. The result being that in subsequent letters, a few more experiences are revealed that could not have been written about before.

Also, Philip Kerrigan now joins my father's adventure. Philip Kerrigan was a native of Chicago where he attended the Hyde Park School. His family originally moved to Haverhill for the purpose of joining up with the shoe manufacturing business. When war was declared, the Kerrigan boys, Philip and Eugene, thought they would return to Chicago and join the Army there and serve with their boyhood friends, but they joined up with the Yankee Division and Battery A of the 102nd Field Artillery in Haverhill instead. Eugene Kerrigan was also gassed while serving with the battery during the summer of 1918 and, upon his recovery, was transferred to the postal service.

Dear Dad and Mother

It is past mid-night and I guess just about every living soul in the peaceful town of Mayet is asleep but I have so blame much on my mind that until I get it off there is no use in my hitting the white bed which is waiting for me. I have been rushed to death all day with one thing or another but this letter must be written tonight so here goes.

As you must know by this time I am not returning to the States with the 26th and this fact may surprise you somewhat and I dare say cause you to feel a bit disappointed. Hence I am writing this note tonight in order to get it off by one of the men tomorrow who is returning. I am afraid it is going to be pretty hard for me to explain why I have taken this step so that you and Mother will understand it but I know that if everything is not made clear in this letter it will be after you have talked to Ben Pitman and Lanigan. If everything is not clear then I want you both to trust in my judgment which it is to my advantage and for my own benefit that I am remaining for further service in France. I now shall try to explain things as best I can with a pencil and on paper.

On March 20th luck took a very sudden turn in my favor and I along with all other graduates from officer's schools rose from our present rank to second lieutenants. At first none of the men wanted their commissions because they thought they could not return home with the divisions but this matter was quickly cleared up by the General who told us we all would be sent back to our regiments and returned to the States with them unless we desired to remain in France. After receiving my commission the idea of staying over here grew stronger and stronger so I talked the matter over with several men who are pretty well up in the military world and who knew more of the present conditions and the chances for the future than I did. Having gotten their views of the matter plus several other lieutenants' I went to my room in the hotel at Ecommoy and alone had a long talk with myself. You, Mother, and the family being the center of my thoughts. I looked at all sides of the question from every angle I could and finally decided to remain over here and carry on military work for a few months more so put in at once for a transfer to the S.O.S. (Service of Supplies) which came through this morning. Another man from the battery who was also commissioned at the same time I was also saw chances over here and is going with me. We leave the regiment tomorrow morning for Le Mans where we will be assigned to duty somewhere in France. Now I want to tell you some of the reasons why I am doing this and I hope both you and Mother will back me up in the step I have taken.

The very first picture that comes into my mind is Mother feeling that I do not appreciate the wonderful home I have waiting for me. Well, darling, God alone knows I do and it is for that home that I am remaining here. Yes, I may have done my part in the war already but there is more to be done yet and I want to help do it. I am young, the life over here holds a charm for me and I must be worth something to the government or I never would be wearing a Sam Browne Belt and a gold bar. There will be lots of cheering and yelling with bands playing and other mothers and fathers weeping with joy to see their sons home and both of you may feel a little touch of grief because your boy is not there. But all those cheers will pass away, the band will stop and your son will be learning more and slowly but surely pushing his way over the rough road to success while others waste their summer in good times. A new world has opened before me - I do not expect to be with the troops as before but am to take up the business end of the Army if you know what I mean. I shall meet a higher class of men and lead an easier life in the line of comforts than before and every day shall be learning. I have worked hard for the chance to go up and now I have it - let's push on. As I said before I left home this will be my college education and no man should finish at twenty-one. I remember Dad one night said in a joking way that I might like the Army so much I would stay in it. Well, I guess it is not quite that bad but since the shells have ceased whizzing and death and danger have been ruled out for a while I must confess it isn't half bad. It isn't all fun by any means but neither is the outside world, and for a young man it is better than ten years of college for a real look at life and experiences. I know several men today who told me only this past week that they were jealous of my chance and wished they were my age or single. I do not seem to be able to tell you just how I feel on paper but if you were only here with me I could do it no time. Perhaps some who return can do a better job to show you that I have done what is best and wise. All I want is to hear from you both saying that you are proud of me and are behind me to the very end. I am coming home when my work is done and a prouder man will never enter the city of Haverhill.

Just how long I shall be in Le Mans I do not know but will give you my address there and your letter ought to follow me.

American Embarkation Center

A.P.O. 762

The reason I did not cable you was because I only had fifty francs to my name and Ev will tell you how far that goes when you are an officer.

Speaking about Ev makes me think of one other thing I want to speak about - the wedding. I suppose there may be some doubt in your minds as to just what to do now Johnny is not returning. I know Sister will wonder what her older brother will think if she does not wait until he comes home so I am going to air my views if I may. Of course I should like to be there but having decided the way I have about staying here I do not want you to wait. It has been a long, hard wait already and I know both Ev and Sister are anxious to be married so please do not hold things up for me.

Well I am afraid I have not cleared everything up yet but it is late and I must get to bed.

Please let me hear from you right away telling me your real opinions of what I have done. If you disapprove say so and Johnny makes moves to give up his work and head for home. If you approve I shall keep up the good work until I feel that I have really finished it. You will hear from me again within a very few days.

All the love in the world to everyone.
Johnny

Dearest Sister

It is just three o'clock in the afternoon and our train does not pull out for Le Mans until eight tonight so I am going to drop you a few lines which I will mail when I arrive at Le Mans as the mail here is closed.

I suppose, darling, that you are pretty nearly heartbroken that your older brother is not returning home with the 26th. It was pretty hard to say good-bye to all the men I have fought with. This morning when it came time to leave, some of the older members of the battery were pretty sorry to see me leave but all of my close friends realized it was for the best and in many ways to my advantage to remain here and wished me the best luck in the world and a "bon voyage" home when my work was done. I know, dear, that for a few days while the big time in Boston is taking place that you will all miss me a great deal but, Sister, I feel sure that once those little griefs have passed that you will say you are glad. I have found my place and remained in France until I felt the job was done up to a brown finish. I gave a short note to Al Houle for Dad this morning which he said he would give to him just as soon as he landed. All I want now is to hear from you, dear, and Mother and Dad saying that you understand my move and approve. You, Sister, must write me just how you feel in the matter not sparing my feelings in the least. If everyone at home is to be all cut up and disappointed why I intend to give up my dream and hopes which I am now working for and return home just as quick as I can. Somehow, however, I have a feeling away down in my heart that you all are going to agree with me that I have done the wise thing but until I do hear from you I must confess I shall be a bit anxious so please write very soon.

As I told Mother and Dad in my note I do not want you and Ev to put off the wedding one day on my account. I know, dear, you will miss me that day more than all the rest put together but I want you to bear in mind that I am happy, thinking of you and we can make up for lost time when I do get back, whereas I would never make up for the chance I have now if I should let it go by. Be sure to send me your picture in your wedding dress and write me all the details of the wedding. Tell Ev for me that he does not want to forget that promise he made Lanigan if he would get him back to the division. Charlie did all in his power for Ev and yesterday told me it was impossible to work. When I told him Ev was on his way home he was very much pleased. Tell Ev also please to save out one bottle of Champagne for my return. You might also tell him if he desires a bottle of very choice French wine to name the brand and I will bring it home to him. Just at present cash is very low and I find it pretty hard to make both ends meet but pay is coming and if you will give me a few weeks' warning beforehand I intend to send you a real wedding present if I have to go dead broke for two months.

A picture is coming. I have got to have one taken for an identification card and will have a good one taken for the family at the same time.

Well, darling, some men are waiting for me so I must close.

Please give Ev my very best and have him kiss the bride a thousand times for me.

Give my love to all the family and keep a lot for yourself.
Johnny

Dearest Mother

Just a few hasty lines tonight while I am waiting for Kerrigan to come back just to let you know what has taken place within the past three days.

We left the battery at Mayet on March 27th and came down here to Le Mans. I had a little trouble about my baggage so we did not get off on the morning train as we had planned but waited until the nine o'clock train that night. Mr. Brown's son was going on the morning train and very kindly got us a room at the officer's club so when we blew in about ten that night we were all set. After a light, before-bed repast consisting of one egg and one cheese sandwich plus a cup or two of coffee, we made our way up to bed. Oh but it did seem good to be able to fall in between nice white sheets and not have a thousand men or more yelling all around. We pulled our lazy bodies out about eight, enjoyed a bully breakfast and then went up to report at the Headquarters of the American Embarkation Center. We were told there that our orders would be ready at eleven so we gave Le Mans the once over plus doing a little business in regard to pay. At eleven we got our orders to report to the Spur Camp which is about two miles out from Le Mans. There is a truck that runs back and forth every half hour to carry people in and out so after lunch we jumped that. The officer's quarters were too full for comfort so after reporting to the camp commander we hit back to the club for the night, coming back here early this morning. I'll bet not one of you not even Ev can guess what kind of a job we have. It makes me laugh myself when I think of it so I expect you all will do the same. This camp is made up of any number of companies who do all kinds of quartermaster work and I have full charge of one of them. Company Commander as it were and it is just the same as being a captain only you wear gold bars instead of silver. Your word is law. My work as far as I can dope it out is to make sure that the top sergeant gets his details out and then I have to attend to all the paperwork about which I know almost nothing. I have Company 49 and Kerrigan has 52. His is at one end of the camp and I am at the other and the camp is one of the biggest in France but the officer's mess and club is in the center so we ought to see each other often. The two lieutenants who command the company next to mine are bully good lads and have offered to help me all they could until I got on to the ropes. I am eating out with them at a sort of private officer's mess which is better than the big one. You can go into Le Mans any time you want to and from all I can gather we have landed a "boss job." Each officer has his own orderly from his company to shine his shoes, run errands and keep the fire going plus any other stuff you may want done. Not bad, hey what? When I first took command one of the old officers had them send for my top sergeant to whom all I had to do was tell him to send me a man to fix up my bed and in no time Johnny was all set. I guess I will have my troubles before I'm through but I shouldn't fret because as one man said a few weeks ago, "Army troubles and worries all come out in the wash so why fret?"

Most of the officers here are doughboys and red around a man's cap is a rare sight. Two Y.M. girls sitting at the big mess where I ate this noon and who had only been over here about a month fell in love with the red and asked me what it stood for and what division I was from. When I told them it stood for artillery and that I was from the 26th I found myself sitting on the world for fair. I was a real hero and had to laugh when one of them said, "Oh, lieutenant, please tell us some of your experiences at the front and how it feels to be under fire." I explained that it was not a very cheerful subject to talk about but they insisted on hearing about Seicheprey and Chateau-Thierry if no other battles so I was the goat and kept both of them plus a doughboy lieutenant who had only been over here a short while amused all through lunch. After lunch the two girls nailed me here in the reading room and wanted me to attend some large officer's dance in Le Mans with them tonight. I did not feel that I had better leave camp so soon so told them that I would love to go to one later on with them. Three service stripes and a wound stripe sure make a hit here. I swear I would like to have gone with them and would have if I had known things were to be so quiet tonight.

Well, darling, things are starting off good and after I hear from you and dad that you are not awfully disappointed in your son for the move he has made I shall feel OK.

My address is at the top of the letter so write "toot sweet" as they say over here.

If things can be arranged this summer I want Dad to give up business for awhile and take a trip over here and bring Art with him. I should like to ask you but fear it would be rather hard to handle a lady. However, things may break so that I can arrange for you also. I will have another permission due about July and that is about when I shall want Dad to visit France and see with his own eyes why his son has fallen in love with it. If the trip appeals to Dad and Art, please let me know and I will be on the lookout for a good time for them to come and will let them know when it is best for me. It certainly would be an education of Art, and Dad would open his eyes with wonder at some of the sights. As for me my heart would beat double time and about four years added to my life at the chance of seeing them on French soil and showing them if possible some of the places I fought. I know of two boys whose fathers came over so if they really want to come I guess there is a way. I am speaking of this trip several months ahead of time so that we all can arrange things in advance and not have to make our plans in a hurry. Ask them both please, Mother, what they think of the idea. If I can see my way clear so that you will not have to rough it at all but can have all the comforts and ease a lady should have I want you to come but I certainly want everything tip top before I ask you over.

Well, Phil has just come in so I will close as we are going up to my quarters to talk things over.

Please give my love to all the family and keep a heap for your dear little self.
Johnny

Le Mans, France
Depot Service Co No. 49 A.S.C.
A.P.O. 762
A.E.F
March 31, 1919

Dearest Mother

This is just a short but sweet note to let you all know what Johnny is up to. I have been more than busy of late and will be so for a few days more until I get things in hand after which I hope to have a little more time to myself.

Both Lieutenant Kerrigan and I have been assigned to Spur Camp just outside of Le Mans. This is a big quartermaster center and mark my word it is a big one. The camp is made up of a lot of companies of men, each company doing certain kinds of work such as loading, checking, packing, truck driving, etc. Each company has its own commander who is in complete charge of the paperwork and seeing that all details are gotten out on time, that the quarters are kept clean and that discipline is maintained. Everything rests with him - he can make and break non-coms and has full power to use whatever form of punishment he may see fit if necessary. For some reason they are using first and second lieutenants for company commanders and that is the job I hold now. I am really a Captain only wearing gold bars and downing a second's pay. It is all old stuff to me except the paperwork and after retreat tonight I heard one of the men say, "Buddy, there's a man we've got to soldier under. He wears three service stripes and a wound stripe and I'll bet my last franc he knows this Army game." Most of the men and officers here have been over a few months and three gold stripes look big to them. Slowly but surely I am getting the reins in my hands and by the end of the week ought to be sitting on the world as they say. I've got a bully top sergeant and a fine clerk so there is not a lot to worry about. There are two other companies alongside of mine who are commanded by two fine lads who are giving me a helping hand where I need it until I get underway. We all sleep in tents with wooden floors and wooden walls half way up. Cold I should say not.

We roast to death most of the time as the orderlies insist on keeping the stove red hot and you know how a tent holds heat. Instead of eating at the big mess which is about six or seven minute's walk away we have our own little mess and mark my word it is good. Breakfast is from seven up to lunchtime and you eat in your underclothes or as you see fit. We get up when we blame please according to how much work we have on hand for the day. I dragged out at nine this morning as there was no work for me until ten when I had issued orders I would inspect tents. I have a busy day tomorrow so told my orderly to wake me at 7:30. I have a barber in my outfit who does all our barber work. Just imagine, dearest, coming in just before lunch or before supper tired out and your brain going full tilt over this, that or the other thing and saying, "Bill, send the barber to my quarters." In he comes with all his outfit, salutes and asks if you sent for him. "Yes, I want a shave, a head rub, a haircut" or whatever I may desire. "Yes, Sir!" is the answer and all you have to do is fall into a chair and he fixes you up fine. You have nothing to do but your own work and others take care of your bed, shoes and little wants. There is a truck from camp every half hour in to Le Mans from 7 a.m. to 12 p.m. and officers can go and come as they please. The men must have passes in order to come in and are not allowed to give these except when a man has business in Le Mans or we see fit. There is a fine officer's club here at Le Mans where I am now, and a small one out at camp. Kerrigan and I came in to shop a little this evening and are now waiting for the grill to open so that we can have a bite to eat before returning. There are two other D men at camp and two men from the old battery who left us to do M.P. work. I'm the happiest man in the world, darling, and I hope they leave me right where I am for a while. All I want now is to hear from you and Dad that you both approve of what I have done and are not disappointed in your son for not returning home just yet.

Well, dear, I must close, eat and get back to camp.

Please give my love to all the family and keep a lot for yourself.
Johnny
P.S.
My address is at the top of letter.

Dearest Mother

This has certainly been a busy day for me but now that retreat is over and supper eaten I find that I can call my day's work done and can sit down alone in my tent and write a real, true letter home. There is no one around to bother me and the only sound I can hear is some of the men out in the company street having an after-supper ball game.

By the time this letter reaches you I suppose you will have received the two notes I sent home by some of the battery men as well as the letter I wrote you from the officer's club in Le Mans a few nights ago. Yes, by this time you ought to have heard about the whole story of my seemingly strange move and I guess there is more than one letter on its way overseas to me. Oh how I wonder what those letters are going to bring. Are they to say that you are heartbroken because I have remained or are they to bring the glad news that whereas you were a little disappointed not to see me with the old crowd you feel that I know best and you are glad I am taking advantage of the chances given to me. I really feel that both you and Dad are going to look at the matter the same as I do but until I get a letter from one of you I must confess I shall feel like a little kid who was told to come home from a party at five and because he was having such a good time stayed until seven and is wondering what his mother is going to say when he gets home. If I were the kid you could spank me and send me to bed without supper or some such thing as that but since I am too old for that sort of punishment there is only about one thing left and to me it would be worse than five lickings - a letter from you saying that you were really all cut up and disappointed because I failed to return from the party at five. Yes, darling, that would really hurt and hurt for a long time. Well it will not be many more days now until that letter comes and I will know how you feel and can stop wondering.

I have decided, dear, that now is the time to send home what few little things I have as souvenirs of the war so am putting them in a separate envelope which I shall mail with this letter. They do not amount to a great deal, Mother, but at the same time mean a great deal to me. They consist chiefly of a few papers and an identification tag. I have a few papers I should like to send but am afraid I may have to use them someday so am holding on to them. The little amount of the Seicheprey fight whereas you have no doubt seen one before is a proof that your boy was there if any one tries to tell you otherwise. Major General Edwards and I being "bunkies" (?) you will notice that he calls me Johnny only puts it John E. Hobson for looks' sake??? [The Citation misspelled his name - John E. Hobson instead of John L. Hobson.] I am also enclosing a few of the exams I had to take while at Saumur. These will be all Greek to you all I guess but just ask Ev about them and he will explain any of the questions so they will be very clear to you?? Oh, yes, if he doesn't I miss my guess because I have had more training in artillery than he has and I have forgotten a lot of it and would have to dazzle some little time before I would work some of the problems out now. If Ev cannot think of any other excuse tell him to say you need range tables and he has none. The identification tag has a long, funny and yet sad story to it which I will not go into here. The little thing has seen action however and really ought to be kept. I did have the first sergeant's stripes I wore and which have been all through the war with me including the hospital but they seem to have gone off on a little trip tonight so I cannot send them along with the rest of this stuff. I fear they are A.W.O.L. and may not come back. Well, darling, these few little things will show you all that your boy was really one of the many who have faced death that the world might be a little better place to live in. I know you and the family will be proud of them but please do not try to make me out a hero because I am far from one. If possible I should very much like to have you have the two papers on Seicheprey framed. One because it gives an account of the battle itself and the other because General Edwards has signed it himself. Some of you might like to wear the YD but please be sure to ask Ev just where it should be worn. The identification tag I fear is too cheap an affair for any of you to want to put on your wrist but do so if you want. The gold bar is the first one I ever wore on my shoulder and you, darling may be able to find some place to put it. I wanted to send you a small one such as we wear on our caps but was unable to buy one in Ecommoy or Mayet with a pin clasp. The one I got has two pins on it which you punch through the cloth and bend. I guess this is all I have to send you just now so will go on to the next subject - why I did not cable you I had been commissioned and was not returning home with the 26th.

This question I guess you have asked yourself a good many times and I have intended to speak of it before but have forgotten it every time. These commissions came through so blame quick that no one had time to write, cable or save money for the big event. The result was that everyone was nearly flat. I had just an even 300 francs I believe at the time and my letter of credit all gone. I had to buy a uniform which I can assure you was nothing like the one I had ordered for me when I graduated from school last November but a good deal better looking than the one I had on at the time which had seen its best days some weeks before. This of course made a fairly large hole in that 300. While in Ecommoy waiting our commissions to come from Chaumont we were billeted in an attic which was cold, dusty and full of rats. Kerrigan and I decided that that was no place for gentlemen to sleep so like so many of the others got a room in a tired, cheap hotel. It was better than the hard floor anyhow as we had a fine, soft bed. By that time I didn't have enough francs to buy the armhole of a vest so returned to the regiment with my commission, the trench coat I bought at school and about four cents in my pocket. I was assigned to Battery F for duty and when my transfer came through was at a loss as to how I was to pay my officer's mess bill which amounted to only five francs. I couldn't get my final statements as the quartermaster was closed and so I tried to figure out who owed me money or who might have some. At last I thought of one man who owed me twenty francs and as luck would have it he had it. Three cheers! I was rich again and paid my mess bill. I didn't have enough to cable however. That noon I met George Croston by chance and not having seen him for ages asked him out to lunch with me. We had a bully feed but when paid for left me afloat again as far as money went. I was leaving Mayet that night for Le Mans with

Lieutenant Kerrigan and he also was broke so the future about eight that evening as we were waiting for the train looked rather hard. Neither of us were worrying however as money or no money we intended to get along somehow. Well, Mother, just as that train was breezing down the track one hour late as usual in comes a man all out of breath waving 50 big francs in the air. "Gee, Jack, I thought you had left," he said, "and I wanted to pay you the money you loaned me last August before you left as you may need it." "May" was not the word he wanted to use then I fear. That fifty went like dust under the wheels of a fast car when both Phil [Kerrigan] and I had to live on it for 48 hours and before either of us knew it we were in that blissful condition known as broke again. Well we were all assigned then and did not need any money for a few days. Somehow the helpless feeling of not having anything but the good luck coin you sent me a year ago last Xmas in my pockets made me feel cheap so I decided I would try my luck on drawing my final statements here, also the 13 days officer's pay due me April first. My company payrolls, having been labored and worked on half of last night by the clerk and myself, were in ok shape and ready to be taken into Le Mans to the quartermaster so when I opened my blue, sleepy eyes this a.m. I saw millions of francs floating before me - in fancy. While dressing I turned to Gentile, my orderly - who, by the way, is a Greek, not a Jew - and said, "Gentile, I have got to go into Le Mans this morning. See if you can find me a side car." "Yes, Sir." He came back in about five minutes with the welcome news he had found one and the driver would be at my tent ready to go in half an hour. I got to Le Mans, turned my payrolls in and then headed for the officer's Q.M. Great, I would get my final statements right away but would have to wait two days for that 13 days' pay. Well that was all right, I could get nearly 200 francs at once which was enough for my cable. Once all that money was in my hand I went out so fast I forgot to take my discharge papers with me and had to go back later for them. I jumped into that side car so fast and so hard I nearly knocked the driver off the motorcycle. "Where next, Sir?" he asked starting the engine. "Paris, Tour, Bordeaux, anywhere I can get a cable off to the States," I answered. He drives me up to the cable office here and I dash into that place on all fours. A most beautiful girl sat up behind the desk so I head for her. She must have been in love or out late last night because my cablegram did not interest her in the least so I called for the boss who was a rather fat man full of pep and life with a big smile on his face. Surely he will take an interest, I thought, and he did but it would be impossible to get my cable out for at least a week as they were all tied up with official business. I thought mine was official enough so offered him a bonus of twenty francs to get it through for me right away. Alas he did not see how it would be done even if he did figure on papers, books and even the desk itself for five minutes. Hence, darling, you see it was really impossible to let you know any quicker than I have. Needless to say, I did not hit that "bath tub" [the side car of the motorcycle] so hard or eagerly when I went out.

If you are not bored to death reading this stuff I will tell you of an experience I had a few days ago which makes me laugh every time I think of it. About the middle of the afternoon an order comes in to the officers of Co.s 47, 48 and 49, my company, which had to be attended to at once and someone had to go into Le Mans. The other two officers were away from here at the time so I would handle the whole thing and save them a call-down perhaps for not being here. I chartered a side car and headed for the city telling the top sergeant of the 47th and 48th to tell their commanding officers when they returned that I would attend to the whole thing so not to worry about it. I got the business done and walked up to the Officer's Club where a car was to meet me. Being a little early and the car not there I went inside to buy some cigarettes and ran into a lieutenant from camp I knew with two YMCA girls. "Just the man we want to make the fourth one to our party." he said, introducing me to the girls. "Business or pleasure brings you into the city this afternoon lieutenant?" asks one. Up to then I had not a chance to open my mouth. I explained that it was business and that I expected my sidecar any minute to take me back to camp. The driver could surely wait they said an hour while I had tea with them but I had a non-com's meeting at 5:30 and some orders to get out before six so told them I really had to return to camp. Just then in walks the driver with the news he had a blow out. "There now, you surely will sip tea with us until that is fixed." "Delighted!" I said fishing in my empty pockets for money - this was before I became so rich from these final statements. During tea, one of the girls told me about this most wonderful dance coming off at some hotel "Demain Soir" I believe she said and asked me to attend after which the four of us would have a jolly (get that) little supper. That was too much for me and I dove into my pockets to see if some 1,000 franc note had not grown in the past half hour. I did all in my power to get out of it but excuses were in vain so I said I would be there hoping against hope I could beg, borrow or win a few francs between then and eight the next night. Next I had to promise I would tell her all about my experiences at the front and how I was wounded. I swear I am going to take those service stripes and wound stripe off if people keep on asking me how it feels to be under fire, etc. Most of them around here have only been over here three or four months as I believe I told you in one of my letters a few days ago. Well when my driver came in and said the tire was fixed I said good-bye to the other lieutenant and his girl but mine insisted on coming out to the car with me telling me all the way not to forget "Demain Soir." The other lieutenant paid for the tea thank goodness. "Demain Soir" finds me all set for the big affair when orders blow in for this, that, or the other thing so I had to call the party off. I saw the other lieutenant and explained things to him before he went in. Now they want a dinner party Sunday night. These YM girls come from New York and surely are pretty.

Court Martial No. 1

This must be my last story for tonight about life in the S.O.S. because it is getting late and you must be getting tired. A couple of mornings ago the top sergeant came into my tent with the morning orders and a long face. "What's the matter sergeant?" I asked when I saw his face. "Are you sick or have we got a real day's work ahead of us?" "Neither, Sir." He answered only "we have an order here from the captain to prefer charges against -Blank- for being out of camp without a pass and I do not like to see any of our boys get into trouble." This made me smile but I managed to hide it behind a towel. After looking over the rest of the orders I had -Blank- sent to my tent and got the whole story from him while the first sergeant listened. The whole thing was so blame small that I wanted to let him go in the worst way but I had warned the men against this sort of thing only a few nights before and told them that any break of this rule would mean that I would have to punish the offender and I did not like to do that. After thinking about the matter over a few minutes while -Blank- and the sergeant looked at me as if I ruled the whole earth I said, "Blank- you are confined to the company street for a period of 30 days. You are relieved from the easy job you have now as telephone operator and are to be put on hard labor for the same time, 30 days." I then turned to the top sergeant when -Blank- had left and told him to get out a company order telling of -Blank's- confinement and read it at retreat and put it up on the board outside the office. That had to be done by regulations as well as for some personal reasons of my own. "Shall I make out these charges also Lieutenant and on what Articles of War do you want him tried?" "To Hell with the charges and Articles of War" I said, "Get that order out toot sweet and I'll tell you when I want the charges made out and on what Article." He had that order down here for me to sign in no time and up on the board quicker. I played this Army game just long enough to know that courts martial are bad things and certainly do not approve of them except in rare cases. It mars a man's record and lots of times I think their sentences are more than they deserve. Certainly no man I could help out of one was going to get it if it was in my power to prevent it. I knew I would have to appear on the scene and I certainly have no desire wasting my time over a trial I felt sure would fall flatter than a ton of bricks. I had had several talks with the Captain and knew he was a good scout so I just made up my mind to fight before it was too late. That morning when he came around to look the place over as he does daily, I took the matter up with him telling him what I had done and giving my reasons for wanting to check the thing where it was. Oh joy, oh bliss, after talk-ing my head off and pulling every half dead brain cell I ever had to life for half an hour he smiled and said something about he guessed I could hand hard punishment out all right and he would let the matter drop. Mother, I was never so thankful to anybody before in my life as I was to him because I do hate to see a man's neck deep in trouble over nothing but what one lieutenant can handle without messing up his records. The top was so pleased when I told him all was well along the coast that he came down that noon with four cigars for me

- but mark my word -Blank- is paying for being out of camp without a pass and I am seeing to it that my order of hard labor is carried out - his service record is clear and a lot of red tape saved for another day as well as a charge sheet when both may be needed. The whole blame gang step double-time now when I appear.

Well, darling, tomorrow is checking day which means work here so I must close and get to bed.

Please give my love to all and keep a heap for yourself.

Johnny
P.S.
I hope you can read this letter as the writing is anything but good.

Le Mans, France
Depot Service Co. 49
Spur Camp
A.P.O. 762
April 12, 1919
PAY DAY

Dearest Mother

This has indeed been a busy day for your boy and now that the last franc has been paid and the hands on my watch read eight I must confess I am tired. Not bodily, but mentally. You see this was payday and as one of the other lieutenants was away on a fourteen day leave I had to pay his company as well as my own. Another lieutenant and I left here with saddle pockets thrown over our shoulders at 7:30 a.m. to go into Le Mans for the money. What I knew about drawing money for payrolls was pretty small I can assure you but where there's a will there's a way you know so before I went to the Major to get it I had found out just what had to be done on my part as near as I could and figured the rest out for myself. I blows in there bigger than life with this other lieutenant and throws my payrolls under the gold leafer's eyes as if I was some old experienced captain who had done nothing all his life but draw pay for his men. The other lieutenant who was only drawing for one company gave his rolls to a wise looking sergeant who stood nearby. "You are drawing pay for two companies?" asked the old Major. "Yes, Sir. My own and a lieutenant's who is away on leave and whose company has been turned over to me while he is away." "You are pretty young, Lieutenant, I should say, to have two companies on your youthful hands when one is a handful for an older man," he said laughing.

This struck the American girl who was playing Pay Day or Home Sweet Home on the typewriter in the corner funny and she looked at me in a most pleasing way and tried to hold back a laugh which finally after a few seconds' struggle broke out. "What have you got to say about the matter Miss Some One?" asked the Major as he dove down into a huge chest and pulled out a roll of 100 franc notes which nearly set me on the stove. I never knew there was so much money in one place in France before in my life.

"I have to laugh the way you kid these poor lieutenants along, Major, who are doing captain's work on $1,700 a year," she said. "Tough on them," replied the Major planting his lean form into a chair and throwing all the money in France around over his desk. It could not have been quite all that because I remember the sergeant dove into that chest and came out with a few odd francs for the lieutenant with me. "This will make it, sir," he said as he handed the francs to my friend who was already lost trying to figure up how much he had. I swear I saw that man count one pile of tens four times and I began to wonder where in the name of heaven I was going to get off when I began counting money for two outfits. Just then the Major said, "Let's go lieutenant." And off we went or rather off he went and I followed about 700 or 800 francs in the rear. I was gaining about five francs on every pile and was figuring that before long I would be right up there with him when he bellows out, "$3,000 dollars, 17,400 francs! (The rate being 5.80 on the dollar just now)" That got me, Mother, I just gave up. He looked up at me once but my lips were moving so I guess he thought I was following but in reality I was trying to figure out where on God's green earth all that money had sprung from. I was almost tempted to ask him if I could look into that chest but realizing that the shock would kill me, I did not.

"There you are, lieutenant," he finally said, "Now will you please sign these two papers?" I looked them all over and finally just to please him signed them, doing so in a most carefree manner as if all I had done in my youthful life was to sign papers and carry off cart loads of cash. By the time I had over $3,000 dollars put away in my bag the other lieutenant was ready so we saluted and walked out. Once outside that done, almost at the same minute we reached into our trenchcoat pockets, pulled out our 45's and put a slug into the chamber - then put them on safety - returned them to our pockets and headed for camp. If dad could only see his son now, I thought as I walked through the crowds, he would wonder where he had made all his money. We got back to camp OK.

While at lunch I sent my orderly out after the top sergeant of my second company whom I told to have his men lined up for pay in ten minutes. My own company was all at work so I would not pay them until after supper. Well, darling, you should have been here to see Johnny pay off for the first time. If my faithful old pipe had not been well set between my teeth I never would have got away with it. After I got the first twenty paid I felt at home but up to then I was a bit shaky and I will confess it. Over $3,000 dollars was more than I ever really handled in cold cash before in all my life and I knew if I made a mistake it would have to come out of my pocket. After I got through the top sergeant said the company had never been paid off so fast before since they had been here which made me feel pretty good. But the blow came when I walked into mess that night and the other lieutenant looked up from a piece of pie and asked, "How did you come out on your paying?" "Fine and dandy up to date" I said, "but I have my own company to pay off after supper and may run short."

"Well, I ran short just an even 60 francs" he said "and of course had to dig it out of my own pocket." "Ye Gods", I thought and he counted his twice in town this morning and I fell by the wayside at 3,000 and drew out at least once again that much. I dug into my pocketbook, found the large sum of ten francs and wondered what I was to do if after supper upon paying my company I ran short over ten.

Well, darling, I pushed the pipe into my mouth again at 6:30 p.m. and fell to handing out money like a cook would hand out bread - only my brain was going full blast. Finally the top calls out Pvt. Blank - 66 francs - I paid him and waited for the next man. "That cleans them all up, Lieutenant," he said. "Cleans them all up?" I asked looking at the neat piles of cash still in front of me. "Yes, Sir", he said "and I guess you came out ahead of the game instead of behind as the lieutenant in 48 did." "Hush, Sergeant, not a word until we fill those envelopes for the men in the woods." Well, we did this and all was well - I was square with the board and my own ten francs safe. Wait until the other lieutenant comes back from the show tonight and I certainly will give him a grand laugh.

Thus ends payday - also this letter.

Please give my love to all and keep a heap for yourself.
Johnny

Undated

Arthur L. Hobson sent the following cable:

We received your letter of March 31st to Mother telling us what you were doing and concluded you had landed in a feather bed. We are of course disappointed not to see you but am glad to have you stay and get the experience and a little fun too. The boys are back and we have seen a few of them - Houle was at the house last night and told us quite a lot.

Hope you got my cablegram congratulating you on your commission. We are behind you.

With lots of love from all.
Dad

Le Mans, France
Depot Service Co 49 A.S.C.
Spur Camp
A.P.O. 762
April 14, 1919

Dear Dad

Your cablegram was handed to me this noon at lunch by my orderly and the joy and relief it brought with it can only be appreciated by one who is thousands of miles from home and has done something which might on the face of it seem foolish. No, it has not worried me for a single minute because I felt I was doing what was the best thing but I was a bit anxious to know how you and the family were going to take it. How was the news broken to you? Did you hear it before the division docked or was one of the letters I sent home by the men handed to you as you stood looking vainly over the happy throng for me? I know the first letter from home will answer these questions and can hardly wait for them to arrive. When your cable was first handed to me the expression on my face changed from a smile to sorrow and when the two other lieutenants saw this they stopped eating and just looked at me without saying a word. I did not really expect to hear from you so soon but was expecting a wire from a very close friend of mine who is in trouble. I was afraid worse had come to worse and he had passed out of this beautiful world of ours forever. When I broke the seal however and read the first word my expression changed "toot sweet" and I jumped out of that chair like a wild man letting out a yell. The orderly picked up the chair and looked at me as if he thought I had gone mad. Then I broke the news to the other two lieutenants who shook my hand as if it was a cable announcing my engagement. We had been talking about it only yesterday afternoon and were wondering how you all were going to take it. They both agreed that I must have the finest father and mother possible and that it was clear you both were heart and soul behind your son. I could not have felt happier if I had been engaged to the finest girl in the world. In fact, Dad, I fear I would be unhappy if any girl had any strings on me while this roaming and adventure seeking germ is in my blood. All I want is the great outdoors and bang, bang, bang. At times I have a longing for a home to walk into at night where I know there will be a big, hot supper waiting for me where all I have to do is push a button and on goes the light, where I can walk on rugs and sit in a big, soft easy chair - but somehow these do not last long and that feeling for the little crude homes I make for myself drives the other away. Take tonight for instance. I had to work until late and hence when I got around to eat, my supper was a little cold but oh how good it tasted. Rip off your blouse and belt, sling your hat anywheres it may or may not land on a cot but no matter - rip open the old OD shirt, let out the waist belt, roll up your sleeves and eat, eat, eat. Then after supper a smoke, talk with the other lieutenants for a little while. The subject consisting of anything from business to our innermost thoughts. A little more work and then down here to the tent to write you. When I first came in I looked at the sides all bare except for a few papers hung on a nail such as orders, etc. A wooden floor with no polish and a bit rough in places. A little stove red hot and a bunk in the corner neatly covered with OD blankets. A candle on the table with matches beside it and a box of Fatima cigarettes. A small box of candy from the mess sergeant on the one and only chair and my orderly curled up by the stove on a bag shining my shoes. Then, Dad, I began to think of the men at home and what they must be having and I wondered who were the happiest - those who lived in style and rode around in big cars and took beautiful girls to dinners, dances, etc. who said they would be "charmed" (with the accent in the "r') or "bored" (same accent) the same as Johnny did once, or myself in a canvas tent. Which of us are the happiest and gaining the most. I am a thousand times more so. They do not even know what real life is any more than I did two years ago. Yes, they have an awfully good time at the dances and it is fun to carry on a summer's romance with some nice, interesting dark-eyed or light-eyed girl and I expect to do it all over again and have more fun out of it than before but I never shall forget the time I spent in my Uncle's Army. I hope every young man from now on has to do at least six months in the Army where he can get out and rough it and really live. If your lumber camps, Dad, are anything like the Army for life, just put my name in for an upper bunk right away. A growing man needs raw meat and black coffee to really put the fight into him - a little hot soup will keep his heart warm and a good, rich hash made out of the week's pick ups will keep his brain half alive trying to figure out what isn't in it. If he desires to keep his wits real sharp just reverse the problem and figure out what is in it. Don't forget now, Dad, an upper bunk, food and work.

Now I want to ask you a question which I am in dead earnest about even if I have fooled a bit for the past three or four lines. Would it be possible and would you like to take a trip over here to see me? I will be due for another leave about the first of July or a little before and there is nothing I would enjoy more than having you with me. My idea would be to have you bring Art along also so that he might get a chance to see France before all the battlefields are all fixed up. I should like to have Mother and the rest come also but am afraid that under the present conditions they would not enjoy it a great deal, but I think I can show you and Art a pretty good time. It certainly would be an education for Art and I really believe I could find enough new things for you to see and hear to keep you interested and busy. Personally, I am very anxious, indeed, for you to come over and see what there is left of the great war and get a glimpse, no matter how small, of the life, both work and play, which has carried off the heart and soul of your son for the past year and a half. There really isn't much to tell when you come down to rock bottom facts but oh what a lot to see. To read or hear someone tell about the battlefields or the leftovers here means little or nothing to a man unless he has seen it - then he will be able to appreciate what the U.S. has been up against and what great things she has done. One lieutenant right here would not believe there were shell holes big enough for a horse and team to drive into until he visited Chateau-Thierry and went through the Belleau Wood a few days ago. When he got back you would have thought he was a two-year-old home from his first theater where he had seen someone fly. He has been after me ever since to tell more and more of my experiences up on the lines and he can now understand what I mean when I say we faced Hell at times. These are the sights I want you to see before it is too late. The ruined villages - the bare waste of country with only a dead tree here and there - the dugouts - a few shells lying around a few trenches and the ground torn up for miles with shell holes. Then, Dad, and only then, will you fully realize what this war was for those who were there when it all took place. They already have started to clean up at Chateau-Thierry and I imagine at other places also but there will be a lot to see the first of July. These sights may not sound very cheerful to look at but you become so interested that part if not all of the dark side is forgotten. Don't worry, I will not show you any poor bodies of either side torn to threads - that you can read about and realize, but Dad, I do want you to see the rest. If you have any trouble getting transportation across, Mr. Fuller or some of his friends ought to be able to help you. Tell them you have a son over here near death or anything but get here. Please think this idea over in some of your spare minutes and see if you cannot arrange it. Someone has just got to handle that business for you, that's all there is to it and I want you to forget everything but your own pleasure. I know blame well you want to come and Lord knows I want you to so somehow it just must be worked out. If I could only hear you singing "I'm in the Army now. I'm not behind that desk" I would be the happiest man alive. I will make you forget the office and business, Dad, for a few weeks if you will only "pack up those troubles in your old suit case and visit your son in France". Please, Dad, think it over and let me know your thoughts. Just as quick as I hear from you that you can come I will start making plans over here.

Well I guess I have written enough for tonight so will close.

Please give my love to all the family and keep a lot for yourself.
Johnny

Dearest Mother

It is Easter Sunday morning and one of those nice spring days which makes a man feel that life is really worth living after all. Not hot or not cold but just a nice cool, clear day. But in spite of the day I could not help letting my memory wander back over the past twelve months and see as if in a moving picture the Easter of a year ago. It was pouring rain and the battery was slowly moving along over muddy roads on its way to the Toul Sector. I left them about four o'clock in the afternoon to go forward up to the lines with the Major, one officer from each battery and about twenty men to take over the telephones and make ready for the battery when she would pull in a few days later. We went up on big trucks and the experiences and thoughts which passed through my mind will never be forgotten. At first the towns we passed through looked fine and the country was beautiful - then as darkness set in and the steady bang, bang of the truck brought on a sleepy feeling we all fell off into catnaps only waking up when the truck was brought to a sudden stop for some reason. The little towns were dimly lighted and every now and again as we passed some small house I could catch a glimpse of the fine rain still falling. Having been in the saddle all day up to four o'clock I began to feel the need of real sleep so pulled myself down between two big bedding rolls and lit my good-night cigarette. I could not help thinking of Kid, my horse, and wondering how she was making out on this hellish night. We both had had a long, hard day the day before when I had been in the saddle from seven a.m. up to five p.m. and from eight until twelve that night and I knew that after Easter Sunday's long hard hike in the rain she must be stiff, tired and hungry just as I was. I had left orders that just as quick as the battery put up for the night Kid was to be well rubbed down, fed and covered with every blanket that could be had. Kid, being sort or a pet of every man in the detail, I knew she would be cared for so I fell off into the wonderful land of dreams. How long I slept I do not know but all of a sudden the truck stopped with an awful jerk and I woke up. All was darker than ink and a few good-natured swear words greeted my ears from men who had been roughly thrown against the side of the truck. Then I heard the voice of the driver bellow out, "Get those ---- caissons out of the way!" Next I heard the Major yell out a command. "Shoot the ---- horse if he will not get up and drag him off the ---- road but for God's sake don't block the road in this hell hole!" I heard the driver sing out. "Make it fast!" called out the captain. "We have got to get through!" I stuck my head out under the canvas and tried to see what all the fuss was about but all I could make out was a few men hurrying here and there. Then a pistol shot - a groan and we moved on. About ten minutes later we stopped in some farmyard where a bunch of new trucks awaited us. We changed, only this time each captain took a truck and after packing his detail in it, started off all in different directions. The Major was with us. Where oh where were we going? I tried to hear what the officers were saying to the driver but the truck made too much racket so I gave it up. About eleven that night we stopped and got orders from the Major to unload all the baggage as quick as possible. He had not any more than got the words out of his mouth when they started to come. I saw the Major, the Captain and the driver all disappear over the bank at the side of the road head first and decided to follow. That idea was knocked out of my head before I went two feet however and found myself all covered with mud and dirt laying beside the road. I swear, Mother, I thought I was dead but I heard the motor still running in the truck so decided I had merely been roughly knocked down by one of those shells which now were falling like rain. Not feeling it was wise to stay where I was, I decided to crawl on my belly over to the truck and get under it. I was making fine progress on my long, lean belly towards that truck when I heard the Major say "Is everybody here?" "I think that fourth shell got Sergeant Hobson" I heard someone say. "He fell like a ton of lead just as I came over the bank." The Major muttered some cuss words about those ---- Germans and the next thing I knew he was standing over me laughing his head off. "Where did you learn to swim on dry land?" he asked as I made another healthy over handstroke on my belly for that truck. I was all set by then, cool as could be so stood up and explained I was heading for under the truck - whereupon he laughed again and said I had better join the rest of them in the little dugout. I thanked him but said I feared it would be a bit crowded in the dugout and as I was tired I wanted to stretch out and sleep and could do this under the truck fine. He could not see my idea at all for a few minutes but finally did, so returned to the dugout while I shut the motor off and crawled underneath the old boat. I was asleep in no time and never entered my head that the road was hard. Someone woke me up about two and said as they had started to throw over gas the Major wanted me in the dugout. I felt a bit rested by then so made a dive for the dugout. The rest of the night was just one grand concentration of gas and big shells. That is the way I spent last Easter and this year I am up one more step in the military world and enjoying a bright, sunny day. I suppose you all have been to church and let us hope put up a humble little prayer for your son who has not been there for ages. However, darling, I have not forgotten my God who has brought me safely through the fire and Hell of this war and every night I pray to Him to help, guard and protect my youthful steps as well as those of others until such time as He may call us to His home above.

I have just had a visit from a YMCA man who wants one of the boys in my company to work in his canteen which is near here. He certainly was a jolly old bird but rather simple looking. I gave him the man, however, and that pleased him nearly to death. I'm going down and hit him up for a cake this p.m. for our mess. I even asked him to eat with us this noon which he could not do, he said, as he was going to Le Mans for lunch so I swear I do not see why he should not come across with a cake, do you?

Well, darling, lunch is ready so I must close as I have to inspect the mess. I got apple pie for all the men this noon and I want to see how it goes.

Please give my love to all the family and keep just heaps for yourself.
Johnny

Dearest Sister

Having written several letters home of late there really is not a great deal of news to tell you. However, before rolling into bed for the night I think I will drop you just a few hasty lines so that the postman will not pass 129 Arlington St. by without leaving at least one overseas letter. Now that Ev is home and about all the rest from around Haverhill I guess my letters are about the only ones which arrive at our house from across the deep blue sea. You may, of course, have some friends still over here whom I do not know but I guess most of them are safe and sound in the U.S. by now. I will be there also someday, dear, if I can ever get this love for the open air and a roaming life out of my blood. I am just having the time of my young life and no one over here needs to talk home to me until the last gun is fired now that I have heard Dad and the rest of you are behind me. I want to land just about in the middle of next September so that I can enjoy one or two weeks of horseback riding, walking and autoing at Rye. Then for a few weeks of pleasure around Haverhill with one or two short trips and I guess Johnny will be ready to put the saddle on again and work. There is no use in planning ahead these days however because I have given my heart and soul to the flag and where it leads I must follow until I feel that my duty is fully done and have given the government all I can and it in return has given me the same.

I do not doubt in the least, darling, but what at times you wonder if you really have an older brother at all and if so just what he looks like. The picture in Dad's den must have become old by now and you regard it as one of these old pictures of some boy you knew away back in the days you were at Bradford and whom you may have had a summer's flirtation with but have not seen for years and do not expect to see for years more. Darling, I look just the same as when that picture was taken and am more worthy to be called your brother than at that time. Everything about me is the same except my heart and soul which have been made richer and larger by my experiences of the past year and a half. Nevertheless, dear, the second week in May is the week set for me to visit Le Mans and have another one taken. My pay voucher has already gone in and I have been promised my check on the first. Just as quick as I get that I order a new uniform which will take about a week to make and then for my picture. I will get them off to you just as quick as they are done so you can take the old one down and put up the new one up which will reassure you in minutes of doubt that you really have an older brother even if you have not kissed him or told him he smoked too much for over a year and a half. And, speaking of smoking too much, who am I going to kid about powdering their pug nose too much when I get back? Ev will very likely be the one to inspect the powder situation for you when I get back and I will not have anyone to give the once over before starting out for the dances. Oh, yes, I will at that - dear little "K" will have to take your place and be the object at which my mean remarks fly. Well, if she has as good a stock of comebacks as her older sister had some nights I can remember I guess it will be to my advantage to keep still. I have enjoyed many a quiet laugh to myself over here when I have stopped and thought of how I would come into your room just as you were heaping the sixth or seventh layer of powder on your nose or face. The expression on your face when I would appear in the door and your opening barrage of words have given me many minutes of pleasure as I have looked back on it all. Those days are over, darling, but their memory can never be forgotten. Times may have changed us both but as I told you in a letter a long time ago to me you will always be the same little girl who used to run and cry on my shoulder when we were little kids. You, darling, had a lot to do with the framing and building up of my love for home and the spirit which eighteen months ago sent me to France to fight that that home and millions of others might not suffer what some have over here. If all girls would only take the personal interest in their brothers that you have in yours the brothers would be better men and the sisters better women - but I am sorry to say some brothers and sisters never seem to learn to really know each other until after the real early stages of youth are over and the best, happiest days of such love are half gone. We both have lots of good times coming together in the future but we are older and they will be a lot different than before. We may have many a heart-to-heart talk in the days to come but they will be different than those we used to have. I have thanked God more than once, darling, that he gave me a sister not merely in name but in actions and who was not afraid to let the whole world know that I was her brother.

I suppose just about this time the 26th is getting ready for its big parade in Boston. Poor little old Bean Town ought to be slightly overcrowded that day I should judge. I know you and the rest of the family will take it in and shall expect some long interesting letters giving me all the details of the day. We have some kind of a big review here Sunday and I suppose I have to command this dashing company of mine. Some general is to give us the once-over and hence I am studying up on infantry drill regulations. Can't you picture me commanding a whole company at a general review? Cheer up. I fooled one general last January and may be able to make this one think I know a little something. Just so long as I do not give "squads left" when I mean right as I saw one Captain in a review do and ball the whole thing up all will be fine and dandy.

Well, darling, I must close and sleep a while. Here's hoping I hear from you before many days as there is lots of little things I am anxious to hear about home. I wrote Ev a short time ago and hope he takes a few minutes to answer. Why don't you write me a joint letter some evening when he is up?

Give my love to everyone and keep a lot for one of the dearest little sisters in the world - yourself.
Johnny

Six months had passed since the shooting in Europe had stopped and life in Boston had returned to a normal pace. Spring had arrived in New England. However, Bostonians were enthusiastically preparing for the 26th Division's homecoming parade. Newspaper headlines of the week showed that Boston had moved on. Captivating the fascination of the citizenry of Boston at this time were the exploits of two flyers, Frederick Raynham of Britain in a Martinsyde "flying machine," and an Australian, Harry Hawker, in a Sopwith biplane, who had taken up the challenge of the $50,000 prize offered by the London Daily Mail for a successful trans-Atlantic flight. With the world watching and waiting, the two pilots, their navigators and their "flying machines" were waiting out the weather at St. Johns, Newfoundland, and might take off at any moment to attempt an Atlantic crossing. It would be eight more years, the spring of 1927, before Charles Lindberg would successfully make his historical solo Atlantic crossing.

On the day of the parade, the citizens of Boston took a break from the trauma of a labor strike that threatened to bring the city and businesses to a halt to celebrate the 26th Division's homecoming. On strike were local telephone operators, who felt their jobs were threatened by the introduction of a new invention - the dial telephone.

On 20 April, a party was held for the officers of the 26th Division at the City Club in Boston. On 22 April, the 20,000 soldiers of the Division that had landed in Boston were reviewed at Camp Devens in Devens, Massachusetts.

Camp Devens had opened in August 1917. The military facility sat on five thousand acres northwest of Boston and was carved out of the farmland and forest along the Nashua River and it served as a temporary cantonment area for training troops during the First World War. In 1932, the facility became permanent and the name was changed from Camp Devens to Fort Devens.

The Governors of each of the six New England States and 250,000 people attended the division's review. In the ceremony, Major General Harry C. Hale and Major General Clarence R. Edwards decorated the red battle flag of the 102nd Field Artillery Regiment with streamers and battle ribbons of the six campaigns it had fought: Chemin des Dames, Toul, Aisne-Marne, St. Mihiel, Troyon and Meuse-Argonne. The battle flag of the 102nd Field Artillery Regiment was the first flag decorated of the 250 battle flags of the Yankee Division.

The following day, the 26th Division was put aboard trains at Camp Devens and transported 35 miles east to downtown Boston where the soldiers were billeted at armories and halls around the city to await the celebratory parade.

Beginning at noon on Friday, 25 April, the men of the 26th Division were honored at a parade through the streets of Boston where they were viewed and cheered by over one million spectators, including the Hobson family.

The homecoming parade in Boston on 25 April was just as my father imagined it would be. It was just as he had portrayed it in the letters expressing his hopes and dreams sent to his family during the darkest days of the fighting in France. However, now that the dream was reality, he wasn't there to triumphantly ride a horse down Tremont Street as he had promised his family he would someday.

Through these massed ranks of spectators, miles and miles of steel-helmeted men swinging forward beneath a sea of bristling bayonets marched along a five and a half mile parade route starting on Beacon Street. They marched down Beacon Street, up Beacon Hill and past the State House. The parade turned down Park Street and marched along Tremont, Boylston, Charles Street, and then up and down Commonwealth Avenue. They crossed over at Arlington Street and went back up Boylston Street to Massachusetts Avenue and down Columbus Avenue back to Park Square.

The parade stretched out in a great wavy ribbon and moved along under a score of flags suspended by wires over the center of the narrow streets of Boston. Nineteen bands joined the wild tumult striking up The Battle Hymn of the Republic, When Johnny Comes Marching Home Again, Pack Up Your Troubles, Keep the Home Fires Burning, and Till We Meet Again.

Confetti showered down on the parade from the windows of the buildings along the parade route. Pigeons and balloons were released upward from the street.

There was a biting, early spring wind that day and the many flags and banners that hung over the streets, some large enough to partially hide the buildings, snapped sharply in the wind. Snow showers had fallen on the city that morning. Nobody seemed to mind the brisk weather.

Forty-two viewing stands were erected along the parade route using hundreds of thousands of board feet of lumber; 17 miles of rope restrained the cheering crowd along the parade route. Immediately following the parade, there was a mammoth sale by the City of Boston of the rope and lumber used for the parade.

General Hale and General Edwards led the triumphal march. The horse that Edwards had ridden in France and brought home to the States with him was still in quarantine, so for this parade, Edwards mounted a magnificent,

16.2 hands high (a "hand" is four inches), dapple-gray horse re-named Y-D. This steed was a Huntsman and descendant of a local famous horse of the time, Alexander Higginson's Stud at South Lincoln.

Edwards started the parade, rode at its head for a while and then observed the rest of the parade from a Park Square viewing stand on Canton Street. As he passed by, Edwards was heartily cheered by mothers and fathers who looked upon him as a savior, the man who had lead their sons into battle and then delivered them home again.

Following their respective units, the Division's officers followed, each mounted on a dark horse with a glistening coat that had been brushed to the appearance of shiny velvet, bearing polished leather saddles and tack.

There were 24 units of the Yankee Division represented: infantry, artillery and support units. It was a virtual sea of men, 20,000 strong, marching in perfect formation through the streets of Boston.

The measured cadence, the tramp, tramp, tramp of marching men, was delivered by the thick-soled, hob-nailed trench boots on the historic cobbled streets of Boston. Wave after wave of soldiers marched past the shining gold dome of the Massachusetts State House with the warming afternoon spring sun glinting on shouldered rifles, fixed bayonets and trench helmets. Had he been there, Father would have loved it!

The wounded men who could manage it rode in automobiles. The spectators cheered the loudest for them.

Young's Hotel in downtown Boston displayed a historic Union flag that had been hand-stitched by the proprietor's sister who had welcomed New England soldiers in New Boston, New Hampshire, back from the American Civil War.

It all must have been a joyous, spectacular sight.

But a hush fell among the crowd as the clattering horses of General Edwards' staff passed by a very large, white, silken flag with a single gold star beneath the number 1,760, a memorial to the men of the division who had been killed in the fighting. As they passed, the mounted officers in their saddles stiffened their backs to attention, turned their heads toward the waving flag and snapped a sharp salute.

And, as the soldiers of Battery A of the 102nd Field Artillery Regiment silently marched past the memorial flag, the thoughts of every man in the battery was of their comrades who had been killed in action or had died of disease while fighting in France: Alexander Booth, Frank J. Coughlin, Karl F. Pitcher, Herbert G. Raymond, Melvin T. Rice, and Herbert G. Whiting. These men had given the last full measure so that liberty would not perish from the earth.

On 29 April, the soldiers of the 26th Division and 102nd Field Artillery Regiment who had landed in Boston at this time were discharged from the Army at Camp Devens.

26th Division Homecoming Parade - Looking down Tremont Street,
Boston, with the Massachusetts State House in the background, 25 April, 1919.
Boston Public Library Archives - Boston Globe photograph

26th Division Parade on Commonwealth Avenue, Boston, 25 April 1919.
Boston Public Library Archives - Boston Globe photograph

Dearest Mother

There is no news to tell you of interest as nothing very exciting has taken place for some little time outside of my regular work. I have been kept fairly busy and as a result have not been into Le Mans in the evening for almost ten days. Yesterday I went in in a sidecar for about an hour on business but aside from that have been sticking pretty close to camp. Next week I shall have two days of touring again in a Dodge or sidecar having this month's payroll signed up by men working out in the woods. These trips are good fun if you get a good car but very tiresome in a poor one.

Our review which I wrote Sister about a few nights ago comes off tomorrow morning. We got our final orders on it last evening in regard to the formations. Both Phil and I are lost with these infantry formations and hence tonight one of the doughboy lieutenants is going to explain it all out to us. We both told the commanding officer he ought to change it to the artillery formation which we both know like an open book. Well, I guess we both will get by some way.

Phil received some mail from home a couple of days ago in answer to letters he had written from here so I am expecting some tonight or tomorrow. His folks say the 26th is home safe and sound and that paper clippings were on the way. We both are looking forward to seeing these needless to say. We both are very happy in our new work and can now say that we have things fairly well in hand. We often speak of the old crowd and now are wondering just what kind of reception they received upon their return to home sweet home. I imagine most of them are out of the service by now but will bet it will not be many weeks before they wish they were back in again. The Army, Mother, is a funny thing - very much like school days in many ways - some men do not like it while in it but once out you will find a large percent wishing they were back in uniform again. I have seen several who have come to me on bended knees and asked me to approve their application for return to the States and when it comes back from headquarters with their passports home really hate to leave. Just like school - you want that slip to get out but when you get it you hate to leave. I know that is the way I am going to feel when my discharge is handed to me. If my chances in the business world were not what they are I swear, darling, I think I would sign up with the regular Army. Dad was right when he said give Plattsburgh a try - you do not even know what the Army is like and it may be more fun than you think.

By the time this letter reaches you Dad ought to have received my letter asking him to come over here about the first of July and bring Art with him. What do you think of my idea, Mother? It strikes me it would be a bully experience for both of them.

What are the big plans laid out for the wedding? I am very anxious indeed to hear about them so please give me all the little details. I'll bet both Sister and Ev are the happiest people in Haverhill to be near each other again. I can picture Sister when the news arrived that he would be home at zero hour. I'll bet she couldn't eat, sleep or keep still a minute. The trip from Boston to Haverhill must have seemed hours long to Ev and I know blame well he only hit one step on the way to the front door. Love must be Hell when you are so near and yet so far from the one you love and the train does not leave for two hours.

Well, darling, I must close as it is time to leave for officer's meeting.

My love to all and heaps for yourself.
Johnny

Le Mans, France
Depot Service Co 49 A.S.C.
Spur Camp
A.P.O. 762
April 27, 1919

Dear Dad

Another week has passed and Sunday has come around again. It seems only yesterday that I wrote out a bunch of Sunday passes and yet I was at it again this noon. Time certainly is flying by on wings of gold and before we know it summer will be gone and another fall and winter looking us in the face. Before I fully realize it I will have been gone from home for two whole years and yet somehow it seems as if I had been gone four at least now. So much has happened, such big changes have taken place and I have seen and learned so much that it does not seem possible it would all happen in so short a time. Many new and interesting changes must have taken place at home also during my absence and upon the day of my return I guess we all are going to notice marked changes in each other. You and I, Dad, will be closer and nearer each other than before and will be able to appreciate the good points of each other's makeup as only time and experience can make us. It will be a happy day for us all, Dad, and is coming just as quick as the work is cleaned up over here.

My orderly has just returned from Le Mans with the paper and I notice that Italy is kind of getting overheated. I should hate to see a small sideshow break out down there now that the big one is all over but if it does I will be the real Johnny on the spot and not have to come over here again. Who knows, I might have a chance to use some of the stuff I picked up at Saumur after all but I guess the chances are pretty small. Another game of dice with Life and Death over a small disagreement would not please me but should the old battle flag with the stars and stripes on it lead the way to the dice game I will gladly follow. That flag has become a part of my life and means more to me right now than it ever did before. Every time I see it floating to the breeze over post headquarters it is as if America had been moved over here and when I get back and see it floating on the flag pole at the beach it will bring back wonderful memories. Let us hope it does not have to lead men to death and suffering again.

We had our review this morning and would you believe it I got away with it in fine style. Just before I reached the receiving stand marching like a general at the head of my company I glanced over my shoulder and saw that my company line was leaking a little in the middle - one sharp sentence and I had them straight however and when I gave "Eyes Right!" and came up to a salute myself as we passed everything was tip-top. There were four Red Cross girls in the stand and one of them must have seen that break in the line just before I passed because she smiled as if amused and made some remark to the general. I wanted to smile back but did not have the nerve as the old general was looking right at me. After the thing was all over they took a picture of all the officers. I will try to get one if they come out for sale. I wish you and Mother had been there to see the review as it was very pretty even if the band was poor. I believe we are to have another one in a week or so which ought to be better than today's as both the officers and the men will have had more drilling. Some of the men have had very little and many of the officers have forgotten a lot since they have not used it for so long. A little brushing up with the drill book brings it all back again however to those of us who did at one time know a little about squads East and West.

I was over in Phil's [Kerrigan] tent after the review and he and another lieutenant are fixing up or rather thinking of fixing up a nice two weeks trip to England and want me to join them. We all are going to want a week or ten days before putting in for it so that we can see how things are breaking the middle of next month. If all looks good our request is going in - if not we wait a while. Don't worry, Dad, I have not forgot you and Art and only last night had my big map of France out figuring out about what trip we wanted to take if you can get over. All ought to be ok if Italy will only lay dead as I think she will.

I was right in my prime this afternoon when I dug up a book of Robert Services' poems - Rhymes of a Red Cross Man. You have it at the house I am sure because I remember reading it before leaving and have referred to one or two of these poems in letters before. Sister gave you three of his books one Xmas and his works have found a very soft spot in my heart. I have tried to buy these books over here but with no luck. Every time I meet a man who has one of them as I have from time to time I always borrow it and spend most of my spare time reading and re-reading different poems which I like best. I have Rhymes of a Red Cross Man here on my desk now so am going to give you the names of a few I just love and can fully appreciate:

The Fool - Page 13
Young Fellow, My Lad - Page 73
On the Wire - Page 80
Over the Parapet - Page 108
Pilgrims - Page 124
Faith - Page 173
My Foe - Page 181

There are others which are mighty good but these seven stand out as best in my opinion. The Lone Trail in one of his other books is a peach and fits me to the dot in a way. Read some of these, Dad, and I think you will agree with me that they are fine.

The rate of exchange as perhaps you know is 5.80 now and so this payday all will be pretty rich men. I expect my check Thursday which will amount to about $140 minus insurance and 30 days' rations. If I could go from $45 a month to $140 a month on a proportion basis in the business world I would not be so very bad would I? I am fully self-supporting now just so long as I stay in the Army but fear I will need your aid a bit when I get out and put my shoulder up against a new wheel. Cheer up, if I stick at it the way I have in this game I may someday be self-supporting in business also.

Well, Dad, we are going into the movies this evening for a change as all of us have stayed pretty close to camp for some little time and feel a change would do us good - hence I must close and pull on my boots and fix up a bit because one never can tell what one may run into in Le Mans and "Y" girls or Red Cross nurses might be in the party so it would never do to look too slack.

Please give my love to all the family and keep a lot for yourself.
Johnny

Le Mans, France
Depot Service Co 49 A.S.C.
Spur Camp
A.P.O. 762
May 4, 1919

Dearest Mother

There was another review today and after it was all over and I was laying out on my cot taking life easy, who should come in but my orderly with three letters for me. Darling, I nearly went wild with joy because this is the first mail I have received from home since I left the battery.

There was one letter from you and one from Sister both written April 22nd and one from Elouise which Sister had forwarded. You cannot imagine how eagerly I tore them open to get at the precious contents inside. There were lots of things of interest in all of them and when I read what Sis had to say about George as a society man I had to laugh out loud. That struck me funny for fair.

Your letter made me feel like a low-down cuss in places for not returning with the battery. You did not speak your innermost feelings right out but I could read between the lines as only a son can when he reads his mother's letter. I could picture you all standing there on the dock early in the morning straining your eyes for the first sight of The Mongolia which you all thought was bringing your boy back to you. When she appeared I know just how that little heart of yours must have beat and I could almost see the tears of joy standing out in those soft brown eyes of yours. Then when the boys started to land I know how vainly you must have looked for the face of the one and only one in that crowd who could stop that heart pounding with excitement by his kisses. And, dear, to hear that he was not among the returning heroes must have sent a pang of pretty deep grief into that little heart and soul which have prayed for his safety and speedy return. These thoughts haunt me and I am not one bit ashamed to confess brought two big salty tears into my eyes. Darling, those must have been painful minutes for you all and I was the cause of them. I know a big reception was waiting for everyone and knew you had fixed up something a little extra for your boy and perhaps I should have returned and not caused you the pain of disappointment. But, dearest, as you said in your letter and have said before, I have my own life to live and work out and you never will stand in the way - no, dear, you never would, you would suffer yourself before you would see any one of your children fail to get success and happiness. I may have caused you some disappointment just now - I know I have in fact because a mother who did not feel a keen disappointment when her son failed to return when he might would not be a real mother - but, darling, someday I shall repay that debt and in the years to come you will say, "He may have caused me months of worry and hours of disappointment but he's a real man." You are proud of me now just as you say in your letter and what we may have missed by not returning for the big reception will be made up for a thousand times over by our own quiet little party when I do return. What's in a reception - what is a reception anyhow? Darling, the big outlay of bands, streets packed with millions of people as the troops pass by cheering, yelling, crying all at once means little or nothing to me. There are only a few in that crowd I know or give a darn about and the rest are show as far as I am concerned who do not interest me at all. My reception will be my idea of a real one. When my work is done and I return home and lose myself in the arms and kisses of those who really care for me - I will be able to enjoy and appreciate the love which is waiting for me and give out that which I have without a band playing or people yelling. Just walk in as Dad would after a business trip - hang my hat in the closet and give and receive the blessings of a wonderful home. I agree with the man who was asked by his future bride upon his return to tell her all about the war and his brave deeds - he answered, "There is nothing to tell. I did my duty and no man should sing his own praise. Let the past be forgotten. What I want is love, love, love with no big showing." We will have our own little time together, darling, you, the family, and I someday and you just wait and see if it does not beat the big time the rest may have had in a thousand ways.

This barracks bag story is a long one and a funny one. I doubt if I ever laughed so much as I did over the news that my bag was home. I will most certainly put charges in against it for being Absent

Without Leave when I get home. What right had it to return before its master, that's what I want to know? It's the same old bag that left Boxford with me and at which you all enjoyed a good laugh one evening. Heave her in a closet under lock and key until I get there to put in my charges. The story as I said is a long one so I will only outline it to you and hope you can imagine the rest.

After I received my commission I was sent out for duty with Battery F, 102nd Regiment. They were some little distance from Mayet and in a regular mud hole. When the orders came in one noon for me to report to Le Mans I decided that before I left I must pull a sort of good-bye party so decided to leave that P.M. for Mayet, pull the party and leave with Phil on an early train the next morning. (How I got the money for this party is another story which you will hear some day.) The ration wagon had left in the morning so I could not send my bag in to Mayet on that and it looked as if I was to have to call the party off and wait until the next day before I left. There was, however, a Frenchman who lived next to the officer's mess who owned one of the two-wheeled French wagons and to him through an interpreter I told my story. He finally agreed to bring the bag in for me if I would pay him five francs and be at the station at ten o'clock. I agreed and said he would get his money when the bag was at the depot - a wise move on my part. I was there at ten, he may have been but I'll be hanged if I saw either him or his wagon. The morning train was packed so Phil and I decided to stay over until the night train and see if we could not locate that bag. I phoned out to the battery and did everything I could think of to spot it but all in vain. The bags of the regiment were all piled up in a freight shed and I never looked them over. Finally I got mad and said I was leaving bag or no bag and asked one of the sergeants to keep an eye out for it and if he saw it to push it off when they came through Le Mans the next day. Some how the blame thing must have skipped everyone's notice and got by. There is nothing in it I need or cared much about except the pictures of the family and the letters which I had saved. These are all safe however and whereas I would like the pictures I am glad the letters are in a safe place because I do think a lot of some of them. If those O.D. blankets are still in it I wish you would have them steamed first to make sure no cooties are in them and then hide them until I get home. I have been trying to figure out how I was going to hook a few and if some inspecting officer has not already lifted them I guess the problem is solved. Now for the worst blow of all. The sofa pillow you spoke of as being so frenchy and a few other little things do not belong to me at all. One of the men in my section by the name of Webster hurt his leg last December and was sent to the base hospital. He did not have time or he wasn't able to take care of that stuff so I decided he would appreciate it if I as his sergeant looked out for it for him. I turned all his government stuff in per orders but his personal belongings - diary, sofa pillow, etc. - I put in my own bag for safekeeping. Land only knows where he is now but I believe he was sent home before the division so ought to be in Haverhill now. I have forgotten his first name but know he would appreciate it if that stuff was returned to him. Sergeant P.P. Hugs may still have a list of the sections at that time and can tell you his first name and where he lives. Webster is a good, honest boy and could very likely tell you just what belonged to him if you care to look him up. If not, wait until I get back and I will attend to it. I just remembered, I still have my roll call and have looked up his full name which is Herbert M. Webster. When I get my money conditions a bit settled I will buy you some of these French fancy pieces. I hope Dad has not tried drinking the contents of those bottles thinking it might be French wine as it is some stuff I used on a couple of mustard gas burns which kept breaking out and bothering me every now and then. Throw the stuff away for heaven's sake because it is old but save the beer bottle as I had one awful time capturing that. I do not remember just what was in that bag of interest, nothing I guess, but do know that had I known it was to reach home safe it would have been full of junk for all of you.

This Lieutenant Brown whom I sent that letter home by was in my class at Saumur and is an awfully fine lad. He stood one of the highest in the class and certainly knows the artillery game. If you ever happen to meet him as you very likely will please give him my best and tell him I still have his address and will use it "toot sweet".

Now about these pictures. They're coming, darling, and by the end of the month ought to arrive at the house. My new uniform will be done the tenth and I have my picture taken the eleventh or twelfth.

You shall have at least four of them, dear, in the family and one will be sent to each of the grandparents besides. I expect to go to Paris for three or four days of pleasure about the middle of the month if my 1,035 francs are not all gone and will have some more taken there if these in LeMans are not fairly good. I realize the newspapers might want one but what in the name of heaven do the magazines want my picture for? I'm no General Pershing or Mr. Wilson. Keep the pictures dark, dear, when you get them as far as these papers etc. are concerned - if they yell for one make sure they are not going to have big headlines about me but just some small article and if you can gracefully get out of giving it to them at all by all means do so.

The other night I had a telephone call from Headquarters asking me if I wanted to go on a trip. I said it was not my habit to turn those things down and then I was told what was up. It seems there are two leave trains going from here each week taking men to leave areas. One officer takes charge of the entire train and men on the way to and from the area. He stays there the seven days and just enjoys himself. In other words all he has to do is get them there and bring them back. I expect to leave next Sunday or the Sunday after on one of these trips. It is duty and hence does not count as a leave for the officer and all his expenses are paid.

Well, dear, mess is ready so I must close. Give my love to all and keep a heap for your own little true blue heart.
Johnny

Dear Dad

Upon my return to camp this evening after a long day's auto trip with payrolls, etc. I found two letters waiting for me from you. One was dated April 11th and the other April 16th. There is no need to tell you how welcome they were and with what eager fingers they were torn open. There also was a letter from the Societe Generale in Paris sending me a postal order amounting to 1,180 francs in compliance with instructions from Brown Brothers & Co - Boston. The part of the letter where it said, "By order of" was not filled in but there is no doubt in my mind who sent me the money.

Dad, I do not know how to thank you for this money since words cannot do it enough. I was just taken off my feet when I opened the letter and found out what it was because I did not expect any money from home or had the thought ever entered my head to write for any as I had figured out that it was just up to me to scrape and save until I had enough to buy what few little things I need. This first pay as a second lieutenant gave me enough money to buy a new suit, which will be done next week, and a foot locker. Up to date I have been unable to find one but have the money ready when one does turn up. The rest of my pay was to go to my mess bill, etc. When these expenses were met I would have just a little left over to save as you advised me to do. I am usually too tired or have too much work to do to go into Le Mans in the evenings now except Saturday nights when we all go into the theater or movies. My expenses for a little while will be fairly heavy until I get what stuff I really need as an officer and which I figured would take me two months to get on my pay. I am not getting any extra stuff at all as I do not figure I will be in the service long enough to need it. The money you sent me is going to help out a whole lot and I most certainly appreciate it from the bottom of my heart. You said in your letter you did not know just what my expenses as a lieutenant would be so I will tell you. It all depends, Dad, on where you are stationed. Here we draw rations from the company's kitchen and have it taken out of our pay vouchers. This is much cheaper and easier the way we are situated than buying our food from outside. Every officer puts in a few francs for extras, such as eggs, canned fruit, canned peas, etc. which we buy from time to time. This amounts up to about 100 francs a month. In other places your mess bill may be a great deal more all depending upon what sort of a mess you have to eat at. The officers here who do not eat with their companies or who are not in command companies pay 5 francs a day for their mess and do not eat as well as we do unless the food has come up since I ate at the main mess which was some little time ago when I first came here and was not assigned to any company. Then comes the bill from pressing your clothes. As you of course know it is up to an officer to have a clean and neat appearance at all times when on duty. The enlisted man is not expected to have his clothes pressed and spotless but an officer is as far as possible. Around camp they are not as fussy about this as in some places but when you go off on other business or pleasure you are expected to look tip-top. These bills are not very large but large enough to count a lot when you come to figure. Then it is up to you to pay your orderly a little something each month. This is left entirely up to the officers here as to how much they will give their orderlies. If you have a lot of work from him and keep him on the go most of the time you should pay fairly well. Our orderlies here do very, very little and are excused from all other work is the custom. I only have two pairs of shoes and one pair of semi-dress boots to be shined which is nothing side of some officers who have once again that number plus leather leggings. He has then really only one pair of shoes to shine a day except when I wear the semi-dress which is only once or twice a week. I have very few errands for him and on the whole he has a pretty easy time of it. I pay him about 20 to 25 francs a month. Then these parties which just at present I am not very strong for but have to go on a few of them for politeness sake. These are just what you would make them. It is really pretty cheap for an officer to live here but in other places it costs like everything. The government gives you almost nothing so you can figure my expenses to be just about the same as a man in business supporting himself.

The advice you gave me in your letter dated April 16th is most certainly well worth heeding and will not hurt me a bit. I know just the spirit it was given and a letter just like that every now and then will not do me any harm at all. I realize now as never before how young I am and will be first to confess that lots of things which come in the course of the day's work puzzle me whereas the older men handle the same thing with ease. But, I've got to learn to meet these questions and solve them sooner or later and there is no time like the present. My eyes and ears have not been shut on the past eighteen months and now I am having a chance to work out in what I have learned from the other men's mistakes in running a Company or Battery. Just as you advised in your letter it might be well to go slow and I have. "Make sure you are right and then go ahead" is my motto and I have been making doubly sure since I got my commission. Right now I am expecting a telephone call from the Major about a very, very small matter I called him up about a short time ago and he was not in. It does not really amount to a row of pins in a way and yet might mean a whole lot. I feel certain I know what to do but there is a little doubt going on in my mind as to just what was meant by a certain order upon which my decision rests and whereas all the lieutenants here feel half sure I am right I am going to make sure before going ahead. Do not worry, Dad, about my losing interest in my work or laying down. A man can lose his interest - no one can stop him from that - but he cannot lay down around here for one second without about half the camp on his neck. That is one of the big lessons of the Army in my opinion - you have got to stick, got to keep going or be put in a place where you will have to. If I had ever thought my interest was going to die out or I would have to force myself to do the day's work I never would have remained over here. Captain Morrison may have had his faults but by God he was a worker and he made every man under him work. I learnt in a double quick time from him to work first and play afterwards.

There has been very little going on around camp of late except our regular work. I have been spending all my time here except when called off on business as I was today. In fact I do not expect to leave until next week when Doris the girl I met after the review a week ago last Sunday and I have a little farewell party. She leaves for the States a week from Saturday and has fixed up a good-bye party.

Everything is going tip-top, Dad, and now that I have really heard from home I feel that everything is OK all around.

It is getting late so I must close and get to bed. Please let me hear from you every chance you get to write even if it's just a few lines.

Give my love to all the family and keep a lot for yourself.
Johnny

Le Mans, France
Depot Service Co. 49 A.S.C.
Spur Camp
A.P.O. 762
May 9, 1919

Dearest "K"

I was laying on my cot a few minutes before lunch this noon when my orderly came in and handed me a letter. I looked at it, squinted my eyes and said to myself I wonder what girl this is from? Whoever she may be she most certainly writes a good hand. Then I opened the letter and found it was from you. Darling, I was more than pleased. Now what I want to know is what have you been doing to get so expert with that little right hand of yours? You write better than I do and I studied or was supposed to have studied writing at Bryant & Stratton. I can easily see that all of my brothers and sisters are beating me out along some lines. I guess even little Buster will be telling his older brother what's what along some lines when I get back.

There really is not a great deal of news to tell you of real live interest but there may be one or two little things which will keep this letter from being too dry reading and force you to throw it away half read.

Last Wednesday another lieutenant and I left camp about eight in the morning in a Dodge touring car for a day's trip out into the woods to have our payrolls signed by the men we had out there. To be sure, our Dodge was nothing like the beautiful Marmon I understand from Art the family are to buy, but nevertheless it could roll right along. Just as we were making our first stop about noon it began to rain and hail great guns. The roads around these camps are very poor anyhow being all torn up by the heavy trucks and when it rains they are all but impassable. Well, we banged along until we reached the camp getting there OK but I do not see why we did not break all four springs and a few wheels. After our business was done the lieutenant there very kindly asked us to stay for lunch which we did. It certainly was a fine meal too. There are lots of colored men there who cut the wood and mark my word "K" they know how to cook. We had an apple pie fit for any king and a batch of French fried potatoes which would have done your heart good just to look at. Then there was meat, biscuits and jam and, of course, a cup of the old Army jet black coffee which I stopped drinking ages ago. After lunch we started off again, the sun out nice and bright. The country is in full bloom over here now and some of the pretty sights we saw made me think I was back home. There is one thing however you rarely see in the States and that is a real true castle. There are lots of them over here and at this time of year the vast grounds around them are just wonderful. They would make a fine place to have a big house party, "K". Most all of them have a big ballroom right in them and even a church. If we only had one Sister could have her wedding and reception and dance all under the same roof with ease. Someday, dear, I hope you have a chance to see some of these places. I have seen very, very little of the States but I doubt if you can find anything more beautiful anywhere than these big estates. We of course could not stop and really look them over as we had a big distance to cover but I have visited them at other times in other parts of France and know how pretty they are. We had a fine day outside of that shower and returned to camp about six o'clock tired, dusty and dirty but very much pleased with our day. We got a lot of work done and on the way got a show much of interest.

I am glad to hear that you expect to enter Bradford next fall. Are you going to live over there as Sister did or go over every day?

Yes, dear, I imagine the young people on the hill your age are just having the time of their lives with dances, etc. Please remember me to them all and I shall expect an invitation to one of your dances when I get back. You and I will go together in the Marmon filling the back seat up with two other couples. Ask Art or Dad which ever is boss of the car if you and I can take it out some evening next fall. We want to get it all dated up ahead of time you know, "K", as there must be a big demand for it. I will drive so tell Art he will not have to give up his evening or if I am not experienced enough at the wheel by then you can do the driving.

I have just got a new cot which arrived today with springs in it. All the officers over here on the hill asked to be furnished one and for some reason our request was granted and they arrived this afternoon. I am very anxious to try mine out so I guess I had better close and fall into it.

Be careful, "K", not to break too many hearts with those big brown eyes of yours. Make them behave if possible which I very much doubt.

Johnny

Dearest Mother

As perhaps you know May 11th has been set aside from all the other days of this year as Mother's Day. Every American soldier in the A.E.F. is supposed to take a few minutes on this day and write a few lines to his mother or, if she is gone to the world where pain is not known, to some other boy's mother. These letters are all to be turned into Headquarters tomorrow morning and pushed to the U.S. with all possible speed. I opened up an attack on my company last Monday evening by talking to them right from the shoulder on the matter. Tuesday evening right after mess I called all my non-coms together and talked to them about the duty they owed to the woman who had brought them into this world who had cared and suffered for them while they were young boys and whose heart had been broken when they were called to serve overseas. Lots of us remembered her for a while after we landed on foreign soil, I said, but somehow as the days rolled by into months and we all became a real active part of the great machine of war many of us kind of forgot her. We did not intend to but it was easier to go out at night than to write when there was very little to say and the first thing we knew many days and perhaps weeks had gone by and we had not written the woman who was most anxious to hear from us. While the fighting was taking place, I told them, no one in this world can appreciate the struggle which must have taken place in the hearts and souls of every mother who had a son over here and those who knew their boys were up in the lines subject to instant death at any minute must have suffered more than the boy she had sent with a proud but heavy heart to answer his country's call. Think it over men - you can have a million friends both male and female but only one mother. Those of you who have lost their mother know even better than those of us who have not what a friend she is and those of us who have allowed the

Army to harden our hearts and souls to such an extent that a deeper love for her has not been created are not fit to be called men. I do not hold myself up as an example for any man to follow but I am proud to make the statement during the months I was in the lines I wrote home to her every week and sometimes twice a week. When I was wounded at Chateau-Thierry and sent to the base I passed into a dead faint while in one dressing station and in spite of all the Hell, blood and death I had seen and which was naturally in my mind's eye the first person I saw in a vision as I started to come to was my mother, and men I am not ashamed to tell you I called for her not to myself but out loud. That's what my mother means to me and what I know yours means to you. Now men go out and see to it that every man in your squad writes home to her this week as he never has before. Tell them what I have told you and it will make those who might have forgotten stop and think. I will check all these letters off on the company roster and the men who do not write will hear from me.

Well, darling, every man wrote and two who could not write came to my tent and asked me to write their letters for them. They told me what to say and I wrote it down for them. Now having gotten all the men to write I guess it is up to their company commander to get busy and write his Mother's Letter.

There is to be another review tomorrow after which all the men will be given a chance to attend services in the big YMCA hut which will be dedicated to the mothers. A big altar has been built and every man who has a picture of his mother can place it on the altar during the services. I only have a snapshot of you, dear, but it will be among the pictures of the mothers who gave up their boys that this world might be a safer place to live. I certainly will feel proud when I see your picture among that lot of faces of mothers whose sons now are serving overseas.

Things have been quiet around camp as far as real excitement go but I have been so busy that outside excitement has little or no place to fit into my life just now. Today has been a peach. Rushed to the limit from right after breakfast until supper. Maybe I will not sleep tonight. Tomorrow I am officer of the day which means another busy day all day. My paperwork is nearly in shape and by the end of next week we will be ready to pick up and pull out. This will be a big load off of my mind needless to say.

Darling, do not worry about me asking for an inspection of you or your little army of helpers. You are the commander there at home and I fear any inspection I might make would be a failure. If my Army was half as well in order and picked up as yours I would never have to make a tour of inspection.

The bellybands, dear, you spoke about and which I forgot to tell you about in my last letter surely have been the cause of many a family laugh as far as I can figure it all out. All but the ones you found in my A.W.O.L. bag were used for cleaners and covers. They make excellent covers and were equally as good for cleaning purposes. Do not feel offended I did not use them before for the right thing but I swear I did not need them and hated to see them not being used for something.

They have just started to issue a new kind of meat or rather the same meat cut differently. It is called "boneless meat" and is just what the name implies, the bones have all been taken out and the meat comes packed in boxes ready to roast, make stews out of or put in hamburg, etc. The boxes are marked on the outside roast, hamburg or whatever the cut may be and the cooks just have to open up the box and they have just the cut they want. It is bully meat and very tender.

Well, darling, I am tired so am going to close and go to bed.

I shall be thinking of you, dear, more than usual tomorrow and wish you might be here to see your boy lead a company past the reviewing stand in a review.

Please give my love to all the family and an extra amount goes to you on Mother's Day if I have more to send than ever before.

Johnny

Dearest Mother

By rights I ought to hit the little old cot as it is fairly late and I have had a busy day but I guess I have one more duty to perform before we can really call it a day so here goes.

There is almost no news to tell you all but just the same I know you will be looking for a letter no matter how dry reading it may be and I intend to see that you are not disappointed.

Your two letters written from New York reached me a few days ago and I do not remember any news that has pleased me more than that contained in these letters that Ev was due to dock within a few hours. Gee, but I am glad to hear it and Sister must have been wild from the time she received his cable right on up to the time she saw him. I guess even then her excitement did not let up a great deal. Ev too must have experienced some rather odd heart flutters as that transport drew nearer and nearer to the dock. I am certainly glad for them both that they are together again at last after a year and a half separation. Ev has certainly been true to her and many a night has longed to see her. Sis has been the same way I guess and now all I pray is that they waste no time in pulling off the big day. I guess by the time this reaches you a date will be set and plans under way. Do tell me about them, dear, as best you can on paper and what little detail you may leave out I will fill in in my imagination.

I had a little hard luck this week on my new uniform. It was to be ready for me last Wednesday night but as is very apt to be the case with these French tailors it was late and I could not get it until Saturday evening. That was the day I was to pose for my picture but of course could not without the new uniform. It is impossible to get into Le Mans now except after supper with the exception of Saturday p.m. as there is work piled up sky high every other day. I am having another lieutenant assigned to my company to help me out this week and so may be able to shove enough work over on him to get up before Saturday. Every company is getting another officer. They have just made a bunch of new ones and enough are being sent out here so that every company can have two officers. They are all green the Major said and for a while the older officers would have to check up on their work and help them a bit until they got the ropes where they would handle them. If they are any greener than I was when I first hit here may the good lord help them. The present company commanders will still hold their command and these new lieutenants are to work under them as the commander sees fit. Thank goodness I will not lose my command of my company because I love them and have everything going fine and should hate to have some new man come in and change everything around right under my eyes. These new officers we have been advised to put on drill, carry on inspections, etc., while we give our time to the paperwork and generally oversee that all goes along as it should. This will be a big help as we all have had just about twice as much as we could do and do it right. Aside from my company work I have the big kitchen out of which four companies are fed to look after and under the present working conditions I have my hands full to keep it clean and in order. I was over two hours straightening out the ration returns tonight which somehow got all balled up.

I am sorry to hear that you do not think Dad will attempt the trip over here. I know he does not like the water but had hoped he would muster up all his courage and try it. If, however, he does not feel that he had better for business reasons or otherwise I would suggest that you and Art come. I do not believe you would be able to stand the trip I had laid out in my mind but that is only a small thing to change. We will only make what plans are absolutely necessary and leave the rest to be made when you arrive. These will all depend upon your strength and desires. Art can take side trips either alone or with officers we will find heading for places he may like to see where you do not feel like going while you and I play around the big cities where I am sure you will have a good room and good food. Don't worry, dear, I have seen a lot of France and will be perfectly happy to go just where you want to or stay in one place and enjoy having you with me in my second country. It will be your trip and I will see to it that your slightest whims are gratified as far as

I can. Tell Dad Art will look out for you on the way over and after you meet me you will be turned over to my care until you leave for home when I will give you back to Art. Just let me know a little in advance when you are coming so I can arrange where to meet you and get a leave.

Well, darling, I am getting sleepy so guess I had better get to bed.

Give my love to all and keep a heap for yourself.
Johnny

Le Mans, France
Depot Service Co. 49
Spur Camp
A.O.P. 762
May 28, 1919

Dearest Mother

It seems as if life had never been so full of happiness and held so many charms for me as it has since I received my gold bar and took up my duties as a second lieutenant. The days just seem to fly by and every one brings new chances and new ideas with it. I am lost in my work and now that I have mastered the big things of my daily work find that the smaller ones are cleaning up fast. Never have I met a better lot of men than I am now working with and if you and the family were only near enough so that I could see you every night or weekend my happiness would be complete. Well, darling, your son is just gaining in every way and whereas both you and Dad may miss him please always bear in mind that he is taking advantage of a wonderful chance and that it will not be very long before he will come sailing back.

The picture has been taken, dear, but I fear they are not going to turn out very good. I hurt my ankle catching behind the bat and was not able to get into Le Mans as soon as I wanted to. When I finally was able to move around a lot I looked the city all over for a real high tone place to go but could not find one. I contented myself with the best I could find however, figuring that I had been forced to put it off long enough. They will be ready next week and sent to you at once.

I now have two officers under me in the company and hence have been able to get a lot of little details such as inspection of quarters, etc. off my hands. This gives me more time to put in on the paperwork and general management of the company. They are both bully good men and have taken ahold of the work I have given them to do in fine shape. One of them nearly cost me $120.00 the other night when I paid the company off but we all make mistakes once in a while. I was paying and he was checking the men's names off as I paid them. He failed to check one man who was drawing $120.00 and when I came to check the whole payroll up to figure out just how much was to be turned in, etc. I found myself short a large number of francs. This has to come out of the commanding officer's pocket and I did not cherish the idea of paying out any sum like that for a mistake. After checking every way I knew how I found the mistake and also found that I had come out to the good. When I told the officer about it he worried his poor head off for the rest of the day.

I expect to leave here for Paris June 4th to be gone there three or four days. Phil is going with me and also another lieutenant. I hope to find something there to buy Sister and Ev for a wedding present. What my luck will be remains to be seen. I do not know what they need or might like that will not be given to them by their friends over there but I hope to find some little gift which will please them.

Tomorrow afternoon I go off in a sidecar to get this month's payroll signed by three or four men who are stationed about an hour's ride from Le Mans. I cannot say I am looking forward to the trip with a great deal of pleasure because I fear it will be a dusty one. I could have gotten a car but can make better time in a sidecar since it is not a long trip.

We are having beautiful weather now - not too hot but just right to go around in our shirtsleeves.

Well, dear, I must close for this time but one of you will hear from me again very soon.

Love to all and heaps for yourself.

Please give my very best to Ev.
Johnny

2nd Lieutenant John Lambert Hobson II, Le Mans, France, 1919.
Stephen G. Hobson Collection -Hobson family photograph

Dearest Mother

These pictures are certainly awfully poor but they are the best I could have taken at the time. I fear you will all think after one look at them that your boy is sick or was at the time they were taken. Such was not the case at all I can assure you. I told the young lady who took them I thought she had the camera too far away but she said no so I let her shoot and here are the results. I only had half a dozen made up as I did not consider them worth spending more money on. You folks keep all you want and if there are any extra give them to whomever you want to. If the chance presents itself I shall try to have more taken - if not I shall wait until I get home and then have some good ones taken before I put aside my uniform and don the long pants again. I have spent many happy months in Uncle Sam's clothes and shall never forget them.

I understand that officers returning from overseas duty are not allowed to wear their Sam Browne Belts after landing. I am sorry to hear this because all my uniforms and all other officers' who have served over here are cut for the belt and look bad without it. I will not feel fully dressed without mine even if I have only worn it a few short months. They most certainly set an officer off and whereas they are hard to keep clean and shined up it is worth the trouble for the appearance they give.

These pictures, dear, have been a long time coming and now that they have arrived will no doubt be a little disappointment to you since they are so poor but let us hope will serve to stop some of that longing around your little heart to see your boy. I am sending these to the beach figuring that by the time they get there you will have opened up the house.

Please give my love to all the family and tell them not to judge my real looks by these pictures because if they do they have got a mighty sickly looking brother whereas in reality he never was better in his life.

Lots of love and kisses for yourself.
Johnny

Dearest Mother

Ever since I returned from Paris last week I have done nothing but work, work, work. I did however find time to write you eleven pages about my time in the big city which you must have received by now. It was a wonderful trip and we all had a fine time as I guess you know from my last letter. Just now I am up to a new game and it is a very exciting but uncertain one. I have not time to go into details now as I have a business engagement in two minutes and shall be busy the rest of the day. This is just a note to say hello and send my love to you all. Just as quick as things ease up a bit you will receive another long letter from me but for the present this little note will have to carry my love and kisses to you all. Here comes the other lieutenant so I must close and fall to the work again.

Love, love, love, love and kisses, kisses, kisses for you all.
Johnny

Dear Dad

There have been so blame many little things to attend to of late and I have been banging around from one place to another that I have not had a minute in which to write anyone. Last Sunday I got just a short note off to Mother to let you know that I was well and happy but aside from that and the long letter telling you all about my Paris trip I fear I have fallen down a bit. I now have a little time to myself however and so am going to try to make up for lost time.

The Depot Service Co. I was with has left for the coast and, Dad, maybe we did not all have to work to get them ready. For three days and three nights every officer slaved his head off to get every little detail just right. Records had to be checked and re-checked - arrangements made for turning in extra clothes, kitchen equipment, etc. We all worked together like clockwork however and when the time came to leave the men were all equipped and their records in A No. 1 shape. I turned my command over to another lieutenant just before they left and started out on a new trail with several other officers who wanted to remain in France until fall. We had no idea where we were going or what kind of work we were to do until yesterday when orders came in for us to report to Saint-Nazaire to do embarkation work. A bunch of us leave early tomorrow morning for that little city where I first saw French life and started my career as a soldier on foreign soil. How long we shall be there I do not know but unless Germany refuses to sign the peace terms and we are all called up into the lines again I guess you will see me blowing into home around the middle of September and perhaps before. I have never been happier in my life, Dad, and just so long as you dear ones at home are not missing your son too much I shall stay over until fall. It is really surprising how many officers do want to stay over and are doing so. The older men figure that business conditions are none too good at home and that they are to be the gainers in the long run by remaining over until all is cleaned up. With me it is merely the fact that I love the life and feel that in spite of the roughness of the path once in a while I am making good. I have had my hand in a lot of different kinds of work and feel that each and every one has taught me something. Be patient, dear Dad, and when your boy does come back you will be all the gladder to see him.

I had a letter from Jeanne a few days ago in which she told me that Dr. Walker was at Base 52 here in Le Mans. I found him last Sunday and we enjoyed a very fine supper together and talked over old times. He is a Major as perhaps you know. Why I have not seen him before I cannot understand as he is staying at the officer's hotel and I run in there very often. I confess I fear I should not have known him all dressed up as a Major so perhaps we have seen each other several times. He sends his very best to you all.

I suppose the talk is all of the wedding now. It does not seem possible that I am going to return to find my older sister married and perhaps "K" engaged. How about it "Little Brown Eyes." I shall be thinking of you all on the 28th and wondering how every little carefully planned detail is going. Where are they going on their honeymoon? Wish they would come over here for a few weeks.

Well, Dad, I have got to pack my locker so will close. I will cable you my address as soon as I know it.

Please give my love to all and keep a lot for yourself.
Johnny

CHAPTER SIXTEEN

Embarkation Camp

Saint-Nazaire, France

"Every time I see a transport pull out through the locks my heart just sinks into my boots when I realize that perhaps I should be on her instead of chasing my own selfish desire for adventure all over France."

2ND LIEUTENANT JOHN L. HOBSON II

The Embarkation Camp at Saint-Nazaire of 1919 was certainly a different scene from that which greeted the 26th Division when they first landed in France in the fall of 1917.

The Embarkation Camp was located three miles from the railroad station and about the same distance from the docks. But the camp now had a billeting capacity for approximately 17,000 people being processed and transported out of France.

There were actually three camps now: two main camps and an Isolation Camp. There were two parade grounds, two mess halls, administration headquarters, delousing plant, sales commissaries, Quartermaster stores, amusement halls, clubs, souvenir stores and a post office, all connected by boardwalks so that soldiers could get from one place to another without wading through mud as they had done upon landing here in 1917.

Twenty years later, during the Second World War, Saint-Nazaire harbor would become the home of the impenetrable submarine pens of Hitler's Third Reich.

Saint-Nazaire, France
American Embarkation Camp No. 1
A.P.O. 701
(Undated)

Dearest Mother

I suppose you have all been more than anxious to hear from me since you received my last letter to Dad saying that I had been transferred to Saint-Nazaire. I know you are all just crazy to hear what your boy is up to now and no doubt are wondering a little where his wild adventure seeking spirit is going to finally land him. Well, darling, you know the greatest game of chance ever played is life itself and you can mark my word your son is really living and playing the game for all that is in him. It is wild and hard at times but oh, dearest, how I do love it all and how happy I am in all of my work and play realizing that it is all my own work and each little mark I may make on the course of the week is made by my own efforts. Well, dear, I know you are anxious for me to get started on some real facts so I will begin.

We arrived here last Saturday morning after spending a very comfortable night on the train coming from Le Mans. There were two other officers with me who were playing the fortunes of war with me and who were both commanding Depot Service Co. at Le Mans. One of them lived in the next tent to me at the Spur Camp so you see, darling, I am not alone on my trip. We all had lunch in town that noon and took the one o'clock bus out to camp No. 1 where our orders called for us to report. This camp is the very camp Battery A spent her first few days in France in and all the way out fond memories kept coming back to me as the bus rolled along. The place, however, has changed a lot since 1917 when the battery was here and now instead of a mud hole there is a real honest to God camp here. Lots of buildings have gone up and the place has been improved in a thousand different little details. These of course did not interest the other officers very much but I looked for every bush and tree that were here two years ago. We reported and were shown to a big barrack with 20 or 30 little rooms in it with one officer in each room and we were given one of these each and told to report for orders the next morning. This we did and of course all got different work. I have officer work and that is just what I like. The paperwork is along the same line as I had to do when I was commanding the company so I am not lost as I would have been had I not had that experience with paperwork at Le Mans. There are two of us in the office and one of us can get off almost every afternoon as the work lets up there as a rule and one man can handle it easy. The reports coming in in the morning keep us both pretty busy and when noon comes along I am ready to eat. Just how long we shall remain here is a question. We are all attached to what is known as the Army Service Corps and were sent here as far as we can figure it out just to mark time until they get ready to use us when we will be sent elsewhere. Well there is no use trying to figure out what will happen or where we shall be sent because we will stay here until further orders arrive and so why figure ahead.

There is one sight here, darling, I really wish you could see and that is the Hostess House where the French brides of American soldiers stay while waiting to be transported to the States. The husbands of these girls are in most cases here in camp also waiting ships to carry them homeward and an order came out a couple of days ago saying that husband and wife must go on the same vessel which has not been the case up to now as a rule. The men do their work during the day and visit with their brides in the evening. Mother I really feel sorry for most of these girls from the bottom of my heart. Some of them are of a very low type and are not worth feeling sorry for but others look like very nice, well brought up girls and these are the ones I pity. They are living in a seventh heaven now being treated like queens by the U.S. Government but I fear that many of them are going to be very, very unhappy when the men are discharged and take them to the farm to live. Many have got the idea they are going to live in some big city like New York and ride in soft cushioned autos where in reality they are to ride on hay loads, etc. Then again very few speak English and I fear their path will be a rough one for a good many months and they will wish they had not left France. I am wondering just how the American people are going to receive them and what the outcome of these marriages will be. If you happen to know anything about it I wish you would write me the news. Do not worry, darling, your boy will never, never marry over here. In the first place I have not seen any girl I should care to call my wife in France and in the second place I do not approve of these marriages except in a few very rare cases. There is a little girl waiting for me somewhere in the good old U.S. with real American blood flowing in her veins and until I find her or she finds me I stay single. In fact, darling, I have an idea I shall do so for some little time to come. A single life is not half bad but of course I have never tried the double.

I suppose when this reaches you I shall no longer have a sister whom I can call Miss Alice Hobson but it will be Mrs. Everett Bradley. "K" will then be Miss Hobson I believe if my memory of American customs has not failed me. The saddest words of tongue or pen are these, "By gosh, I'm broke again" hence my cable to Sister will be a few days late. The pictures are on the way all addressed to you and I wish you would give one to Sis and the others to those you think best. They turned out so poor that I only had half a dozen made up but will let you all see how I look as an officer but my face and eyes look as if I had been sick for years when in truth I never was better in my life.

Every time I see a transport pull out through the locks my heart just sinks into my boots when I realize that perhaps I should be on her instead of chasing my own selfish desire for adventure all over France. But I intend to make up for my pleasures when I return by just pulling you and Dad right with me every place I go and thus adding to my joys and putting a new and different light on my adventure-seeking young life. Are you game to follow where I head? If you had rather you shall lead and I give you my word as a man you will find your son right by your side. You have been with me in spirit over here and before long you shall be with me in person also.

Goodnight, dear, and may God guard and watch over you.
Johnny

Dear Dad

We have been very busy all the morning but things have let up now and as there is about an hour left before lunch I have decided to drop you just a few hasty lines. There really is not a great deal of news but just the same I know a few lines of love will be appreciated by you all.

Things here at camp are going along in first class shape as far as I am concerned. I like my work even better than that I was doing at Le Mans but had I not had that experience with paperwork I would have been lost in this office. There really is not a great deal to Army paperwork after you get the idea of it but until you do it all seems like one big muddle. When orders, etc. are handed to me now I know what to do with them and where to look for the information I want. Some things here are a little different than they were at the Spur Camp but the idea is the same and all I have to do is remember the new forms. There is one thing I do like about office work - you see all orders and notices and in that way are able to keep up with all doings around camp and all things of importance which take place in the A.E.F. After the company left I of course missed several orders so the first thing I did when I landed in here was to read up on all back orders I had missed. Some of these orders are very interesting and I like to try to figure out just what those higher up are working for when they issue some orders. Sometimes I see through it and sometimes I do not but there is always another order out a few days later to let me know how my guess came out. I am more than happy, Dad, and if I only had you and Mother here to stroll up and down the beach with in the evening my happiness would be complete. A nice quiet walk and talk with you over a cigar would seem pretty good to me these days.

There is all kinds of social life around this camp. The officers who are working here have one of the finest clubs I ever saw. Casual officers [officers not stationed at the camp] are not allowed in except as guests but have a small club of their own. Our club has a big reading room which is cleaned out every Sunday afternoon for dancing and the tables and chairs make their way to the walls again every Wednesday night when there is dancing. We have a big dining room where every officer has his own place so he will not have to wait for his meals by standing in line and buying meal tickets as the casuals do. French girls wait on tables and they certainly do it up brown. For eleven francs you can buy at the club office books which entitle you to have beer or wine for supper if you so desire. But, Dad, the cost of eating there is sky high and it is really the only place officers stationed here can eat and get back to their work on time. Nine francs a day for meals is what they charge and ten francs a month for the club. When you stop and figure it all up and then stack it up against some officer's messes it makes it pretty steep. Well the expense has got to be met while I am here so I have started to figure out how much I am going to have left of my June check for cigarettes, candy, etc. A soldier does not get much money, he spends a lot but, Dad, you very, very rarely see one broke for more than a couple of days. They get it somehow if they need it.

Last night one of the officers who was at the Spur Camp with us blew in here with a company to wait on a boat to take them home. About four in the afternoon word came down that he would go aboard today and the boat would leave this evening. He wanted to give the other two officers who are stationed here with me and myself a farewell dinner. We went to the Grand Hotel and lordy, lordy what a meal we had. Fine music played while we ate and a nice cool breeze from the ocean blew across the courtyard. We had just about everything from soup to nuts and when I got through I could hardly walk. At ten o'clock we danced and just as the clock struck mid-night started back to camp. So you see, Dad, that life in the Army is not all work when the shells have ceased flying. We have lots of good times in the evenings and very, very few are cut and dried. We just start out after office hours and pleasure finds us, we do not have to seek her. When the orderly knocks on the door the next morning we all hit the floor full of pep and ready for the day's work. Lots of evenings we just sit around and talk in our rooms or at the club and read. We are always happy and that is the chief thing in life.

There are of course a lot of naval men around town and there is where you can always find fun and hear interesting reports of the big land over there. The officers are awful nice and will do anything they can for you. Some one of these days I think I will ask one to slip me under his bunk on the return trip. This would give me a chance to say hello folks and give you all a kiss. George Stevenson is on a boat now I understand and I am hoping he docks here one of these days. I have sent him my address and told him where he can find me if he should drop into Saint-Nazaire by chance. The Mongolia steamed in here yesterday and loads today leaving for Boston tomorrow I believe.

Well, Dad, it is time to eat so I must close.

Please give my love to all the family and remember me to all the young people at the beach.

Lots of love for yourself.
Johnny

Dearest Mother

Now that the excitement is all over and we have all fallen back
into the old road of work again I am going to drop you a few lines
relating in a brief way how the signing of peace was celebrated here.

Saturday as of course you know was Peace Day. I suppose that
in what I call the outside world or civil life all work was called off
on that day but over here in the army we had to keep our shoulders to
the wheel as best we could all day. About four o'clock however that
afternoon we closed up the office and hurried to our rooms to dress
up for the evening. I took a fine hot shower, put on my best uniform,
boots and spurs, took my crop in my hand and along with another
lieutenant went forth to see the fun. First I gave the two officers
who came here with me a dinner party to celebrate Sister's wedding.
This was at the hotel where Ev and I ate our first French meal when
we landed over here with the battery. After supper we took a walk
down to the docks to see how many boats were in and if by chance
one was going out. There was a big liner just heading into the locks
as we arrived loaded with American troops all yelling their throats
sore. We watched them get under way and then turned our foot steps
for the officer's café. There was a big crowd there and it looked sort
of dead so we just fazed right out and went to the Café du Ocean
another officer's hang out. There we found more doing. The band
was playing good old American music - beautiful French girls with
American officers were sitting all around sipping their drinks and
talking. The place was all fixed up with flags and, darling, the whole
place was well worth seeing and I could have listened to that band
all night. We found a table and sat down and just fully enjoyed the
place until it got dark outside. Then the big parade started so we
went out to see it. With the exception of Armistice Night at Saumur
I have never seen more fun in my life. A French band lead the way
followed by a handful of French soldiers and behind them about

everybody in the city dancing, yelling and shooting off fire works. Very few Americans took part in the parade. The enlisted men not being allowed in town after 9:30 and it was ten then and whereas the streets were filled with officers none seemed to care to join in the yelling mob. I did however see a few enlisted men and sailors in the crowd who had got special passes or over stayed their regular one. We watched the parade pass and then went into the Grande café which is for officers only. That place was a mad house for sure. Majors at least forty years old had gay little French girls with them and the colonels were not letting anyone slip anything over on them. All were well armed with fire works including the girls. Firecrackers were banging all around in the place under chairs, on the tables and in mid air. Even rockets were shooting madly across the room while flares of every color shot up from every corner and table in the place. I met a 26th Division colonel out of the 103rd Artillery who shook my hand long and hard saying, "Boy, I am glad to see an officer from a real division here. I know the kind of stuff they are made of and what they have been through and I admire every one of them especially the young men your age who have given up so much to fight for their country - Have a drink on me." We stayed with him for awhile and then went to the Ocean again. By this time that place was a mad house but the good old band was still pounding out American songs for all it was worth. When they struck up "Poor Butterfly" I wondered to myself how many girls in the States were singing that song to themselves having in mind some soldier over here. "The moon and I know that he'll be faithful. He'll come back to me some day. But if he don't come back I just must cry, I just must die - Poor butterfly." About one a.m. they played "Home Sweet Home" and you should have heard that bunch sing as they helped their fair sex on with their coats and went out. Things had let up outside a little by then but we walked around just to watch the crowd that was still at it. We got back to camp about three o'clock Sunday morning and eight o'clock found me at my desk in the office feeling as fresh as a newborn baby. Needless to say, Sunday night I went to bed about eight o'clock but Peace is only signed once in a man's lifetime - that is when he is young enough to really enjoy it - so I consider that my all-night celebration had a just cause. I guess you folks in the States tried to turn the world upside down also and all ex-soldiers who took life easy that night must have been sick.

It is all over now, darling, even the shouting. All that is left to do is get the remaining troops home and clean up over here. There is no danger of any serious trouble breaking out I don't believe. Germany is on her knees and now that I feel certain I shall not get back only to read in the papers that war has broken out again and hence cuss myself for not remaining over ready to jump for the gun at the first poor move that Germany made I am ready to return home feeling that my full duty to my country is well done. Should I have returned last April and trouble had started I never would have been happy but now I can return knowing that I shall not have to sit peacefully in an easy chair on the porch smoking while good American red blood is flowing like water up on the battlefields again while I lay back in ease and comfort. We have all heard a lot about trouble in Mexico and those of us who have taken a fancy to Army life, and there are many more than you would believe have, are now anxious to get back and clean that mess up before we lay aside our uniform and get settled down to work. We might as well make a clean job of it while we are at it and then pull out feeling that we can rest in peace for a few years. Rumor has it that one division was sent right to the border as soon as they landed which gives many of us to believe that trouble may really be starting down there. If it is, Mother, it will be a small job side of this one over here and I hope all the men who did not get enough get into it. I guess however that I shall have to miss that little party as by the time I get back it will more than likely be over if it ever even starts. I guess however it is just as well because if I kept on attending these shooting banquets someone would sooner or later spell my name right and not half right as the Huns did and J.L. 2nd would be no more except in memory.

Now I suppose you are asking yourself more than ever, "When, oh when, is my dear boy coming back to me?" Well, darling, that all depends upon how quick the Army Service Corps can clean up its work over here. The port at Saint-Nazaire is due to close about the middle of July unless orders change. By the end of July all men here not in the Army Service Corps ought to be home. Some on the A.S.C. will also be home but will I be one of them is the question. I am wearing three stripes on my left sleeve and that may send me home - it will if my services can be spared. The A.S.C. however needs officers to handle guard companies, paperwork and other things so it is rather doubtful if I get back in July but you can never tell. There is one thing sure, dear, I will be home early next fall because they are rushing things to the limit now that Germany has decided to behave and we know where we stand. Thousands of troops are due in here this week and just as fast as the boats arrive and can be loaded they will be shipped out. Things are going to move very fast now, Mother, and we have been all ready to put on the extra speed for some time but could not do so until peace was signed. Now that speed will start. Just keep smiling and cheerful as you have in the past, dearest, and before you know it you will hear my voice on the phone saying, "The black sheep has returned to the fold. Put on an extra place at the table tonight as I shall be home for supper." Or perhaps you would rather I would let you know if possible where and on what date I am to land so that you can meet me at the dock. You can rest assured, dear, that I will let you know either by wire or phone just as quick as I hit U.S. soil and if you desire I will try to arrange it so you can get to the dock to see the transport pull in. If you are at the beach I think the best plan is for me to get to Boston without saying a word and phone you from there. Then none of you will have to worry about getting to me at some camp. You will get the phone call and then just send the auto to meet me at the depot - the next thing you know I will be at the house. No excitement - no anxious hours or days of waiting. Let me know what you want me to do and I will try to carry your wishes out.

Well, darling, I guess I have written enough for this time so will close.

Please give my love to all the family and remember me to all the crowd at the beach.

We'll see you all before many months.

Love and heaps of kisses.
Johnny

Dearest Mother

Well I suppose by this time the excitement of the wedding is just about a thing of the past and you are now anxiously awaiting the return of the bride and groom from their honeymoon. There has naturally been some delay in my mail since I moved from Le Mans down here and whereas a little breezed in a couple of days ago it was all written three or four weeks before the 28th. I sent you a cable from here giving you my new address so I ought to begin to receive letters direct before very long which will tell me all about the big doings. I have pictured it all out in my mind and now am wondering if my mental paintings were right. Sister must have looked pretty all dressed up in her bridal dress and Ev I feel certain cut a fine figure all polished up for the big affair. In the letter from Sister which I received she did not know where they were going on their trip and has got me guessing. I expected a trip up through the mountains in the States would be their plan but from what Sister said I doubt if I was right. Well, I hope the letter telling me all about it will arrive before long.

Things with me, darling, are going along just the same as usual. Every morning including Sunday finds me in the office ready for the day's work and every evening finds me ready to have a good time. I am more than happy and things are coming before my eyes which are certainly teaching me a lot. Plans for the future and golden chances are coming up every week and I am listening, watching and waiting and learning all the time. These two officers I am with, darling, are two of the finest men I ever met and the three of us have stuck together like glue ever since I went to Le Mans last March. "Every man for himself and all for the crowd" is our motto. You always see us together and when they went to Le Mans on leave last week and I for several reasons did not go they said the first question they were asked by people who knew us was, "Where is the 'grand lieutenant'?" One of them is very short hence he is known as "Le Petit lieutenant." "Le Petit lieutenant" disappeared yesterday and has not been seen since. I left him right after breakfast and when I met the other lieutenant after lunch at the club as we always do, Joe never showed up. I looked high and low for him after supper and finally gave up and went to bed. About ten o'clock this other officer wakes me up and wants to know what in the name of heaven I had done with "Le Petit?" I told him I had not seen him since breakfast and we both got anxious right away because he had not been able to find him either. We looked in his room this morning and his bed had not been slept in so we both start off on a hunt today. I fear he is in the hospital because he made the remark in the morning he felt rotten. I am taking a YMCA girl out for lunch this noon followed by a dance and if I don't find or get some word of Joe I fear she will have to wait for me at the hotel because I must find him before I leave camp.

This YMCA girl is a French girl who is doing "Y" work with the American Army. She was with the 28th Division for a long time and has done lots of work up near the lines. She speaks English as well as I do and the first night I met her asked her what part of the States she was from. You can imagine how surprised I was to find out she had never been to the States at all. She is going over in September to visit some friends in Boston and "Pa." [Pennsylvania] My but it was funny to hear her talk of Brookline and Newton. She asked me a lot of questions about the customs over there. She is a beautiful dancer and loads of fun. After lunch we are coming out here to the dance at the officer's club. She is staying at a summer resort about six miles from camp with a lot of other YMCA workers and after the dance we go out there and join some other girls and officers for supper and another dance. It is Sunday, darling, I know but that is the big day in the Army and just about the only day we can get off in the p.m. so please do not judge me too hard. The other two officers think it is a fine joke for Jack to be taking a girl out for lunch and swear they are coming in and eat at the next table to us at the hotel. Neither of them dance so I am all set there.

One of these officers has really fallen in love - not Joe or Jack because we couldn't but the third one - and, darling, he has got a beautiful girl. He is going to visit her in her home in Paris the last of this month and the wedding will follow if everything is all right with her father who is a captain in the French Army. Gee, but she is pretty and just as nice as she can be. She speaks no English but he can make her understand all he says in broken French. I have had supper with them several times and, Mother, she certainly is a peach.

Well, I must close and start out looking for "Le Petit."

Love to all and heaps for yourself.
Johnny

Saint-Nazaire, France
Embarkation Camp No. 1
A.P.O. 701
July 9, 1919

Dearest Mother

I suppose by now the beach is going full blast - everybody is there and no doubt many new faces have appeared which last summer were facing shell fire over here. Sister will be back from her honeymoon before long and will be dropping in for supper with you every now and then. Art I believe is off boating this month and will more than likely return brown and happy. "K" is enjoying the bathing and dances. Buster is the only one of the family I cannot quite picture in his daily fun. He must have grown a lot in the past two years and for all I know is one of the big men at the dances and around the beach. You and Dad I can fancy as going along just as you did when I was there - enjoying every day and taking in most of the dances. At times I kind of wish I were back there with you all and yet I know I would not be home more than a couple of weeks before I would want to be back over here again helping in this cleanup work. To be sure I cannot just eat, sleep and be merry as I could at Rye all this summer but, darling, I am so happy in my work that I look forward with pleasure to each day. I am also getting enough fun in the evenings to make life seem really worthwhile. Last Sunday was one of the best days I have had since I arrived at Saint-Nazaire.

I met that French YMCA girl at noon in town and we had lunch together at the Grande Hotel. After lunch we walked up and down the ocean front until four when we came out here to camp for the dance. Oh, Mother, how that girl could dance - it was just great. After the dance we went back to the city again, found a taxi and went out to the summer resort where she is staying which is about six miles from here. She wanted me to stay all night and I had fallen so madly in love with the place that I got a room. After washing up we started out to find a nice cozy little place to eat and I never laughed so in my life as I did over that hunt. There are hundreds of nice little places where you can eat under the trees but every one she liked I didn't and every one I liked she didn't. Finally after walking nearly two miles we both decided we were hungry enough to eat anywhere we could get food so went into the first place we came to. It was eight o'clock then so you can imagine how hungry we were not having eaten since noon. Darling, I wish you could have seen your boy that night sitting out in a beautiful garden eating supper with a "Y" girl. After supper we stayed around a while and talked, then started for the hotel. When we got there we found a movie picture show on but for some reason neither of us wanted to go so found two nice chairs carried them down to the beach and just sat and listened to the moaning of the waves, and watched the moon. This girl has been doing work with our "Y" for over a year, speaks fine English and is most interesting to talk with. We talked about America and compared our customs with theirs. Then we talked the war all over and finally about one a.m. decided it was time to say goodnight. I took the 6:45 train back to the city the next morning. Right off the reel at eight o'clock the Major breezes in with four court martial cases for me to look into and make out the papers for the trials. One of the three cases was an attempt at murder and that proved to be a hard one. I had to have everything ready by noon the next day and, Mother, I certainly did work. But the papers were ready at ten o'clock the next morning and one of them is on trial now. I was plugging away for dear life with an old coon Monday night after supper and must admit he along with some other hard ones I had talked with during the day had me in a very poor frame of mind. He would tell me nothing and for two solid hours I had been asking him questions to try and get some connected story out of him. After a while it got on my nerves and I told him if he did not come across and make a clean story of the whole thing I was going to see he was put in a position where he would be only too glad to tell all he knew. He thought it all over and finally started in from the very beginning and told me all. He was nearly through and was going over a talk he and another coon had which was not made up of the sweetest words I have heard when the office door opened behind me and I heard a girl laugh, then utter a frightened yell and the door banged. I turned to the orderly and asked him who that was at the door. He didn't know except it was a girl all dressed up in evening clothes. Just then an officer I knew came in all shined up like a door handle, "Busy, Jack?" he asked. "Yes, but I will be through in a few minutes," I said. "Sit down." When I finished up with that coon and the guard had taken him out, this officer began to laugh his head off while I pushed my cap back on my head and sunk down into my chair a few more feet - all in!! "Have you been listening to that stuff all day?" he asked when he got through laughing. "Yes, and worse than that." I replied. "Well then you need to join our party and forget some of it because if any man could cuss worse than that coon and has before you, you must be all in." I showed him some of the stories of a few men I had there and he agreed with me that my mind and brain must be all in. I asked him what the party was. It seems that he had been out to this summer resort for supper with an American "Y" girl and had met my friend. The three of them had got a big American auto and were going to a dance about twenty miles out of town. They wanted another officer and my little friend suggested me. They had gone to my barracks only to learn that I was at the office. This French girl thought she would steal in and surprise me but did not like my company - in fact, was really afraid when she heard the coon raving and saw the guard standing behind him with a gun. Hence I missed being very nicely surprised by a girl. I sent the orderly out to tell the young ladies to come in and they did but I noticed they looked all around just as if they expected some colored gentleman to jump out at them. After talking the matter all over I finally decided to go with them and we all had a bully time before the night was over and I forgot all about my rough room friends until the next morning. This French girl said she would never, never try to surprise me again in the office if I kept animals like that around.

Well, dear, I guess I will close and walk over to the officer's club for a couple of hours as they are having a dance and I want to see the fun.

Please give my best to all.

Love and kisses for yourself.
Johnny

CHAPTER SEVENTEEN

Little Boar's Head - And Beyond
Johnny Comes Marching Home

"...everything noble, loving and true."

ALICE CARY (GALE) HOBSON

"Having a bully time with Dad"

JOHN LAMBERT HOBSON II, CIVILIAN

That was the last letter my father wrote from France.

True to his expectation about how rapidly things were progressing, within four days of writing that last letter, it was determined that his job at the Saint-Nazaire Embarkation Camp was complete and the Army decided it was time for him to go home and be discharged.

Along with 90 officers, two nurses and 1,990 enlisted men, Father boarded a troop transport ship, the USS Pastores, and at 5 o'clock in the morning on 14 July 1919, the Pastores steamed through Saint-Nazaire's harbor basin and locks and began the 3,243 nautical mile voyage to Hoboken, New Jersey, USA.

Twenty-two months had passed since my father first landed at Saint-Nazaire in the cold rain in the fall of 1917. Then, he stepped off the gang-plank of a troop ship onto muddy French soil as a wide-eyed and uncertain rookie Corporal, his worldly possessions in a duffle bag slung over his shoulder. He was clad in an ill-fitting uniform, covered with a poncho, capped by a slouching campaign hat and wearing hobnailed, ankle-high boots with puttees wrapped around his lower legs.

Now, as he stood on the ship's deck leaning against the rail of the Pastores as the ship steamed west toward the shores of the United States, he watched the French coast disappear in the sunrise. It was as if the past two years had all been but a dream. How things had changed. Now his worldly possessions were in a steamer trunk placed in his "stateroom" by an orderly, his name, rank and home address neatly stenciled on the trunk's lid. He was dressed in a tailored, dress officer's uniform, capped with an overseas cap and booted with handmade leather riding boots that had been polished to a mirror finish. It all was topped by a trench coat.

On the high, stiff collar of his uniform there was the brass U.S. pin on one side and on the other side a pin with crossed cannon, marking him as a United States soldier serving in the artillery. The buttons of his uniform were of brass with the American eagle on each. On the sleeve of his uniform were two gold service stripes, one for each year of service, a gold chevron for overseas duty and a red wound chevron. That wound chevron would become the Purple Heart medal. On each shoulder and on the overseas cap there was a single gold bar indicating his rank as a second lieutenant. On the right shoulder of the uniform was the division's patch, the blue YD letters on a brown field. And across his chest was the leather Sam Browne belt, polished to a high reflection. These were the outward trappings, the symbols of his service to his country in the United States Army artillery with the 26th Division fighting in a foreign land, and those of a soldier who had been wounded in combat and one who had been commissioned an officer and attained the rank of second lieutenant. That résumé was all displayed on the outside.

On the inside, in his heart, there must have been more - much, much more. He had proven himself to the world as an officer and a gentleman, a leader of men, and now he was anything but wide-eyed and uncertain. He was wiser now and proud, to be sure, but he was also forever humble. He had, after all, answered the call of his country and thrown himself into the breach in defense of democracy and freedom. He had experienced and survived the fighting. He had seen and experienced horrible things. He had a few brushes with death in the process. He had been wounded in the line of duty. He had endured the pain and suffering of mustard gas burns. He had been struck by lightning. He had been blown up in an observation post that was hit by German artillery and for a moment mistakenly declared dead. His convoy was shelled by artillery while he sought safety under a truck. The horrible memory of the death and destruction of war would never leave him completely. But, he also knew full well that he had survived the carnage of this war only by the grace of God. Others were not so fortunate. He was humble. But, at this moment, he must have taken strength and confidence from the feeling that whatever lay ahead in life for him, any hardship he encountered would not exceed what he had seen and experienced over the past twenty-two months.

In this adventure he had given a lot, but he had received more. And, best of all, he was now going home. Ah, yes. Home, sweet home!

The uniform and military trappings would soon be put away into the trunk and stored in the attic, but not the life lessons and experiences. Those he would carry around with him in his mind and heart for the rest of his life, and they would be far more enduring and valuable. They would serve him better than the uniform.

The USS Pastores which carried father back home again had a length of 495 feet and a beam of 55 feet. She was a twin-screw type of transport ship with a speed of 15 knots per hour. She was built in 1912 at the Werkman, Clark & Co. Ltd. yard in Belfast, Ireland. She originally flew the British flag plying the United Fruit Company's trade among New York, West Indies and Central and South America. When Britain entered the war in 1914, her registry was transferred to the United States and she became one of the first ships taken over for the transportation of American troops, making her first convoy from New York to Saint-Nazaire, France, in June of 1917. This voyage of July 14, 1919 was her twentieth trip, with only one minor incident in her history. On her tenth voyage, in August of 1918, while approaching New York, a German submarine fired upon her. She returned fire and, after firing nine shots from her afterdeck, the submarine disappeared.

Unlike the voyage to France on the Finland two years earlier, the course the Pastores sailed on the voyage home was straight ahead, not a zig-zag course to avoid enemy submarines, and the ship was not blacked out at night. The weather on the voyage home was fair and windy. After a nine-day voyage without incident, the USS Pastores docked at Hoboken, New Jersey on 23 July. One can only imagine the emotion my father and thousands of other returning soldiers felt upon steaming past the Statue of Liberty.

This time, before leaving France, my father had cabled his family about his return. However, he had also told them he felt there was no sense or need for the family to greet him at the dock when he landed in New Jersey. He felt it was an unnecessary fuss for them to make the trip to meet him and, even if they did come to meet him, he couldn't immediately return home with them because there was the discharging processing to go through before he would be allowed to leave. The family would only have to wait in the New York area, possibly for several days, while the discharging process took place. He told them he would phone them from the train depot when he arrived home.

On 25 July 1919, two days after the ship docked, Second Lieutenant John Lambert Hobson was honorably discharged from the United States Army at Camp Dix in New Jersey.

When he was discharged, my father sent a telegram to the family summer residence at Little Boar's Head. The telegram simply stated: "Will be home Saturday. Johnny"

WHEN JOHNNY COMES MARCHING HOME
Patrick Gilmore

When Johnny comes matching home again, hurrah, hurrah!
We'll give him a hearty welcome then, hurrah, hurrah!
The men will cheer, and the boys will shout,
And the ladies, they will all turn out,
And we'll all feel gay, when Johnny comes matching home.

Two months after his return from France, my father began his next adventure, a career in the paper manufacturing business.

He was always restless. He liked being "in harness." His Yankee work ethic discouraged too long a period of leisure. A dilettante's life did not appeal to him, even for a brief time. In August 1919, at the age of twenty-two, he and his father leisurely drove to Woodland, Maine, where, during the fall of that year, my father would begin learning the paper manufacturing business from the bottom up. He started his career by working in the woods for the St. Croix Paper Company. Forty-three years later, he would retire from the company as Chairman of the Board.

While driving to Woodland with his father that August, they took their time. Father and son stopped along the way to do some fishing together. The two of them had some catching up to do and plenty of experiences to share.

While on that road trip, my father sent a post card to his mother, who was at the summer residence at Little Boar's Head. The post card was post-marked Beddington, Maine, a remote little town, population fewer than 50, located on the ninety-mile, dirt Air Line road, officially Route 9, that runs from Brewer to Calais. On the post card was a picture of a modest fishing cabin with an inviting hammock to one side and written on the post card was a note boasting of catching four fish and that he was, "Having a bully time with Dad." He did finally get to have some time alone with his father, time that he so longed for and dreamed about while serving in France.

That "bully time" turned out to be more time with Dad than he originally thought. For the next 27 years, until his father's death in 1946, father and son would become a well-respected and beloved team in the paper manufacturing business and the Boston business community. Newspaper-publishing custom-ers supported their product and the Boston banking and business community valued their business acumen. The St. Croix Paper Company personnel affec-tionately referred to the father and son team as "A.L." and "J.L.".

While active in business, John served on the board of directors of the Towle Manufacturing Company, The National Bank of Haverhill and the Shawmut Bank. He was a Trustee of Bradford Junior College.

In 1920, Alice Cary Gale Hobson gifted a parcel of land in Exeter to the Town of Exeter, New Hampshire. The land was to be the site of Gale Memorial Park, a park she dedicated to her father's memory. Stephen H. Gale had died that year. She made the donation of the land for the purpose of the site to be used for a Soldier's Monument for the Soldiers of the World War.

Daniel Chester French, who was born in Exeter and had that same year sculpted the statue of the sitting Abraham Lincoln at the Lincoln Memorial in Washington, DC, sculpted a magnificent bronze statue that would be erected there in Gale Memorial Park.

The statue represents the mother resolute, inspired to undergo her sacrifice, pointing out the path of duty to her intrepid soldier son. The inscription on the base of the statue reads:

"With veneration for those who have died, gratitude to those who live, trust in the patriotism of those who come after, the Town of Exeter dedicates this Memorial to her Sons and Daughters of the World War."

The World War Soldier's Memorial was dedicated at Gale Memorial Park in Exeter on 4 July 1922. The dedication ceremony was concluded by the bugle call of Taps.

Gale Park, Exeter, NH, 2003. Stephen G. Hobson Collection - Stephen G. Hobson photograph

John Lambert Hobson II and his mother, Alice Cary (Gale) Hobson on the occasion of her 80ᵗʰ Birthday, Little Boar's Head, Rye Beach, NH, 1952. Stephen G. Hobson Collection

In 1925 at the age of 28, John married Helena Gailey in Woodland, Maine. The marriage didn't last and ended in divorce several years later. There were no children from that marriage.

In 1940 at the age of 43, John would marry again to Louise Mary Tarling of Portland, Maine. That marriage would happily last 27 years until John's passing.

There were three children from his marriage to Louise Tarling: Mary Louise (Hobson) Wollerscheid born in 1941, John Lambert Hobson III born in 1943, and Stephen Gale Hobson born in 1946.

Left to right: Louise Mary (Tarling) Hobson, John Lambert Hobson III,
Mary Louise (Hobson) Wollerscheid, and Stephen Gale Hobson - 1992 -
Stephen G. Hobson Collection - Stephen G. Hobson photograph

On the evening of 4 July 1967, at age 69 and just one month before his seventieth birthday, John Lambert Hobson II died of cancer in Wolfeboro, New Hampshire.

He is buried with his father, mother, brothers and sisters at the Hobson family cemetery plot in Linwood Cemetery in Haverhill, Massachusetts.

To his family, friends and all that knew him he was, indeed, what his mother had said about him when he was a young man in 1916. Throughout his life he was, "…everything noble, loving and true."

TAPS

Composed by Major General Daniel Butterfield
Army of the Potomac, American Civil War

"Fading light dims the sight,
And a star gems the sky, gleaming bright.
From afar drawing nigh - Falls the night.

"Day is done, gone the sun,
From the lake, from the hills, from the sky.
All is well, safely rest, God is nigh.

"Then good night, peaceful night,
Till the light of the dawn shineth bright,
God is near, do not fear - Friend, good night."

John Lambert Hobson II, 1954. Stephen G. Hobson Collection - Stephen G. Hobson photograph

MEET THE MANAGEMENT
ARTICLE FROM ST. CROIX OBSERVER
FEBRUARY 1, 1954

President John L. Hobson is the third member of the Hobson family to take an active part in the management of the St. Croix Paper Company. His grandfather, John L. Hobson, 1st was one of the organizers and a director of the Glen Manufacturing Company which built and operated a newsprint mill in Berlin, NH about 1880. His son, Arthur L. Hobson, graduated from Harvard in 1895 and went to work in the mill in Berlin. He worked in every department and was made General Manager, a position which he held until the property was acquired by the International Paper Company in 1898. With a knowledge of paper making and a love for the industry, it was a natural for them to become interested in the formation of the St. Croix Paper Company in 1904 and both father and son became directors of the new company. "A.L." was Treasurer of the company until 1926 when he became President and Treasurer.

Our President, John L. 2nd, visited the mill in Woodland several times when he was in his early teens. His entry into the paper industry was delayed by World War I. He served two years in France, ten months on the firing line, was gassed in the battle of Chateau-Thierry, and was commissioned 2nd Lieutenant after graduating from Saumur Artillery School in France.

Following his discharge from the service, he enjoyed a two months rest and came to Woodland in the fall of 1919 [Age 22]. He spent one year in the woods, cutting scaling, etc. He spent one year in the Accounting Department and then was made Asst. General Manager. He went to the Boston office as Asst. Treasurer on November 1, 1928 [Age 31], and was elected President in the fall of 1946 [Age 49] after the death of his father, Arthur L. Hobson, and continues as head of the Company.

In Woodland John took a keen interest in local affairs. He served as Second Selectman of the Town of Baileyville for one year, was Commander of W. T. Wren Post, American Legion for one year, and was president of the St. Croix Baseball League for two or three years.

He has taken an active part in the affairs of the paper industry and served as president of the Newsprint Service Bureau for several years. He also served as Vice Chairman of the newsprint industry committees of OPA (Office of Price Administration) and WPB (War Production Board) and was chairman of both committees for the last six or eight months before they were dissolved.

He has one hobby, his home and family. At their attractive home in Swampscott, he forgets the many problems of the office and spends every possible moment with his wife, Louise, and their three children, Mary Louise, John L. 3rd, and Stephen. A well-trained dog and cat complete the family circle.

He modestly refers to the success of the St. Croix Paper Company as due to the splendid organization behind him, and the splendid organization that preceded him. He is following in that tradition of his grandfather and his father, who were responsible for the inscription on the bell which rang out from the old mill in Berlin and now calls the people of Woodland to worship in St. Luke's Church: "THE CONSUMPTION OF PAPER IS THE MEASURE OF A PEOPLE'S PROGRESS."

EPILOGUE

Going Back to the Front

"When you go home, tell them of us, and say, for your tomorrow, we gave you our today."

ALLIED CEMETERY EPITAPH

"This is their cathedral and theirs alone"

STEPHEN GALE HOBSON

"Brothers, we are treading where the saints have trod."

ONWARD, CHRISTIAN SOLDIERS

7 October 2004: Exactly eighty-seven years and one day after my father landed at the port of Saint-Nazaire and walked down the gangplank of a troop ship, stepping onto French soil as a Corporal in the United States Army, I stepped off an Air France A 330 Airbus jet airliner at Charles De Gaulle airport in Paris. The purpose of my visit was to trace my father's footsteps. I wanted to walk in the forests and fields of the Ardennes and

through the scenic villages in the valleys of the Marne, Meuse and Aisne where eighty-seven years before my father had walked in the deadly serious work of war.

I had researched and written about it. Now I wanted to stand where my father had fought with his artillery regiment of A.E.F. National Guard volunteers, shoulder to shoulder with the Allied forces during three campaigns of the First World War, two of the campaigns being decisive in the war. With my father's battle maps in hand, I wanted to stand where he had stood. I wanted to see it. I wanted to feel it. I wanted to experience it. Yes, it was a pilgrimage of sorts. But, it was more a trip made out of curiosity: a desire for confirmation of what I imagined it to be. I was not disappointed.

What was it like to be there, to walk the paths my father walked and to stand exactly where he had stood in those hallowed fields? It left a great impression.

My father did not fight on battlefields that were subsequently decorated or acknowledged with monuments or plaques. His battlefields today are simply ordinary fields, woods and hillsides. What happened there is what makes those places special. The monuments, statues and plaques were elsewhere close by, and there are a lot of them around this part of France that commemorate both sides. Being there reminded me of the many monuments and plaques in the United States that commemorate the battlefields of the American Civil War. When I see those, I am always wondering about the fight that took place in the adjacent, unmarked farmer's field. After all, Revolutionary War's Bunker Hill Monument in Charlestown, Massachusetts, is located on the wrong hill.

I was struck with how this countryside in France had not changed in eighty-seven years. It is truly beautiful: rolling fields interspersed with patches of woods. In 1918, these same beautiful woods and cultivated fields that I was now looking at were a trenched, cratered, pocked and deeply scarred moonscape created from years of trench war, exploding bombs and artillery shells that left gaping holes in the earth described as ranging in size from that of a barrel to that of a house cellar. The forests were all shattered stumps, the standing trees having been clipped off, mown down by artillery. The scene back then was described by flying ace Eddie Rickenbacker in his book "Fighting the Flying Circus" as he first flew over this same ground on his first mission as,

The trenches in this sector were quite old and had remained in practically the same position for three years of warfare. To my inexperienced view there appeared to be nothing below me but old battered trenches, trench work and billions of shell holes which had dug up the whole surface of the earth for four or five miles on either side of me. Not a tree, not a fence, no sign of any familiar occupation of mankind, nothing but a chaos of ruin and desolation. The awfulness of the thing was truly appalling."

Today, the open wounds of war are almost gone. The trees have grown back. The fields are cultivated again, fruitful and beautiful. However, there are still scars. In the woods and unplowed fields there are still remains of trenches and shell holes, but their contours have been softened by the passing of time. Standing in the remains of the trenches and looking over what was No Man's Land yields an eerie reminder of what took place here.

Battle trash - shrapnel, spent bullets, shell casings, barbed wire, unexploded bombs, artillery shells and soldiers' equipment - is scattered everywhere in the countryside like acorns, and the locals place about as much value on it. When I spoke of my surprise that this hadn't been cleaned up after all these years, I was reminded by one of the locals that hundreds of thousands of tons of bombs, artillery shells and bullets rained down on this land and there was an equal amount of military equipment and human refuse left behind by retreating and advancing armies or the dead. He said he wasn't surprised that I didn't understand. Americans don't understand what it is to have a protracted war of world proportion fought on their homeland. The American Revolution and Civil War combined don't qualify.

*26ᵗʰ Division marching through wrecked Vaux, 21 July 1918. 26ᵗʰ Division,
A.E.F. Division Histories, Vol. 2*

Vaux, October 2004. Stephen G. Hobson Collection - Stephen G. Hobson photograph
*This photograph was taken from the road leading into town and from the same direction as the
previous July 1918 photograph, just from the other side of the street. The house on the left side of this
photograph is also pictured in the 1918 photograph as the wrecked first house on the left on the road
leading into town and all the rest of the houses going down the road are the same as well. Note the
same wood in the upper right corner on the hill on the other side of the town that is now fuller.*

Many existing houses and buildings still bear the scars of war where a machine gun strafed a wall or shrapnel exploded and left its mark in a wall or the side of a house. In some cases, the locals proudly point these out.

I reminded myself that an entire generation of flowering French and British manhood was killed in this war, and 117,000 American boys as well. I thought how sad it is that we will never know what genius could have come from this loss; perhaps another Einstein, Shakespeare, a researcher who finds the cure for cancer or a world leader who brings world peace?

I was told a story by a Frenchman I encountered one day near the Chemin des Dames when I stopped at a café looking for directions. Right out of central casting, this gentleman was of slight build, sported a large, thick, drooping black moustache and possessed prodigious, bushy, black eyebrows. He was wearing corduroy pants, a sweater and, in deference to the muddy walking conditions of that day, wore rubber shoes. Fortunately, he spoke excellent English. He was quietly sipping his afternoon coffee when an accommodating wait person, who was patient but frustrated with my lack of conversant French and my finger pointing at a map and sincerely wanted to be helpful with my request for directions, introduced us. This man had the most marvelous twinkle in his eyes.

When my English-speaking savior discovered my mission, he told me about an incident he had witnessed on a WWI battlefield tour he used to conduct at the Caverne du Dragon, or as the Germans called these chalk caves, the Dragon Lair or Drachenhohle. As an aside, when preparing for this trip, I had researched battlefield tours. In the process I discovered a rather ghastly marketing reality. There are very few battlefield tours in the area I was in - what is referred to as the American Sectors - even though it was decisive in the war, because there hadn't been enough men killed there to attract the tourists like there had been at the Somme.

This Frenchman's story was about two men he encountered on the tour, a German and a Frenchman. They had served their respective countries in the infantry in the First World War. Coincidently, but unknown to the other, they both fought at the same time on the very field where they were standing. Returning to this ground, coincidence, fate and nostalgia overtook these two veterans.

Memories rekindled and dragging family members behind them, each instinctively took respective positions where the opposing trenches had been that they had defended 60 years before. They started reliving the attack.

They began retracing their steps across what was then a killing field. They gestured, using their walking sticks as imaginary bayonet tipped rifles. They shouted, one speaking German, the other French. They cursed the charging enemy. They muttered to comrades of long ago who were in their memory dying again as they fell in the mud beside them as they courageously charged across the broken ground at the opposing trenches into the enemy's rolling artillery barrage and machine gunfire. Both veterans were caught up in emotion and completely unaware of each other's presence. That is, until they met in the middle.

Confronting each other face-to-face again in the middle of No Man's Land, they stopped mid-sentence and mid-gesture and froze in their tracks. They stared at each other for a moment while the reverie dissipated and they gradually mentally digested what was really happening here. Then, these reunited strangers who 60 years before were trying to kill each other, burst into tears and embraced. My narrator said it was not just a quick, light "how nice to meet you" embrace. It was a long, sobbing, bone crushing, emotional catharsis kind of embrace. It was an embrace that expended 60 years of pent up, conflicted emotion.

Who knows if this story is true? I suppose a similar story can be told about many veterans returning to their battlefields. But it does make a point about the retrospect of war. And this Frenchman's story had an impact on me, which, I suppose, is why he told it to me, and I know it is why I am retelling it here. Wars are fought by soldiers who are human, and the horror of it all, mentally or physically, makes every combat soldier a casualty of war.

My directions received and our conversation over too soon, as I parted from this hospitable man, he warmly shook my hand, clasping mine in both of his. He looked deeply into my eyes and he thanked me for what my father had done for his homeland. I subsequently received this expression of gratification many times while in France from people ranging from the mayors of towns, farmers whose permission I sought to walk through their fields, Museum directors and staff in the village Mairie (town hall) who assisted me with research, and wait staff in cafes and restaurants who, while I was dining alone, curiously inquired about my poring over books, maps and making notes. But, at this particular moment, and each time this happened, I felt humble and proud. Speechless and choked with emotion, I felt my eyes well up. I could only acknowledge his kind words with a nod. I cast my moist eyes to heaven in hope that my father was listening.

Comparing the regiment's battle maps of 1918 to my modern 2004 Michelin road map, I was constantly surprised that the landscape and roads had not changed since my father walked, rode horseback or bumped along in a motorized troop transport truck, ambulance, or the sidecar of a motorcycle across this ground 87 years earlier. It made my search for Battery A's gun positions remarkably easy. The roads have not been added to, subtracted from or widened or paved over. They matched the old battle maps perfectly.

The back roads are narrow, winding and charming. They traverse beautiful countryside and clearly are designed for travel on foot or by horse-drawn carts and certainly not by high-performance BMWs like my transportation. The byways beckon you to stop, spread a blanket in a field beside the road and have a picnic and enjoy the serenity. However, the distances between sectors and fronts that took the Yankee Division and its 102nd Field Artillery Regiment days and weeks to transport to by rail, truck, foot and horseback, I traversed in minutes traveling in my car on France's perfectly surfaced major highways at the legal speed limits in excess of 100 mph, a speed attained in 1918 by only the fastest fighter planes of that era.

Remarkably, the contour and boundaries of the fields and woods are, like the roads, exactly as they were in 1918, too. It was like going back in time.

You have to see the pictures of the destruction of the villages and towns wrecked by both armies during the First World War, what it was like when my father was there, to appreciate the rebuilding that has taken place since. The new building construction is not quite the same classic design as before, which looked then like something out of a story book, like it was when Clovis was king. But, the new construction is in keeping with the surroundings and acceptable to the eye. I found this a reassurance. I took heart that some beautiful places don't change and are not ruined by ugly developments and awful looking, sprawling shopping malls.

The towns and villages where I spent time, Allemant, Pinon, Soissons, Reims, Rambucourt, Xivray, Vaux, Domptin, Chateau-Thierry, and many of the other beautiful towns and villages I drove through in the valleys of the Marne, Meuse and Aisne while touring (a euphemism for being lost!) were destroyed during the war. The realization of the destruction left me as appalled as Eddie Rickenbacker was flying over it for the first time. There were more than four thousand French villages and towns completely or partially destroyed during this war.

This ground east of Paris was heavily fought over in the First World War. There were two battles fought in some locations, once when the Germans came through on their way west, and another when they were pushed back. And, of course, there was the stalemated fighting that took place for several years that literally ground to dust the villages and towns along the Hindenburg Line. For example, there was a First Battle of the Marne in 1914, and then there was the Second Battle of the Marne in 1918. Both battles were fought on the same ground. And both were big, decisive, destructive fights. Between 1914 and 1918, there were holding actions along the Western Front where neither side's progress could be measured in a full kilometer. There were some local trench warfare skirmishes and fights that lasted for almost four years.

When I stood in the battery's position where my father stood, I had the regimental battle map in my hand. I would orient myself toward the direction in which the battery's guns were firing and from where the enemy's artillery or infantry charges might be coming at them. I placed myself in the scene. Orienting gave me a more complete sense of what it was like.

Standing there oriented, it was impossible for me not to use my imagination and think back to my father's stories and descriptions. Vividly coming to mind were images of night artillery duels: the flashes of the artillery's muzzle blasts cleaving the night, the brilliant colors, and the explosions of wrecking destruction as the shells found their targets.

For a moment, just a moment, in my mind the ghosts would appear. I could imagine the clamor of war. My senses came alive. In my imagination I heard the bark of Battery A's guns. I could see in my reverie the fog of war.

I could see the gun crews laboring in their dance of repeatedly firing the French 75 mm guns, sweating, pouring round after round of path-making destruction ahead of the infantry who, on the signal of whistles blowing at a synchronized time, "jumped the bags" and went "over the top" from their forward positioned trenches and charged headlong, bent forward with bayoneted rifles thrust in front across No Man's Land.

I could imagine the battery pausing in their dance briefly for a sight adjustment, the instruction possibly being relayed from my father positioned in a crude observation tower, to allow for the infantry's progress or regress across No Man's Land, or to redirect the destruction on another target that required attention.

In my reverie I could feel the concussion of the enemy's incoming explosive artillery shells pounding the earth as they landed, and seeing the gas shells bursting in the fields setting off a cloud of drifting horror. I could smell the acrid cordite of the artillery rounds being fired and imagined the garlic odor I had been told about of the incoming mustard gas.

I could hear a bell ringing frantically, alerting the artillery soldiers that a gas attack was underway and to put on their gas masks. I could see artillery men wearing steel trench helmets scurrying around on urgent missions and errands running bent over as if shielding themselves from a hail storm, protecting themselves from the rain of shrapnel from incoming fragmentation shells bursting overhead. And all the while about their mission, playing Russian Roulette with the random chance of being directly hit by the incoming, creeping, artillery barrage and having a limb blown off or becoming a bloody mist.

Above the deafening roar of the outgoing artillery and the bursting incoming rounds, I could hear men shouting, screaming the profane exclamations of war: commands repositioning artillery pieces and horse drawn limbers, the confusion, the chaos... and the fear.

But, this surreal scene flashed through my imagination for only a moment. As quickly as they appeared, the ghosts vanished.

I realized that, unless I was actually there in the fight in 1918, I couldn't possibly reconstruct in my mind the true horror and destruction that happened here. I don't have the ability to fully comprehend it. No matter how many stories I've been told or books and letters I've read, my mind has no true frame of reference for it. That regrettable ability is reserved for those who were actually there. This place is their cathedral and theirs alone.

I realized that my father, and many men like him, paid a very heavy price for me to be able to stand here. I felt respectful. I felt like a visitor to a church of a religion into which I hadn't quite been baptized.

I realized that I can, however, appreciate what happened here. I can be aware of why they fought and what they were fighting for.

I can appreciate the sacrifice they made. And, in my time, I can do what I can to not allow what they did here to become in any way diminished, tarnished or forgotten.

Walking out of those beautiful woods and fields where other men on another day courageously stood and fought for their way of life and bequeathed what became mine, I did not take quite as much of what I have in this life for granted as I had when I walked in.

And, now that I am back home in the United States surrounded by my life's rewards, I feel that if this realization is the only thing I got from this trip, it was worth everything.

Remarkable, isn't it? Somehow, our parents never stop teaching us, even after they're gone.

Stephen G. Hobson, standing in the field by Boise La Croisette, Chateau-Thierry sector, October 2004. Stephen G. Hobson Collection - Stephen G. Hobson photograph

During the Second Battle of the Marne while in the Chateau-Thierry sector defending against the enemy's final grand offensive of the First World War, on the night of 14—15 July 1918 while repairing a broken communication wire my father was caught out during a Mustard Gas barrage in this field which is adjacent to Boise La Croisette. The 26th Division's Gas Officer reported that 1,500 77 mm gas shells rained down on this field and Boise La Croisette that night. Trapped in a shell hole for half an hour while the gas shells rained down on him and another man who accompanied my father on this mission, my father was drenched with Mustard Gas. Badly burned by the caustic Mustard Gas, my father was taken off the front line. His recovery from the burns he received that night would take several months in a rear position hospital.

In this picture, Battery A's 75 mm guns were positioned in the wood (Boise La Croisette) on the left in the clearing just beyond the 4-wheel vehicle. The 26th Division's 101st Infantry, the 102nd Machine Gun Battalion and the 101st Engineers were dug in along the edge of the wood on the left. The trenches and fox holes are still there. At the top of this picture on the far side of the field, the Paris—Metz Road runs in an east—west direction along the ridge. Just beyond the Paris—Metz Road were the German occupied villages of Belleau, Vaux and Bouresches from where the attack came.

Ils n'ont pas passe! (They did not pass!)

FINI

APPRECIATION

"Appreciation is a wonderful thing. It makes what is excellent in others belong to us as well."

VOLTAIRE

I owe gratitude to the following people. Without their contribution, this would have been a lesser work.

It was said in a quote somewhere of the letters my father wrote to his mother that, "It took a remarkable man of twenty to write these, but it took an even more remarkable woman to deserve it." I would like to extend that sentiment to all of my father's family. You make us proud and appreciative of the life you gave us and the values you instilled.

Anita Gaunt, the editor of this work. Anita's discipline and expertise has greatly enhanced this work. Through this process, Anita has become a friend. I am fortunate to have discovered her. When I initially interviewed Anita for the job, after she read a draft of the manuscript, I asked Anita why she would be interested in spending time working with material that relates to the First World War, a subject most people would find boring. She responded that her son had served with the military and was wounded in Iraq. She said that my father's letters "spoke to her."

Tad Lyford, a talented artist who drew several of the maps for this work.

The following for their encouragement and advice: my wife Pamela, John H. Staples, Joseph T. Dunn, and John J. Bingenheimer.

573

Martha Clark, Archivist, Boxford Document Center, Boxford, Massachusetts, for the pictures and historical information on Camp Curtis Guild, Jr. and the 26th (Yankee) Division.

Greg Laing of the Historical Department - Special Collections, Haverhill Public Library, Haverhill, Massachusetts, for the information on the Hobson and Gale families and the period's pictures of the Haverhill family homes.

George Rollins of East Boxford, Massachusetts, and his family who live in the house that was built from the original East Boxford train station. They extended their hospitality to a complete stranger (me) who was searching for where his father and the 102nd F.A. boarded a troop train bound for New York and then on to the battlefields of France. I was cordially invited into their beautiful home and they gave to me the picture of the East Boxford train station as it appeared in 1929. It meant a great deal to me to stand where my father had departed to begin his adventure.

Gilles Lagin of the Belleau Wood Museum, Marigny en Orxois, France, who provided hospitality, a tour and showed me the places my father wrote about while serving in the Chateau Thierry Sector, including where the battery's guns were located while serving in this sector, the field on the edge of Boise la Croissette Wood in Domptin where my father was gassed, the field hospitals in Bezu Le Guery and Luzanzy where my father was taken for treatment after being gassed and the 102nd F.A.'s command post in Villers-sur-Marne. Also thanks to Gilles for providing pictures and information about the Chateau-Thierry sector.

Jean and Catherine Noulard, owners of their family's St. Guilein Farm in Vaudesson, France. They kindly gave me permission to walk their land in search of Battery A's position at the Chemin des Dames Sector. When the rain came, Jean and Catherine welcomed me hospitably into their home and served coffee on two occasions. I should also thank the Noulard's Brittany Spaniel who enthusiastically lead the way through the thickets, keeping me company during my exploration and shared with me in the field the croissants left over from my breakfast picnic that were in my pack.

Colette and Bernard Carle of Rambucourt, France, who, upon discovering me early one October morning in 2004 with battle maps in hand wandering in the fields around their home searching for Battery A's positions in the Toul Sector, politely asked if I was lost. Upon discovering my mission, they spent the entire day with me showing me around Rambucourt. They opened the town hall and shared historical photographs with me. At the end of the day they served me "café" and home baked cookies. They provided a period sketch of the grain silo in Rambucourt, used as an observation post, that my father was in when it was hit by German artillery.

I am appreciative of the many men and women I encountered perchance in cafés, shops, villages and towns while traveling in France, who went out of their way for a non-French speaking wayward traveler, readily offering help with directions, shared stories and local history. Their hospitality and patience was a credit to France. Whenever my mission was revealed, they all sincerely thanked me for my father's service on behalf of their country. One town official in Bezu Le Guery, a town just outside of Domptin where, after being burned by mustard gas, my father was delivered to a triage station, said to me, "There is no division between the people of our countries. It is the politicians that create the division."

Mostly, I am appreciative of the men and women of all the nations of the Allied forces who fought for freedom, many of whom gave their lives for the cause. Thank you for our today.

SOURCES

The information obtained for this work about the history and positions of the regiment and the battery came primarily from the journal and battle maps from a privately published book, "History of the 102nd Field Artillery", printed by the Lawrence Press, Inc., in Boston in 1927. Its detailed descriptions of the movements of the regiment are selectively used throughout the book as the bases for the background of my father's letters. Information about the division came from "The History of the 26th Yankee Division - 1917 - 1919", published by the Yankee Division Veterans Association, and "A Brief History of the Fighting Yankee Division - A.E.F. - On The Battlefront - February 5, 1918 - November 11, 1918", by John Nelson, which was reprinted from "The Worcester Evening Gazette" in 1919. Information reporting the 26th Division's homecoming parade in Boston was obtained from the Boston Public Library's collection of past editions of "The Boston Globe".

My grandmother's private collection and related newspaper clippings from "The Haverhill Gazette" from 1917 - 1919 on a variety of related topics provided much information. And finally, my personal collection of photographs and my father's memorabilia have also helped provide details

Berry, Henry. "Make the Kaiser Dance". New York: Doubleday & Company, Inc. 1978

Boston Globe, Various editions 1918 - 1919

Cooper, Captain Edwin H. "Pictorial History of the 26th Division United States Army". Boston: Ball Publishing Company, 1920

Gang Plank News

Gardner, Joseph L., Josephy, Alvin M. Jr., Marshall, General S. L. A. "The American Heritage History of World War I". New York: American Heritage Publishing Company, Inc. 1964

"[The] History of the 26th Yankee Division 1917 - 1919", 2e. Salem: Deschamps Bros. 1919

"History of the 102nd Field Artillery July 1917 - April 1919". Boston: Lawrence Press, Inc. 1927

Nelson, John. "A Brief History of the Fighting Yankee Division A.E.F." Worcester: Worcester Gazette Company, 1919.

Service, Robert. "Rhymes of a Red Cross Man" New York: Barse & Hopkins, 1916.

Sibley, Frank P. "With The Yankee Division in France". Boston: Little, Brown, and Company. 1919

Walker, Thomas J. "Gen. Stephen H. Gale", Concord: *The Granite Monthly*, August, 1906

www.worldwar1.nl/

John L. Hobson II's original letters written home during the First World War from 1916 - 1919 and the newspaper clippings and photographs have been gifted for the purpose of preservation and public viewing to the Haverhill Public Library, Special Collections Department at 99 Main Street Haverhill, MA 01830.

More information about this book and additional photographs can be obtained and viewed at the book's website aflagunfurled.com or on Facebook at A Flag Unfurled – The War Letters of John L. Hobson.

ABOUT THE AUTHOR

Stephen Gale Hobson was born in Boston, Massachusetts, and grew up on the North Shore in Swampscott, Massachusetts. He was graduated from the Shore Country Day School in Beverly, Massachusetts, Proctor Academy in Andover, New Hampshire, attended Boston University and was graduated from Burdett Business School in Boston. His graduate studies were conducted with attendance at Yale's School of Organization and Management in New Haven, Connecticut.

Hobson was in business for 44 years, first in the paper industry in sales and senior sales management and later in financial services in wealth and investment management and consulting. He serves the community though volunteering at SCORE (Service Core of Retired Executives) and volunteers and has served on the Board of Directors at the Maine Maritime Museum in Bath, Maine. He lives in Cumberland Foreside, Maine where his primary interests are his wife Pamela and his three sons and five grandchildren. He is an outdoor enthusiast and fly fisherman.

Made in the USA
Charleston, SC
25 April 2013